The Nuclear Crisis

Protest, Culture and Society

General editors:
Kathrin Fahlenbrach, Institute for Media and Communication, University of Hamburg
Martin Klimke, New York University Abu Dhabi
Joachim Scharloth, Waseda University, Japan

Protest movements have been recognized as significant contributors to processes of political participation and transformations of culture and value systems, as well as to the development of both a national and transnational civil society.

This series brings together the various innovative approaches to phenomena of social change, protest and dissent which have emerged in recent years, from an interdisciplinary perspective. It contextualizes social protest and cultures of dissent in larger political processes and socio-cultural transformations by examining the influence of historical trajectories and the response of various segments of society, political and legal institutions on a national and international level. In doing so, the series offers a more comprehensive and multi-dimensional view of historical and cultural change in the twentieth and twenty-first century.

Volume 1
*Voices of the Valley, Voices of the Straits:
How Protest Creates Communities*
Donatella Della Porta and Gianni Piazza

Volume 2
Transformations and Crises: The Left and the Nation in Denmark and Sweden, 1956–1980
Thomas Ekman Jørgensen

Volume 3
*Changing the World, Changing Oneself:
Political Protest and Collective Identities in West Germany and the U.S. in the 1960s and 1970s*
Edited by Belinda Davis, Wilfried Mausbach, Martin Klimke, and Carla MacDougall

Volume 4
The Transnational Condition: Protest Dynamics in an Entangled Europe
Edited by Simon Teune

Volume 5
Protest Beyond Borders: Revisiting Social Mobilization in Europe after 1945
Edited by Hara Kouki and Eduardo Romanos

Volume 6
*Between the Avantgarde and the Everyday:
Subversive Politics in Europe, 1958–2008*
Edited by Timothy Brown and Lorena Anton

Volume 7
*Between Prague Spring and French May:
Opposition and Revolt in Europe 1960–1980*
Edited by Martin Klimke, Jacco Pekelder, and Joachim Scharloth

Volume 8
The Third World in the Global 1960s
Edited by Samantha Christiansen and Zachary A. Scarlett

Volume 9
The German Student Movement and the Literary Imagination: Transnational Memories of Protest and Dissent
Susanne Rinner

Volume 10
Children of the Dictatorship: Student Resistance, Cultural Politics, and the "Long 1960s" in Greece
Kostis Kornetis

Volume 11
Media and Revolt: Strategies and Performances from the 1960s to the Present
Edited by Kathrin Fahlenbrach, Erling Sivertsen, and Rolf Werenskjold

Volume 12
Europeanizing Contention: The Protest Against 'Fortress Europe' in France and Germany
Pierre Monforte

Volume 13
Militant Around the Clock? Left-Wing Youth Politics, Leisure, and Sexuality in Post-Dictatorship in Greece, 1974–1981
Nikolaos Papadogiannis

Volume 14
Protest in Hitler's 'National Community': Popular Unrest and the Nazi Response
Edited by Nathan Stoltzfus and Birgit Maier-Katkin

Volume 15
Comrades of Color: East Germany in the Cold War World
Edited by Quinn Slobodian

Volume 16
Social Movement Studies in Europe: The State of the Art
Edited by Olivier Fillieule and Guya Accornero

Volume 17
Protest Cultures: A Companion
Edited by Kathrin Fahlenbrach, Martin Klimke, and Joachim Scharloth

Volume 18
The Revolution before the Revolution: Late Authoritarianism and Student Protest in Portugal
Guya Accornero

Volume 19
The Nuclear Crisis: The Arms Race, Cold War Anxiety, and the German Peace Movement of the 1980s
Edited by Christoph Becker-Schaum, Philipp Gassert, Martin Klimke, Wilfried Mausbach, and Marianne Zepp

The Nuclear Crisis

The Arms Race, Cold War Anxiety, and the German Peace Movement of the 1980s

Edited by

Christoph Becker-Schaum, Philipp Gassert,
Martin Klimke, Wilfried Mausbach,
and Marianne Zepp

berghahn
NEW YORK • OXFORD
www.berghahnbooks.com

First published in 2016 by
Berghahn Books
www.berghahnbooks.com

© 2016, 2020 Edited by Christoph Becker-Schaum, Philipp Gassert,
Martin Klimke, Wilfried Mausbach, and Marianne Zepp
First paperback edition published in 2020

All rights reserved. Except for the quotation of short passages
for the purposes of criticism and review, no part of this book
may be reproduced in any form or by any means, electronic or
mechanical, including photocopying, recording, or any information
storage and retrieval system now known or to be invented,
without written permission of the publisher.

Library of Congress Cataloging-in-Publication Data

Names: Becker-Schaum, Christoph, 1952– editor of compilation. | Gassert, Philipp, editor of compilation. | Klimke, Martin, editor of compilation.
Title: The nuclear crisis : the arms race, Cold War anxiety, and the German peace movement of the 1980s / edited by Christoph Becker-Schaum, Philipp Gassert, Martin Klimke, Wilfried Mausbach, and Marianne Zepp.
Description: New York : Berghahn Books, 2016. | Series: Protest, culture and society ; volume 19 | Includes bibliographical references and index.
Identifiers: LCCN 2016019721| ISBN 9781785332678 (hardback : alkaline paper) | ISBN 9781785332685 (ebook)
Subjects: LCSH: Peace movements—Germany—History—20th century. | Antinuclear movement—Germany—History—20th century. | Protest movements—Germany—History—20th century. | Cold War—Social aspects—Germany—History—20th century. | Germany (West)—Social conditions. | Germany (East)—Social conditions. | North Atlantic Treaty Organization—History—20th century. | Nuclear weapons—Europe—History—20th century. | Nuclear disarmament—Europe—History—20th century. | Arms race—Europe—History—20th century.
Classification: LCC JZ5584.G3 N83 2016 | DDC 327.1/747094309048—dc23
LC record available at https://lccn.loc.gov/2016019721

British Library Cataloguing in Publication Data

A catalogue record for this book is available from the British Library

ISBN 978-1-78533-267-8 hardback
ISBN 978-1-78920-509-1 paperback
ISBN 978-1-78533-268-5 ebook

Contents

List of Figures — vii

Abbreviations — xii

Acknowledgments — xviii

Introduction. The Nuclear Crisis, NATO's Double-Track Decision, and the Peace Movement of the 1980s — 1
Christoph Becker-Schaum, Philipp Gassert, Martin Klimke, Wilfried Mausbach, and Marianne Zepp

Chapter 1. From Helsinki to Afghanistan: The CSCE Process and the Beginning of the Second Cold War — 37
Anja Hanisch

Chapter 2. The NATO Double-Track Decision: Genesis and Implementation — 52
Tim Geiger

Chapter 3. SS-20 and Pershing II: Weapon Systems and the Dynamization of East-West Relations — 70
Oliver Bange

Chapter 4. NATO's Double-Track Decision and East-West German Relations — 87
Hermann Wentker

Chapter 5. Political Parties — 104
Jan Hansen

Chapter 6. Eco-pacifism: The Environmental Movement as a Source for the Peace Movement — 119
Silke Mende and Birgit Metzger

Chapter 7. Rationality of Fear: The Intellectual Foundations of the Peace Movement — 138
Marianne Zepp

Chapter 8. The Institutional Organization of the Peace Movement — 154
Christoph Becker-Schaum

Chapter 9. The Spaces and Places of the Peace Movement 173
Susanne Schregel

Chapter 10. The Protagonists of the Peace Movement 189
Saskia Richter

Chapter 11. The Independent Peace Movement in East Germany 207
Rainer Eckert

Chapter 12. Visual and Media Strategies of the Peace Movement 222
Kathrin Fahlenbrach and Laura Stapane

Chapter 13. The Churches 242
Sebastian Kalden and Jan Ole Wiechmann

Chapter 14. Trade Unions 258
Dietmar Süss

Chapter 15. The Police 274
Michael Sturm

Chapter 16. "Men Build Missiles": The Women's Peace Movement 290
Reinhild Kreis

Chapter 17. Nuclear Attack and Civil Defense: Preparing for the Worst-Case Scenario
in Politics and Science 306
Claudia Kemper

Chapter 18. Nuclear Doomsday Scenarios in Film, Literature, and Music 322
Philipp Baur

Chapter 19. A Triumph of Disarmament? The 1980s and the International Political System 338
Florian Pressler

Index 352

Figures

Figure 0.1. Meetings of foreign and defense ministers of NATO member states on 12 December 1979 in Brussels, Belgium (NATO photos) — 5

Figure 0.2. Demonstrators with banner in front of the Memorial Church on the Kurfürstendamm in West Berlin on 10 June 1982 protesting against the visit of US President Ronald Reagan (ullstein bild / Stark-Otto) — 17

Figure 1.1. The Conference on Security and Cooperation in Europe (CSCE) in Helsinki in the summer of 1975 was the first attempt by Eastern and Western states, including the United States and Canada, to secure détente by means of multilateral cooperation. The photo shows the First Secretary of the Central Committee of the SED (Socialist Unity Party of Germany), Erich Honecker (front left), and Chancellor of the Federal Republic, Helmut Schmidt (front right), before the conference on 30 July 1975 (BArch B 145 Bild-00009689 / Engelbert Reineke) — 40

Figure 1.2. Singer songwriter and human rights activist Wolf Biermann at a civil rights meeting for Charter 77 in Frankfurt's trade union building on 26 March 1977. In the background (left to right) Rudi Dutschke, Jiri Pelikan, and Adam Mischnik (ullstein bild / dpa) — 42

Figure 2.1. "The Last Stand," 26 September 1983 (DER SPIEGEL 39/1983, 173) — 55

Figure 2.2. Jimmy Carter (USA), Valéry Giscard d'Estaing (France), James Callaghan (UK), and Helmut Schmidt (FRG) at their meeting in French Guadeloupe on 5/6 January 1979 (Jimmy Carter Library, Atlanta, GA) — 60

Figure 2.3. "The Arms Race—How and Where?" (Globus Grafik / Picture-Alliance) — 66

Figure 3.1. East German graphic showing the reach-diameters of Western nuclear systems, Department of Military Intelligence, National People's Army (BArch, Abteilung Militärarchiv (Abt. MA)) — 77

Figure 3.2. Caricature "Arms race: help, I've been followed" (Horst Haitzinger) — 79

Figure 4.1. US President Gerald Ford (right) in conversation with the first secretary of the Central Committee of the SED, East Germany, Erich Honecker on 1 August 1975 at the Conference on Security and Cooperation in Europe (CSCE) in Helsinki, Finland (BArch B 145 Bild-00003774 / Engelbert Reinecke) — 90

Figure 4.2. A poster protesting against the NATO Double-Track Decision in front of a house destroyed during World War II on Fehrbelliner Str.-Schönhauser Allee in East Berlin, 9 June 1985 (ullstein bild-CARO / Page Pijorr) — 97

Figure 5.1. CDU peace conference in the Konrad Adenauer House held under the slogan "Peace with Fewer Weapons" on 3 February 1983 in Bonn (BArch B 145 Bild-F065003-0012 / Engelbert Reineke) — 107

Figure 5.2. SPD election poster for the parliamentary elections in 1983 (BArch Plak 104-PM0357-013) — 112

Figure 6.1. Caricature "It's not so bad, one forest dies, another one takes its place" (Horst Haitzinger, Pershingwald, 1983 / Museum of Contemporary History, Bonn) — 127

Figure 6.2. Poster "Defend yourselves! Against the nuclear threat," a map indicating nuclear installations by the Green Party, 1981 (Archiv Grünes Gedächtnis, Berlin) — 128

Figure 7.1. The writer and scholar Robert Jungk during a meeting of the Second European Conference on Nuclear Disarmament in the International Congress Centre, Berlin, on 9 May 1983 (ullstein bild / Rieth) — 143

Figure 8.1. Forms of interest aggregation and decision-making in the peace movement (Adapted from Thomas Leif, *Die professionelle Bewegung: Die Friedensbewegung von innen* [Bonn, 1985].) — 157

Figure 8.2. Poster Menschen- und Aktionskette für Frieden & Arbeit von Duisburg nach Hasselbach 20. Oktober 1984 (Human chain for peace & work from Duisburg to Hasselbach, 20 October 1984) (BArch Plak 007-021-040) — 166

Figure 9.1. Demonstrators in front of the US military base in Mutlangen holding a banner with the inscription *Pershing macht frei*

(Pershing makes you free) (Hans Günter Lambertz / Haus der Geschichte, BaWü, DLG 0449/053) 177

Figure 9.2. Rally outside the US military base in Mutlangen on 3 September 1983 including a child's stroller that has been declared a "nuclear weapon-free zone" (ullstein bild / Rieth) 180

Figure 10.1. Petra Kelly (Green Party, Die Grünen) blocking access to a missile depot of the US military base in Mutlangen on 1 September 1983. She is wearing a steel helmet decorated with cut flowers (ullstein bild / Krewitt) 196

Figure 10.2. Record cover: "Sonne statt Reagan" (Sun instead of Reagan) the eponymous single by Joseph Beuys, 1982 (VG Bild-Kunst) 199

Figure 11.1. Der Wittenberger Friedenskreis (The Wittenberg Peace Group) invited the participants of a church convention on September 24, 1983, to a meeting at the Lutherhof. Approximately 2,000 mostly young people gathered in an ancient monastery after sunset to watch a blacksmith forge a sword into a plowshare (epd-bild / Bernd Bohm). 211

Figure 11.2. East German civil rights activist Bärbel Bohley holding a banner declaring "We hunger for disarmament. Fasting for Life" at an event named Fasting for Peace in the East Berlin Redeemer Church in August 1983 (Roland Jahn / Gustav Havemann Gesellschaft, Berlin). 213

Figure 12.1. Poster "Scrap Nuclear Missiles," "Pershing II—Cruise Missiles—No!" (Netzwerk Friedenskooperative / Stuttgart, Wurttemberg State Library) 227

Figure 12.2. Protesters form a 108-kilometer-long human chain along Bundesstrasse 10 between Stuttgart and Neu-Ulm protesting against the deployment of new nuclear weapons in the Federal Republic of Germany on 22 October 1983. Recorded near Lonsee (Picture-Alliance) 230

Figure 12.3. Protesters beginning to perform a mass die-in in front of the US military base Wiley Barracks in Neu-Ulm to express opposition to the deployment of new nuclear weapons in the Federal Republic of Germany on 22 October 1983 (Picture-Alliance) 230

Figure 12.4. Heinrich Böll, surrounded by Oskar Lafontaine, Annemarie Böll, Gert Bastian, Petra Kelly, and others, on the occasion of the "celebrity blockade" directed against the deployment of medium-range missiles at the US military base in Mutlangen in 1983 (Barbara Klemm / Deutsches Historisches Museum, Berlin) 233

Figure 13.1. Cover "The New Peace Movement—Protesting against Armor," 15 June 1981 (DER SPIEGEL 25/1981) 245

Figure 13.2. Participants of the German Lutheran Church Congress in June 1983 displaying violet scarves imprinted with the motto "Return to Life: The Time Has Come—For a No without Any Yes to Weapons of Mass Destruction" (epd-bild / Norbert Neetz) 247

Figure 14.1. A poster "Give Peace a Chance! Antiwar Day 1981, DGB-Youth North Rhine-Westphalia" (DGB Jugend NRW / Stuttgart, Wuerttemberg State Library) 264

Figure 14.2. A Poster "We want to live! No more nuclear missiles in Central Europe. Peace Walk of the trade union IG Metall and Initiative Ludwigsburg Days for Peace (Initiative Ludwigsburger Friedenstage) for Disarmament in East and West," 09/25/1983 (IG Metall Ludwigsburg / Stuttgart, Wuerttemberg State Library) 267

Figure 15.1. Federal border officials guard the barracks of the US Carl Schurz Barracks in Bremerhaven on 15 October 1983 (ullstein bild / Pflaum) 277

Figure 15.2. Blockade of the US Andrews Barracks in West Berlin, Lichterfelde on 15 October 1983. Dirk Schneider, member of parliament for Berlin (Alternative List), is being carried by police officers in order to clear the street (ullstein bild / Harry Hampel) 281

Figure 16.1. Women and children protesters blocking a road between the US military base in Mutlangen and Schwäbisch Gmünd on 3 September 1983 (ullstein bild / R. Janke) 296

Figure 16.2. Poster "Stand up for Peace!" (Netzwerk Friedenskooperative / FFBIZ Archive, Berlin) 299

Figure 17.1. Triage System (Doctors' Initiative in the City of Ulm) 313

Figure 17.2. Civil protection practice: a safe room shelter for women and children, about 1975/1980 (BArch B 422 Bild-0140 / Kurt Hilberath) 315

Figure 18.1. Cover of "Die letzten Kinder von Schewenborn" (The last children of Schewenborn) by Gudrun Pausewang, 1983 (Ravensburger Verlag) — 328

Figure 18.2. Poster "Künstler für den Frieden" (Artists for Peace) major event in support of the Appeal of Krefeld, 1982 (BArch Plak 006-030-003) — 331

Figure 19.1. US President Ronald Reagan and Soviet General Secretary of the CPSU Mikhail Gorbachev during their summit on 19–20 November 1985 in Geneva, Switzerland (Ronald Reagan Presidential Library, Ventura, CA) — 343

Abbreviations

AAPD	Akten zur Auswärtigen Politik der Bundesrepublik Deutschland, Files on the Foreign Policy of the Federal Republic of Germany
ABC	American Broadcast Channel
ABM	Anti-Ballistic Missile
ACDP	Archiv für Christlich-Demokratische Politik, Archive for Christian Democratic Politics
AdG	Archiv der Gegenwart, Archive of the Present
AdL	Archiv des Liberalismus, Archive of Liberalism
AdsD	Archiv der sozialen Demokratie, Archive of Social Democracy
AFK	Arbeitsgemeinschaft für Friedens- und Konfliktforschung, Association for Peace and Conflict Research
AfS	Archiv für Sozialgeschichte, Archive for Social History
AGG	Archiv Grüner Gedächtnis, Green Memory Archive
AGDF	Aktionsgemeinschaft Dienst für den Frieden, Action Committee Service for Peace
AKH	Aktionskreis Halle, Action Group of Halle
AP	Associated Press
APuZ	Aus Politik und Zeitgeschichte
ASF	Aktion Sühnezeichen/Friedensdienste, Action Reconciliation Service for Peace
AsF	Arbeitsgemeinschaft sozialdemokratischer Frauen, Association of Social Democratic Women
AT-1/-2	Anti-Tank (mine systems)
BArch	Bundesarchiv, Federal Archives
BAF	Bundeskongress Autonomer Friedensinitiativen, Federal Congress of Autonomous Peace Initiatives
BBU	Bundesverband Bürgerinitiativen Umweltschutz, Association of Citizens' Initiatives for Environmental Protection

BDKJ	Bund der Deutschen Katholischen Jugend, Federation of German Catholic Youth
BEK	Bund der Evangelischen Kirchen der DDR, Federation of Protestant Churches in East Germany
BfZ	Bundesamt für Zivilschutz, Federal Office for Civil Protection
BGM	Boosted Guided Missile
BHA	Federal Executive Board and Bundeshauptausschuss, Federal Committee
BM	Truck Mounted Multiple Rocket Launcher (boyevaya mashina - combat vehicle)
BRD	Bundesrepublik Deutschland, Federal Republic of Germany (West Germany)
BT-Protokolle	Bundestagsprotokolle, Protocols of the Parliament of the Federal Republic of Germany
BUF	Bundeskonferenz Unabhängiger Friedensgruppen, Federal Conference of Independent Peace Groups
BUKO	Bundeskongress Entwicklungspolitischer Aktionsgruppen, Federal Congress of Development Policy Action Groups
BUND	Bund für Umwelt und Naturschutz Deutschland, Union for the Environment and Nature Conservation
BVS	Bundesverband für den Selbstschutz, Federal Association for Self-protection
BzB	Bundesamt für zivilen Bevölkerungsschutz, Federal Agency for the Protection of the Civilian Population
CASTOR	Cask for storage and transport of radioactive material
CDU	Christlich Demokratische Union Deutschlands, Christian Democratic Union
CFK	Christlichen Friedenskonferenz, Christian Peace Conference
CIS	Commonwealth of Independent States (formerly USSR)
CND	Campaign for Nuclear Disarmament
CPSU	Communist Party of the Soviet Union
CSCE	Conference on Security and Cooperation in Europe, KSZE Konferenz über Sicherheit und Zusammenarbeit in Europa
CSU	Christlich-Soziale Union in Bayern e.V., Christian Social Union of Bavaria

CSSR	Czechoslovak Socialist Republic
DDR	Deutsche Demokratische Republik, German Democratic Republic (East Germany)
DFG-VK	Deutsche Friedensgesellschaft-Vereinigte KriegsdienstgegnerInnen, German Peace Society / United War Resisters
DGFK	Deutschen Gesellschaft Für Friedens- und Konfliktforschung, German Society for Peace
DfuL	Dokumentationsstelle für unkonventionelle Literatur, Documentation Center for Unconventional Literature
DFU	Deutsche Friedensunion, German Peace Union
DGB	Deutscher Gewerkschaftbund, Confederation of German Trade Union
DKP	Deutsche Kommunistische Partei, German Communist Party
DM	Deutsche Mark, German Mark (West)
dpa	Deutsche Presse-Agentur
DS	Demokratische Sozialisten, Democratic Socialists
EKD	Evangelischen Kirche in Deutschland, Protestant Church in Germany
EMP	Electromagnetic Pulse
END	European Nuclear Disarmament
epd	Evangelischer Pressedienst
ERW	Enhanced Radiation Weapon (neutron bomb)
ESG	Evangelische Studentengemeinden, Protestant Student Communities
EZA	Evangelisches Zentralarchiv Berlin, Protestant Central Archive Berlin
FAZ	*Frankfurter Allgemeine Zeitung*
FBS	Forward Based Systems
FDJ	Freie Deutsche Jugend, Free German Youth
FDP	Freie Demokratische Partei, Free Democratic Party (Liberal Party)
FFBIZ	Frauenforschungs-, bildungs- und -informationszentrum e.V., Women's Research, Education and Information Center

FÖGA	Föderation gewaltfreier Aktionsgruppen, Federation of Nonviolent Action Groups
FRG	Federal Republic of Germany (West Germany)
GdP	Gewerkschaft der Polizei, Trade Union of the Police
GDR	German Democratic Republic (East Germany)
GLCM	Ground-Launched Cruise Missiles
HLG	High Level Group (one of the LTDP's task forces)
ICBM	Intercontinental Ballistic Missile
IDK	Internationale der Kriegsgegner, War Resisters International
IG	Interessengemeinschaft, Syndicate
IISS	International Institute for Strategic Studies
IKV	Interkerkelijk Vredesberaad, Interchurch Peace Council
IKvu	Initiative Kirche von Unten, Initiative Church from Below
INF	Intermediate-Range Nuclear Forces
IPPNW	International Physicians for the Prevention of Nuclear War
JEF	Jung Europäische Föderalisten, Young European Federalists
KOFAZ	Komitee für Frieden, Abrüstung und Zusammenarbeit, Committee for Peace, Disarmament, and Cooperation
LARS	Light Artillery Rocket System
LD	Liberal Demokraten, Liberal Democrats
LTDP	Long-Term Defense Program
MAD	Mutual Assured Destruction
MARV	Maneuverable Reentry Vehicle
MBFR	Mutual and Balanced Force Reductions
MGM	Mobile Guided Missile
MiG	Mikoyan-Gurevich (Soviet aircraft company)
MIRV	Multiple Independently Targetable Re-entry Vehicle
MP	Member of Parliament
MRCA	Multi-Role Combat Aircraft
N + N	Neutral and Nonaligned States
NATO	North Atlantic Treaty Organization
NVA	Nationale Volksarmee, National People's Army (East Germany)
Ökopax	*Ökopazifismus,* Eco-pacifism
ORL	Ohne Rüstung Leben, Living without Arms

PAH	Anti-Tank Helicopter (Panzerabwehrhubschrauber)
PKA	Petra Kelly Archive
PUWP	Polish United Workers' Party
RAF	Rote Armee Fraktion, Red Army Fraction
RMA	Revolution in Military Affairs
SALT	Strategic Arms Limitation Talks
SAPMO	Stiftung Archiv der Parteien der Massenorganisationen der DDR im Bundesarchiv, Archive of the Parties and Mass Organizations of the GDR in the Federal Archives
SBZ	Sowjetische Besatzungszone, Soviet Occupation Zone
SDAJ	Sozialistische Deutsche Arbeiterjugend, Socialist German Workers Youth
SDI	Strategic Defense Initiative
SED	Sozialistische Einheitspartei Deutschlands, Socialist Unity Party of Germany
SJD	Sozialistische Jugend Deutschlands-Die Falken, Socialist Youth of Germany-the Falcons
SNF	Short-range Nuclear Forces
SPD	Sozialdemokratische Partei Deutschlands, Social Democratic Party
SS	Surface-to-Surface Missiles (NATO category for Soviet missiles)
START	Strategic Arms Reduction Talks
StGB	Strafgesetzbuch, Penal Code
TAZ	*Die Tageszeitung*
THW	Technisches Hilfswerk, German Technical Emergency Service
TNF	Theater Nuclear Forces
TRADOC	"Training and Doctrine Command" of the US Army
TU	Tupolev (Soviet aircraft company)
UiD	Union in Deutschland, Union in Germany
UK	United Kingdom
UN	United Nations
USSR	Union of Socialist Soviet Republics

VDS	Vereinigte Deutsche Studentenschaften, United German Student Bodies
VfZ	*Vierteljahrshefte für Zeitgeschichte*
WDC	Workers' Defense Committee
ZdK	Zentralkomitee der deutschen Katholiken, Central Committee of German Catholics

Acknowledgments

This volume could not have been realized without the intellectual and financial support of several institutions. The German Historical Institute (GHI) in Washington, DC was instrumental in acquiring the copyrights for many of the images in this volume. Together with the Heidelberg Center for American Studies (HCA) it hosted a workshop with our contributors, which significantly advanced the creation of this volume. We therefore thank the directors of both institutions, Hartmut Berghoff as well as Detlef Junker, for their support not only in the realization of this book, but also for their help in launching a digital archive on the nuclear crisis of the 1980s (www.nuclearcrisis.org).

Furthermore, our thanks go to New York University Abu Dhabi, the chair for the History of European-Transatlantic Culture at the University of Augsburg, the Heinrich Böll Foundation, as well as The Society for the Promotion of the Schurman Library for American History at the University of Heidelberg for their financial support of this endeavor.

Special thanks also go to the excellent and tireless coordinator of our research project, Laura Stapane, for her unflagging efforts in all aspects of the development and production of this volume and for patiently trying to keep us organized. At Berghahn Books, we are grateful to Marion Berghahn and Chris Chappell for their support of this project, as well as Jessica Murphy and Melissa Gannon for overseeing the final production process.

We would like to dedicate this volume to our dear friend and colleague Saskia Richter. Her academic dedication and intellectual passion will remain an example for us.

Introduction
The Nuclear Crisis, NATO's Double-Track Decision, and the Peace Movement of the 1980s

Christoph Becker-Schaum, Philipp Gassert, Martin Klimke, Wilfried Mausbach, and Marianne Zepp

In the fall of 1983 more than a million people all across West Germany gathered under the motto "No to Nuclear Armament" to protest the implementation of NATO's Double-Track Decision of 12 December 1979 and the resulting deployment of Pershing II and cruise missiles in West Germany and other European countries.[1] The media overflowed with photos of human chains, sit-in blockades, and enormous protest rallies. The impressive range of protest events included street theater performances, protest marches, and blockades of missile depots. During the final days of the campaign there were huge mass protests with several hundred thousand participants, such as the "Fall Action Week 1983" in Bonn on 22 October and a human chain stretching about 108 km from Ulm to Stuttgart. It seemed as if "peace" was the dominant theme all over Germany.[2]

Despite these protests, the West German Bundestag approved the missile deployment with the votes of the governing conservative coalition, thereby concluding one of the longest debates in German parliamentary history.[3] A few days later the first of the so-called Euromissiles were installed in Mutlangen, near Stuttgart, and in Sigonella, on the island of Sicily.[4] The peace movement had failed to attain its short-term political aim. However, after a brief period of reflection, the movement continued to mobilize masses of people for its political peace agenda. Although the government felt its position was strengthened by its handling of the Euromissiles controversy, it nonetheless considered a renewed public debate on the modernization of NATO short-range missiles in the second half of the 1980s infeasible. The "fight for peace" had thus left deep divisions in the political culture of Germany.[5]

The Euromissiles controversy was the chief topic of political debate in the early 1980s.[6] To reduce the conflict to a simple confrontation between the political establishment on the one hand and the peace movement on the other would be to misjudge the complexities on both sides. The peace movement was not only a dazzling, but also a collaborative phenomenon, encompassing a wide range of people from Communist groups to conservative Catholics.[7] At the same time, mainstream political forces were deeply divided. The missile debate thus contributed decisively to a political sea change in Bonn in 1982 with the end of the social-liberal coalition under Chancellor Helmut Schmidt and Helmut Kohl's election as chancellor of a new Christian-liberal government.[8] This volume explores the different stages of this development, analyzes the position of each side, draws attention to some of the leading political personalities, and finally evaluates the consequences for West German society and the implications for the end of the Cold War.

To highlight the societal context of the debate, we have come to use the term "nuclear crisis." We want to stress that the debate about NATO's Double-Track Decision involved far more than questions of international security and foreign relations. During the nuclear crisis, people in West Germany, like those in many other Western societies, sought to come to terms with their own past, present, and future.[9] The dispute about arms deployment was an expression of rapid sociocultural changes that started in the 1960s and continued with the economic transformations in the 1970s. As early as 1982, Erhard Eppler, a member of the Social Democratic Party (SPD) and one of the most outspoken critics of nuclear arms modernization, concluded that the peace movement was "one of several manifestations of a change in social perception and a shift in fundamental values that began in the late sixties among young people. It gained momentum during the 1970s until it was accepted among broader segments of society and continued to spread visibly in the 1980s."[10]

The Issues

So what was the great controversy of the 1980s actually about? In hindsight the causes and effects are obvious to the supporters of the NATO Double-Track Decision. To Hans-Dietrich Genscher, the Foreign Minister of both the social-liberal and the subsequent Christian-liberal coalition, the "Soviet challenge" was the catalyst for a Western arms upgrade—he deliberately coined the term *Nachrüstung* (retrofitting/countervailing strategy). The NATO Double-Track Decision was thus for Genscher both indicative and constitutive of "the period when it was determined whether the Soviet Union would gain political power in Western Europe through military superiority, and whether it would succeed in separating Western Europe from the United States."¹¹ In the eyes of Kohl, the Warsaw Pact had "acquired a substantial military predominance in Europe." Through the deployment of SS-20 missiles NATO's doctrine of a *flexible response* to a possible Soviet attack was undermined. This presented the US president with a dilemma: in an emergency situation he would have to decide whether to stand by his allies and respond with ballistic missiles or tolerate a decoupling of Europe to protect his own country from a retaliatory Soviet intercontinental missile strike.¹²

To see the NATO Double-Track Decision as a direct response to a unilateral nuclear arms threat by the Eastern bloc is only half the story, however. Anyone who really wants to understand its origins has to dig deeper into history. First, as Tim Geiger shows in his contribution to this volume with regard to its roots, the NATO Double-Track Decision was an unintended consequence of détente and the relaxation of Cold War tensions during the 1960s and early 1970s. As Schmidt argued in a speech delivered to the London-based International Institute for Strategic Studies in October 1977 (later glorified as the beginning of the Euromissiles rearmament), the SALT negotiations between the superpowers on intercontinental ballistic missiles had left out the long-range and intermediate-range missiles.¹³ The SS-20 fell into a "grey area" because of its target range of 5,000 km, which mostly threatened Europe and the East Asian allies of the United States. As a result, the SS-20 was not considered to be an intercontinental weapon. This created a problem for NATO as its officially adopted doctrine of *flexible response* from 1967–68 required a measured reaction to military aggression. Since NATO had no weapon equivalent to the SS-20, this inequity in the escalation continuum allegedly destabilized the nuclear balance of power.¹⁴

Even at the time there was considerable skepticism—especially within the strategic community—about the proposition that the SS-20 had divided Western deterrence into two spheres and rendered it unviable. Britain and France both commanded their own quite considerable nuclear capacity. Experts, such as the British chief strategist Sir Michael Quinlan, did not accept the idea that nuclear war could be potentially restricted to Europe as not only Schmidt but also his successor Kohl feared. The experts regarded nuclear weapons as essentially political tools. Nuclear arsenals served as a deterrent, that is to say, they prevented war. If deterrence failed, they promised the rapid termination of a conflict.¹⁵ As MC 14/3—the overall strategic concept adopted by NATO in 1967–68—anticipated, this could mean that a demonstrative detonation of a single bomb or several precision nuclear air strikes against selected targets would lead to a cessation of military action. French President François Mitterrand also did not buy into the strategy of flexible response.¹⁶ But since the main interest of the French was to keep the *force de frappe* out of the negotiations and to keep the Federal Republic of

Germany firmly integrated within the alliance, France supported the NATO Double-Track Decision, albeit without any direct involvement.[17]

Second, the Double-Track Decision was in part the outcome of the "revolution in military affairs" that had taken place during the late 1960s and the early 1970s. Both NATO and the Warsaw Pact were forced to respond to technological innovations. According to NATO's Harmel Report of 1967, the Western alliance followed a policy of détente and defense through deterrence. It sought to find a diplomatic way to come to an understanding with the East and thus improve security via détente while simultaneously continuing to modernize its technology. Since the 1950s, NATO and the United States had pursued technological solutions and nuclear deterrence because these were cheaper and less burdensome to taxpayers. For a long time, nuclear weapons had been seen as politically more acceptable than large-scale conventional armament ("more bang for the buck"). The drawback to this cost-saving strategy was NATO's relative inferiority when it came to conventional arms. Moscow thwarted this calculation as it gradually improved its arms and, after the 1960s, increasingly reached nuclear parity.

In his survey of the weapons systems developed on both sides of the Iron Curtain since the late 1960s, Oliver Bange discusses the political consequences of technological innovation. NATO planned new conventional and nuclear weapons systems long before the SS-20 turned into a military and political problem for the West. Research and construction on Pershing II and cruise missiles had been in progress since 1969 and 1970. In 1972 the construction of the neutron bomb was resumed after it had been stopped in 1958. Both military alliance systems developed new aircraft that revolutionized warfare: the MRCA Tornado displayed high-performance electronics and was capable of transporting nuclear and conventional weapons at low altitudes behind enemy lines. The Soviet "Backfire" bombers, on the other hand, worried US officials since these weapons could potentially serve as intercontinental bombers. In addition, there was also a new generation of artillery and battle tanks like the German Leopard 2. Bange argues that these new weapons profoundly transformed a strategic perception of war that was shaped by the "major and decisive tank battles" of World War II.

These mutual observations and threat perceptions are crucial for an understanding of the Cold War.[18] Despite the increased access to historical sources and archives, a variety of interpretations remain with regard to Moscow's motives and reasoning. According to Bange, the Soviet Union was at all times well informed about NATO plans and proceedings. It seems to have partially anticipated NATO's arms modernization. Convinced that the West pursued inherently aggressive goals,[19] the Kremlin had been expecting the introduction of cruise missiles and Pershing II since their design in 1970 and had thus preemptively counteracted by introducing new weapons such as the SS-20. Moscow took the view that the SS-20 was merely the result of regular modernization efforts. Other authors point out that during the end of the Brezhnev era the Soviet Union's "military-industrial complex" ultimately acted outside political parameters. The orthodox interpretation assumes that the Soviet Union harbored aggressive motives.[20]

The third element to consider when reviewing the complex history behind the Double-Track Decision is that the decision was in part the result of internal Western disagreements over strategy. While the decision eventually strengthened the internal bonds and cohesion among Western allies, it at first sought to heal a rift caused by a deep crisis in US-German relations in particular and transatlantic relationships generally, an ongoing predicament that had come to the forefront during the late 1970s.[21] This was partly the result of increased confidence among the political elites in the two German states. Some thirty years after the end of World War II the leaders of both states were concerned that Germany would again turn into a battlefield. Such worry contributed to a certain convergence of interests between East and West Germany. Hermann Wentker shows that despite a revival of East-West tensions after the Soviet invasion of Afghanistan in 1979, neither side wanted to cut the thread of their bilateral discussions. Although West Germany had been a driving force behind the Double-Track Decision, even hardline conservative Christian Democratic politicians were not inclined

Figure 0.1. Meetings of foreign and defense ministers of NATO member states on 12 December 1979 in Brussels, Belgium (NATO photos)

to use the aggressive anticommunist rhetoric of American neoconservatives around President Ronald Reagan. Anja Hanisch points out that Europeans living on the demarcation line of the East-West conflict valued détente substantially more than US decision-makers. Caught in the middle, these everyday citizens were therefore more likely to support, albeit in part rhetorical, concessions to the East.

The growing tensions within the Western alliance were exemplified by Chancellor Schmidt's confident admonitions to the Americans, who seemed to have become forgetful of their contractual obligations within NATO, as well as by divergent perspectives on the Conference for Security and Cooperation in Europe (CSCE) and détente. Political scientist Helga Haftendorn argued early on that the Double-Track Decision was partly based on a US-German misunderstanding. Following the tradition of his predecessors Kiesinger and Adenauer, Chancellor Schmidt was beset by a lingering nightmare that the superpowers would act in complicity at the expense of West German security. The progress that the United States and the USSR had made in the SALT negotiations was of little use to the West Germans. Chancellor Schmidt's 1977 London speech was a sharp reminder to the Americans that SALT could produce potential imbalances and create more insecurity in Europe. The embattled Carter administration took this as a call for more arms. Now the German Federal government faced a dilemma to which the NATO Double-Track Decision seemed to offer a resolution. As Geiger explains, in his contribution to this volume, the threat to deploy medium-range missiles (i.e., Pershing II and cruise missiles) was combined with an offer to continue disarmament negotiations.

The Double-Track Decision can therefore be seen as an attempt to bridge divergent interests within NATO and to strengthen transatlantic cohesion. The Western alliance had seriously suffered during the turmoil of the Vietnam War.[22] Furthermore, Europeans and Americans drew different conclusions from détente.[23] After US President Jimmy Carter's coming into office there was little hope of an improvement in German-American relations, since at least Chancellor Schmidt considered the new president's efforts at international politics amateurish.[24] The Double-Track Decision was supposed to demonstrate the unity of NATO, which wanted to prevent the appearance of West German nuclear isolation. As a consequence, the cruise missiles were planned to be stationed not only in West Germany but also in Great Britain, the Netherlands, Belgium, and Italy (Pershing II missiles, more limited in range, were placed exclusively on German territory). Helmut Kohl, Chancellor Schmidt's successor, also attached extraordinary significance to the implementation of this decision with respect to the political alliance. He bluntly accused the peace movement of being anti-American and conjured up an image of transatlantic estrangement caused by ungrateful Germans toward disappointed Americans.[25] For Chancellor Kohl, the political struggle over the missiles was also a struggle for the soul of the alliance.

The Protagonists of the Conflict

Who were the protagonists? The "front line" was more uneven than it appears in retrospect. At the height of the controversy over the weapons modernization in the fall of 1983, two relatively clearly identifiable camps seemed irreconcilably opposed to each other: on the one side, the government led by Helmut Kohl since the autumn of 1982, his coalition parties, the CDU/CSU, the FDP, and its supporters; on the other side, the peace movement as well as the parliamentary opposition (which, after the general election on 6 March 1983, included the Green Party). The two sides had come into formation when NATO made its fundamental decision in December 1979. That it would not be easy for the moderately left or social democratic fathers of the Double-Track Decision—Chancellor Schmidt in Germany, Prime Minister Callaghan in the United Kingdom, President Carter in the United States—to convince their own political following of the necessity of modernizing their nuclear arsenals had been obvious since the controversy about the neutron bomb in 1977; hence, the latter is often regarded as having been a kind of test run for the subsequent Euromissiles controversy.[26]

The contribution by Jan Hansen on the political parties in West Germany highlights that politicians not only from the Social Democratic Party (SPD), but also from the Free Democratic Party (FDP), and even among the conservative Christian Democratic Union (CDU) (though hardly any in the Christian Social Union, CSU), showed an understanding for the concerns of the peace movement, even if they held no outright sympathy. In an address to the national convention of the CDU in Hamburg in 1981, a 22-year-old Christian Wulff, who later would become president of the Federal Republic of Germany, caught national attention when he demanded that everyone "take into account that many people in this country, both young and old, are afraid."[27] The deepest division undoubtedly existed among the Social Democrats. The proponents of the implementation of the Double-Track Decision gathered around Chancellor Schmidt, who insisted on a clear distinction between his own position and that of the peace movement, but found their support diminishing and were soon in the minority. Even though the controversy was seemingly about foreign policy, domestically the SPD faced the prime challenge of integrating the new social movements that had emerged from the student protests of the late 1960s. Party Chairman Willy Brandt and Party Secretary Egon Bahr, both outspoken critics of nuclear rearmament and proponents of a strong peace policy, tried hard to build bridges to the New Left in the area of foreign policy.[28]

A similar line of conflict existed among the labor unions, as Dietmar Süß shows. Divisions among its members for and against the peace movement followed comparable age and lifestyle demographics. When the question arose as to how to respond to the new social movements, it seemed to touch on central notions of political identity.[29] Despite longstanding antimilitarist traditions within the unions, the attitude of conservative union members, for example Hermann Rappe (chairman of the trade union representing workers in the chemical industry), proved very similar to that of Chancellor Schmidt and his pragmatic and consensual liberal-minded social democrats, and showed little understanding of the peace movement's organization, its forms of protest, or its grassroots political orientation. In addition, the moderate left displayed a knee-jerk anticommunist reaction. As firmly established, powerful institutions, the labor unions in this respect were comparable to the Christian churches and the political parties, and they saw little reason to get involved with the colorful and politically intangible networks of a green and alternative peace movement.

Sebastian Kalden and Jan Ole Wiechmann analyze how the established churches, despite being divided on the "peace issue," provided "one of the most important platforms for the peace and security policy debates in West Germany around 1980." The social changes of the 1960s and 1970s did not pass without leaving its mark on the churches.[30] Only a small fraction of the congregations of these churches felt an affinity toward the peace movement. Nonetheless, the great mass meetings of the Protestant churches—that is to say the church congresses in Hamburg (1981) and in Hanover (1983)—turned into central events shaping the public debate, as the opponents to the Euromissiles were able to make effective use of the media coverage.[31] The churches provided an important organizational structure for transnational communication on the topic of peace. Mainly among the Reformed Protestants (to a far less extent among Lutherans), a close exchange of ideas took place, both internally and with other denominations, for example, with the Dutch Reformed Church.[32] On the Catholic side, pastoral letters of the US Conference of Catholic Bishops that officially rejected deterrence in 1982 turned into key documents for church discussions in Germany. Even many non-Christian and non-Catholic members of the peace movement followed the words from the American bishops with great interest.

Despite such internal divisions, political parties, trade unions, and churches served as institutionalized forums for the public debate about the Euromissiles. Notwithstanding a lack of research in this area, the same is likely to be true for public opinion, as polls show a wide spectrum of views. Opponents of the NATO Double-Track Decision claimed that West Germans supported the transatlantic alliance but rejected a defense system based on nuclear weapons.[33] Confronted with the issue of nuclear defense, the majority of West Germans opted for a policy of "better red than dead." Conversely, Helmut Kohl's electoral victory in 1983 is often considered a victory for supporters of the Double-Track Decision. Yet other factors played at least an equally if not more significant role in this result. The journalist Josef Joffe commented even then that a chief reason for the political failure of the peace movement was the lesser significance of foreign policy issues in comparison with economic and social issues and the fact that nuclear doomsday scenarios themselves were insufficient to determine electoral outcome.[34]

The Peace Movement

A peculiar feature of the peace movement of the 1980s is that, as a protest movement, it was characterized by cooperation as well as some competition among influential organizations and established social actors such as political parties, churches, and trade unions, and among other social movements. This meant, in Christoph Becker-Schaum's view, "an increase in resources and a heightened capacity to rally people." At the same time, it implied "the danger of dependency," a worry that was discussed at the time in light of the participation of communists within the movement.[35] To balance diverging interests and political traditions, the peace movement created its own organizational structure with a Coordination Committee led by an executive office and various central and regional conferences. As a result, the movement's dynamic now also influenced traditional organizations. Indeed, the peace movement grew into the largest protest movement in the history of West Germany by adopting structures from the "New Social Movements"[36] and the alternative culture of the 1970s. With the end of protests after the deployment of the Euromissiles starting in late 1983, its institutional structure, however, largely dissolved.

The peace movement drew on various sources and realms of experience: first and foremost among these were the ecology and environmental movements of the 1970s. Silke Mende and Birgit Metzger explore how the fight against civilian use of nuclear power "provided significant human and institutional resources" for the peace movement. The environmental movement had already successfully influenced existing institutions such as churches and political parties. Following its lead, the peace movement manifested a comprehensive "perception of a social crisis and its criticism," which subsequently led to the intellectual basis of a fundamental critique of "existing conditions" and the perceived lack of problem-solving skills within the incumbent "party state."[37] Marianne Zepp then discusses how "Eco-pacifism" and approaches of academic peace and conflict studies served as additional intellectual foundations and precursors. Institutionalized during the era of the social-liberal coalition, peace and conflict research bracketed the peace movement with the support of academic institutions, such as research organizations and universities.[38] As a consequence of their advanced research, the peace movement could ground its arguments at the onset of the debate about NATO's Double-Track Decision in a systematic and science-based critique of the idea of "deterrence." In many cases, its members appeared better informed on political, military, and moral implications of certain weapons systems than those in favor of the arms upgrade.[39]

Who then belonged to the peace movement of the 1980s? Next to the traditional institutions already mentioned, ranging from churches to trade unions and the Communist Party, the movement comprised of peace organizations with longstanding traditions (e.g., the Deutsche Friedensgesellschaft-Vereinte Kriegsdienstgegner [German Peace Society-United Conscientious Objectors])—some dating back to the time of the German Empire. Certain membership groups modeled on the British Campaign for Nuclear Disarmament from the 1960s made up the Easter March movement. Finally, participants in social phenomena such as the squatter scene and the ecological movement need to be included. In his contribution, Christoph Becker-Schaum points out that the peace movement showed all the characteristics of a youth movement, albeit less explicitly than the student movement of the 1960s. Participants were slightly older, often in their twenties and occasionally in their early thirties, whose formative years had been during the often-depressing social upheavals of the 1970s that were marked by anxiety and deep crisis ("No Future"). Active members were also closely aligned with the alternative milieu.[40] They formed the movement's bulk and its active core. In the early 1980s, they were thus younger than the former activists of the 1968 generation and regarded the Green Party as representing their point of view, but kept the Old Left, including all communists, at bay.

The peace movement of the 1980s encompasses an astonishingly broad spectrum not only of institutions, but also individual members. Irrespective of the high proportion of young adults, its following was less clearly defined than the protest movements of the late 1960s, because it cut across generational lines. Compared to 1950s antinuclear activism, which was strongly grounded in the labor movement and Protestant milieus, the social background of the 1980s peace movement was more heterogeneous. Reinhild Kreis describes how women in particular were able to play an independent and socially salient role in the peace movement—which contrasted sharply with their less visible participation in the strikingly male-dominated 1968 protests and 1950s campaigns against rearmament.[41] Not surprisingly, female as well as male members of the peace movement sought to highlight this important position of women in the media coverage. Saskia Richter's chapter shows the incredibly diverse range of prominent personalities involved in the movement. They include former Chancellor and SPD chairman Willy Brandt and the circle of his ambitious SPD successors, such as Oskar Lafontaine (himself a future SPD chairman), but also former army general Gert Bastian, conservative journalist Franz Alt, as well as Eva Quistorp, cofounder of the women's peace movement. Petra Kelly may be singled out among the immensely diverse group of activists in that she was a charismatic politician with a US background and a completely different political and organizational style.

Similar to proponents of the NATO Double-Track Decision who enacted a show of international solidarity at summits and state visits, the opponents of the arms upgrade also engaged in international exchanges among likeminded groups. Facilitated by national and international church organizations, scientific groups such as the International Physicians for the Prevention of Nuclear War, artistic and cultural initiatives, and more institutionalized and regular platforms hosted by groups such as European Nuclear Disarmament (END), among others, the connections among nuclear disarmament activists intensified rapidly from the beginning of the 1980s. This development fostered joint protest actions and the swift dissemination of relevant literature, protest strategies and techniques, as well cultural practices and visual representations of antinuclear activism across national borders.[42] Although often mediated by individuals with international contacts and experience (such as Petra Kelly or Mary Kaldor), these relationships could also rely on a well-established global nuclear disarmament movement that had come into being after World War II.[43] Nonetheless, these transnational networks were frequently caught in the conflicting priorities of local and transnational issues and needs, as the ultimate aims of these national movements differed considerably.[44]

The European line of demarcation known as the "Iron Curtain" did not prevent a regular exchange of ideas and people. Next to a multitude of transatlantic meetings, there were international ties within Western Europe and between Westerners and dissidents in Eastern Europe. The latter played a highly symbolic role in the publicity generated by the visit of Green Party members from Bonn to dissidents of the German Democratic Republic in 1983. Rainer Eckert explains that participants in the independent peace movement in East Germany were rarely in a position to participate actively in international networks yet perceived themselves, just like their Western counterparts, as members of a pan-European and global movement.[45] With Polish and Czech dissidents they shared a belief that international peace was impossible without the right to domestic freedom and democracy.[46]

The Forms of Conflict

How did the peace movement communicate its protest? Kathrin Fahlenbrach and Laura Stapane reveal how contemporary images displayed certain patterns. Photos, posters, and film footage persistently showed a cross-section of society—adults, children, teenagers, and grandparents—demonstrating side by side. It has already been mentioned that the ideology of the peace movement grew out of the social movements of the 1970s and the practices of peace activism followed the traditions of the protest movement of 1968.[47] This also holds true for its aesthetic dimension and general character. Posters deliberately copied the style of the student movement and, according to Fahlenbrach and Stapane's analysis, members symbolically emphasized their ideological distance from the norms and styles of conventional politics by wearing casual clothes and publicly employing expressive modes of communication like dance and stylized movement. Such provocative antiestablishment aesthetics sometimes alienated proponents of the Double-Track Decision. Interestingly enough, the conservative CDU copied the format of protest events with a campaign of "10,000 days of peace," but deliberately chose a different set of aesthetics for it.[48]

The choice of location and social space for each protest was a central element in the communication strategy of the peace movement: opponents to the Euromissiles preferred to draw on the "local" dimension and made use of a personal environment, which Susanne Schregel defines as "local space" in the struggle for peace. Crowd-drawing demonstrations were staged in central venues, although many small regional protest events took place as well. Some of these locations certainly attracted more than local media attention, taking on national and international significance, especially the missile depot near the village of Mutlangen close to Stuttgart and Waldheide near Heilbronn, as well as corresponding hotspots of missile deployment in other European countries. The local blockades literally performed "body politics" and drew attention to the spatial and regional threat of the arms upgrade to neighborhoods. A novel concept of a nuclear-free zone was developed that deliberately set "realms of peace" apart from "military settings." Despite this focus on local landmarks, international twin partnerships developed as well. In this respect, the peace movement anticipated a subsequent global justice movement that stresses the importance of local developments in relation to global processes.

This pronounced localization and simultaneous interconnection between local and regional with international and global events are also characteristics of nuclear doomsday scenarios portrayed in the arts and popular media during the 1980s. The film *The Day After* (1983), for example, chooses a seemingly arbitrary city from the American Midwest as the site of a nuclear apocalypse and Gudrun Pausewang's popular novel *The Last Children of Schewenborn* situates a nuclear war in a small town setting. This new focus on local environments was a marked shift in popular culture dealing with nuclear disaster—and it was not the only one, as Philipp Baur points out. Fiction took a turn to the serious in the sense that most narratives did not offer an escapist happy ending like the one in the movie *War Games* (1983). Films like *The Day After* and *When the Wind Blows* (1986) terminate in real-time disaster. The early 1980s also saw the rise of "nuclear pop."[49] This type of popular music communicated anxiety and served as a mouthpiece to artists who identified with the peace movement for its aims and purposes. Up to a certain degree this music may even be understood as a social mechanism for coping with the nuclear crisis.[50]

Scientists of various disciplinary backgrounds played a prominent role in the public debates about the nuclear threat covered by the media. In her chapter Marianne Zepp analyzes networks of scholars from the social sciences who specialized in peace and conflict studies. These scientists were highly skilled in communicating information and had privileged access to print and broadcast media; thus, they had no trouble arguing their case in the public domain. Among these experts, there were both proponents and opponents of the Euromissiles. Claudia Kemper argues, for example, that specialist knowledge—such as the principles of civil defense and first-hand experience in dealing with emergencies and catastrophes, as well as familiarity with military war planning—was used for legitimizing as well as rejecting NATO's planned nuclear weapons upgrade. Science therefore became a central arena of conflict. This is reflected in the media history of the nuclear crisis, in which the experts' discourse and its reception mirror the public debate on the looming "nuclear holocaust." Nuclear disaster scenarios developed by civil defense experts often found their way into fictional texts, such as Anton-Andreas Guha's *Ende: Diary of a Third World War* (1986, German edition 1983) and Raymond Briggs' graphic novel *When the Wind Blows* (1982). These national networks of experts were thus part of international and transnational communicative contexts.

The peace movement's communication strategy directed toward media coverage took on various forms, including demonstrations, parliamentary debates, party congresses, publications, and the physical obstruction of missile transports. The strategy at times involved deliberate conflicts with the police and the judiciary. This struggle was an essential element of the peace movement as a whole. Court cases about sit-ins in Mutlangen or the "arms tax boycott" passed through the entire court system right up to the Federal Constitutional Court. The courts by and large adopted the reasoning of the proponents of the NATO Double-Track Decision and the logic of the necessity of an upgraded arms threat. At the same time, the principle of freedom of assembly was strengthened. Security laws were tightened in part, and the police union started an internal debate questioning the legality of blockades. Moreover, as Michael Sturm shows, the police gradually revised their methods. A comprehensive process of learning had been initiated that assumed a form of "citizen orientation" and a more relaxed attitude. Ultimately the police developed new techniques (protest policing) to adapt to these new forms of protest.[51]

History and the Movement's Legacy

The historical consequences of the nuclear crisis have not yet been systematically explored by scholars. Contemporaries were arguing intensely about the impact the social movements of the 1980s exerted on security policy. They asked whether the grand debate on security in the early 1980s over the NATO Double-Track Decision had a lasting impact on the strategic culture of West Germany and what its enduring heritage might be.[52] Contemporary fears were formulated, for example, by the political scientist and Adenauer biographer Hans-Peter Schwarz, who suggested that the German *Machtbesessenheit* (obsession with power) during the first half of the twentieth century had mutated into a *Machtvergessenheit* (being oblivious to power) and hence a shift toward denouncing all responsibility for international politics.[53] Drawing upon these arguments, historians such as Peter Graf Kielmansegg, Heinrich August Winkler, Jeffrey Herf, and Eckart Conze have argued that the refusal of the peace movement to back the NATO Double-Track Decision broke an accepted consensus about security concerns that "had held for two decades."[54]

With regard to the impact of the nuclear crisis, four questions seem particularly pertinent:

First, contemporary conservatives wondered about the "fortification/ militancy of democracy" (*Wehrhaftigkeit der Demokratie*) and the strength of democratic systems to resist totalitarian challenges. With regard to the politics of memory, this argument is fraught with danger: it compares the appeasement policies of the 1930s with actions by the seemingly powerless executives of democratically elected governments in the face of the Soviet challenge. This sharply contrasts with the argument that the debate over the Double-Track Decision enhanced the roots of democratic culture in West Germany[55] and was a sign of a consolidated post-fascist cultural consensus that was tightly interwoven with a self-definition of Germany as a peace-oriented society, thus demonstrating another phase of the country's continuous liberalization.[56]

Second, a closely related and equally controversial question, is whether the critique of the arms upgrade via the Euromissiles debate led to a retreat to nationalist attitudes and positions—and thus had an alienating effect on West Germany in relation to other Western democracies—and whether the peace movement can be found guilty of a prejudiced anti-Americanism. Opponents to the Euromissiles again take the opposite view and point out that due to multiple pan-European and transatlantic contacts the peace movement resulted in an increased Western integration of the Federal Republic of Germany and, perhaps even more importantly, its protests, just like the 1960s protests[57] served as a gateway for Western influences, thus contributing to a larger "Westernization" process (Anselm Doering-Manteuffel).

Third, some historians question whether the nuclear crisis had an overall impact on institutional party politics and the general potential of social movements to influence political decision-making within and outside parliament. The prevailing view is that the peace movement failed in its self-imposed task to prevent the implementation of the NATO Double-Track Decision and, as a consequence, has not left deep marks in the fabric of West German democracy. Yet the Green Party's election into parliament institutionalized the protest movement, which certainly had a tremendous impact on the political landscape and the ability to create majorities for government.

Finally, the fourth question is whether the 1980s debate about security policy in general and the NATO Double-Track Decision in particular played a role in bringing about the end of the Cold War. There are again very different and opposing perspectives on this complex matter. Some argue that the uncompromising attitude of Western governments forced the Soviet Union into giving in to an arms agreement. Others, by contrast, claim that the ostracization of nuclear weapons and an emerging peace consensus set the ground for more relaxed international relations in the second half of the 1980s, which in turn led to the collapse of communist regimes, therefore making a significant contribution to the end of the Cold War.

Politics of Memory

With regard to our first question, the "fortification/militancy of democracy" (*Wehrhaftigkeit der Demokratie*) and the coming to terms with the National

Socialist past, Helmut Kohl justified his support for the NATO Double-Track Decision with reference to an "ethical responsibility" stating that "we all ... learned a lesson from history in two terrible wars, with displaced persons and refugees, survivors and the fallen of two world wars." Policy should "prevent the apocalypse with the help of historical experience and practical common sense [and] it needs to prevent an extortion that harbors the possibility of unleashing an inferno."[58] In a fierce rhetorical skirmish delivered in parliament in June 1983, the general secretary of the conservative Christian Democratic Party, Heiner Geissler, accused Green politician Joschka Fischer of being responsible for the ethics of pacifism in the 1980s, which resembled those of the appeasement policy of the 1930s that "had made Auschwitz possible." According to Geissler, the death of millions of people could have been prevented "if the weakness of liberal democracies had not made it so easy for the dictator of the Nazi regime to start the war. This is the truth."[59]

Supporters of the NATO Double-Track Decision belabored historical analogies to justify taking a "firm stand" against the Soviet Union. However, Geissler's antagonist Fischer had employed similar rhetoric only a few days earlier when he gave an interview to the political journal *Der Spiegel*. Fischer argued that it was "morally appalling that in the logical system of modernity after Auschwitz [that] there was still no taboo against preparing for mass destruction."[60] Fischer had also warned against false analogies between Nazi crimes and the East-West conflict. But his own comments were representative of similar rhetorical devices used by large segments of the peace movement. Slogans like "No More War" and recalling the memory of the German genocide of the Jews in the 1940s had become increasingly widespread and were supposed to boost motivation to engage in current political action. Time and again memories of World War II were invoked in order to support a "resistance against nuclear missiles" and score political points. Memorial days such as 8 May (Victory in Europe Day, day of German surrender), the "Antiwar Day" on 1 September, and ceremonies held in memory of anti-Nazi resistance fighters invoked the past for the political purpose of rallying the public to a pacifist stance.[61]

Opponents of the Euromissiles considered it their duty, in the spirit of a "militant/fortified democracy," to engage in "resistance" to accelerated arms production and deployment, using precisely this term due to its strong historic connotations. Günter Grass, author and subsequent winner of the Nobel Prize for literature, characterized the underlying logic of nuclear armament as a "cynical abandonment of fundamental values of human ethics ... , which had back then led to the Wannsee Conference and the decision for the final solution—nowadays it results in military simulation games which assume worst-case scenarios with casualty figures of fifty or eighty million deaths

Figure 0.2. Demonstrators with banner in front of the Memorial Church on the Kurfürstendamm in West Berlin on 10 June 1982 protesting against the visit of US President Ronald Reagan (ullstein bild / Stark-Otto)

as inevitable fallout."[62] Supposed parallels to a "nuclear holocaust" (a term that was in high circulation) or "Shoah" were drawn countless times in word and picture as well as expressed by symbolic actions (demonstrators wearing concentration camp clothes, posters displaying slogans such as "Pershing sets you free").[63]

Given the importance of Holocaust remembrance in Western societies in the 1980s as a central moral point of reference, both sides of the conflict emphasized—with an almost disconcerting harshness from today's perspective—that the issue of armament was much more than a simple question of security policy. The change of government and the conservative turn in the Federal Republic of Germany in 1982–83 only intensified both sides' polemical rhetoric in this debate, which was also about the future of society; more specifically, the question was posed if a "left-liberal political hegemony" would successfully withstand a "neo-conservative reversal." It was the time of the decade-long dispute in intellectual circles and among historians known as the *Historikerstreit* (historians' dispute) and there would be no consensus about which lessons could be learned from history. The German theologian Dorothee Soelle, who taught in New York, described the Pershing II missiles in Mutlangen as "flying incinerators";[64] a verdict, which in retrospect is perhaps not quite so shocking if one bears in mind that members of the Ploughshares movement in the United States used similarly drastic historical analogies.[65]

"We want to learn from history. We never again want to make the mistakes that led to Nazi barbarism," said Kohl in November 1981.[66] It would have been unthinkable that this frank announcement, which certainly also hides more than it reveals, could have been uttered by a Christian Democratic or conservative politician in the 1950s.[67] Although the antagonists did not agree regarding the way Hitler and Nazi Germany constituted a warning and what political conclusions or moral proscriptions might be deduced from the Holocaust, there was a firm understanding on all sides that the identity of West Germany was based on an acceptance of crimes committed "from German soil" and a wholehearted rejection of these atrocities. This consensus was expressed subsequently by Federal President Richard von Weizsäcker in his famous speech delivered on the occasion of the fortieth anniversary of the end of World War II in 1985.

Western Ties and Anti-Americanism

The second question raised earlier relates to whether there was a consolidation or a disengagement of "Western ties,"[68] and how this affected "Germany's position in the world." Again we find a surprising bitterness in the aggressive clashes of opposing opinions. Ultimately, however, the frequent mutual visits across the Atlantic and within Europe that occurred during this time only further enhanced West Germany's integration into the West. Euromissile opponents were regularly accused of an "alienation from the democracies of the West,"[69] even though many of them were deeply influenced and inspired by Henry David Thoreau, Martin Luther King, Jr, Mahatma Gandhi, and other protagonists of nonviolent resistance equally revered by the US peace movement. In a sense they served as agents of a "Westernization" and proliferation of a democratic culture of protest of American origins even acknowledged by Chancellor Kohl.[70] The peace movement in West Germany therefore ensured that its mass gatherings and large demonstrations included well-known figures from the United States, Britain, and the Netherlands who held speeches and were prominently placed on the podium to demonstrate internationalism accordingly.[71]

Members of the peace movement in Germany vehemently denied the charge that they were "anti-American." Quite a few, however, readily made a bogeyman out of US President Reagan and regarded themselves, together with their friends in the United States, as part of an anti-Reagan movement.[72] Officials of the Reagan administration, on the other hand, also firmly relied on crude enemy images, which in the American domestic context was not without precedent and was thus less sharp in its tone for US audiences than in German translation.[73] Such linguistic misunderstandings in transatlantic communications are likely to have escalated the struggle regarding the Double-Track Decision. The Krefeld Appeal (1980)—a plea directed at the West German government, formulated by various opponents of the Double-Track Decision, to refrain from deploying the Euromissiles—for example, equally rejected the Euromissiles, because Germany should not be at the mercy of an "American decision" based on the assumption that "a limited nuclear war in Europe is feasible."[74] The Appeal of Bielefeld—put forward by the SPD's youth organization—made a similar plea. Ironically, it was precisely this sentiment that had been the motive for Chancellor Schmidt as well as others in their support of the Double-Track Decision: to prevent a solitary decision by the Americans. Interviews given by senior American politicians and projections by American military planners who claimed that "victory is possible" were therefore grist for the mill for opponents of the Euromissiles and found their way into numerous pamphlets and speeches delivered at peace demonstrations.[75]

The security plans of the Reagan administration provoked a lasting debate about Germany's position within the transatlantic alliance among intellectual leaders of the peace movement as well as numerous local or regional grassroots initiatives. Did the alliance still serve German interests and should German-American relations continue to form a "second constitution" for the Federal Republic? The historical irony of this was, of course, that in the process of this debate the initial involvement of the Federal Government and Chancellor Schmidt's role in initiating the NATO Double-Track Decision gradually vanished and the decision came to be reinterpreted as an American imposition.[76] In this context, Pastor Heinrich Albertz, a member of the SPD and former mayor of Berlin, coined the well-known phrase that Germany remained an "occupied country,"[77] which further indicated the national fervor with which the political situation of the divided country was observed by some representatives of the peace movement. Certain opponents of the Euromissiles at the same time hoped for a reformulation of the German question and for more national political autonomy; their sentiments were summed up by the motto "The FRG is El Salvador."[78]

Faced by a renewed nuclear arms race and a strategic realignment of US politics toward a tough anti-Soviet confrontation, the question of national interest was therefore raised anew: "Who are we really, and in what situation do we find ourselves as Germans in the middle of Europe and with respect to the superpowers that dominate the world? How much freedom do we have to make our own decisions and how tight is the network of dependencies? Is our position different from that of our European neighbors in the East or the West?"[79] The state of being "occupied" was graphically illustrated on covers of respective publications, which displayed representations of missile deployments and nuclear explosions on West German territory, or the extensive maps of the *Militarization Atlas of West Germany*; one chapter of this book by Alfred Mechtersheimer, a social scientist and peace researcher, was in fact titled "An Occupied Country."[80]

A basic narrative that portrays Germany as a victim of a superpower conflict, particularly at the hands of an "American imperialism" aggravated by Reagan, forms a leitmotif for many publications of the peace movement and sympathetic intellectuals during the 1980s. Not only the Krefeld Appeal, initiated by communists shortly after Reagan's election, called for the government in Bonn to unilaterally prevent the creation of "a modernization of nuclear weapons in Central Europe as a nuclear arms platform for the United States."[81] Other perhaps more balanced publications that also directed criticism toward the Soviet Union nonetheless adopted and spread perceptions of Europe as a quasi-colonial protectorate of imperial superpowers. Albertz and Eppler, for example, made it perfectly clear that they judged the Soviet arms upgrade as great a problem as that of the West. Yet their formulations generally attacked Western positions more severely because, in their view, there was less chance of influencing Moscow from Western Europe.[82]

Given the harsh criticism of the plans of the US administration on the part of many members of the peace movement, their opponents regularly made pointed and polemical accusations that the movement paid homage to an undifferentiated and prejudiced anti-Americanism.[83] That certainly struck a nerve, and leading figures of the movement reacted in the strongest terms.

Nobel Laureate for Literature Heinrich Böll, for example, said at a demonstration in Bonn on 10 October 1981, that as a writer in 1945 he had, like many of his colleagues, been "liberated by American literature." He was more pro-American than the conservative parties of CDU/CSU, where American politics were even "less controversial" than "in America itself."[84] "No, it is not anti-American," argued Walter Jens, professor of rhetoric in Tübingen, "to declare, in agreement with the proclamations of the [US] civil rights movement, the hubris of the Reagan regime" and to highlight salient differences between German and American survival plans. To place oneself in the position of the Soviet Union, which was surrounded on all sides by the West, was also, according to Jens, not an indication of anti-American sentiment.[85]

Conversely, for the governing conservative coalition parties the massive and often unfounded criticism aimed at President Reagan and the United States in general was a most welcome opportunity to display faithful political allegiance and to act pro-American. Like Konrad Adenauer before him, the leader of the Christian Democrats and chancellor, Helmut Kohl, warned of the "illusion of a third way," in other words, a "special role for Germany" between East and West.[86] The SPD, he claimed, was cultivating "the evil spirit of anti-Americanism."[87] The conflict about the adequate security policy generated a "bad mood" in American-German relations and would promote isolationist tendencies in the United States. Left-wing leaders like Lafontaine and Eppler were "more Soviet than the Soviets" and statements by the Social Democratic chairman Herbert Wehner were disqualified by Kohl as "outright assistance" to the USSR.[88] Opponents to the Double-Track Decision conjured up fears of war, but his Union stood equally "for peace."[89] It was not the morality of deterrence that was open to debate, but the defense of Western values and the principles of democracy, freedom, justice, and human rights. More specifically, for Kohl the task was to defend a future in "a community of free peoples" in which they are able to create "jointly with our friends our destiny in peace and freedom."[90]

It would be misleading to consider the Euromissiles debate an example of an "alienation from Western democracies." The fact that the degree to which the Germans deemed themselves to be with the "West" was subject to debate ultimately consolidated cultural and political ties within the West. Both sides of the Double-Track Decision saw themselves as part of a transatlantic political community that provided different solutions to the problem of how the security issues relating to nuclear deterrence and the East-West conflict should be dealt with. There was no consensus on foreign policy in the United States during the Reagan administration, and neither was there any in West Germany. Chancellor Kohl expressed regret that during his visits to the United States he had to answer "nagging questions" of his American friends as to "where the path of West Germany [was] leading?"[91] Petra Kelly pointed out that she and her American friends "struggled for hope,"[92] and Willy Brandt explained to his friends in the United States that the rejection of new missiles was not anti-American but in line with the demands of the American freeze movement.[93]

The Impact on Party Politics

The third question about the political impact and the consequences of the nuclear crisis for the West German political system seems to be the easiest one, answered once the Schmidt government was replaced in 1982 at the height of the "missile debate." However, we need to avoid the false straightforward link between chronology on the one hand, and cause and effect on the other. Indeed, the social-liberal coalition did not primarily collapse because of the nuclear crisis, but due to profound disagreements in economic and social policy as well. The nuclear crisis was more significant, however, for the success of the Green Party in these elections and their mandate to enter into parliament in March 1983. But even in this case the controversy about the Euromissiles was merely one among several factors, and the extent to which it was decisive for the electoral success of this new party remains controversial.[94] However, as Mende and Metzger argue, the issue of nuclear weapons was more compatible with other goals than the objectives of the antinuclear energy lobby and the environmental movements. The debate about the NATO Double-Track Decision thus seems to have had the most profound effect upon the party system of West Germany ever since the 1950s, even if the precise impact is impossible to measure by social scientific standards. After all, one result was the permanent expansion to a four-party system.

The nuclear crisis therefore did not alter the fundamental structure of the political culture in Germany in its orientation toward the West or its post-Nazi consensus; rather, both experienced a certain consolidation. The nuclear crisis did nonetheless affect everyday party politics and changed the configuration of power relations in parliament. Similarly, the breakup of the social-liberal coalition under Schmidt and Genscher was connected to the "missile controversy," even if this was by no means the sole reason for the departure of the Free Democratic Party from government.[95] Right after the change of the governing coalition, the Double-Track Decision served like an appeal to the internal solidarity of the newly formed alliance and as a unifying bond between the new coalition partners despite a rather heterogeneous spectrum of opinions. The Green Party's electoral success, on the other hand, is evidence of the SPD's failure to integrate the votes from the left-alternative movements.

At the same time, however, it enhanced internal party cohesion and determination and had a calming internal effect among Social Democrats, which, as a result, would probably have returned the party to power in the 1991 elections if it had not been for the historic German unification in 1989–90.[96]

In sum, West German politics and its major parties were yet again, despite serious disputes and conflicts on foreign policy, fundamentally united to a remarkably high level on issues of domestic and social policy. The differences pertaining to foreign policies, however, helped to secure and legitimize new coalition governments, as they did in 1969. It was a manifestation of West German normalcy that the various political camps—unlike, for example, in the United Kingdom and the United States—accentuated their political profile with the help of foreign rather than domestic policy. Consequently, the dispute on nuclear deterrence continued well after 1983 because it allowed for an antagonistic positioning of both camps without infringing on the great democratic consensus that entailed, above all, issues of social policy. It may thus not be unreasonable to argue that the nuclear crisis did ultimately not so much fracture but further a basic consensus in West German society.[97]

The End of the Cold War

And finally, the fourth question: What is the connection between the nuclear crisis and the end of the Cold War? Historians are reluctant to explain historical developments with reference to single issues or events. The question can therefore not be satisfactorily answered when phrased in this limited way. In his contribution to this volume, Florian Pressler underlines that the "victory of arms control" in the second half of the 1980s had many fathers and mothers. Following the argument of the doyen of the history of the global peace movement since 1945, Lawrence S. Wittner, it is possible that protests indeed exerted pressure on the US administration and its European allies.[98] President Reagan personally had a deep-seated aversion to nuclear weapons (which explains his enthusiasm for the Strategic Defense Initiative, or SDI) and increasingly revealed himself from 1983–84 onward to be a radical nuclear abolitionist.[99] At the same time, the conservative supporters of a "Cold War triumphalism"—but not only those—are probably right in their assessment that Gorbachev had to respond, as he himself wrote, to the fact that the USSR was "pressed into an exhausting arms race to which it was nearly led to the brink of ruin."[100]

The Soviet Union reacted to the Double-Track Decision with various diplomatic and security policies, as Oliver Bange explores in his contribution to this volume. These included indirect and concealed strategies—through the "peace policy" of allied countries such as East Germany—but also partially open and direct financial and logistical support for the Western peace movement. This "infiltration" does not, however, explain the phenomenon of the peace movement in all its heterogeneity. Ultimately, the movement had to compete and resonate in an open, pluralistic society and to succeed in a free market system of Western media.[101] Moreover, the USSR and the Warsaw Pact had adapted their military plans early on and managed to adjust to the new strategic realities that were created by the stationing of Pershing II and cruise missiles in Europe. Recent research recognizes in this period a transition to an increasingly defensive-minded strategy by the Warsaw Pact and, with the Berlin Declaration of May 1987, a complete shift toward defensive planning.

The renewed intensification in the East-West confrontation since the late 1970s—the invasion of Afghanistan by the Soviet Union marks an important date in this process—was one of the roots of the resurgence of the peace movement in the early 1980s. News about multiple instances of near-war emergencies that could be prevented only at the very last minute resulted in a major rethinking on the part of the USSR as well as the United States.[102] Unlike in the 1950s, Europeans in the East and West during the 1980s were no longer prepared to readily accept the severe confrontational rhetoric of the superpowers. The sudden return of a nuclear threat that many had believed gone and that popular culture had helped to discredit provoked a serious shock. Against this background both President Reagan as well as his Soviet counterpart Mikhail Gorbachev, General Secretary of the Communist Party, gave in. After their first meeting in Geneva in 1985, a second encounter in Reykjavik in 1986 almost resulted in a sensational disarmament deal.[103]

It is hard to imagine that the East-West conflict would have found such a dramatic but peaceful end with the fall of the Berlin Wall in 1989–90 if there had been no prior phase of serious progress in the area of détente. The INF Treaty of 1987 abolished all medium-range missiles on both sides, representing the implementation of the disarmament part of the NATO Double-Track Decision, and provided an important psychological breakthrough. It was, however, embedded in numerous other steps toward détente in Europe and beyond, including the Soviet withdrawal from Afghanistan. Both Reagan and Gorbachev primarily kept in mind their domestic situation when embarking on these initiatives. Consequently, their drastic steps toward a rapprochement provoked skepticism on the part of their allies, who considered this reversal to be too fast.[104] Curiously, in 1987–88, shortly before the end of the Cold War, these differences even led the American government to question the solidarity of the West German government, one of its foremost political allies.[105]

The debate about the Double-Track Decision prepared the way for the reunification of Europe in spirit, if not in quantifiable terms or as a specific causal event. The nascent independence of the Europeans in the East and West from the two dominant superpowers has already been referred to. But there is another point to be made: peace organizations like the British European Nuclear Disarmament (END) early on engaged in a dialogue across the frontiers of the Cold War. They systematically communicated not only with the official, that is, the state-sponsored peace movement of the East, but also with members of human rights groups, which had emerged in countries such as Czechoslovakia, Poland, and Hungary because of the Helsinki process. Initially, considerable tensions developed as the Western members of the peace movement insisted on discussing disarmament while their Eastern activist counterparts refused to separate external peace from civil liberties and personal freedom on a domestic level. To these activists, human and civil rights in their own countries were a prerequisite and a guarantee for détente and peace at large. One of the most burning issues of our days thus first emerged in the context of the nuclear crisis in a way that cut across the ideological blocs of East and West.

These contacts and relationships were neither void of conflict nor restricted to the political "leaders" of each side; instead, they were ever-expanding and embraced by constantly widening social forces. The thriving social ties between the Western peace movement and Eastern civil rights activists in the context of the nuclear crisis during the 1980s thus substantially helped pave the way for the great turning point of 1989–90 and the subsequent growing together of all of Europe. The resumption of talks, meetings, and general communication based on these transnational networks and relationships of peace movements in the East and West[106] also built a common European identity and, in the case of Germany, a novel identity for all German citizens. Eventually the "nuclear crisis" also provided a path to this larger socio-cultural transformation, just as it helped strengthen an internal democratic consensus.

Christoph Becker-Schaum is Research Associate at the Leibniz Center of Contemporary History in Potsdam. He has previously taught courses on European parties and party systems at the Otto-Suhr-Institute of Political Science at the Free University of Berlin. His publications include *Arnold Herrmann Ludwig Heeren: Ein Beitrag zur Geschichte der Geschichtswissenschaft zwischen Aufklärung und Historismus* (1993); "Von der Protestbewegung zur demokratischen Alternative: Die Grünen Hessen 1979–2004," in *Hessen: 60 Jahre Demokratie. Beiträge zum Landesjubiläum*, ed. Helmut Berding and Klaus Eiler (2006), 151–87.

Philipp Gassert is professor of contemporary history at the University of Mannheim. Previously he worked and taught at the German Historical Institute in Washington, DC, the University of Heidelberg, the University of Pennsylvania in Philadelphia, PA, and the University of Augsburg. He has also been a visiting professor at the University of Haifa and Sir Peter Ustinov Visiting Professor at the University of Vienna. Since 2011 he has been the Executive Director of the German Association for American Studies. Gassert specializes in twentieth century transatlantic and international history. Selected publications include *Kurt Georg Kiesinger, 1904–1988: Kanzler zwischen den Zeiten* (2006), *Kleine Geschichte der USA* (together with Mark Häberlein and Michael Wala, 2007/08), *Zweiter Kalter Krieg und Friedensbewegung: Der NATO-Doppelbeschluss in deutschdeutscher und internationaler Perspektive* (coedited with Tim Geiger and Hermann Wentker, 2011), *Amerikas Kriege* (2014). He is one of the codirectors of the research project "The Nuclear Crisis: Cold War Cultures and the Politics of Peace and Security, 1975–1990" (www.nuclearcrisis.org) and is currently working on a global history of protest marches and street demonstrations.

Martin Klimke is Vice Provost for Academic Policies and Governance and Associate Professor of History at New York University Abu Dhabi. His research explores the intersections of political and cultural, diplomatic and transnational history. It is dedicated to the role of America in the world with an emphasis on processes of transnational exchange in US-European relations in the twentieth century, and more particularly in the period of the Cold War. Klimke is the author of *The Other Alliance: Global Protest and Student Unrest in West Germany and the US, 1962–1972* (2010) and coauthor of *A Breath of Freedom: The Civil Rights Struggle, African-American GIs, and Germany* (2010). He is a coeditor of the Protest, Culture, and Society publication series at Berghahn Books and of several collected volumes on various aspects of transatlantic and transnational history, as well as the Cold War, most recently *"Trust, but Verify": The Politics of Uncertainty & the Transformation of the Cold War Order, 1969–1991* (2016) and *Nuclear Threats, Nuclear Fear and the Cold War of the 1980s* (2016). He is also an associated researcher at the Heidelberg Center for American Studies (HCA) and codirector of the research project "The Nuclear Crisis: Cold War Cultures and the Politics of Peace and Security, 1975–1990" (www.nuclearcrisis.org).

Wilfried Mausbach is the Executive of the Heidelberg Center for American Studies (HCA) at the University of Heidelberg. He is the author of a book on American economic postwar policy toward Germany, *Zwischen Morgenthau und Marshall: Das wirtschaftspolitische Deutschlandkonzept der USA*

1944–1947 (Düsseldorf: Droste, 1996), coeditor of *America, the Vietnam War, and the World: Comparative and International Perspectives* (New York: Cambridge University Press, 2003), and an adjunct editor of *The United States and Germany in the Era of the Cold War, 1945–1990: A Handbook*, 2 vols. (New York: Cambridge University Press, 2004). He is the codirector of the research project The Nuclear Crisis: Cold War Cultures and the Politics of Peace and Security, 1975–1990 (www.nuclearcrisis.org).

Marianne Zepp received her MA at the Johannes-Gutenberg-University of Mainz in history, sociology, and German literature and her PhD at the Technical University, Berlin, in contemporary history in 2006. Her research focuses on contemporary history, politics of memory, European and international development of democracy, as well as gender politics. She is the author of *Redefining Germany: Reeducation, Staatsbürgerschaft und Frauenpolitik im US-amerikanisch besetzten Nachkriegsdeutschland* (2007); "Weiblichkeit als politisches Argument: Frieden und Demokratie im Übergang zu einer deutschen Nachkriegsgesellschaft," in *Frieden durch Demokratie: Genese, Wirkung und Kritik eines Deutungsmusters*, ed. Jost Dülffer and Gottfried Niedhart (2011), 187–205. Zepp worked with the Heinrich-Böll-Foundation for over fifteen years in Berlin as a program director for Contemporary History and Democratic Development before joining the foundation's Tel Aviv office as a program director for Israeli-German relations and relations with Europe in 2011.

Notes

1. NATO's Dual-Track Decision, 12 December 1979, http://www.nato.int/cps/en/natolive/official_texts_27040.htm?selectedLocale=en
2. Rundbrief des Koordinationsausschusses für die Herbstaktion vom 15.–22.10.1983, Nr. 1, July 1983, Archiv Grünes Gedächtnis (hereafter AGG), Berlin ZS 8389.
3. Proceedings of the German Parliament, Stenographische Berichte, 10. Wahlperiode, 36. Session, 2590.
4. Archiv der Gegenwart (hereafter AdG), 26 November 1983, 27213.
5. Jeffrey Herf, *War by Other Means: Soviet Power, West German Resistance, and the Battle of the Euromissiles* (New York, 1991); Eckart Conze, *Die Suche nach Sicherheit: Eine Geschichte der Bundesrepublik Deutschland von 1949 bis in die Gegenwart* (Munich, 2009), 623–33.
6. For an international perspective, see Leopoldo Nuti et al., eds., *The Euromissile Crisis and the End of the Cold War* (Washington, DC, 2015).
7. Thomas Leif, *Die strategische (Ohn-)Macht der Friedensbewegung: Kommunikations- und Entscheidungsstrukturen in den achtziger Jahren* (Opladen, 1990), 32–55.

8. The significance of the Double-Track Decision for the end of the Schmidt-Genscher government has been contentious. See the contribution of Jan Hansen in this volume.
9. Philipp Gassert, "Arbeit am Konsens im Streit um den Frieden: Die Nuklearkrise der 1980er Jahre als Medium gesellschaftlicher Selbstverständigung," Archiv für Sozialgeschichte (hereafter AfS) 52 (2012): 491–516.
10. Erhard Eppler, "Friedensbewegung," in *In letzter Stunde: Aufruf zum Frieden*, ed. Walter Jens (Munich, 1982), 143–66, especially 152.
11 Hans-Dietrich Genscher, *Rebuilding a House Divided: A Memoir by the Architect of Germany's Reunification* (New York, 1997), 154; 164. For an introduction to the Euromissile Crisis, see also David Holloway, "The Dynamics of the Euromissile Crisis, 1977–1983," in Nuti, et al., *The Euromissile Crisis*, 11–28.
12. Helmut Kohl, *Erinnerungen 1982–1990* (Munich, 2005), 140.
13. Helmut Schmidt, "The 1977 Alastair Buchan Memorial Lecture," in *Survival* (1978), 2–10. See also NC homepage: https://www.box.com/shared/266gfclxsf.
14. The concept of "flexible response" harks back to the late 1950s. It became official policy in December 1967 through MC 14/3, compare the Report of the Military Committee of NATO, 16.1.1968, http://www.nato.int/docu/stratdoc/eng/a680116a.pdf; on Schmidt's geopolitical nightmares, see Philipp Gassert, "Did Transatlantic Drift Help European Integration? The Euromissiles Crisis, the Strategic Defense Initiative, and the Quest for Political Cooperation," in *European Integration and the Atlantic Community in the 1980s*, ed. Kiran Patel and Kenneth Weisbrode (New York, 2013), 161–62.
15. Beatrice Heuser and Kristan Stoddart, "Großbritannien zwischen Doppelbeschluss und Anti-Kernwaffen-Protestbewegungen," in *Zweiter Kalter Krieg und Friedensbewegung: Der NATO-Doppelbeschluss in deutsch-deutscher und internationaler Perspektive*, ed. Philipp Gassert, Tim Geiger, and Hermann Wentker (Munich, 2011), 316f. See also Kristan Stoddart, "Creating the 'Seamless Robe of Deterrence': Great Britain's Role in NATO's INF Debate," in Nuti et al., *The Euromissile Crisis*, 176–95.
16. Hans-Peter Schwarz, *Helmut Kohl: Eine politische Biographie* (Munich, 2012), 428.
17. Georges-Henri Soutou, "Mitläufer der Allianz? Frankreich und der NATO-Doppelbeschluss," in Gassert, Geiger, and Wentker, *Zweiter Kalter Krieg*, 363–76; Frédéric Bozo, "France, the Euromissiles, and the End of the Cold War," in Nuti et al., *The Euromissile Crisis*, 196–212.
18. Gottfried Niedhart, "Selektive Wahrnehmung und politisches Handeln: Internationale Beziehungen im Perzeptionsparadigma," in *Internationale Geschichte: Themen—Ergebnisse—Aussichten*, ed. Winfried Loth and Jürgen Osterhammel (Munich, 2000), 141–57.
19. See also Gerhard Wettig, "Sowjetische Euroraketenrüstung und Auseinandersetzung mit den Reaktionen des Westens. Motivationen und Entscheidungen," in Gassert, Geiger, and Wentker, *Zweiter Kalter Krieg*, 49–64.
20. Herf, *War by Other Means*. That the Soviet hegemony was actually weakening has been argued by Vladislav M. Zubok, "The Soviet Union and Europe in the 1970s," in *Europe in the International Arena during the 1970s: Entering a Different World*, ed. Antonio Varsori and Guia Magni (Brussels, 2011), 143–58. See also Jonathan Haslam, "Moscow's Misjudgment in Deploying SS-20 Missiles," in Nuti, et al., *The Euromissile Crisis*, 31–48.

21. Matthias Schulz and Thomas A. Schwartz, eds., *The Strained Alliance: U.S.-European Relations from Nixon to Carter* (New York, 2009); Kristina Spohr Readman, "Conflict and Cooperation in Intra-alliance Nuclear Politics: Western Europe, America and the Genesis of Nato's Dual-Track Decision, 1977–1979," *Journal of Cold War Studies* 13, no. 2 (2011): 39–89; Matthias Schulz and Thomas A. Schwartz, "NATO's Nuclear Politics and the Schmidt-Carter Rift," in Nuti et al., *The Euromissile Crisis*, 139–57; William Burr, "A Question of Confidence: Theater Nuclear Forces, US Policy toward Germany, and the Origins of the Euromissile Crisis, 1975–76," in Nuti et al., *The Euromissile Crisis*, 123–38.
22. Andreas W. Daum, Wilfried Mausbach, and Lloyd C. Gardner, eds., *America, the Vietnam War, and the World: Comparative and International Perspectives* (New York, 2003).
23. Leopoldo Nuti, ed., *The Crisis of Détente in Europe: From Helsinki to Gorbachev, 1975–1985* (London, 2009); Schulz and Schwartz, eds., *The Strained Alliance*.
24. Klaus Wiegrefe, *Das Zerwürfnis: Helmut Schmidt, Jimmy Carter und die Krise der deutsch-amerikanischen Beziehungen* (Berlin, 2005).
25. "Bericht des Parteivorsitzenden Dr. Helmut Kohl," 29. Bundesparteitag der Christlich Demokratischen Union Deutschlands (Niederschrift), Mannheim, 9.–10.3.1981, Ms. Bonn 1981, 34–35.
26. Tim Geiger, "Die Regierung Schmidt-Genscher und der NATO-Doppelbeschluss," in Gassert, Geiger, and Wentker, *Zweiter Kalter Krieg*, 95–122, especially 100–105; Philipp Gassert, "Viel Lärm um Nichts? Der NATO-Doppelbeschluss als Katalysator gesellschaftlicher Selbstverständigung in der Bundesrepublik," in Gassert, Geiger, and Wentker, *Zweiter Kalter Krieg*, 175–202.
27. Protokoll des CDU-Bundesparteitages 1981 in Hamburg, 60, quoted after Hansen in this volume.
28. According to Boll and Hansen, "Doppelbeschluss und Nachrüstung als innerparteiliches Problem der SPD" in Gassert, Geiger, and Wentker, *Zweiter Kalter Krieg*; see also Bernd Faulenbach, *Das sozialdemokratische Jahrzehnt: Von der Reformeuphorie zur neuen Unübersichtlichkeit. Die SPD 1969–1982* (Bonn, 2012). On the repercussions for Social Democratic parties across Europe, see Bernd Rother, "Family Row: The Dual-Track Decision and Its Consequences for European Social Democratic Cooperation," in Nuti et al., *The Euromissile Crisis*, 331–47.
29. See also Wolfgang Schröder, "Gewerkschaft als soziale Bewegung. Soziale Bewegung in den Gewerkschaften in den Siebzigerjahren," in *AfS* 44 (2004): 243–57.
30. Bernd Hey, *1968 und die Kirchen* (Gütersloh, 2008).
31. Hans-Jochen Luhmann and Gundel Neveling, *Deutscher Evangelischer Kirchentag* (Hamburg, 1981); *Dokumente* (Stuttgart, 1981); Susanne Schregel, "Konjunktur der Angst: 'Politik der Subjektivität' und 'neue Friedensbewegung,' 1979–1983," in *Angst im Kalten Krieg*, ed. Bernd Greiner, Christian Th. Müller, and Dierk Walter (Hamburg, 2009), 495–520.
32. Sebastian Kalden, "A Case of Hollanditis: The Interchurch Peace Council in the Netherlands and the Christian Peace Movement in Western Europe," in *Nuclear Threats, Nuclear Fear and the Cold War of the 1980s*, ed. Eckart Conze, Martin Klimke, and Jeremy Varon (New York, 2016), 251–267.
33. Ralf Zoll, "Sicherheitspolitik und Streitkräfte im Spiegel öffentlicher Meinung in den Vereinigten Staaten von Amerika und der Bundesrepublik Deutschland," in *Genese,*

Struktur und Wandel von Meinungsbildern in Militär und Gesellschaft: Ergebnisse und Analyseansätze im internationalen Vergleich, ed. Ralf Zoll (Opladen, 1982), 33–65; Thomas Risse-Kappen, *Die Krise der Sicherheitspolitik: Neuorientierung der Entscheidungsprozesse im politischen System der Bundesrepublik Deutschland* (Mainz 1988), 194. On public opinion across Western Europe, see Maria Eleonora Guasconi, "Public Opinion and the Euromissile Crisis," in Nuti et al., *The Euromissile Crisis*, 271–90.

34. Josef Joffe, "Peace and Populism: Why the European Anti-Nuclear Movement Failed," *International Security* 11 (1987): 3–40.

35. For a brief overview of the German peace movement, see also Holger Nehring, "The Last Battle of the Cold War: Peace Movements and German Politics in the 1980s," in Nuti et al., *The Euromissile Crisis*, 309–30. On the "infiltrated" peace movement, see Udo Baron, *Kalter Krieg und heißer Frieden: Der Einfluß der SED und ihrer westdeutschen Verbündeten auf die Partei "Die Grünen"* (Münster, 2003); Michael Ploetz and Hans-Peter Müller, *Ferngelenkte Friedensbewegung? DDR und UdSSR im Kampf gegen den NATO-Doppelbeschluss* (Münster, 2004); for a critical reexamination of the "fifth column thesis" see Holger Nehring and Benjamin Ziemann, "Do All Paths Lead to Moscow? The NATO-Dual-Track Decision and the Peace Movement—A Critique," in *Cold War History* 12, no. 1 (2012): 1–24.

36. A term that only gained traction in Germany during the 1980s; compare Wilfried Mausbach, "The Present's Past: Recent Perspectives on Peace and Protest in Germany, 1945–1973," *Mitteilungsblatt des Instituts für Soziale Bewegungen* 32 (2004): 67–98, especially 68; Roland Roth and Dieter Rucht, eds., *Die sozialen Bewegungen in Deutschland seit 1945: Ein Handbuch* (Frankfurt am Main, 2008), 640–41.

37. On the environmental dimension, see also Wilfried Mausbach, "Nuclear Winter: Prophecies of Doom and Images of Desolation During the Second Cold War" and Stephen Milder, "The Example of Wyhl: How Grassroots Protest in the Rhine Valley Shaped the West German Anti-Nuclear Movement," both in Conze et al., *Nuclear Threats*, 27–54; 167–185.

38. Ulrike Wasmuht, *Friedensbewegungen der 80er Jahre: Zur Analyse ihrer strukturellen und aktuellen Entstehungsbedingungen in der Bundesrepublik Deutschland und den Vereinigten Staaten von Amerika nach 1945* (Giessen, 1987); see also Benjamin Ziemann, "Perspektiven der historischen Friedensforschung," in *Perspektiven der historischen Friedensforschung*, ed. Benjamin Ziemann (Essen, 2002), 13–39, esp. 14–15; David J. Dunn, *The First Fifty Years of Peace Research: A Survey and Interpretation* (Aldershot, 2005).

39. Andreas Rödder, "Bündnissolidarität und Rüstungskontrollpolitik: Die Regierung Kohl-Genscher, der NATO-Doppelbeschluss und die Innenseite der Außenpolitik," in Gassert, Geiger and Wentker, *Zweiter Kalter Krieg*, 123–36, especially 125.

40. See Sven Reichardt and Detlef Siegfried, eds. *Das Alternative Milieu: Antibürgerlicher Lebensstil und linke Politik in der Bundesrepublik Deutschland und Europa 1968–1983* (Göttingen, 2010); Hanno Balz and Jan-Henrik Friederichs, eds., *"All We Ever Wanted …" Eine Kulturgeschichte europäischer Protestbewegungen der 1980er Jahre* (Berlin, 2012).

41. On the women's movement and 1968, see Kristina Schulz, *Der lange Atem der Provokation. Die Frauenbewegung in Frankreich und der Bundesrepublik, 1968–1976* (Frankfurt am Main, 2002).

42. For transnational connections of church-based activisim, see Sebastian Kalden and Ole Wiechmann's contribution in this volume, as well as Beatrice de Graaf, *Die DDR, die niederländischen Kirchen und die Friedensbewegung* (Münster, 2007). For END, see Patrick Burke, "A Transcontinental Movement of Citizens? Strategic Debates in the 1980s Western Peace Movement," in *Transnational Moments of Change: Europe 1945, 1968, 1989*, ed. Gerd-Rainer Horn and Padraic Kenney (Lanham, MD, 2004), 189–206; Patrick Burke, "European Nuclear Disarmament: Transnational Peace Campaigning in the 1980s," in Conze et al., *Nuclear Threats*, 227–250. On the spread of "Nuclear Free Zones," see Susanne Schregel, "Global Micropolitics: Towards a Transnational History of Grassroots Nuclear Free Zones," in Conze et al., *Nuclear Threats*, 206–226. For transnational linkages in a more general perspective, please see Matthew Evangelista, *Unarmed Forces: The Transnational Movement to End the Cold War* (Ithaca, NY, 1999).

43. On individuals such as Petra Kelly, see Stephen Milder, "Between Grassroots Activism and Transnational Aspirations: Anti-Nuclear Protest from the Rhine Valley to the Bundestag, 1974–1983," *Historical Social Research* 39, no. 1 (2014): 191–211. On the global movement against nuclear disarmament, please see the pioneering works by Lawrence Wittner, *Toward Nuclear Abolition: A History of the World Nuclear Disarmament Movement, 1979 to the Present*, vol. 3 of *The Struggle against the Bomb* (Stanford, CA, 2003); *One World or None: A History of the World Nuclear Disarmament Movement through 1953* vol. 1, of *The Struggle against the Bomb* (Stanford, CA, 1993); and *Resisting the Bomb: A History of the World Nuclear Disarmament Movement 1954–1970*, vol. 2 of *The Struggle against the Bomb* (Stanford, CA, 1997).

44. On transatlantic differences, see Wilfried Mausbach, "Vereint marschieren, getrennt schlagen? Die amerikanische Friedensbewegung und der Widerstand gegen den NATO-Doppelbeschluss," in Gassert, Geiger and Wentker, *Zweiter Kalter Krieg*, 283–304; Kyle Harvey, "The Promise of Internationalism: US Anti-Nuclear Activism and the European Challenge," in *Making Sense of the Americas: How Protest Related to America in the 1980s and Beyond*, ed. Jan Hansen, Christian Helm, and Frank Reichherzer (Frankfurt am Main, 2015), 225–244; Dario Fazzi, "The Nuclear Freeze Generation: The Early 1980s Anti-Nuclear Youth Revolt between 'Carter's Vietnam' and 'Euroshima'," in *A European Youth Revolt: European Perspectives on Youth Protest and Social Movements in the 1980s*, ed. Knud Andresen and Bart van der Steen (Basingstoke, 2016), 145–158.

45. See the contribution by Rainer Eckert in this volume. See also Thomas Goldstein, "A Tenuous Peace: International Anti-Nuclear Activism in the East German Writers Union in the 1980s," in Conze, et al., *Nuclear Threats*, 142–164.

46. See also Malcolm Byrne, "The Warsaw Pact and the Euromissile Crisis, 1977–1983," in Nuti, et al., *The Euromissile Crisis*, 104–120; Idesbald Godeeris and Malgorzata Świder, "Peace or Solidarity? Poland, the Euromissile Crisis, and the 1980s Peace Movement," in Nuti, et al., *The Euromissile Crisis*, 291–308; Christie Miedema, *Vrede of Vrijheid? Dilemma's, dialoog en misverstanden tussen Nederlandse en West-Duitse linkse organisaties en de Poolse oppositie in de jaren tachtig* (Amsterdam, 2015); Christie Miedema, "'Hätten wir doch mehr auf die polnischen Ratschläge gehört': Die Grünen und die polnische Opposition in den 1980er Jahren," in Heinrich-Böll-Stiftung, *Grünes Gedächtnis 2015*, 59–82.

47. For the various forms of protest in the peace movement, see Tim Warneke, "Aktionsformen und Politikverständnis der Friedensbewegung: Radikaler Humanismus und die Pathosformel des Menschlichen," in Reichardt and Siegfried, *Das Alternative Milieu*, 445–72.
48. Aktionszeitung, "5. Juni, Hofgarten in Bonn—Großdemonstration Gemeinsam für Frieden und Freiheit, ACDP, CDU, Bundespartei, Ordner 2/20, 2/207 Broschüren und Flugblätter Jan.1982–Aug.1983; eine Übersicht zur Kamapagne 10.000 Friedenstag in Übersicht," in Union in Deutschland (hereafter UiD) 26 (1983): 1.9.1983; Deutsches Monatsblatt, 7/8 (1983).
49. Martin Klimke and Laura Stapane, "From Artists for Peace to the Green Caterpillar: Cultural Activism and Electoral Politics in 1980s West Germany," in Conze, et al., *Nuclear Threats*, 116–141.
50. See also William Knoblauch, "Will You Sing About the Missiles? British Anti-Nuclear Protest Music of the 1980s," in Conze, et al., *Nuclear Threats*, 101–115. On the politics of emotions, see Schregel, "Konjunktur der Angst."
51. See the contribution by Michael Sturm in this volume.
52. For a summary, see Risse-Kappen, *Die Krise der Sicherheitspolitik*.
53. Hans-Peter Schwarz, *Die gezähmten Deutschen: Von der Machtbesessenheit zur Machtvergessenheit* (Stuttgart, 1985).
54. Peter Graf Kielmansegg, *Nach der Katastrophe: Eine Geschichte des geteilten Deutschland* (Berlin, 2000), 234; Eckart Conze: *Suche*, 544; Heinrich August Winkler, *Der lange Weg nach Westen: Deutsche Geschichte vom "Dritten Reich" bis zur Wiedervereinigung*, Band 2 (Munich, 2000), 370f.; Herf, *War by Other Means*, 27, does not only see the security and foreign policy but also the democratic consensus in jeopardy overall.
55. See the contribution by Marianne Zepp in this volume.
56. The following remarks on points 1 through 3 draw on Gassert, "Viel Lärm um Nichts?"
57. For the transatlantic dimension of protest, see Martin Klimke, *The Other Alliance: Student Protest in West Germany and the United States in the Global Sixties* (Princeton, NJ, 2010).
58. Grundsatzrede des Vorsitzenden der CDU Deutschlands, Helmut Kohl, auf dem 30. CDU-Bundesparteitag, Hamburg, 2.–5.11.1981, 28–51, especially 33–34.
59. Deutscher Bundestag, Stenographische Berichte, 10. WP, 13. Sitzung, 15.6.1983, 755.
60. "Wir sind ein schöner Unkrautgarten," Spiegel-Gespräch mit Joschka Fischer und Otto Schily, *Der Spiegel* 24, 13 June 1983, 23–27, especially 26.
61. See, for example, the flyer of the Peace Initiative Wilmersdorf in Fritz Teppich, ed., *Flugblätter und Dokumente der Westberliner Friedensbewegung: 1980–1985* (Berlin, 1985), 25.
62. Günter Grass, "Vom Recht auf Widerstand: Rede auf der Gedenkveranstaltung der SPD zum 50. Jahrestag der Machtergreifung Hitlers in Frankfurt," in Grass, *Essays und Reden III, 1980–1997* (Göttingen, 1997), 63–70.
63. For the illustrations, see Volker Nick, Volker Scheub, and Christof Then, *Mutlangen 1983–1987: Die Stationierung der Pershing II und die Kampagne Ziviler Ungehorsam bis zur Abrüstung* (Mutlangen, 1993). See also Eckart Conze, "Modernitätsskepsis und die Utopie der Sicherheit: NATO-Nachrüstung und Friedensbewegung in der Ges-

chichte der Bundesrepublik" in *Zeithistorische Forschungen/Studies in Contemporary History,* Online-Ausgabe, 7 (2010): H. 2, http://www.zeithistorische-forschungen .de/16126041-Conze-2-2010.
64. Nick, Scheub, and Then, *Mutlangen 1983–1987,* 6. For references to Nazi Germany in general, see Eckart Conze, "Missile Bases as Concentration Camps: The Role of National Socialism, the Second World War, and the Holocaust in the West German Discourse on Nuclear Armament," in Conze, et al., *Nuclear Threats,* 79–97.
65. Mausbach, "Vereint marschieren, getrennt schlagen."
66. Helmut Kohl auf dem 30. Bundesparteitag der CDU in Hamburg, 2.–5.11.1981, 30.
67. Philipp Gassert, "Zwischen 'Beschweigen' und 'Bewältigen': Die Auseinandersetzung mit dem Nationalsozialismus in der Ära Adenauer," in *Epoche im Widerspruch. Ideelle und kulturelle Umbrüche der Adenauerzeit* (25. Rhöndorfer Gespräch), ed. Michael Hochgeschwender (Bonn, 2011), 183–205.
68. Heinz Bude and Bernd Greiner, eds., *Westbindungen: Amerika in der Bundesrepublik* (Hamburg, 1999); Mary Nolan, *The Transatlantic Century: Europe and America 1890–2010* (New York, 2012), 302–10.
69. Winkler, *Der lange Weg nach Westen,* 373, turns his contemporary criticism from within the party into an academic argument supported by empirical evidence. Compare the contemporary contributions by Winkler, Gesine Schwan, and others, in Jürgen Maruhn and Manfred Wilke, eds., *Wohin treibt die SPD? Wende oder Kontinuität sozialdemokratischer Sicherheitspolitik* (Munich, 1984). In a similar vein see the highly tendential description in Hans-Ulrich Wehler, *Deutsche Gesellschaftsgeschichte,* Bd. 5, (Munich, 2008), 250.
70. Kohl stressed repeatedly that the Americans "truly do not lack democratic understanding for demonstrations of free citizens for goals that deviate from those of the government." See CDU-Bundesparteitag Hamburg 1981, 33.
71. See photos as well as press coverage in *Aktion Sühnezeichen,* Bonn 10.10 1981.
72. See, for example, Petra Kelly "'Sie sollen sich Sorgen machen': Rede auf dem zweiten Forum der Krefelder Initiative, Dortmund, 21.11.1981," printed in Petra Kelly, *Um Hoffnung kämpfen: Gewaltfrei in eine grüne Zukunft* (Cologne, 1983), 69–71.
73. The crusade metaphor is often misunderstood in Germany, since in the United States "crusades" or "wars" are traditional terms stemming from the Christian social reform movement of the nineteenth century for campaigns against poverty, racial discrimination, etc. Along the same lines, many German commentators took the religious dimension of Reagan's "evil empire" rhetoric literally and saw its significance in Reagan's move toward the evangelical spectrum of the Republican Party, which had been partially critical of the "Reagan Revolution" and its domestic policies. See Werner Schmidt, "Die außenpolitische Rhetorik Ronald Reagans und die politische Kultur der USA," in *Rekonstruktion amerikanischer Stärke. Sicherheits- und Rüstungskontrollpolitik der USA während der Reagan-Administration,* ed. Helga Haftendorn and Jakob Schissler (Berlin, 1988), 87–100; Matthew Avery Sutton has noted that "While premillenialism had little (if any) direct influence on [Reagan's] actual foreign policy, it provided him with the rhetorical tools for mobilizing the American people to wage the Cold War." *American Apocalypse: A History of Modern Evangelicalism* (Cambridge, MA, 2014), 355.

74. "Bielefelder Appell" (Dezember 1980), abgedruckt in *Vorwärts*, 14.5.1981, online verfügbar unter, http://germanhistorydocs.ghi-dc.org/pdf/deu/Chapter12Doc7KM.pdf.
75. See Alfred Mechtersheimer and Peter Barth, eds., *Den Atomkrieg führbar und gewinnbar machen? Dokumente zur Nachrüstung*, vol. 2 (Reinbek, 1983), 59, 73, 79, for example, which includes explanations by members of the Reagan administration. See also Robert Scheer, *Und brennend stürzen die Vögel vom Himmel. Reagan und der 'begrenzte' Atomkrieg*. (Munich, 1983).
76. For more detail, see Herf, *War by Other Means*, 119f.
77. Heinrich Albertz, Panel Discussion "Wie christlich kann Politik sein?," 19.6.1981, Sporthalle Alsterdorf, in Luhmann and Nevelin, *Kirchentag*, 692.
78. Philipp Gassert, "Anti-Amerikaner? Die deutsche Neue Linke und die USA," in *Anti-Amerikanismus im 20. Jahrhundert. Studien zu Ost- und Westeuropa*, ed. Jan C. Behrends, Árpád von Klimo, and Patrice G. Poutrus (Bonn, 2005), 250–67.
79. Heinrich Albertz, "Von der Nation und von Wichtigerem," in Jens, *In letzter Stunde*, 135–42, especially 135.
80. Alfred Mechtersheimer and Peter Barth, ed., *Militarisierungsatlas der Bundesrepublik. Streitkräfte, Waffen und Standorte. Kosten und Risiken* (Darmstadt, 1986), 13.
81. "Krefelder Appell," in *Nachrüsten? Dokumente und Positionen zum NATO-Doppelbeschluß*, ed. Alfred Mechtersheimer (Reinbek, 1981), 250; available online in Michael Schmid, "Der Krefelder Appell," in 100(0) Schlüsseldokumente, http://mdzx.bib-bvb.de/cocoon/de1000dok/dok_0023_kre.pdf?lang=de.
82. This victimization discourse is palpable in a series of articles by the left/liberal magazines *Der Spiegel, Stern*, and *Die Zeit*. See, for example, the title of the *Spiegel* cover of July 1981: "Deutschland—Schießplatz der Supermächte" (Germany–Shooting Range of the Superpowers), which adopted Albertz's phrase from the panel discussion of the church congress. The series was published as Wilhelm Bittorf, ed., *Nachrüstung. Der Atomkrieg rückt näher* (Hamburg, 1982).
83. For a contemporary response to the claims, compare Emil-Peter Müller, *Antiamerikanismus in Deutschland: Zwischen Care-Paket und Cruise Missile* (Cologne, 1986; see also Reinhild Kreis, "'Eine Welt, ein Kampf, ein Feind'? Amerikakritik in den Protesten der 1980er Jahre," in Balz and Friedrichs *"All We Ever Wanted"*, 135–55.
84. Heinrich Böll, "Dieser Tag ist eine große Ermutigung," in *Bonn 10.10.1981*, 159–62, especially 159.
85. Walter Jens, "Appell in letzter Stunde," in Jens, *In letzter Stunde*, 7–26, especially 13.
86. "Bericht des Parteivorsitzenden Dr. Helmut Kohl," 29. Bundesparteitag der Christlich Demokratischen Union Deutschlands (Niederschrift), Mannheim, 9.–10.3.1981, Ms. Bonn 1981, 34f.
87. Ibid.
88. Kohl calls statements by Herbert Wehner a "sheer relief operation for the Soviet Union." *Frankfurter Allgemeine Zeitung*, 9 February 1979. For the other quotations, see Weber, *Zwischen Nachrüstung und Abrüstung*, 132.
89. As Kohl stated on the thirtieth national party convention of the CDU, "We are part of the German peace movement," Protokoll des 30. Bundesparteitags in Hamburg, 2–5.11.1981, 33.

90. "Frieden und Freiheit: Resolution zur aktuellen Friedensdiskussion. Verabschiedet vom Bundesausschuss der CDU am 15. Juni 1981," printed in Mechtersheimer, *Nachrüsten?* 182–89, quotation at 186, 189. On the transatlantic relationship, see also Reinhild Kreis, "Trust through Familiarity: Transatlantic Relations and Public Diplomacy in the 1980s," in *"Trust, but Verify" The Politics of Uncertainty & the Transformation of the Cold War Order, 1969–1991,* ed. Martin Klimke, Reinhild Kreis, and Christian Ostermann (Redwood City, CA, 2016), 218–234.
91. Helmut Kohl auf dem 30. Bundesparteitag der CDU in Hamburg, 2.–5.11.1981, 33.
92. See the title of her book, *Petra Kelly: Um Hoffnung kämpfen. Gewaltfrei in eine grüne Zukunft* (Bornheim-Merten, 1983).
93. Offener Brief des Vorsitzenden der SPD, Brandt, auf Fragen amerikanischer Freunde, 7.8.1983. In *Willy Brandt: Gemeinsame Sicherheit. Internationale Beziehungen und deutsche Frage 1982–1992,* ed. Uwe Mai, Bernd Rother, and Wolfgang Schmidt (Bonn, 2009), doc. 6, 142–46.
94. See Silke Mende, *Nicht rechts, nicht links, sondern vorn: Eine Geschichte der Gründungsgrünen* (Munich, 2011), as well as Andrei S. Markovits and Philip S. Gorski, *Red, Green, and Beyond* (New York, 1993), 106–12.
95. Genscher, *Erinnerungen,* 447f., talks about "compelling domestic and international causes," whereas "everything else" was increasingly "covered" by the NATO Double-Track Decision. See also Tim Geiger and Jan Hansen, "Did Protest Matter? The Influence of the Peace Movement on the West German Government and the Social Democratic Party, 1977–1983," in Conze et al., *Nuclear Threats,* 290–315.
96. Boll and Hansen, "Doppelbeschluss und Nachrüstung," in Gassert, Geiger and Wentker, *Zweiter Kalter Krieg,* 203–28.
97. Philipp Gassert, "Arbeit am Konsens."
98. Lawrence S. Wittner, *Toward Nuclear Abolition: A History of the World Nuclear Disarmament Movement, 1971 to the Present* (Stanford, CA, 2003), esp. 369–404. See also Matthew Evangelista, *Unarmed Forces: The Transnational Movement to End the Cold War* (Ithaca, NY, 1999).
99. See Beth A. Fischer, *The Reagan Reversal: Foreign Policy and the End of the Cold War* (Columbia, MO, 1997), 102–43; Paul Lettow, *Ronald Reagan and His Quest to Abolish Nuclear Weapons* (New York, 2005).
100. Michail Gorbatschow, *Gipfelgespräche: Geheime Protokoll aus meiner Amtszeit* (Berlin, 1993), 9 (cited by Pressler). For the argument that the Soviet Union fell victim to the arms race with the United States, see the summary by Richard Pipes, "Misinterpreting the Cold War: The Hardliners Had It Right," *Foreign Affairs* 74 (1995): 154–60.
101. Helge Heidemeyer, "NATO-Doppelbeschluss, westdeutsche Friedensbewegung und der Einfluss der DDR," in Gassert, Geiger, and Wentker, *Zweiter Kalter Krieg,* 247–68; Holger Nehring and Benjamin Ziemann, "Führen alle Wege nach Moskau? Der NATO-Doppelbeschluss und die Friedensbewegung. Eine Kritik," in *VfZ* 59 (2010): 81–100.
102. See *The Able Archer 83 Sourcebook,* posted 7 November 2013, The National Security Archive, retrieved 19 November 2014 from http://www2.gwu.edu/~nsarchiv/nukevault/ablearcher/; Vojtech Mastny, "How Able was 'Able Archer'?" *Journal of*

Cold War Studies 11 (Winter 2009): 108–23; Georg Schild, *1983: Das gefährlichste Jahr des Kalten Krieges* (Paderborn, 2013); Dmitry (Dima) Adamsky, "'Not Crying Wolf': Soviet Intelligence and the 1983 War Scare," in Nuti, et al., *The Euromissile Crisis*, 49–65; Conze, et al., eds., *Nuclear Threats*, passim.

103. On the impact of Reykjavík, see Elizabeth Charles, "Gorbachev and the Decision to Decouple the Arms Control Package: How the Breakdown of the Reykjavik Summit Led to the Elimination of the Euromissiles," in Nuti, et al., *The Euromissile Crisis*, 66–84.

104. Hermann Wentker, *Außenpolitik in engen Grenzen: Die DDR im internationalen System 1949–1989* (Munich, 2007).

105. Michael Broer, "The NATO Double Track Decision, the INF Treaty, and the SNF Controversy: German-American Relations between Consensus and Conflict," in *The United States and Germany in the Era of the Cold War, 1945–1990: A Handbook*, 2 vols., ed. Detlef Junker et al. (New York, 2004), 2: 148–54.

106. Kacper Szulecki, "'Hijacked Ideas.' Human Rights, Peace and Environmentalism in Czechoslovak and Polish Dissident Discourses," *East European Politics and Societies* 25, no. 2 (2011): 272–95.

Chapter 1

From Helsinki to Afghanistan: The CSCE Process and the Beginning of the Second Cold War

Anja Hanisch

In the summer of 1975 the Finnish capital witnessed a meeting the likes of which had not been seen in Europe since the Vienna Congress in 1815. Diplomats from thirty-five countries, senior representatives and journalists from across Europe and around the world traveled to Helsinki to attend the signing of the Final Act of the Conference on Security and Cooperation in Europe, or CSCE, on 1 August 1975. In one sense, the document denoted the ceremonial conclusion to long years of tough negotiation. In another sense, it marked a beginning.

The CSCE process is uniquely linked to the history of the Cold War. It reflects the complicated interdependencies that were characteristic of the postwar world order, and therefore features a complex web of bi- and multilateral relations and developments, as well as transnational actors and opposition groups. Processes of societal transformation, particularly in Eastern Europe, were an important result of this international conference diplomacy.

In the turbulent 1970s and 1980s the CSCE process, despite a dramatic deterioration in East-West relations after the Soviet invasion of Afghanistan, offered an ongoing discussion platform for maintaining relationships and dialogue, while other forums of international diplomacy and negotiation such as SALT (Strategic Arms Limitation Talks) or MBFR (Mutual and Balanced Force Reductions) increasingly faltered. The scope of topics raised in the CSCE went well beyond military aspects. In the CSCE, humanitarian concerns were integrated with those of security, and it was precisely this conjunction that helped bring about lasting change in the international relations of the 1980s.

Equally lasting were the changes inspired in East European societies by the CSCE. Whether these were obvious, or more subtle, as in an increased awareness of humanitarian concerns and human rights, by the end of the

Cold War it became impossible to ignore these changes. The CSCE also raised Western consciousness of humanitarian issues. However, it did not so much serve as a basis for protests against the wrongdoings of its own governments as it led to greater interest in observing how Eastern Europe complied with its provisions.

The Conference on Security and Cooperation in Europe

As early as the 1950s the USSR had attempted to launch a European conference that would seek to deal with security on an international level. However, the West suspected, and rightly so, that the USSR's prime motivation was to prevent the integration of the Federal Republic of Germany into the Western alliance.

From the perspective of the West, and in particular West Germany,[1] certain fundamental questions about the political situation in Europe had to be settled before a conference could be held. This was satisfied with the signing of the German *Ostverträge* (East Treaties) and the ratification of the *Viermächteabkommen* (Quadripartite Agreement) on Berlin. Moreover the Western nations insisted that the agenda be extended to humanitarian issues such as freer movement of people, ideas, and information. In addition, the Western European countries made the inclusion of the United States and Canada a nonnegotiable condition for their participation in such a security conference.[2]

Only after the USSR had met these conditions was the road clear to start thinking about holding a European security conference. As of 22 November 1972, the representatives of thirty-three European states (only Albania abstained), the United States, and Canada gathered in Dipoli (a conference center close to Helsinki), Finland, for multilateral preparatory talks. A first important result of the discussions was that negotiations were to be held outside the respective blocs and that any decisions were to be unanimous. Soon, however, the talks in Dipoli went beyond purely organizational topics.

By January 1973 four thematic areas had been established for the security conference agenda; they were referred to as "Baskets." Basket I dealt with issues of mutual relations and security. Basket II was about cooperation in economic, scientific, technical, and ecological matters. Basket III took shape as a distinct item of the agenda only at the beginning of 1973; it involved cooperation in humanitarian matters such as exchange of information and reunification of families. Lastly, Basket IV concerned questions of follow-up procedures and subsequent meetings. Preliminary talks concluded in the summer of 1973 with the "Blue Book," and its recommendations were ceremoniously adopted by the foreign ministers.[3]

Now the real negotiations of the CSCE could begin. These were to take place in three phases: the ceremonial opening of the conference by the foreign ministers of the participating states in Helsinki, to be followed by the actual negotiations held in Geneva, and the finalization of these in a formal ceremonial conclusion.

The start of the negotiations in Geneva on 18 September 1973 quickly revealed the issues in dispute. Heated debates took place about the wording and placement of the principals of multilateral relations in Basket I, dealing with sovereign equality among states, respect for human rights, and fundamental freedoms. Nearly up to the end of the negotiations it was still unresolved as to where to insert a sentence demanded by the German Federal Republic and its allies about the possibility of peaceful change of borders: should it come under the principle of the inviolability of borders or the principle of the sovereignty of states? The German Federal Republic considered its inclusion imperative in order to preserve the possibility of German unification.[4]

Additional complications arose from strategies of tactical negotiation. Eastern delegations under the leadership of the USSR pressed for speedy progress on the topics in Basket I, while the Western delegations sought to delay any agreement in this Basket until progress in Basket III was tangible. Swift agreement was reached about cultural and educational cooperation, but information exchange and human contacts, both sensitive areas for the Eastern bloc states, remained contentious.

The negotiations on economic, scientific, technical, and environmental cooperation in Basket II were comparatively straightforward. Initially the East pursued the ambitious goal of establishing a permanent institution for handling follow-up procedures, a concern raised in Basket IV. However, the Western states at first showed little interest in Basket IV and opposed the idea of a permanent institution for the CSCE. Given the tortuous development of the negotiations in Basket III, the Eastern states soon dropped the idea of a permanent institutionalized body. Their then significantly more defensive line was to avoid establishing an institution that could serve as "an appeal body for Basket III."

After nearly two years of negotiations, what came to be called the Helsinki Final Act was ceremoniously signed.

The four Baskets woven in Dipoli had now been filled. Basket I contained ten principles for the design of multilateral relations of the members of the CSCE, including sovereign equality, inviolability of borders, territorial integrity of states, nonintervention in internal affairs, and respect for human rights and for fundamental freedoms. In Basket III, agreement had been reached on wide-ranging formulations such as "favorably" considering

Figure 1.1. The Conference on Security and Cooperation in Europe (CSCE) in Helsinki in the summer of 1975 was the first attempt by Eastern and Western states, including the United States and Canada, to secure détente by means of multilateral cooperation. The photo shows the First Secretary of the Central Committee of the SED (Socialist Unity Party of Germany), Erich Honecker (front left), and Chancellor of the Federal Republic, Helmut Schmidt (front right), before the conference on 30 July 1975 (BArch B 145 Bild-00009689 / Engelbert Reineke)

visa applications and viewing requests for family member reunifications in a "positive and humanitarian spirit."[5]

From the perspective of international law, the Final Act did not represent a binding contract. However, it did represent a high level of official commitment as thirty-five high-ranking state representatives, among them US President Gerald Ford and Soviet Secretary General Leonid Brezhnev, vested it with political authority. In the eyes of the Eastern bloc states, the document cemented the status quo of the postwar order in Europe. At the same time it also included dynamic elements: first, the ratification of the Final Act provided the CSCE process with a structural base as the participating states had consented to congregate for a follow-up meeting in Belgrade in 1977; and second, Basket III presented for the first time a detailed map for the implementation of the human rights and basic liberties recognized and acknowledged in Basket I.[6]

Were the Eastern states aware of the risk they were taking when they signed the Helsinki Final Act? Neither the USSR nor East Germany was completely naïve about the possible consequences of the recommendations of Basket III or the principles on human rights in Basket I. This had become clear during tough negotiations. Indeed Moscow and East Berlin viewed with suspicion the potential political consequences of the agreement right after the signing of the Final Act.[7]

Many quarters in the West regarded the Final Act not as a diplomatic achievement but rather as a colossal concession to the hegemonic aspirations of the USSR. Under the headline "Jerry, Don't Go" the *Wall Street Journal* urged President Gerald Ford not to travel to the signing of the Final Act in Helsinki.[8]

Societal Implications of the Helsinki Final Act

Delegates of the participating states, senior government officials, and journalists had hardly left Finland when a fierce controversy about the interpretation of the Helsinki Final Act broke out. All participating states had agreed to publish the wording of the Final Act. East Germany and the USSR, for example, printed the text in major daily newspapers such as *Neues Deutschland* (New Germany) and *Pravda* respectively.[9] Feeling the need to justify the alleged concessions they made to the territorial aspirations of the USSR and the order of Yalta, the Western states underlined the importance of Basket III. In contrast, the Eastern states stressed the results of Basket I and in particular the principles of the "inviolability of frontiers," "sovereignty," and "nonintervention in internal affairs," which softened the cutting edge of Basket III and its humanitarian recommendations.

Eastern state propaganda could not, however, prevent many in Eastern Europe from drawing hope in various ways from the Final Act. In the Baltic republics groups called confidently on the principle of "self-determination of peoples" referred to in Basket I while in the USSR, Poland, the CSSR (Czechoslovak Socialist Republic), and East Germany, persons mainly responded to Basket III. Moscow saw the formation of an opposition group around the nuclear physicist Yuri Orlov and other well-known opponents in May 1976. It was known as the Moscow Helsinki Group and sought to inform the public as well as governments of CSCE-member states about violations made by the USSR to the recommendations of the Final Act and to document such violations.

Initially, the Kremlin reacted relatively moderately; it attempted to publicly compromise the Moscow Helsinki Group. At the beginning of 1977, however, repressions became more intense. Several members of the group were arrested and sentenced to years of imprisonment and exile. The CSCE process hence influenced the attitude of the Kremlin in two ways: immediately after the summit in Helsinki, the CPSU (Communist Party of the Soviet Union) avoided incidents that could trigger Western criticism, which explains the relatively soft stance it took toward the Moscow Helsinki Group. As the follow-up meeting in Belgrade drew closer, this approach posed risks as it provided the Moscow Helsinki Group with an international platform for making its concerns public. From the perspective of Moscow this urgently needed to be prevented.[10]

Some citizens of the Czechoslovak Socialist Republic proclaimed the so-called Charter 77 at the beginning of 1977. They based their demands on the Final Act of Helsinki and called for respect of human and civil rights. By April 1979 nearly a thousand people had signed this appeal. Similar to the goals of the Moscow Helsinki Group, the intention was to direct attention to individual cases of human and civil rights violation. Drawing upon the CSCE Final Act, Charter 77 put forth the idea that "peace cannot be divided." Therefore peace could prevail between states only if and when these states upheld peace among their own citizens by respecting their rights. De-

Figure 1.2. Singer songwriter and human rights activist Wolf Biermann at a civil rights meeting for Charter 77 in Frankfurt's trade union building on 26 March 1977. In the background (left to right) Rudi Dutschke, Jiri Pelikan, and Adam Mischnik (ullstein bild / dpa)

spite the fact that Charter 77 did not expressly refer to itself as an opposition group and acknowledged the authority of the Communist Party, its mere existence posed a threat to the regime.[11]

In 1977 there were also attempts made in the GDR to refer to the CSCE Final Act in a similar way as Charter 77. These attempts were repressed by the authorities relatively quickly. However, in a different vein, those GDR citizens who desired to emigrate realized the potential of the Final Act for their aspirations. Since the building of the Berlin Wall in 1961 there had been hardly any opportunities to leave East Germany legally. The number of emigration applications in which people referred to the recommendations of Basket III as the basis for their request rocketed, and East Germany could not control the growing number of applications right up until 1989 and the fall of the Wall. The response by the Socialist Unity Party of Germany (SED) mirrored that of the Kremlin: initially the party tried to avoid public criticism directly after the Helsinki agreement and allowed the emigration of several thousand applicants. This measure served to maintain domestic tranquility. Yet with the approaching follow-up meeting in Belgrade, tensions grew and at the same time, repressive measures against applicants were introduced.[12]

The Final Act was also a point of reference for the oppositional milieu in Poland. Initially intellectuals were the primary implementers. They cited the CSCE when protesting against the constitutional amendment of 1975, which was to assert the leading role of the communist Polish United Workers' Party (PUWP). Gradually workers also became aware of the Final Act. As food prices in Poland soared in 1976, activists founded the Workers' Defense Committee (WDC) and with it established an organizational framework for their objectives. Seen from an organizational and methodological point of view, the WDC was inspired by the Moscow Helsinki Group and became an important forerunner for founding the trade union Solidarność (Solidarity) in August 1980. As in the other countries, the CSCE process had a moderating influence on those in power.[13]

In the West the CSCE process provoked increasing awareness of human and civil rights as a powerful political catalyst. Although the initial stance of the United States on the CSCE process, under the government of Gerald Ford and Henry Kissinger, was largely skeptical,[14] this attitude gradually changed as events in Eastern Europe unfolded. The United States began to pursue a distinctly active human rights policy toward the Eastern bloc states with the inauguration of US President Jimmy Carter in January 1977, who was influenced by his Polish-born security advisor Zbigniew Brzezinski.[15] In 1975 the US Congress formed a Commission on Security and Cooperation in Europe to place the growing interest in the CSCE process in government setting.[16] In Western Europe, Helsinki groups were established with the purpose of monitoring compliance to the CSCE recommendations and offering contacts for critics and opposition figures.[17]

From Détente to Confrontation: The CSCE Follow-up Meeting in Belgrade 1977–78

As Soviet-American relations began to deteriorate, it was clear that international détente was past its peak. SALT II and MBFR negotiations faltered. Then, contrary to standard diplomatic practice between the superpowers, the new US Secretary of State Cyrus Vance raised the issue of human rights. This increased the ill humor of a Kremlin that had already become suspicious during the SALT negotiations. Conversely NATO observed the deployment of modern SS-20 missiles by the USSR with critical eyes.[18]

Seen in this light, the initial conditions for the first CSCE follow-up meeting starting in Belgrade on 4 October 1977 were notably poor. The members of NATO had agreed not to endanger the process of détente or to create a provocative atmosphere. However, it proved a difficult balancing act to maintain détente on the one hand and on the other to exert moderate pressure on the Eastern bloc states to permanently ameliorate human rights as envisaged in Basket III.[19] A feeling of insecurity among the Alliance was increased by the appointment of a former Federal Supreme Court judge and US ambassador to the United Nations, Arthur Goldberg, to the position of head of the US delegation. President Carter had instructed Goldberg to pursue human rights issues vigorously.[20] Goldberg denounced specific cases of human rights violations, naming, among other instances, the treatment of Alexander Ginsburg and Yuri Orlov. Predictably, the Eastern delegations reacted defensively. Even within the Alliance, the Goldberg strategy at first did not receive support. Only gradually did the other NATO partners fall in line with the Americans, driven less out of conviction than by a desire to show unanimity on the side of the Western states.[21]

Eastern attitudes were not significantly changed by the harsh American criticism on human rights. Prior to Belgrade, the states of the Warsaw Pact had decided not to compromise their position any further. They would accept only a brief, final declaration for the Belgrade meeting. They were also prepared to end the conference without any final document. Furthermore, they wanted to keep the planned debate on the implementation of the Helsinki Final Act as brief as possible because they anticipated criticism on their human rights record regarding their failure to implement the recommendations in Basket III.[22]

Against this background, little progress was made at the Belgrade meeting. While the Eastern bloc primarily made proposals for Basket II, the Western states focused on questions dealing with humanitarian cooperation.[23] Some proposals by Warsaw Pact states (the Warsaw Treaty Organization of Friendship, Cooperation, and Mutual Assistance) relating to Basket I and Basket III were made only to circumvent unwelcome Western propositions.[24] As every effort to develop a substantive final document failed because of the Eastern blockade, the Western and neutral states focused on finding agreement on a short draft for a final document as of February 1978. This was intended to demonstrate that no substantial progress in détente had been achieved in Belgrade.[25] In early March all parties adopted this brief declaration. The document stated that diverging opinions existed about the implementation of the CSCE Final Act and that there was no agreement on further recommendations.[26]

Although the final document of the first follow-up meeting was disappointing compared to the Helsinki meeting, it was not seen as an outright failure by Western contemporary reviews.[27] Two important results had been achieved: first, it reaffirmed a commitment to the Helsinki Final Act as a framework for multilateral cooperation, and second, a further follow-up meeting was to be held in Madrid in the fall of 1980. Thus it ensured the continuity of the CSCE process.

The East also viewed the results of Belgrade in a positive light, but for somewhat different reasons. Although the USSR and its allies clearly felt disaffected about criticism from the West with respect to human rights issues and humanitarian cooperation, the USSR, like the West, did support a continuation of the CSCE process. Moreover, by producing such a brief agreement, the Eastern bloc had achieved its goal of not giving in to further concessions with respect to humanitarian issues.[28]

Poised between Crisis and Compromise: The CSCE Follow-up Meeting of Madrid in 1980

Irrespective of the relatively positive assessments of the Belgrade CSCE follow-up meeting, the second follow-up meeting in Madrid on 11 November 1980 took place in circumstances of dramatically worsening East-West relations. The initial euphoria had dissipated. Polemical rhetoric increased in the face of Soviet nuclear armament, the invasion of the Red Army in Afghanistan, and, in the West, a revival of US anticommunism. Nevertheless, not least because of the international developments at the end of the 1970s, the meeting confounded all expectations and closed with a substantial document. NATO's Double-Track Decision—involving an offer for negotiations to the Warsaw Pact regarding mutual limitations on the number of medium-range ballistic missiles on the one hand, and, on the other, a modernization of US missiles and their deployment to Western Europe—had exerted pressure on the USSR, which responded by trying to use the CSCE process for its own purposes of military détente. The Soviet's main interest was an agreed-upon mandate for a disarmament conference. To achieve this end they were willing to make concessions on humanitarian issues.

France had already proposed a European Conference on Disarmament in 1978, with a section on confidence-building measures and a second part on disarmament. The idea had been to conduct negotiations in the style of the old Gaullist tradition, which defined Europe "from the Atlantic to the Urals" and therefore encompassed a geographically larger area of negotiation than did the Helsinki Final Act. In 1979 France suggested that the proposal, which had originally been tabled outside the CSCE process, be considered at the Madrid follow-up meeting.[29] NATO supported the French idea, but made it clear, well before the follow-up meeting, that a decision on a disarmament conference could only be part of a "balanced outcome," that is, in return for humanitarian concessions.[30]

The French and Soviet ideas differed mainly with respect to the geographical dimensions. Moscow took the view that only the regions specified in the Final Act should be affected. Moscow envisaged humanitarian concessions particularly in the easing of regulations for the reunion of family members and marriages. These concessions involved faster processing of such requests, lower application fees, and better working conditions for accredited foreign journalists. These Soviet concessions went especially against the interests of East Berlin, which saw its security threatened by an expansion of humanitarian CSCE recommendations.[31]

Although this initial situation promised fruitful negotiations, the subsequent discussions in Madrid between the fall of 1980 and the summer of 1983 turned out to be tense. The first part of the Madrid agenda, a debate on the current state of the implementation of the Final Act, continued for four weeks until mid-December 1980. Western countries especially criticized the Czechoslovak Socialist Republic, the USSR, and East Germany. The subsequent discussion of the second item on the agenda of the Madrid meeting concerned a deepening of mutual relations. Both France and the USSR soon put forward their respective proposals for a disarmament conference.

Talks initially made swift progress after the Christmas break, with the USSR promptly expressing willingness to compromise on humanitarian issues as well as on the geographical scope defined by France in its proposal for disarmament. The USSR's position was met with the extreme displeasure of East Germany. By the end of March 1981, the group of neutral and nonaligned (N + N) states submitted a first comprehensive draft for a final document. It served as the basis for subesequent discussions.[32] At this point, there was no agreement on the geographical scope of the confidence-building measures (despite the USSR's initial flexibility on the issue), the wording on the principles of human rights and the freedom of religion had yet to be formulated, and no progress had been made on the exchange of information or on the reunification of families.[33] The United States summarized the state of negotiations in June 1981 and presented this summary as a comprehensive proposal to the USSR. The US representatives demanded further concessions from the USSR on such matters as convening a group of experts to work on reuniting families, ending radio jamming, and allowing Helsinki Groups to monitor and document the implementation of the CSCE recommendations independently of state institutions. The USSR immediately rejected this American document.[34] Thus, despite a good start, the Madrid negotiations were deadlocked by the summer of 1981 as both sides of the "Disarmament versus Humanitarian Concessions" debate felt the cost of compromise was too high.

After the summer break in 1981, discussions continued to revolve around the same problem. Now, however, external factors influenced the process of negotiation. In the winter of 1981 recent developments in Poland caught up with the Madrid talks after General Wojciech Jaruzelski declared martial law on 13 December 1981 in order to combat the trade union movement Solidarity. Nonetheless, the USSR seemed willing to make concessions.[35] When Western countries raised the Polish situation in the Madrid discussions, the USSR rejected a compromise draft on 17 December.[36] The developments in Poland posed significant difficulties for the negotiations. After a Christmas hiatus, progress on the resuming talks was so slow that a postponement was inevitable. On 12 March 1982, the delegations departed, but not before agreeing to continue with the talks on 9 November of that year.[37]

It was not until spring 1983 that negotiations gained momentum: after a Christmas break, the Western states indicated that they would adopt a flexible position with respect to the wording of their proposals. The N + N states wanted to assume the role of an intermediary between East and West—but for no more than five weeks—while the USSR desired a speedy conclusion to negotiations. By mid-March the neutral states tabled a compromise version of the original proposal for a final document that helped pave the way to a fruitful conclusion.[38] The USSR accepted this draft as a basis for negotiations. The geographical scope for confidence-building measures included all of Europe and adjacent seas.[39]

Nevertheless the meeting hit a dead end because the USSR categorically refused changes requested by Western states: in particular it refused to accept a ban on radio jammers and a mandate for a meeting of experts on human contacts.[40] For eight weeks the discussions were deadlocked. Then a compromise proposal by the Spanish Prime Minister Felipe Gonzalez on 17 June 1983 opened the way for a resolution: the West would stop insisting on a ban on radio jammers and in return the East would allow a meeting of experts dealing with human contacts.[41]

By 15 July all CSCE participating states agreed on this compromise. The Madrid meeting ended with the signing of a substantive Final Document on 7–9 September 1983, which built a bridge toward more relaxed international relations in the 1980s. Instrumental to this achievement was the negotiated mandate of the Conference on Security and Confidence-Building Measures and Disarmament in Europe, which took place in Stockholm from 1984 to 1986.

Conclusion

The CSCE process provided a continuous platform for discussions between the East and West starting in the mid-1970s. Although exposed to a changing international political climate, ranging from a mood of euphoria during détente to periods of deep distrust, it never ceased to operate. While other negotiations that focused on military matters ground to a halt, the combination of security and humanitarian issues offered by the CSCE process created new negotiating opportunities. Importantly the CSCE played a role not only on an international level, but also on a societal level. Its ideas spread and contributed to societal change, especially in Eastern Europe, where its impact varied considerably from country to country. The linking of social issues to a conflict situation as part of an international negotiation is a unique feature of the CSCE process. At the time of the Madrid follow-up meeting, however, hardly anyone would have anticipated that the CSCE participant states would sign the Paris Charter in November 1990, which declared the end of the Cold War.

Anja Hanisch studied modern and contemporary history with a focus on the history of international relations in Bamberg, Germany, and the US, and completed her dissertation on the "Conference on Security and Cooperation in Europe," which was awarded the Leibniz Association's Young Scientists Award in 2011 at the University of Leipzig. Following her PhD, she completed the Federal Foreign Office's summer school "International Futures," worked for the Center for International Peace Operations in Berlin, the Office of the United Nations in Geneva, and was a Mercator Fellow on International Affairs. She currently works for the KfW Development Bank.

Notes

1. Matthias Peter, *Die Bundesrepublik im KSZE-Prozess 1975–1983: Die Umkehrung der Diplomatie* (Berlin 2015).
2. Petri Hakkarainen, "From Linkage to Freer Movement: The FRG and the Nexus between CSCE Preparations and Deutschlandpolitik, 1969–1972," in *Origins of the European Security System: The Helsinki Process Revisited 1965–75*, ed. Andreas Wenger, Vojtech Mastny, and Christian Nuenlist (Abingdon, 2008), 164–82.
3. The "Blaue Buch" is reproduced by Hermann Volle and Wolfgang Wagner, eds., *KSZE: Konferenz über Sicherheit in Europa in Beiträgen und Dokumenten aus dem Europa-Archiv* (Bonn, 1976), 153–64.
4. Gottfried Niedhart, "Peaceful Change of Frontiers as a Crucial Element in the West German Strategy of Transformation," in *Helsinki 1975 and the Transformation of Europe*, ed. Oliver Bange (New York, 2008), 39–52.
5. Final Act of the Conference on Security and Cooperation in Europe from 1 August 1975. Printed in Volle and Wagner, eds., *KSZE,* 237–84, see 239–244, citations 268 and 269.
6. Ibid., 237–84.
7. Anja Hanisch, *Die DDR im KSZE-Prozess 1972–1985: Zwischen Ostabhängigkeit, Westabgrenzung und Ausreisebewegung* (Munich, 2012), 88–119; and Svetlana Savranskaya, "USSR and CSCE: From Inviolability of Borders to Inalienable Rights," in *From Helsinki to Belgrade: The First CSCE Follow-up Meeting in Belgrade 1977/78*, ed. Vladimir Bilandžić and Milan Kosanović (Belgrade, 2008), 231–55.
8. Sarah Snyder, "'Jerry, Don't Go,' Domestic Opposition to the 1975 Helsinki Final Act," *Journal of American Studies* 44 (2010): 70.
9. *Neues Deutschland*, 2/3 August 1975, 5–10; *Pravda*, 2 August 1975, 2–6.
10. Ernst Wawra, "'Die Beendiung der feindlichen Aktivität?': Staatliche Reaktionen auf die Tätigkeit der Moskauer Helsinki-Gruppe," in *Die KSZE im Ost-West-Konflikt: Internationale Politik und gesellschaftliche Transformation 1975–1990*, ed. Matthias Peter and Hermann Wentker (Munich, 2012), 270–77.
11. Benjamin Müller, "Von der Konfrontation zum Dialog," in *Der KSZE-Prozess: Vom Kalten Krieg zu einem neuen Europa*, ed. Helmut Altrichter and Hermann Wentker (Munich, 2011), 100–101, 104.
12. Ibid., 144–65; and Bernd Eisenfeld, "Die Ausreisebewegung: Eine Erscheinungsform widerständigen Verhaltens," in *Zwischen Selbstbehauptung und Anpassung: Formen des Widerstandes und der Opposition in der DDR*, ed. Ulrike Poppe, Rainer Eckert, and Ilko-Sascha Kowalczuk (Berlin, 1995), 192–223.
13. Gunter Dehnert, "'Eine neue Beschaffenheit der Lage:' Die Rolle des KSZE-Prozesses in der Formierung der polnischen Opposition und ihrem Durchbruch zur Massenbewegung (1975–1989)," in Altrichter and Wentker, *Der KSZE-Prozess,* 87–98.
14. Jussi Hanhimäki, "They Can Write It in Swahili: Kissinger, the Soviets, and the Helsinki Accords 1973–75," *Journal of Transatlantic Studies* 1 (2003): 37–58.

15. Patrick Vaughn, "Brzezinski and the Helsinki Final Act," in *The Crisis of Détente in Europe: From Helsinki to Gorbachev, 1975–1985*, ed. Leopoldo Nuti (London, 2009), 11–25, see esp. 11, 12, and 14.
16. Sarah B. Snyder, *Human Rights Activism and the End of the Cold War: A Transnational History of the Helsinki Network* (Cambridge, 2011), 3852.
17. Sylvia Rohde-Liebenau, *Menschenrechte und internationaler Wandel: Der Einfluss des KSZE-Menschenrechtsregimes auf den Wandel des internationalen Systems in Europa* (Baden-Baden, 1996), 67–70.
18. See Tim Geiger's contribution in this volume.
19. Ambassador Pauls, Brüssel (NATO), to the Foreign Office on 1 July 1977 in Akten zur Auswärtigen Politik der Bundesrepublik Deutschland 1977/II, document no. 170: 876–880.
20. Breck Walker, "'Neither Shy nor Demagogic': The Carter Administration Goes to Belgrade," in Bilandžić and Kosanović, *From Helsinki to Belgrade*, 207–30, see esp. 225.
21. Snyder, *Human Rights Activism and the End of the Cold War*, see 101, 104.
22. Hanisch, *Die DDR im KSZE-Prozess 1972–1985*, 188–97.
23. Notes recorded by the Assistant Secretary of State Blech on 11 November 1977 in Akten zur Auswärtigen Politik der Bundesrepublik Deutschland 1977/II, document no. 320: 1537–41, see esp. 1538 and 1539.
24. Hanisch, *Die DDR im KSZE-Prozess 1972–1985*, 204.
25. Benjamin Gilde, "Keine neutralen Vermittler: Die Gruppe der neutralen und nicht-paktgebundenen Staaten und das Belgrader KSZE-Folgetreffen 1977/78," in *Vierteljahrshefte für Zeitgeschichte* 3 (2011): 413–44; and Benjamin Gilde, *Österreich im KSZE-Prozess 1969–1983: neutraler Vermittler in humanitärer Mission* (Munich, 2013).
26. "Closing communique of the Belgrade Conference 1977," in *Das Belgrader KSZE-Folgetreffen: Der Fortgang des Entspannungsprozesses in Europa in Beiträgen und Dokumenten aus dem Europa-Archiv*, ed. Hermann Volle and Wolfgang Wagner (Bonn, 1978), 172–75.
27. For example, see Per Fischer, "Das Ergebnis von Belgrad Ergebnis von Belgrad: Das KSZE-Folgetreffen in seiner Bedeutung für den Entspannungsprozess," in Volle and Wagner, *Das Belgrader KSZE-Folgetreffen*, 23–32.
28. Hanisch, *Die DDR im KSZE-Prozess 1972–1985*, 207–13.
29. Veronika Heyde, "Nicht nur Entspannung und Menschenrechte: Die Entdeckung von Abrüstung und Rüstungskontrolle durch die französische KSZE-Politik," in Peter and Wentker, *Die KZSE im Ost-West-Konflikt*, 92–95.
30. "Kommuniqué über die Ministertagung des Nordatlantikrats in Brüssel" on 13/14 December 1979 in Europa Archiv 2 (1980): D38–D43, see D40, including quotation.
31. Hanisch, *Die DDR im KSZE-Prozess 1972–1985*, 257–86.
32. Jörg Kastl, "Das KSZE-Folgetreffen von Madrid: Verlauf und Schlußdokument aus der Sicht der Bundesrepublik Deutschland," in *Das Madrider KSZE-Folgetreffen*, ed. Hermann Volle and Wolfgang Wagner (Bonn, 1984), 45–54, see esp. 47.
33. Harold Gordon Skilling, "CSCE in Madrid," in *Problems of Communism* 30, no. 4 (1981): 1–16, see esp. 14 and 15.
34. Douglas Selvage, "The Superpowers and the Conference on Security and Cooperation in Europe, 1977–1983: Human Rights, Nuclear Weapons, and Western Europe," in Peter and Wentker, *Die KSZE im Ost-West-Konflikt*, 34.

35. Jörg Kastl, "Das KSZE-Folgetreffen von Madrid aus der Sicht der Bundesrepublik," in *Europa Archiv* 48 (1983): 617–26.
36. Joachim Fesefeldt, *Der Warschauer Pakt auf dem Madrider KSZE-Folgetreffen und auf der KVAE (ohne Rumänien)* (Cologne, 1984), 19; and Leo Mates, "Von Helsinki nach Madrid und zurück: Der KSZE-Prozeß im Schatten der Ost-West-Beziehungen," in Volle and Wagner, *Das Belgrader KSZE-Folgetreffen*, 55–62, see esp. 60.
37. Kastl, "Das KSZE-Folgetreffen von Madrid aus der Sicht der Bundesrepublik," 49.
38. Jan Sizoo and Rudolf Jurrjens, *CSCE Decision-Making: The Madrid Experience* (The Hague, 1984), 163, 164.
39. Archive of the Parties and Mass-Organizations of the GDR in the Federal Archives (henceforth SAPMO), DY30/J IV 2/2/1996: 11–17; Appendix to the Politburo's protocol no. 14/83 dated 19 April 1983: report on the meeting of the Committee of the Ministers of Foreign Affairs of the member states of the Warsaw Pact Treaty on 6–7 April 1983 in Prague, see 13.
40. Sizoo and Jurrjens, *CSCE Decision-Making: The Madrid Experience*, 165, 240–41.
41. William Korey, "Das KSZE-Folgetreffen in Madrid: Ein Beitrag aus amerikanischer Sicht," in Volle and Wagner, *Das Madrider KSZE-Folgetreffen*, 85–92, see esp. 92; and Sizoo and Jurrjens, *CSCE Decision-Making: The Madrid Experience*, 242.

Select Bibliography

Several edited volumes on the CSCE process up until the mid-1980s have been published. Bange and Niedhart and Soutou and Loth are essential for the beginning of the process. Nuti's attention rests on the ensuing years with a focus on military-security issues and less on the CSCE process itself. Recent research is concisely presented in Altrichter and Wentker and Peter and Wentker and includes discussion on societal consequences in Eastern Europe.

Altrichter, Helmut, and Hermann Wentker, eds. *Der KSZE-Prozess: Vom Kalten Krieg zu einem neuen Europa 1975 bis 1990*. Munich, 2011.
Bange, Oliver, and Gottfried Niedhart. *Helsinki 1975 and the Transformation of Europe*. New York, 2008.
Nuti, Leopoldo, ed. *The Crisis of Détente in Europe: From Helsinki to Gorbachev, 1975–1985*. London, 2009.
Peter, Matthias, and Herman Wentker, eds. *Die KSZE im Ost-West-Konflikt: Internationale Politik und gesellschaftliche Transformation 1975–1990*. Munich, 2012.
Soutou, Georges-Henri, and Wilfried Loth, eds. *The Making of Détente: Eastern and Western Europe in the Cold War, 1965–75*. London, 2008.

Chapter 2

The NATO Double-Track Decision: Genesis and Implementation

Tim Geiger

For the "Chancellor of German Reunification," Helmut Kohl, there was no question of the historical significance of the NATO Double-Track Decision:

> "The NATO Double-Track Decision was the single most important decision on the way to German reunification. My predecessor, Helmut Schmidt, went against the will of his own party when he began the process, and I, together with my government, pushed it through in 1983 against fierce resistance in our own country ... I am truly convinced that without the NATO Double-Track Decision, in 1989, the Berlin Wall would not have fallen and we would not have achieved reunification in 1990."[1]

The judgment of contemporary historical research, however, is by no means as clear-cut. Whether and to what degree NATO's Double-Track Decision, made on 12 December 1979 contributed to the dissolution of the Soviet empire, the decline of communist dictatorships in Europe, and the historical changes in 1989–90 remains open. Contemporary observers were hardly aware of the critical nature of NATO's decision in Brussels or of its significance as a historical turning point. The influential West German news magazine *Der Spiegel*, for example, did not select the Double-Track Decision as a cover story that week but devoted its lead article to the possible consequences of private television ("Sex on All Channels?").[2] As far as international news was concerned, the West German media were much more interested in the Soviet military intervention in Afghanistan that started fourteen days later.

The End of the Détente Era

The NATO Double-Track Decision and the Soviet invasion of Afghanistan are both crucial moments in a process that is frequently referred to as the

"Second Cold War." Even as the détente era reached its peak with the CSCE Summit in Helsinki in 1975, the process of decline had already begun.

In the 1970s the socialist states appeared to be on the rise despite the increasing technological and economic-industrial superiority of the West. In Southeast Asia (Vietnam, Cambodia) the United States suffered humiliating setbacks, while Moscow's allies in Africa (Mozambique, Angola, Ethiopia) seemed to be gaining ground. In the United States the view that the USSR was the main beneficiary of détente thus gained prominence. During the presidential campaign of 1976, the incumbent Gerald Ford announced that in the future he would avoid using the term détente.[3] In contrast, Europeans, especially the Germans, enjoyed the fruits of détente in the form of improved opportunities for contact across the "Iron Curtain." Traditional stereotypes and perceptions of enmity between East and West thus began to lose their political strength.

From a Western perspective the military sector was a cause of concern: negotiations in Vienna between senior NATO and Warsaw Pact countries for Mutual and Balanced Force Reductions (MBFR)—pertaining to conventional forces in Central Europe—had reached a dead end soon after talks began in 1973. The US-Soviet negotiations on strategic nuclear weapons had also stagnated. Upon completion of an interim agreement in 1972 (Strategic Arms Limitation Talks, SALT I), Washington had unilaterally allowed Moscow to introduce heavy Intercontinental Ballistic Missiles (ICBMs) because it was confident of the technological superiority of American rockets constructed with Multiple Independently Targetable Re-entry Vehicles (MIRVs). However, the USSR caught up with MIRV technology much faster than expected, an experience that would make subsequent negotiations increasingly difficult.[4] In 1977 the new Carter administration took over negotiations with a much more ambitious disarmament agenda and presented a concept with radical reduction in nuclear arsenals ("Deep Cuts"). As this called into question the previous negotiation results, it was repudiated by the Kremlin wholeheartedly. Distrust and suspicion prevailed on both sides: From Moscow's point of view, Jimmy Carter had tried to deny the USSR its position as an equal superpower—just as he did with his human rights campaign, which was seen as an attempt to undermine the Soviet Union.[5] On the other hand, Washington doubted the Russian will to achieve a sincere disarmament agreement. From a Western perspective, the build-up of a Soviet high seas fleet was as threatening as the improved air defense capability of the Warsaw Pact. The latter diminished the effectiveness of NATO's defense concept that had up to this point primarily relied on aircraft for its tactical nuclear component.

In 1967 the Harmel Report stated that security should be built on defense as well as détente. Accordingly NATO had continuously increased

Western defense capability and thus its deterrent in order to maintain peace. President Ford's government initiated plans for the improvement of conventional forces and a modernization of tactical nuclear weapons. In 1977, on President Carter's initiative, NATO's Council of Heads of State and Government approved the development of a Long-Term Defense Program. The LTDP was supposed to bring allied military policies in tune with the anticipated requirements of the 1980s. The decision was also taken to increase national military spending annually by 3 percent, a figure that was, in fact, rarely reached. One of LTDP's ten task forces, the High Level Group (HLG), was commissioned to review all tactical nuclear forces. Most of the six thousand tactical nuclear weapons stationed in Western Europe dated back to the 1950s and were only capable of covering distances under 100 kilometers. In the event of war, these outmoded Theater Nuclear Forces (TNF) would either be destroyed by the first echelon of the Warsaw Pact or detonate on (West) German territory. In other words, what the Alliance needed was fewer but more potent nuclear weapons, that is, weapons that were capable of traveling long distances and had more precise targeting capabilities.[6]

Technological innovations made this modernization possible. Of special importance was the development of cruise missiles—remote-controlled missiles able to evade enemy radar detection by flying low and using modern satellite and computer technology to hit targets with great precision. In contrast to frequently repeated statements that NATO's TNF modernization was solely a reaction to Soviet SS-20 missiles, it should be noted that plans on TNF modernization had been well under way before the threat of a new generation of Soviet missiles changed the political scene. The NATO Double-Track Decision therefore derived from two originally independent sources.[7]

Since 1975 Western experts had been observing a massive Soviet production of medium-range missiles. This became the decisive and second reason for the Double-Track Decision. Apart from a new nuclear-capable supersonic bomber (Backfire), the sheer increase in the number of Soviet SS-20 missiles was a matter of great concern to the West. Whereas in the past, the SS-4 and SS-5 missiles had been equipped with a single nuclear warhead, the new SS-20 presented an accurate, mobile, and thus virtually "invincible" weapon. It reduced warning time to a few minutes, had a range of up to 5,000 km and was armed with three individually controllable nuclear warheads, comparable to the US MIRV.

The USSR's motives for the momentous decision to increase armament remain controversial and in need of clarification. Was the Kremlin, as the government of West Germany feared, pursuing politically aggressive goals, namely, "to make Western Europe militarily vulnerable and to detach it from the global politico-strategic deterrence umbrella of the United States"?[8]

Or was it, as the Warsaw Pact and the peace movement claimed, simply a matter of routine modernization? If the latter was the case, then the Soviet leadership misjudged the Western European reaction, as it was perceived by NATO as a qualitatively new threat that demanded a response. According to leading Soviet participants commenting in hindsight, this was indeed the case: decisions regarded by the military-industrial complex as necessary were no longer critically questioned by the Politburo of the Communist Party of the Soviet Union (CPSU).[9]

In fact as far as medium-range weapons were concerned, the USSR had clearly been in a superior position ever since the late 1950s. However, with the SS-20 missile this military superiority made a qualitative and quantitative leap forward. Above all, the new missile's range was considered to be critical: even if deployed beyond the Urals, the SS-20 proved to be sufficiently potent to hit targets all over Western Europe, though no targets in the United States. This fact was directly aimed at the most fragile fault of the Atlantic Alliance: it questioned the US guarantee to protect Western Europe with nuclear arms. Would the United States intervene with its strategic nuclear force, even if this led to further escalation and provoked the Soviet Union into nuclear retaliation against America? Conversely would the Soviet

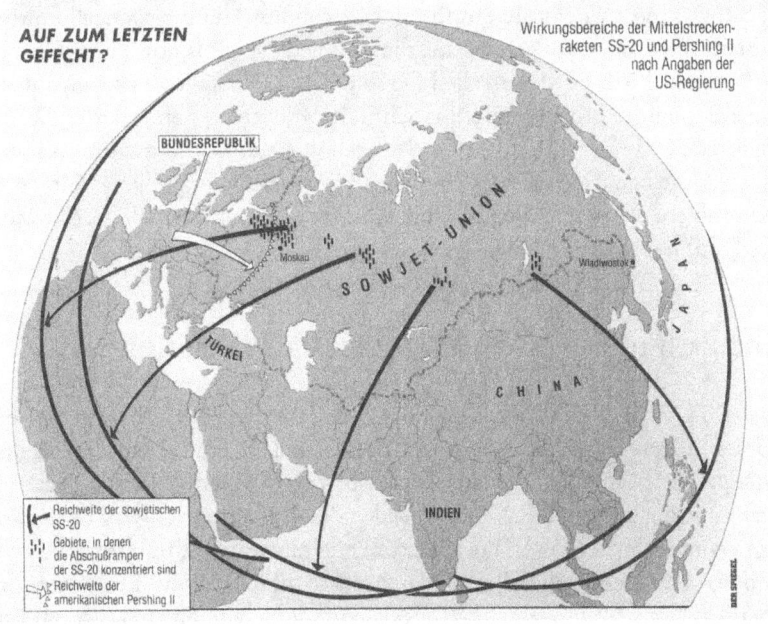

Figure 2.1. "The Last Stand," 26 September 1983 (DER SPIEGEL 39/1983, 173).

Union deliberately try to localize a war in Europe? The SS-20 threatened a detachment of the American nuclear umbrella for Western Europe, which was seen as essential to NATO's strategy of "flexible response" and thus crucial in deterring aggression. Western Europe found itself increasingly open to the risk of political blackmail by the Soviet Union—especially since the SS-20 missiles were not included in either SALT or MBFR negotiations, as they did not belong in either classification and fell into a "gray area."

The government of West Germany and in particular Chancellor Helmut Schmidt pointed this out early on.[10] However, Washington refused to include Soviet medium-range systems in the SALT negotiations. The prospect of an impending agreement on a strategic balance between the superpowers reinforced the dilemma for West Germany: as a front-line state it could fall victim to the USSR's superiority in conventional and medium-range armament.

Chancellor Schmidt raised the subject again in a speech to the International Institute for Strategic Studies (IISS) in London on 28 October 1977: he argued that in order to maintain the credibility of deterrence NATO had to prevent the emergence of disparities in any area of the triad (conventional, tactical, and strategic weapons). The current imbalance could be addressed either by massive Western rearmament or alternatively by mutual disarmament. The chancellor clearly preferred the latter. At no point in his speech, which was mostly dedicated to the global economy, did the chancellor mention SS-20, cruise, or Pershing missiles. Nonetheless it is now considered to be "the true birth of the so-called Double-Track Decision."[11] Participants of the event ensured that Chancellor Schmidt's grievances were heard in Washington, DC. In retrospect, the IISS speech was elevated to manifesto status as it was the first time that a Western head of government publicly pointed to the problem of Soviet medium-range missiles and, in a nutshell, put forward the Double-Track principle.

The Path to the NATO Double-Track Decision

In 1977–78, as NATO was planning to update the TNF (Theater Nuclear Forces), the neutron bomb controversy escalated. In crucial aspects this dispute paralleled many of the later discussions on the Double-Track Decision. The neutron bomb—ERW (enhanced radiation weapon)—was developed from conventional limited-range tactical nuclear weapons. Its narrower focus of destruction reduced "collateral damage." In military terms it was therefore regarded as an "improvement." Especially in densely populated Central Europe it was seen as an effective weapon against the tank armies of the Warsaw Pact. On the other hand, its enhanced precision resulted in a lowering of the nuclear threshold because regionally restricted ERW destruction would not automatically escalate every armed conflict into Armageddon. Using this logic, the planning and execution of war was once again conceivable.

For this very reason Egon Bahr, the foreign policy expert of the SPD (Social Democratic Party of Germany), raised the alarm: he attacked the concept of the neutron bomb as a "perversion of thought" because it kills people but leaves things undamaged.[12] Bahr's outcry triggered a wave of protests against nuclear armament in the Federal Republic of Germany. The Netherlands, the United Kingdom, Denmark, Norway, and the United States also witnessed protests among their citizens against the neutron bomb, which would become a focal point of antinuclear and peace movements.[13] In addition, Eastern propaganda campaigns fuelled the protest.[14]

Faced by such protest, President Carter informed the government of West Germany in November that the United States would produce ERWs only if West Europeans, who would be protected by the new weapon, deployed them in their countries. Chancellor Schmidt did not want the responsibility for this serious armament decision laid on his shoulders, especially as his party voiced massive resistance; he knew it would also negatively impact relations between East and West Germany.

On 20 January 1978, the Bundessicherheitsrat (Federal Security Council) laid down the following fundamental guidelines concerning the neutron bomb. Later these guidelines were also adopted for the NATO Double-Track Decision: (1) only the United States could make a decision about the production of ERWs; (2) should the United States decide to produce neutron bombs, these weapons would also become part of arms control negotiations with the East as a bargaining chip; (3) missiles were not to be installed for two years in order to provide sufficient time for negotiations; and (4) West Germany was not to be the only country where the neutron bomb was installed, other European NATO countries would have to take their share. In view of its politically charged past, West Germany had a special position and was not supposed to become a quasi-nuclear power alongside the United States, the United Kingdom, and France. Its nonnuclear weapons status had to be maintained.[15] Of crucial importance to the West German government was the final guideline, (5) West Germany insisted that the United States should not use West Germany's qualified agreement in any public debate. This meant Carter could not use this argument to justify his decision for arms production domestically by pointing to the requirements of his European allies.[16]

The main obstacle to deployment proved to be guideline number 4. The Scandinavian and Benelux countries as well as Italy were all unwilling to accept neutron bombs. Nonetheless, NATO continued the ERW program.

When President Carter finally and without prior consultation with the Allies stopped the production of neutron weapons in the spring of 1978, the German government was taken by surprise. It felt duped, as the pro-ERW decision had been made against considerable opposition within its own ranks. Confidence in the leadership of the US administration was severely shaken and the competence of the Atlantic Alliance to act effectively was called into question.

To counter these accusations, the Carter administration yielded to requests by its European Allies for cruise missiles as a balance to the Soviet SS-20. European complaints about the inadequate treatment of the "gray area problem" were grist for the mill of those neoconservative US hardliners who increasingly resisted the emerging SALT II agreement with the Soviet Union. The Carter administration primarily wished to restore confidence in its leadership ability. The vigorous promotion of TNF modernization after the summer of 1978 was thus first and foremost a political strategy to return cohesion to the Atlantic Alliance. Washington (like London and Paris) still saw no need for more medium-range missiles. But because the neutron discussion had ended in a fiasco for NATO, it was now imperative that TNF modernization was a political success.

Meanwhile the HLG had reached a consensus about the need for an "evolutionary upward adjustment" of TNF. This would pose an equally credible threat to that of the SS-20 and include systems that for the first time were capable of reaching Soviet territory from Western Europe. The plan was for a mix of cruise missiles, which were difficult for enemy air defense to locate but flew relatively slowly, and Pershing II missiles, which could be comparatively easily detected due to their ballistic trajectory, but that had a short flight time of only a few minutes between launch and impact.[17]

This solution was chosen by the US government who took the view that the European call for a reduction of Soviet superiority in medium-range missiles was a request for more American nuclear weapons. Political scientist Helga Haftendorn described this aptly as a transatlantic "misunderstanding." In fact the German government generally, and indeed specifically on the occasion of the Soviet General Secretary Leonid Brezhnev's visit to Bonn in 1978 emphasized its preference for a disarmament solution without ever ruling out the option of upgrading weapons.[18]

West Germany was now confronted with a self-inflicted dilemma: after repeatedly demanding action in the "gray area," it could hardly now escape modernization without causing a major foreign policy fiasco. If it assumed responsibility for rearmament—which seemed militarily opportune and, in terms of arms control, reasonable (in order to boost its negotiating position versus the USSR)—it risked losing its own domestic political base, given the resistance within the coalition parties.[19] The only way out was an insistence on a simultaneous and balanced nexus between modernization and disarmament.

At the meeting of French President Valéry Giscard d'Estaing, British Prime Minister James Callaghan, President Jimmy Carter, and German Chancellor Helmut Schmidt on the Caribbean island of Guadeloupe in January 1979, this strategy took the form of an agreement: to offer arms control proposals to the USSR with the proviso that should disarmament negotiations fail, NATO would modernize its arsenal of medium-range weapons.[20] However, domestic politics caused difficulties in the Federal Republic of Germany, and other Western European countries encountered considerable grassroots political opposition to a position that irrevocably committed to TNF modernization. Within West Germany, politicians of the governing Social Democratic Party insisted that sea-launched cruise missiles presented an alternative solution.[21] The idea behind that proposal was the hope that a sea-based stationing of new nukes would enable hesitating countries like Belgium, the Netherlands, Norway, and Denmark to take part in this joint rearmament effort. By sharing the burden of nuclear deployment with as many allied countries as possible the West German government hoped to reduce the number of missile systems placed within its borders. However, this hope failed completely. None of these countries favored sea-deployment. Turkey and Greece also refused to take a share. All declined primarily for political reasons. However, military experts preferred land-based missiles anyway: compared with systems stationed at sea, this was cheaper and more efficient, because—and this was the most important aspect of all—it had a much higher deterrence effect. In case of conflict, land-based missiles would more likely be used in order to avoid losing them to the enemy. In a nutshell: all this made the proposition of sea-stationing untenable.[22]

The West German Foreign Ministry, led by Hans-Dietrich Genscher, accepted the American insistence on stationing ground-launched missiles more readily than the Defense Department and the Chancellery. This recurring paradox was due to the German Foreign Ministry's recognition of the necessity for TNF modernization to maintain a balance in the nuclear escalation process, whereas the Ministry of Defense was more concerned with arms control and political negotiations.[23] Ultimately the situation was an expression of different priorities between the two coalition parties, the FDP and SPD.

West Germany warned the Soviet Union and the Eastern bloc countries in vain that if they continued with the installment of SS-20s, NATO would eventually respond. Only a reversal of Soviet military policy could have prevented this escalation. When the CPSU General Secretary Leonid

Figure 2.2. Jimmy Carter (USA), Valéry Giscard d'Estaing (France), James Callaghan (UK), and Helmut Schmidt (FRG) at their meeting in French Guadeloupe on 5/6 January 1979 (Jimmy Carter Library, Atlanta, GA)

Brezhnev finally announced measures for military confidence-building on 6 October 1979 including the withdrawal of twenty thousand Soviet troops and a thousand tanks from East Germany, as well as a redeployment of Soviet medium-range weapons beyond the Urals (from where they still could target all of Western Europe), this was too little, too late. The announcement seemed to the West to be merely a staged propaganda maneuver, not a turning point.[24] Soon after, Soviet Foreign Minister Andrei Gromyko threatened that a NATO pro-missile decision would bring an end to East-West negotiations. Such rhetoric and the supporting propaganda campaign only increased Western resolve.

Within NATO, the United States, the United Kingdom, and West Germany tried hard to reach a common decision. They wanted to demonstrate unity and avoid political division among member states with different defense statuses, even if only a few Allied partners would deploy the new systems. West Germany insisted, in a mantra-like repetition, on the principle of *Nichtsingularisierung* (non-singularization); for reasons of political alliance and détente it should maintain its non-user status (i.e., not be allowed to control nuclear weapons). This status was all the more important because, due to a deliberate technical limitation, the Pershing II had a range of less than 2,000 km and could therefore be installed only in West Germany. Moscow remained just out of reach so that Soviet fears of a "decapitating strike" could be allayed. This technologically determined exception to the principle of non-singularization was compensated by underlining ostentatiously that the sole power over Pershing II remained in the hands of the United States and furthermore that the Pershing IA missiles deployed in West Germany would merely be "upgraded."

Italy's willingness to accept Ground-Launched Cruise Missiles (GLCM) as a nonnuclear power ameliorated West German anxieties of being singled out. Rome's motive was to regain international importance after the meeting of the leading Western powers on Guadeloupe, from which Italy had been excluded.[25] Due to strong domestic resistance, Denmark, Norway, and the two countries where GLCM were also supposed to be stationed, Belgium and the Netherlands, were considered shaky candidates for deployment.[26] At this point the government in Bonn tried at every possible level to win uniform solidarity within the alliance. For example, in a dialogue with the Dutch government it argued that the USSR would be willing to disarm only if the West posed a serious military threat. Instead of backing the package deal proposed by the Netherlands, which made deployment subject to a ratification of the SALT II agreement crafted by the superpowers in June 1979, West Germany pushed for a NATO agreement on TNF modernization that would conversely help to get SALT II ratified by a hostile US Senate.[27] Simultaneously, the German Federal Government urged American leaders to increase their efforts for arms control within the Double-Track Decision by pointing to the social protest movements taking place throughout the West and to the reluctance shown by its European neighbors.

On 12 December 1979, all member states that took part in NATO's military integration adopted the Double-Track Decision: in subsequent years some 108 Pershing II missiles would replace the same number of American Pershing IAs in West Germany. In addition, 464 US GLCMs were stationed in "selected countries." The phrase referred to West Germany, the United Kingdom, Italy, Belgium, and the Netherlands. In order not to "increase the importance of nuclear weapons in NATO," one thousand predominantly shorter-range US nuclear weapons were withdrawn. The overall scope of the modernization was explicitly dependant on the success of prior arms control negotiations between the United States and the USSR.[28]

Despite an outwardly uniform vote, the Netherlands and Belgium had each reserved the right to postpone a final decision on the forty-eight cruise missiles that both countries were supposed to receive. Belgium claimed it would reach its final decision after six months but postponed several times; it finally allowed the deployment of only sixteen GLCMs six years later. In response to growing political and social pressure from the peace movement, the Netherlands did not confirm that it would take its share of the rockets until 1985. Thanks to the Intermediate-range Nuclear Forces Treaty of 1987, which provided for the scrapping of the SS-20 and all US missiles deployed under the Double-Track Decision, the missiles intended for the Netherlands were never actually deployed on Dutch territory.

The Struggle for the Implementation of the Double-Track Decision

Western Europeans believed in the continuation of détente despite verbal threats by the Eastern bloc and a marked deterioration in East-West relations. The West German government tried to reassure its Eastern counterparts that if the three to four years needed to produce the US missiles could be used for determined arms control negotiations, then perhaps the new Western systems would never come into service.[29]

However, the Soviet invasion of Afghanistan on Christmas of 1979 was a severe shock to international relations. The Carter administration, already humiliated by the American embassy staff in Iran being taken hostage, responded abruptly and turned its back on détente. Harsh sanctions were imposed on the Soviet Union and the ratification of SALT II was suspended. There was thus no longer a framework for negotiations about the disarmament component of the Double-Track Decision: if SALT II had come into effect, new arms control discussions would have followed in the SALT III deliberations, which would have included intermediate-range missile systems.

West Germany now faced a dilemma. As its security depended on the military power of the West, it had to follow suit in taking an anti-Soviet stance, even if this was sometimes against its own judgment, as when the United States decided to boycott the Olympic Games in Moscow. Unlike the United States, the German Social-Liberal government considered the past decade to be a success. The 1970s had witnessed relaxed relations and widened political scope between East and West Germany, which had ameliorated the problems brought about by partition in everyday life. To prevent further confrontation, West Germany hoped to persuade the superpowers to resume a dialogue. There was an added complication that it could play no role in direct talks about such arms reduction and could only act indirectly. However, neither superpower displayed much interest in this diplomacy. Moscow hoped that the impact of the Western peace movement would bring an end to the rearmament process and declared that unless SALT II was ratified and the Double-Track Decision annulled no further negotiations would take place.

Having the support of both East and West European leaders in seeking to maintain the momentum of détente, Chancellor Helmut Schmidt proposed a temporary halt to the deployment of medium-range missiles in April 1980. The time gained should be used for negotiations on a mutual limitation of arms. The West risked nothing as it was faced by a de facto Soviet superiority in this category of weapons: if an agreement was reached, the number of Soviet medium-range missiles would no longer increase.[30] In a certain light, this proposal could have been interpreted as a unilateral moratorium at the expense of the Soviet military armament but also as a freeze of an unequal status quo. Schmidt's independent announcement, however, threatened the unity of arms deployment in conjunction with arms reduction envisaged by the Double-Track Decision. It also irritated the United States, the United Kingdom, and Belgium, as well as Schmidt's coalition partner and the opposition. He was forced to make a further statement and explain that in his original proposal he meant a stop of actual deployment, which could be verified, not of production. His proposal therefore covered only the Soviet and not the American systems.

Nonetheless, the Carter administration was dubious of West Germany's commitment to the Double-Track Decision, especially when Bonn announced its chancellor's imminent visit to Moscow. During a regional election campaign in June, Schmidt repeated the idea of a moratorium as a tactical means to appeal to the disarmament wing of his party.[31] Carter responded by sending a rude statement, which was leaked to the press, to make it clear that Washington rejected any softening of the Double-Track Decision. The chancellor felt humiliated and saw a confirmation of his suspicion that the United States would unilaterally accentuate armament as opposed to détente.[32] On the eve of the World Economic Summit in Venice, a confrontational meeting took place that Carter later described as "the most unpleasant personal exchange I ever had with a foreign leader."[33]

Schmidt and Foreign Minister Genscher's meetings in Moscow revealed that the Soviet Union had indeed abandoned its hard-line stance and was willing to negotiate an agreement on intermediate-range missiles.[34] However, the USSR insisted on a point already rejected in SALT: inclusion of all strategic weapons it regarded as pertinent, including the Forward Based Systems (FBS), namely American (and British) nuclear-capable medium-range bombers already deployed in Europe. The FBS issue and the onset of the American presidential election delayed proceedings. Preliminary talks held in Geneva at the end of October 1980 remained inconclusive, especially as President Carter was voted out of office shortly thereafter.[35]

The transition to the presidency of Ronald Reagan intensified the precariousness of the West German government's balancing act. On the one hand, the incoming US administration was even more skeptical toward the Soviets than the preceding one: it resumed a past containment strategy against the Soviets while reverting to a confrontational rhetoric that labeled their government an "evil empire."[36] On the other hand, the West German government had to face the increasing social pressure from a rapidly growing peace movement. The consensus on security among the ruling parties visibly crumbled away. The peace movement and large sections of the governing Social Democratic Party directed massive criticism toward the US government, which was seen as promoting armament rather than disarmament. In this situation, Foreign Minister Genscher, along with his Free Democratic Party (FDP) and the main conservative opposition parties CDU and CSU, raised the political stakes by portraying themselves as guardians of the Atlantic Alliance and left no doubts about their commitment to both parts of the Double-Track Decision. Chancellor Schmidt and Vice Chancellor Genscher (still in coalition) committed their political fate to the Double-Track Decision in May 1981 in order to curb growing intraparty resistance: they threatened to resign if party voting questioned or went against NATO's decision.[37]

In mid-November 1981 the Reagan administration set a new target for the oncoming negotiations on medium-range weapons in Geneva—now called Intermediate-Range Nuclear Forces (INF). The aim was known as the Zero solution: the United States would offer a complete repeal of Pershing II and cruise missiles if the Soviet Union would scrap all its intermediate-range missiles.[38] The government in Bonn had been pushing this proposal for a long time in vain.[39] Hardly anyone regarded the Zero solution as a realistic option—and some Washington hardliners adopted this fairly radical position for this very reason. But the mere fact that two years after the Double-Track Decision had been accepted, talks on arms control finally resumed was well-received by the German Federal government in view of the ever-increasing protests of the peace movement. On Brezhnev's last visit to Bonn in 1981, the Soviet Union was urged to accept the Zero solution. If the superpowers failed to reach such an agreement, West Germany argued, US missiles would definitely be deployed in Europe from 1983 onward. The West German government, irrespective of party or coalition, considered this deployment imperative. This warning was not heeded.[40]

With the onset of the Geneva negotiations (apart from the INF talks, the superpowers had resumed negotiations on strategic weapons, i.e., Strategic Arms Reduction Talks [START] by 1982), the German Federal government had lost its catalytic function as an intermediary or translator. The discussions were limited to the superpowers. In July 1982 Paul Nitze and Yuli Kvitsinsky, the American and Soviet INF negotiators respectively, tried to overcome the stalemate without consulting their governments beforehand: on a hike in the Jura Mountains they came up with their "Walk in the Woods" formula, which stipulated that the medium-range systems of the two superpowers in Europe be limited to seventy-five each and an additional ninety systems for the Soviet Union in Asia. This amounted to an extensive reduction of SS-20s already stationed in the USSR, a renouncement of all Pershing IIs, and a notably reduced deployment of GLCMs on the American side. The leadership in Moscow and Washington rejected this compromise.[41] The Allies first heard of the "Walk in the Woods" proposal after it had fallen through.

In Bonn the social-liberal government coalition collapsed in the fall of 1982, primarily due to differences in economic and financial policy, but also because of foreign and security matters. Chancellor Schmidt's party became in large part increasingly disaffected with the Double-Track Decision. This development promoted incentives for the Liberal Party (FDP) to break off and "turn" toward the opposition parties. On 1 October 1982, the CDU leader, Helmut Kohl, became chancellor after deposing Helmut Schmidt by a vote of no confidence in parliament. Early federal elections in 1983 confirmed the new coalition government consisting of the CDU/CSU and the FDP in office. Partisans of the Double-Track Decision thus claimed a kind of plebiscitary support because the election campaigns were emotionally charged, given the strong opposition to the retrofit of arms. It may well have been called the "missile election campaign." However, even the adversaries of rearmament felt a certain satisfaction in that the Green Party, closely associated with the peace and protest movements, received sufficient votes to enter the Bundestag for the first time.[42]

The Kohl-Genscher government regarded the application of the NATO Double-Track Decision as a litmus test and as a political necessity in terms of foreign relations and alliances. Given the failure of arms control discussions between the superpowers, this meant first and foremost executing the threatened recourse for this situation: the deployment of additional medium-range missiles. However, it also meant stationing these missiles in a country that already had the highest density of nuclear weapons worldwide. Despite numerous mass demonstrations, marches, and "human-chain" protests, the new Christian-Liberal coalition government remained undeterred.[43] After twenty-seven hours of heated debate on 22 November 1983, the majority vote of the West German parliament confirmed the decision to deploy the missiles.[44]

The following day the first Pershing II missiles were delivered to the locations destined for their deployment. Soon afterward the cruise missiles designated for Italy arrived, while the GLCMs for the United Kingdom had already been in position a week before the Bundestag in Bonn had reached

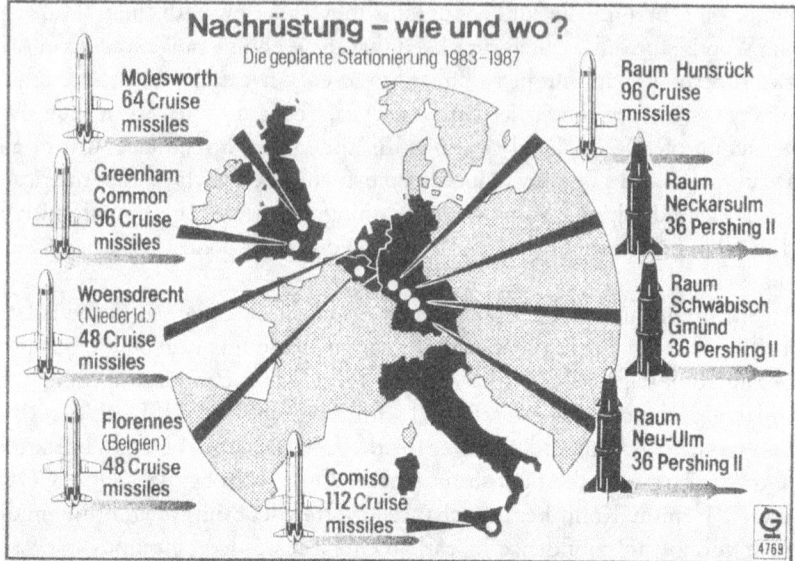

Figure 2.3. "The Arms Race—How and Where?" (Globus Grafik / Picture-Alliance)

its decision. The Soviet Union responded by breaking off negotiations in Geneva. As a counterweight to NATO's new nuclear missiles, additional SS-22 short-range missiles were positioned in the GDR and in Czechoslovakia. An arms race now seemed inevitable, especially after President Reagan announced plans for a space-based missile defense system (Strategic Defense Initiative, SDI) in March 1983.

No one could have predicted that only four years later the renowned anticommunist Reagan would achieve the first real disarmament treaty in collaboration with the new reform-minded Soviet leader Mikhail Gorbachev and usher in the end of the Cold War. The INF agreement sealed the Double-Zero solution, i.e. a Zero Solution for Long-range (LRINF) as well as for Shorter-Range INF (SRINF), and all American and Soviet medium-range missiles, the focus of heated debates for so many years, were scrapped.

Tim Geiger is a research fellow at the Institute of Contemporary History Munich-Berlin (IfZ) in Berlin, working on "Akten zur Auswärtigen Politik der Bundesrepublik Deutschland" in the IfZ branch in the Foreign Office of the Federal Republic in Berlin. He has taught at the Martin Luther University Halle-Wittenberg and Humboldt University Berlin. Geiger is the author of *Atlantiker gegen Gaullisten: Außenpolitischer Konflikt und inner-*

parteilicher Machtkampf in der CDU/CSU, 1958–1969 (2008), which won the German-French Parliamentary Award in 2009, coeditor of *Zweiter Kalter Krieg und Friedensbewegung: Der NATO-Doppelbeschluss in deutschdeutscher und internationaler Perspektive* (2011), as well as an adjunct editor for *Akten zur Auswärtigen Politik der Bundesrepublik Deutschland* (1976, 1977, 1980, 1983) and *Die Einheit: Das Auswärtige Amt, das DDR-Außenministerium und der Zwei-plus-Vier-Prozess* (2015).

Notes

1. Helmut Kohl, "Mauerfall und Wiedervereinigung," *Die Politische Meinung* 54, no. 479 (2009): 9.
2. *Der Spiegel*, 12 December 1979, http://www.spiegel.de/spiegel/print/d-21113118.html.
3. For Ford's remark in his televison interview in Miami, 1 March 1975 see Akten zur Auswärtigen Politik der Bundesrepublik Deutschland (henceforth: AAPD) 1976, Doc. 80; Documents on British Foreign Policy Overseas, Series III, Vol. 3: Détente in Europe, 1972–1976, Doc. 89.
4. Ralph L. Dietl, *Equal Security. Europe and the SALT Process, 1969–1976* (Stuttgart, 2013)
5. Raymond L. Garthoff, *Détente and Confrontation: American-Soviet Relations from Nixon to Reagan* (Washington, DC, 1985), 801–10; Electronic Briefing Book of the National Security Archive's Carter-Brezhnev Project, *SALT II and the Growth of Mistrust,* http://nsarchive.gwu.edu/carterbrezhnev/salt_ii_intro.html
6. Josef Joffe, "Von der Nachrüstung zur Null-Lösung," *Die Zeit*, 27 November 1981, 17; Henry H. Gaffney, "Euromissiles as the Ultimate Evolution of Theater Nuclear Forces in Europe," *Journal of Cold War Studies* 16 (2014):183–1997.
7. Thomas Risse-Kappen, *Null-Lösung: Entscheidungsprozesse zu den Mittelstreckenwaffen 1970–1987* (Frankfurt am Main, 1988), 18–29; Leopoldo Nuti, "The Origins of the 1979 Dual Track Decision," in *Crisis of Détente in Europe: From Helsinki to Gorbachev 1975–1985,* ed. Leopoldo Nuti (London, 2009), 57–61.
8. Gerhard Wettig, "Die Sowjetunion in der Auseinandersetzung über den NATO-Doppelbeschluss 1979–1983," *Vierteljahrshefte für Zeitgeschichte* 57, no. 2 (2009): 218.
9. Mikhail Gorbachev, *Memoirs* (New York, 1995), 443–44; Anatoly Dobrynin, *In Confidence: Moscow's Ambassador to America's Six Cold War Presidents (1962–1986)* (New York, 1995), 430, 432.
10. Tim Geiger, "Die Regierung Schmidt-Genscher und der NATO-Doppelbeschluss," in *Zweiter Kalter Krieg und Friedensbewegung: Der NATO-Doppelbeschluss in deutschdeutscher und internationaler Perspektive,* eds. Philipp Gassert, Tim Geiger, and Hermann Wentker (Munich, 2011), 97–122.
11. Helmut Schmidt, *Menschen und Mächte* (Berlin, 1987), 230.
12. Kristina Spohr Readman, "Germany and the Politics of the Neutron Bomb, 1975–79," *Diplomacy and Statecraft* 21 (2010): 259–85.

13. Lawrence S. Wittner, *Toward Nuclear Abolition: A History of the World Nuclear Disarmament Movement 1971 to the Present* (Stanford, CA, 2003), 22–27.
14. Michael Ploetz, *Wie die Sowjetunion den Kalten Krieg verlor: Von der Nachrüstung zum Mauerfall* (Berlin, 2000), 132–34.
15. Regierungserklärung, 13 April 1978, published in *Bulletin* Nr. 34/1978: 321–26; Risse-Kappen, *Null-Lösung*, 41.
16. Klaus Wiegrefe, *Das Zerwürfnis: Helmut Schmidt, Jimmy Carter und die Krise der deutsch-amerikanischen Beziehungen* (Berlin, 2005), 197.
17. AAPD 1978, Doc. 61, 159. See Kristina Spohr Readman, "Conflict and Cooperation in Intra-Alliance Nuclear Politics: Western Europe, the United States, and the Genesis of NATO's Dual-Track Decision, 1977–1979," *Journal of Cold War Studies* 13, no. 2 (2013): 50–68.
18. AAPD 1978, Doc. 136.
19. AAPD 1978, Doc. 308.
20. Kristina Spohr, "Helmut Schmidt and the Shaping of Western Security in the Late 1970s: The Guadeloupe Summit of 1979," *The International History Review* 37, no. 1 (2015): 167–92.
21. Hans Apel, *Der Abstieg: Politisches Tagebuch eines Jahrzehnts 1978–1988* (Stuttgart, 1990), 77.
22. Presse- und Informationsamt der Bundesregierung, ed., *Aspekte der Friedenspolitik: Argumente zum Doppelbeschluß des Nordatlantischen Bündnisse* (Bonn, 1981), 60–62.
23. Helga Haftendorn, "Das doppelte Mißverständnis: Zur Vorgeschichte des NATO-Doppelbeschlusses von 1979," *Vierteljahrshefte für Zeitgeschichte* 33 (1985): 271.
24. *Europa-Archiv* 1979, D 556–65; English version in Strategic Survey, 1979 (London: International Institute for Strategic Studies, 1980), 102–3, quoted after Maynard W. Glitman, *The Last Battle of the Cold War* (New York, 2006), 239.
25. Lepoldo Nuti, "The Nuclear Debate in Italian Politics in the Late 1970s and the Early 1980s," in *The Euromissile Crisis and the End of the Cold War*, eds. Leopoldo Nuti et al. (Stanford, CA, 2015), 231–50.
26. Vincent Dujardin, "From Helsinki to the Missiles Question: A Minor Role for Small Countries? The Case of Belgium (1973–1985)," in Nuti, *Crisis of Détente*, 72–85; Coreline Boot and Beatrice de Graaf, "'Hollanditis' oder die Niederlande als 'schwaches Glied in der NATO-Kette'? Niederländische Proteste gegen den NATO-Doppelbeschluss 1979–1985," in Gassert, Geiger, and Wentker, *Zweiter Kalter Krieg*, 345–62; Ruud van Dijk, "'A Mass Psychosis': The Netherlands and NATO's Dual-Track Decision, 1978–1979," *Cold War History* 12, no. 3 (2012): 381–405; Giles Scott-Smith, "The Netherlands between East and West: Dutch Politics, Dual Track, and Cruise Missiles," in Nuti et al., *The Euromissile Crisis*, 251–68.
27. Geiger, "Regierung Schmidt," 113.
28. See AAPD 1979, Doc. 373, 375–376. For the NATO communiqué, see http://www.nato.int/cps/en/SID-B49D9CA2-AEA924D7/natolive/official_texts_27040.htm?selectedLocale.
29. AAPD 1979, Doc. 353, 386, 388.
30. Hartmut Soell, *Helmut Schmidt 2* (Munich, 2008), 749–50.
31. AAPD 1980, Doc. 175.
32. Schmidt, *Menschen*, 254–56.

33. Jimmy Carter, *Keeping Faith: Memoirs of a President* (New York, 1982), 537.
34. AAPD 1980, Doc. 192–95.
35. Lothar Rühl, *Mittelstreckenwaffen in Europa* (Baden-Baden, 1987), 242–47.
36. Klaus Schwabe, "Verhandlungen und Stationierung: Die USA und die Implementierung des NATO-Doppelbeschlusses 1981–1987," in Gassert, Geiger, and Wentker, *Zweiter Kalter Krieg*, 65–93.
37. Alfred Mechtersheimer, ed., *Nachrüsten? Dokumente und Positionen zum NATO-Doppelbeschluss* (Reinbek, 1981), 133, 170.
38. Josef Holik, *Die Rüstungskontrolle, Rückblick auf eine kurze Ära* (Berlin, 2009), 51; Marilena Gala, "The Euromissile Crisis and the Centrality of the 'Zero Option'," in Nuti et al., eds., *The Euromissile Crisis*, 158–75.
39. Rühl, *Mittelstreckenwaffen*, 289–96.
40. Hans-Dietrich Genscher, *Erinnerungen* (Berlin, 1995), 424.
41. Christian Tuschhoff, "Der Genfer 'Waldspaziergang' 1982: Paul Nitzes Initiative in den amerikanisch-sowjetischen Abrüstungsgesprächen," *VfZ* 38 (1990): 289–328.
42. Andreas Wirsching, *Abschied vom Provisorium 1982–1990* (Munich, 2006), 17–26.
43. Andreas Rödder, "Bündnissolidarität und Rüstungskontrollpolitik: Die Regierung Kohl-Genscher, der NATO-Doppelbeschluss und die Innenseite der Außenpolitik," in Gassert, Geiger, and Wentker, *Zweiter Kalter Krieg*, 123–36.
44. http://dip21.bundestag.de/dip21/btp/10/10036.pdf.

Select Bibliography

A concise review of the development of the Double-Track Decision is provided by Nuti and Spohr Readman. Essential reading on political perspectives can be found in Haftendorn, Risse-Kappen, and Rühl. Gassert, Geiger, and Wentkers' volume comprises the current state of research, including a discussion of the frequently neglected international dimension. An equivalent in English is the volume of Nuti, Bozo, Rey, and Rother.

Gassert, Philipp, Tim Geiger, and Hermann Wentker, eds. *Zweiter Kalter Krieg und Friedensbewegung: Der NATO-Doppelbeschluss in deutsch-deutscher und internationaler Perspektive*. Munich, 2011.
Haftendorn, Helga. "Das doppelte Mißverständnis: Zur Vorgeschichte des NATO-Doppelbeschlusses von 1979." *Vierteljahrshefte für Zeitgeschichte* 33 (1985), 244–287.
Nuti, Leopoldo. "The Origins of the 1979 Dual Track Decision – a Survey." In *Crisis of Détente in Europe: From Helsinki to Gorbachev 1975–1985*, ed. Leopoldo Nuti. London, 2009, 57–71.
Nuti, Leopoldo, Frédéric Bozo, Marrie-Pierre Rey, Bernd Rother, eds. *The Euromissile Crisis and the End of the Cold War*. Stanford, CA, 2015.
Readman, Kristina Spohr. "Conflict and Cooperation in Intra-Alliance Nuclear Politics: Western Europe, the United States and the Genesis of NATO's Dual-Track Decision, 1977–1979." *Journal of Cold War Studies* 13, no. 2 (2011): 39–89.
Risse-Kappen, Thomas. *Null-Lösung: Entscheidungsprozesse zu den Mittelstreckenwaffen 1970–1987*. Frankfurt am Main, 1988.
Rühl, Lothar. *Mittelstreckenwaffen in Europa*. Baden-Baden, 1987.

Chapter 3

SS-20 and Pershing II: Weapon Systems and the Dynamization of East-West Relations

Oliver Bange

The NATO Double-Track Decision was initiated by the development of new weapons technologies in the early 1970s. SS-20, Pershing II, and cruise missiles shared—despite their very different technical specifications—one common feature: an operational range reaching or even significantly exceeding 2,500 kilometers. They expanded the potential battlefield, previously restricted to the two German states and adjacent areas, to all territory from the Atlantic coastline to Moscow. This changed the scenario of war and military strategy, especially from the perspective of the Warsaw Pact. Perhaps most importantly it created a deep-seated fear among the communist leadership in the Kremlin. From this point onward the USSR's European territories would be devastated by a war in Central Europe—and no longer by only an intercontinental nuclear missile "exchange" with the United States. For Mikhail Gorbachev it was the most important motivation for his disarmament initiatives with the Reagan administration. The resulting treaty on the elimination of intermediate-range nuclear missiles (INF Treaty), however, did not touch on the superabundance of short-range systems, which would have destroyed East and West Germany. Nevertheless it did create a certain kind of trust in mutual reliability that opened up further negotiations about increasingly comprehensive disarmament in Europe after 1989. This in turn implicitly provided a political framework for security essential for German reunification.

By the end of the 1960s the two superpowers had reached an approximate equilibrium in the field of Intercontinental Ballistic Missiles or ICBMs. As early as 1969 Western expertise assumed that the Soviet Union had an assured second-strike capability, in other words, the power to respond with nuclear weapons of a similar magnitude in Western Europe and North America if the United States and NATO were to attack first. Therefore, from that point on, any American president who escalated the use of nuclear weapons from within the confined battlefield of Central Europe to an intercontinental level would also risk destroying the United States by Soviet missiles. However, it had been exactly the threat of this potent escalation that was the foundation of the Western concept of deterrence: if an American president refused to employ intercontinental weapons—because of the existing gap between the intercontinental and intermediate-range missile systems in the West (the Pershing I had a maximum range of 760 kilometers)—the territorial homelands of the superpowers would be detached/separated from a conventional and nuclear war in Europe. The change in conditions under this recently achieved equilibrium raised the question of whether the American "nuclear guarantee" was still credible.

Successive US governments tried to solve this dilemma with a new NATO strategy called "flexible response" in the 1960s–70s. "Flexible response" was meant to introduce an additional continental—that is, purely European—level of nuclear escalation, whereas previously the use of nuclear weapons on the battlefield could only be escalated into a full-blown intercontinental exchange. The purpose of "flexible response," of course, was to provide the US president with as many nuclear options as possible. Ultimately a strategy for preventing war was thus replaced by one for waging it. To facilitate this undertaking, the development and introduction of an entirely new category of nuclear weapons took place in the 1970s: Theater Nuclear Forces (TNFs).

The Development of the Theater Nuclear Forces in the 1970s

During the era of détente in the 1970s both superpowers stipulated the terms of this strategic nuclear realignment. The Strategic Arms Limitation agreements of 1972 and 1979 (SALT I and SALT II) exclusively dealt with intercontinental missile weapon systems and nuclear warheads. As the European TNFs were excluded, the nuclear efforts of both sides increasingly focused on this so-called "grey area." The United States began work on Pershing II missiles in 1969 and on cruise missiles in the 1970s. Both types demonstrated improved accuracy, and the new cruise missiles—with their electronic self-controlled navigation and ground-tracking radar, known in the jargon of the Warsaw Pact as "wing-guided missiles"—gave enemy air defenses little chance of intercepting them.

The initial design for the new generation of cruise missiles was as a submarine-based system with a range of 800 kilometers. A land-based variant followed as the European allies requested an increased range of 2,500 kilometers. Unlike the high extra-atmospheric trajectory of the TNF-missiles (Pershing II, SS-20), the BGM-109G Gryphon design featured a jet engine (turbofan) that was permanently powered, controllable, and therefore extremely precise in striking a target. Although both types of missiles had the same range, up to 2,500 kilometers, the cruise missiles with an average speed of 880 km per hour (550 mph) were significantly slower than the new generation of continental ballistic missiles, the Pershing II and the SS-20. These new cruise missiles were also capable of flying at a very low altitude (depending on terrain, between 30 and 200 meters) and capable of changing direction while showing hardly any infrared radiation. They were therefore almost impossible to locate and, more importantly, to intercept, given the technical standards of the late 1970s. Nor could the armed forces of the Warsaw Pact prevent their launch, because in times of heightened tension the launch-platforms, with four missiles each, could be mounted on a modified truck chassis making them mobile, not stationary.

Almost simultaneously another entirely new weapons system was developed with the Pershing II (the MGM-31B), which was a two-stage rocket traveling at more than eight times the speed of sound and with a range of 1,800 kilometers (considerably more than the Pershing IA), which could reach Moscow within ten minutes. Despite weighing almost twice as much as its predecessor, it was the same size, about 10 meters high and 1 meter wide. Using solid propellant fuel, it was easy to store and to transport on mobile truck-towed launcher platforms. This mobility made the system difficult to spot by enemy reconnaissance but did not impair its battle-ready status, as it was always poised to launch its missiles ("Quick Reaction Alert"). This effectively reduced the warning time for the Warsaw Pact countries to just five minutes. Finally the end stage control system of the warhead, known as a Maneuverable Reentry Vehicle (MARV), was an innovation that achieved significantly greater accuracy than the Pershing IA. This in turn made it possible to use smaller nuclear warheads to accomplish the same military goals.

While the West continued to describe the production and deployment of these systems in the late 1970s and 1980s as a necessary response to the buildup of the Soviet SS-20 force,[1] military experts and commanders of the Warsaw Pact continued to justify the SS-20 program as merely an anticipated response to this threat of Western technological advancement.[2] In fact, the SS-20 (RSD-10) was based on plans for a new intercontinental ballistic missile dating back to the late 1960s. By omitting a propulsion stage, a far-reaching continental weapon was developed that had three atomic and independently controllable multiple warheads (known as MIRVs [Multiple Independently Targetable Reentry Vehicle]) each.[3] Fitted with solid-propellant engines, the SS-20 had a significantly reduced reaction time (instead of requiring one day for preparation, like the SS-4 and SS-5 missiles, it now took only forty to sixty minutes to prepare a launch, or merely six to eight minutes if the weapon were in an alert position). This new Soviet system was also more mobile and hence less easy to track by enemy observation. In addition, its launching platforms were reusable. Depending on estimates, SS-20 missiles could reach objects within a 4,550 to 5,700 kilometer range and carry explosive heads capable of 150 kiloton to 0.5 megaton detonations. MIRV technology also allowed for significantly improved accuracy.[4] Three years after the Pentagon's programs had begun, Soviet development was hastened by a decision taken in April 1973 that led to the deployment of the first SS-20 systems in 1976. Approximately two-thirds of these new Soviet systems were installed within reach of Western Europe.

Technological quantum leaps in computer technology in the late 1960s were the precondition for these new missile systems, including the short-range missiles SS-21, SS-22, SS-23, and ICBM SS-16 and SS-18. The same applies to the development of ground tracking radar and the turbofan techniques of much smaller jet propulsion units. It should therefore be stressed that sea- and land-based cruise missiles, Pershing II and SS-20 missiles, were all developed simultaneously. Even the decision to build cruise missiles and the planning of its use and purpose occurred well before the new Soviet SS-20 intermediate range missiles played a role in political debate.[5]

Innovation in technology inevitably means there will be a lag before production and deployment can commence. Long development and life cycles therefore question whether cruise and Pershing II missiles represent a "response" or a genuine "upgrade" in relation to the SS-20. Recent historical research and access to hitherto restricted documents suggest that production and deployment of new NATO systems would have in any case occurred as part of TNF modernization. For example, the US Senate approved funding to prepare Pershing II for production in the summer of 1976 in order to have missiles ready to be sent to Europe by the summer of 1980. In contrast, the first reference to a potential problem with SS-20 missiles came half a year later at the NATO Council of Ministers in December 1976. However, one can equally challenge the argument that the development of the SS-20 was an anticipatory response to cruise missiles.

This entirely new category of nuclear and, in some circumstances, conventional weapons was introduced in the late 1970s and early 1980s. Their labeling—Theater Nuclear Weapons, Euromissiles, medium-range weapons/INFs, continental missiles, "grey-zone" weapon systems, and so forth—depended on the point of view of the observer. Up to this point, strategic nuclear weapons were designed to achieve political goals (and were oriented toward intercontinental use and toward delivering the greatest possible political and psychological impact), while tactical nuclear weapons were intended to primarily serve military objectives on the battlefield. The introduction of the new systems rendered such long-lasting distinctions useless. With diverse warheads designed to meet differing military requirements, they could serve as a political deterrent or be used selectively against individual tank units, military headquarters, or ships.

In peacetime the efficiency of a new weapon is judged both in terms of its technological development and by the significance that is attributed to it in political-military thinking—not only on the part of those who command it but also by those who may suffer its consequences. It is therefore necessary that such an assessment address a variety of contexts, from the political and social to the military and strategic, particularly for the ongoing conflict between East and West.

The Simultaneous Development of New Military Techniques: The Neutron Bomb, Aircraft Design, Tanks, and Antitank Weapons

The same political and strategic arguments that were behind the development of medium-range missiles with a truly continental reach provided the motivation to consider the development of so-called tailor-made nuclear bombs by US and NATO committees during the early 1970s. Such "tailored" classified warheads were supposed to make it feasible to conduct, depending on the war scenario, a limited or extended nuclear war in Europe. Precision weapons were supposed to replace "big" warheads whose explosive charge was often measured in megatons. Moreover, the various modes of energy-release achieved by a nuclear chain reaction—such as heat, pressure, radiation, and electromagnetic waves—were to be tailored to a specific purpose and thereby were meant to limit loss of life and goods. According to the opinion of Western nuclear experts at the time, such customization was the only politically acceptable way to use nuclear weapons in densely populated Europe. It would also provide the US president with a third nuclear option between the employment of nuclear weapons on the battlefield and intercontinental missile warfare.

Warheads were thus developed that could produce greater heat and pressure waves. These so-called bunker busters were intended to be used against Warsaw Pact headquarters or to block mountain passes outside Europe (especially in the Himalayas). Plans for Europe foresaw the replacement of oversized warheads, which especially threatened the civilian population with their extreme heat and pressure waves, with a new, intense radiation bomb. This enhanced radiation weapon (ERW), also simply known as a neutron bomb, displayed a nearly identical radius of radiation, heat, and pressure. Defense experts believed that the nuclear explosive power of such bombs could deliver the same military-tactical effect but reduce civilian collateral damage by a factor of ten. To this end in 1972, the Americans revived their research on the neutron bomb, which they had stopped in 1958.

Between 1978 and 1983, during the height of the public dispute on the medium-range missiles, both alliances also introduced a number of technologically innovative aircraft. NATO developed a new generation of multi-task fighter planes: the MRCA (Multi-Role Combat Aircraft) Tornado, the General Dynamics F-16 Fighting Falcon, and the McDonnell Douglas F-15 Eagle. The Tornado's flying ability was far outshone by its high-tech electronics and radar components, which enabled it to fly—in air force jargon—"at lowest altitudes." It demonstrated a carrying capacity of about five tons with a range of up to 2,500 kilometers. It was able to carry containers of cluster bombs, antitank weapons, or the nuclear bomb B61. The F-16 had specifications similar to those of the Tornado, but it was better adapted to the role of a bomber and nuclear weapons carrier. Finally the F-15 Eagle could be deployed as a fighter-bomber and an air superiority fighter, but not as a nuclear weapons carrier.

At the time they were introduced, all three aircraft types were equipped with the latest electronics and had significantly increased loading capacity in comparison with other aircraft in the East and West during the late 1970s and early 1980s. The interplay of these design features predestined this new generation of fighter aircraft for NATO missions over the battlefield not only in Germany but also deep into enemy territory.

The Warsaw Pact had already introduced new aircraft, such as the MiG 23 (Flogger), MiG 27 (Flogger D), and Sukhoi 22 (Fitter), in the first half of 1970s, but when compared to their NATO counterparts, they exhibited significantly shorter range, smaller load carrying capacity, and simpler and apparently less reliable electronics. In many respects these planes were more aerodynamic and agile than Tornados and F-15s, but not F-16s. On a more general level the design features of the newer Soviet aircraft followed specifications in developmental and operational doctrine dating back to the 1960s that demanded increased specialization. This principle was adhered to well into the last decade of the systemic conflict between the East and West. For example, the Sukhoi 22 was released in 1976 as a fighter-bomber designed for high speeds near the ground, and in 1983 the MiG 29 (Fulcrum) was a pure air superiority fighter with a short flying range.

Washington paid particular attention to the development and production of the TU-22M (Backfire) bomber. This swing-wing supersonic bomber made its first flight in 1971. The aircraft was designed as a strategic nuclear bomber with a range of up to 7,000 km and, with a top speed of up to 2,300 km per hour, it was as fast as the new NATO Multi-Role Combat Aircraft Tornado. At the end of the 1970s the Americans feared that if the Soviet military adapted their Backfire bomber for midair refueling, it could mutate into a veritable intercontinental weapon.

The "Revolution in Military Affairs" (RMA) in the late 1970s included tank development that was of particular importance to NATO. The Leopard 2, a West German tank, was released in 1980, and the American M1 Abrams was brought out in the same year. The British Challenger was introduced in 1983, and in 1986 came the French Leclerc. The West Germans insisted that the Leopard 2 and the Abrams be equipped with a 120 mm smoothbore cannon, drawing upon intelligence that the Israelis had shared with them regarding the latest Soviet tank equipment. The cannon doubled effective shooting range to almost 4 kilometers. Except for the very first Challengers off the production line, all new NATO tanks employed laser-guided weapon systems for stabilization and tracking to fire and hit targets during travel. And finally, this generation of NATO tanks was fitted with a composite armor casing derived from a variety of materials that offered far more protection for the crew.

The most advanced tank developed by the Soviet Union and deployed in Warsaw Pact armies during the late 1970s was the T-72. Although equipped with a 125 mm cannon, a reloading device, and a laser-controlled firing control system, it had a number of vulnerable points: the turret of the T-72 was molded from cast steel and had no ceramic or other composite armor protection; its weapons were less effective than those of the new western tanks; and there was a significant risk of fire if the interior ammunition storage received a hit. However, the T-80 was supposed to become the primary combat tank and bear the brunt of the fighting with its NATO counterparts. It was produced from 1978 onward and used exclusively by elite tank units in Soviet Guard regiments and Guard tank divisions. Only the second series of the T-80 was fitted with composite armor and a modern weapon stabilization system. Its operating distance was considerably restricted at 335 km, and the great heat of its gas turbine engines could be detected by thermal imaging at a long distance. In this respect it was similar to the American Abrams tank.

Between 1978 and 1981 highly effective new antitank weapons were introduced by both alliances. This had enormous repercussions for projections of a conventional war in Europe. Antitank helicopters appeared on both sides almost simultaneously between 1979 and 1981. These were the Mi-24 (Soviet), the Apache AH-64A (US), and the Bo-105 PAH-1 (West

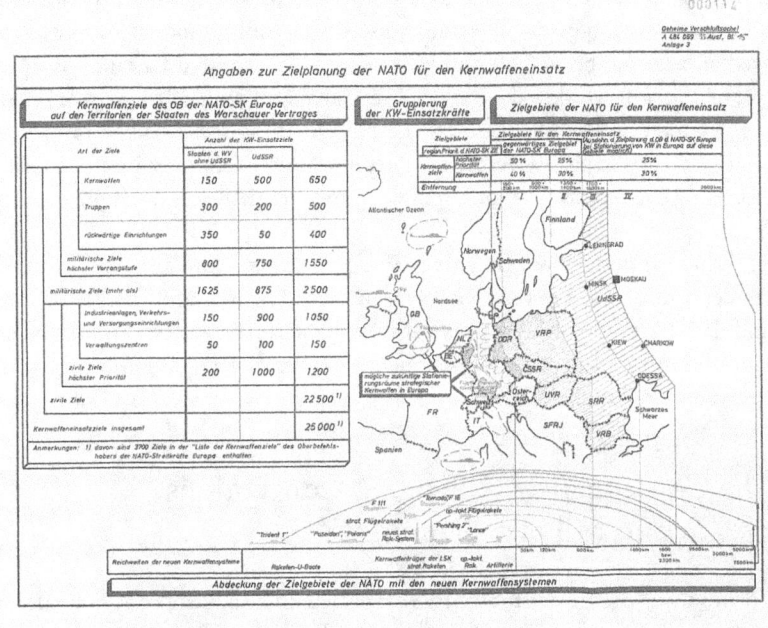

Figure 3.1. East German graphic showing the reach-diameters of Western nuclear systems, Department of Military Intelligence, National People's Army (BArch, Abteilung Militärarchiv (Abt. MA))

German), all specifically designed for this role. These helicopters exerted a tremendous threat to the armored tank units, which until then had continued to dominate thinking about a conventional war in Europe. An Apache helicopter was able to fight sixteen independent targets simultaneously with the help of its sixteen Hellfire missiles and laser-marking. At the same time, artillery shells became an effective means to fight armored tanks due to the introduction of a new type of bomblet munition. This cluster bomb could be fired from conventional tube artillery and aimed directly at the vulnerable thin tops of armored vehicles or be used as antitank mines.

Finally, innovative mine-laying systems, introduced in the early 1980s, also used cluster munitions to fight tanks. The systems, developed in West Germany, were named Skorpion and LARS 1 on the NATO side and BM-27 by the Warsaw Pact. Within just five minutes a single Skorpion-type automatic mine-launching systems could render an area of 1,500 by 50 meters impassable for tank units with 600 antitank mines known as AT-2. A battery of rocket-launching LARS 1 systems could distribute some 2,304 antitank mines of the AT-1 type in barely twenty seconds and up to a distance of 25 kilometers, well beyond the firing range of the tank cannons. Its spread covered an area of about 1,500 by 500 meters. An armored battalion captured by such action would take days to break free and would lose approximately half its men and material. With the help of these technically complex but relatively easy-to-use systems, even reserve units were now in a position to stop and even destroy elite enemy armored tank forces without suffering major losses themselves.

These various developments in weapon systems fundamentally altered a conception of warfare that had been in place for decades. The idea of great and decisive tank battles in Central Europe became obsolete, and the associated assumptions about the strategic advantage of attacking the enemy first became increasingly dubious.

The Consequences: Changing Conceptions of War and Military Planning

The resulting preference for the role of the defender shaped the military dogma and operational planning of the Warsaw Pact. Until then (the late 1970s/early 1980s), the conventional thinking on the part of the Warsaw Pact had assumed that fast tank attacks were the decisive conventional tool. This changed with new weapon systems giving defenders a decisive edge over attackers. The dogmatic image of "aggressive" capitalism and of a "revanchist" Federal Republic of Germany were crucial elements in the East's perception of the West, which would—almost by definition—attack at some future point. The Warsaw Pact intended to stop this kind of Western strike as early as possible and to push the battlefield as quickly as possible back onto NATO territory. In this way most of the destruction, especially the nuclear devastation, would damage the aggressive West. Regardless of the outcome of the war, this development would lead to a weakening of capitalist industry, diminish its resources, and disintegrate Western society. The territory of East Germany and the People's Republic of Poland were regarded as the principle battlefields or as passage terrain and hence of vital importance not only in a possible future military conflict but also during the preparation for such an event.[6]

The main directions of attack, from the perspective of the Eastern bloc countries (until the early 1980s) and as anticipated by the West, would follow the geographical conditions required for tanks: through the North German Plain toward Denmark, the North Sea coast, and the Ruhr region; through the so-called Fulda Gap in the West on to the Middle Rhine in the direction of Luxembourg; along the Bavarian Forest and the Danube toward the Main and the Upper Rhine.[7] Until the late 1970s both the Warsaw Pact and NATO believed that ultimately the war would be decided once the "second wave" of primarily Soviet tank divisions from Eastern Poland and the USSR entered the battle.

Political and military decision-makers of the Warsaw Pact countries were constantly informed by their intelligence services about the latest political and technological developments within NATO.[8] They were in a good position to anticipate future changes quite accurately. It is then no surprise that in 1977–78 Warsaw Pact politicians and military leaders reckoned that a combination of cruise missiles and ERW warheads (neutron bombs) would be introduced. East and West alike calculated that a single cruise missile equipped with a 1 kiloton warhead of ERW could contaminate the area of an armored (tank) division with radiation. The combined elements of the cruise missiles (their range, accuracy, and low production costs), together with the limited resources of the Warsaw Pact to intercept such missiles, posed a grave threat: the cruise missiles could destroy all armored divisions of the "second wave" on their way between Moscow and the German Democratic Republic before they could actually enter the German battlefield. Thus, at least from an Eastern perspective, the decisive factor for a conventional war in Europe increasingly lost its importance. If one further considered the upcoming innovations of NATO in the conventional staples of warfare, such as new tanks, aircraft, helicopters, and antitank technology, one needed to conclude

Figure 3.2. Caricature "Arms race: help, I've been followed" (Horst Haitzinger)

that the divisions of the "first wave"⁹ were to face NATO units of at least equal size and quality. NATO planners pursued precisely this integration of the hinterland into an expanded battlefield during the 1980s with the concepts of "Follow-on Forces Attack" and "Air-Land Battle."¹⁰

The Soviet inability to intercept cruise missiles and Pershing IIs resulted in widespread anxiety both in the USSR and among its Warsaw Pact allies, where there was fear that the military and political leadership would be "decapitated" in their command posts right at the beginning of an armed conflict. In May 1979, six months before the NATO Double-Track Decision, a Polish map demonstrated this new and terrifying war scenario to the state and party leadership. Rather than pushing forward to the Rhine in five to six days and to Paris in just under nine days as envisioned by the Warsaw Pact in its formal training exercises, Polish, East German, and Soviet troops would only reach Hamburg and Hannover after eighteen days, by which time American and West German units would have reached Leipzig in East Germany. Once fully equipped with the latest models, NATO aircraft units would target the area stretching from Western Poland to Warsaw. According to this scenario, the entire area—including all military bases (even the headquarters of the Warsaw Pact in Legnica), the bridges across the Oder-Neisse, the region's ports and transport junctions, as well as the territory of southeastern Poland (where the Soviet tank divisions were supposed to arrive from the Ukraine)—would be, like a carpet, entirely covered with "winged missiles" and their neutron bombs.

At the time none of these weapons or the modern NATO planes actually existed. Nevertheless the potential result of this scenario was wide-reaching nuclear devastation of territories and major flooding of urban areas along rivers. It would be of little consolation to the Polish people that the Soviet leadership apparently planned to strike West Germany and the Benelux countries with potent nuclear bombs. Adapting this Polish scenario to a European scale, thereby including as targets British and French ports and all military units and bases up to Moscow, the result would be similar in that Germany remained the central battleground while the nuclear devastation would expand considerably and reach from the Atlantic coastline to Moscow.

The Reaction of the Warsaw Pact on the Impending Introduction of TNFs

The Eastern Alliance responded to NATO's impending introduction of new nuclear and conventional weapons with varying concepts and intentions. A first adequate strategy to prevent the stationing of missiles in Europe seemed to be direct negotiations between the superpowers. This had had already proved helpful during the Nixon-Ford era, when unofficial contacts had defused several sensitive issues. In order to protect their own interests, Soviet negotiators thus appealed directly to the national interests of the United States between 1977 and 1979. In October 1977 the Soviets went on to offer what amounted to a real "Superpower Deal": the USSR would put a stop to production and deployment of the new generation of its intercontinental ballistic missiles (SS-18) and abandon a midair refueling version of the Backfire bomber (TU-22M). In return the United States would cease the production of neutron bombs and abstain from a deployment of new missiles as well as limit the range of its cruise missiles to 600 km. In this way the predominant powers could protect their respective territories from a nuclear escalation within the Central European battlefield.

This solution, however, presented both strategic and political problems for the allies, especially within NATO, and for this reason partners were not told of the Soviet offer. Even when West German Chancellor Helmut Schmidt in late 1977 made public his not unfounded concerns about a potential agreement between the superpowers to contain a possible war within Europe, US President Jimmy Carter and General Secretary of the CPSU Leonid Brezhnev kept this option secret, not mentioning it until the autumn of 1979. Despite protests from Chancellor Schmidt and many other Western European governments, President Carter, probably in concert with General Secretary Brezhnev, kept the looming problems with the SS-20 and cruise missiles out of the SALT II negotiations, which ended in June 1979.

A second approach was the so-called Peace Policy of the German Democratic Republic. It was an attempt to create among the political left and liberal-left spectrum of the Federal Republic a mass movement against the new intermediate-range NATO missiles and, if not to control then at least to support such organizations. Picturing a kind of reverse domino effect, East Germans hoped that the base of the Social Democratic Party membership would exert pressure on the chancellor. Schmidt in turn would be forced to compromise his position in internal political maneuvering and end up unable to support TNF-deployment within NATO. This would have repercussions not only in Germany but in all the rest of Western Europe, as Bonn's deployment decision was of central importance to other allies. Peace groups in West Germany were thus supported by East Germany, at times without their knowledge. At the time the East German government liked to represent itself at any given occasion on a national or international stage as a "peace-loving country." This strategy was the result of consultations between

East Germany and the highest level of the CPSU and other communist parties of the Warsaw Pact, and it confirmed the special role of the East Germans in influencing the West generally and West German society in particular.[11]

Third, the Soviet Union and its allies sought concurrently to find a nuclear and military-strategic response to Western intermediate-range missiles. One option was to mirror the nuclear strategy of deterrence by NATO as closely as possible. If NATO used its nuclear Pershing II and cruise missiles against the "second wave" in a war, then the USSR would threaten retaliation with a massive launch of its SS-20 missiles against major metropolitan areas in Western Europe. The aim of this threat was supposed to be to maintain the existing advantage in conventional army warfare by the Warsaw Pact and to prevent the "decapitation" or elimination of political and military leadership of the Eastern Alliance at the beginning of a conflict. Thus the Politburo of the CPSU—in anticipation of a deployment decision by NATO—decided in May 1983 to install an additional 270 SS-20 missiles in the western part of the Soviet Union.[12] The East German leadership now had the worrisome prospect of a complete destruction of its territory, even if the official military doctrine of the Warsaw Pact stated that a Western attack would be stopped just before its border.

Fourth, the Warsaw Pact developed new military strategies. It adapted military doctrine as quickly as possible to the needs of new weapons systems and the associated changes in the balance of forces and military war scenarios. The plans of the late 1970s and early 1980s had, as we have seen, initially aimed at maintaining the established doctrine, but as the introduction of the "second wave" onto the Central European battlefield became increasingly dubious it was decided that troops already stationed in the GDR, Czechoslovakia, and western Poland would need to conduct and conclude the war on their own, if necessary.

The conclusions drawn on the basis of these assumptions required more aggressive operations and war planning: so-called Operational Maneuver Groups were now to act as spearheads, breaking the defenses of the West and advancing without assistance to the Rhine. If necessary, nuclear weapons would be used on whatever scale required to achieve this aim. At any sign of an impending NATO attack they would be employed in a preemptive strike. The troops had to be kept constantly at maximum alert. With this tactic, which entailed a high level of political and military risk, the Warsaw Pact managed to conceal changes in the traditional war scenario during the early 1980s, at least theoretically. Thus the East German outline for a large military exercise of the Warsaw Pact, called SOYUS 83, shows at first glance little change compared to the operational doctrine that had been in place from the 1950s right up until the 1970s. The troops of the Warsaw Pact countries would reach the Rhine on the ninth day of the war, just like in earlier plans. A closer inspection, however, reveals the crucial role given to the units deployed in the GDR and Czechoslovakia and the much narrower lines of attack.

Presumably motivated by the increasing volatility of the military situation in the early 1980s, the Soviet General Staff began to initiate changes to its overall strategy after 1983. Proceeding hesitantly at first, the General Staff soon pursued increasingly defensive strategies with more rigor. For example, operational plans of the 5th (East German) Army from 1983 and 1985 specify not only offensive but also defensive operations. A complete reversal was finally reached by the Berlin Declaration of the Warsaw Pact in May 1987.[13] It announced a purely defensive plan with no attack options. In this context it is noteworthy that the Ministry of Defense in Moscow initiated preparations for this change of doctrine six months before Mikhail Gorbachev was appointed General Secretary of the Communist Party of the Soviet Union.[14]

Conclusion

The consequences of the technological revolution in military affairs, which were first trumpeted in the early 1970s but did not show a real impact until the late 1970s and early 1980s, were enormous. It seems, therefore, quite appropriate to perceive the years 1977–83 not only as a period of confrontation but also as a transformation in international relations. Considered from a specific military-strategic perspective, these years constitute indeed a turning point in the second half of the East-West conflict.[15]

Looking at the impact of the NATO Double-Track Decision, or, more generally, the problems surrounding medium-range missiles, two mechanisms appear particularly significant with regard to the "Revolution in Military Affairs" and the collapse of communist regimes in 1989/91. First the deployment of NATO intermediate-range missile systems extended the theater of war from Central Europe, especially East and West Germany, to an entire continent stretching from the Atlantic coastline to Moscow. Second, the effect of this development on the psyche of the leaders of the Warsaw Pact can hardly be overestimated, despite its having been anticipated by the East for years. For the first time in postwar history it seemed that the idea of a quick reversal of a NATO attack was no longer plausible and that even a determined counterattack would not be sufficient to protect Warsaw Pact territory.

Without the dread of the medium-range missiles, Mikhail Gorbachev would have hardly taken the initiative for the Summit of Reykjavík, ratified the Intermediate-Range Nuclear Forces Treaty, or supported the Conventional Forces in Europe negotiations. And again it was a grave concern on the part of the SED leadership that promoted an official "peace policy." This in turn let to a temporary relaxation of pressures on small and mostly unconnected peace groups in the German Democratic Republic. And it was precisely this relative freedom that enabled these groups to form an informal network in March 1983. In the fall of 1989 this network of dissidents organized the mass protests of East Germans. Considered in this light, the transformations in the military and security sphere at the time could be seen as an important factor contributing to the period of change in 1989–90.

Oliver Bange is a senior researcher at the Centre for Military History and Social Sciences of the German MoD (ZMSBw) in Potsdam, where he currently heads the project "Security Policies and the German Armed Forces". He is also a lecturer (Privatdozent) at the University of Mannheim. His publications include *The EEC Crisis of 1963* (London 2000), *Helsinki 1975 and the Transformation of Europe* (co-edited with Gottfried Niedhart, New York 2008), *Wege zur Wiedervereinigung* (co-edited with Bernd Lemke, Munich 2013), *The Long Détente - Changing Concepts of Security and Cooperation in Europe* (co-edited with Poul Villaume, Budapest 2016). His latest monograph deals with the gradual failure of East Germany's external and internal security structures - *Sicherheit und Staat – Die Bündnis- und Militärpolitik der DDR 1969-1990* (Berlin 2016).

Notes

1. The German foreign minister and FDP party chairman wanted to deliberately create an antonym for a term postulated by Egon Bahr, i.e., the "upgrade" of NATO arms. Hans-Dietrich Genscher, *Memoirs* (Munich, 1997), 415.
2. Bernd Biermann, *Offizier, Diplomat und Aufklärer der NVA: Streiflichter aus dem Kalten Krieg* (Berlin, 2008), 243.
3. Stephen J. Zaloga, *The Kremlin's Nuclear Sword: The Rise and Fall of Russia's Strategic Nuclear Forces, 1945–2000* (Washington, DC, 2002); and Pavel Podvig, ed., *Russian Strategic Nuclear Forces* (Cambridge, MA, 2004).
4. For a contemporary source containing technical details deviating from the literature on the subject, see in particular the recordings "Information about the strategic offensive forces' exercises of the USSR noted during the maneuver, SAPAD 81," with initials by Erich Honecker. BA-MA, MSW 1/114493.
5. Leopoldo Nuti, "The Origins of the 1979 Dual Track Decision: A Survey," in *The Crisis of Détente in Europe: From Helsinki to Gorbachev, 1975–1985*, ed. Leopoldo Nuti (London, 2009), 57–71.

6. Rüdiger Wenzke, "Die NVA und die Polnische Armee als Koalitionsstreitkräfte auf dem europäischen Kriegsschauplatz in den 1980er Jahren: Operative Planungen, Konzepte und Entwicklungen," in *Die Streitkräfte der DDR und Polens in der Operationsplanung des Warschauer Paktes*, ed. Rüdiger Wenzke (Potsdam, 2010), 97–125.
7. For a current discussion of operational planing procedures of the Warsaw Pact, see Oliver Bange, "Comments on and Contextualisation of Polish Documents Related to SOYUZ 75 and SHCHIT 88," in Woodrow Wilson Center (Washington, DC, 2010), CWIHP E-Dossier no. 20, Roundtable Discussion on Warsaw Pact Exercises SOYUZ-75 and SHCHIT-88, http://www.wilsoncenter.org/topics/docs/2010-01-25%20Bange%20Comments%20on%20SOJUS%2075%20and%20TARCZA%20882.pdf.
8. Oliver Bange, "Zwischen Bedrohungsperzeption und sozialistischem Selbstverständnis: Die DDR-Staatssicherheit und westliche Transformationsstrategien 1966–1975," in *Militär und Staatssicherheit im Sicherheitskonzept der Warschauer-Pakt-Staaten*, ed. Torsten Diedrich and Walter Sueß (Berlin, 2010), 253–96.
9. "First wave" and "second wave" are terms used in Western publications and by NATO. The NVA referred to the "first wave" as "first and second tactical squadron."
10. Based on the experiences of the Vietnam war and, even more, from the Middle East, the "Training and Doctrine Command" (TRADOC) of the US Army, which had been established in 1973, began to develop concepts for a new defense doctrine for the West. According to this, NATO forces should not only accomplish rearguard action but also, as rapidly as possible, carry out flexible operations against the enemy's armored forces and eliminate enemy reserves in Central and Eastern Europe ("extended battlefield") through extensive air raid strikes. "Air-Land Battle" was officially adopted in 1982 and remained NATO doctrine until the late 1990s. See also John Buckley, *Air Power in the Age of Total War* (London, 1999).
11. See also notes on the meeting of the Central Committee Secretaries Hermann Axen and Boris Ponomarev in Moscow on 1 November 1978, and the speech by Leonid Brezhnev (SAPMO BArch DY 30 / J IV 2/202/572 and DY 30/IV 2/2.035/56) to the Political Consultative Committee of the Warsaw Pact in Moscow on 22 November 1978 (SAPMO BArch: DY 30 / J IV 2/2A/2190). See also the article by Hermann Wentker in this volume.
12. Julij A. Kwizinskij, *Vor dem Sturm: Erinnerungen eines Diplomaten* (Berlin, 1993), 322 and 325.
13. Public declaration of the Political Advisory Committee on military doctrine of the Warsaw Pact, 29 May 1987, copy of a document written in Russian. BA-MA: VA 01/40373.
14. The reorientation of the Soviet Ministry of Defense's new guidelines can also be indirectly observed in the joint Warsaw Pact operational-strategic exercise "Granite 86": given a decidedly defensive position, the forces simulated defense action against NATO's cruise missiles and air attacks. See report and letter by Defense Minister Heinz Kessler to Erich Honecker, 8 April 1984. BA-MA: DVW1-114497.
15. For periodization and terminology see Gottfried Niedhart, "Der Ost-West Konflikt: Konfrontation im Kalten Krieg und Stufen der Deeskalation," *Archiv für Sozialgeschichte* 50 (2010): 557–94.

Select Bibliography

In addition to the references to current research literature provided in this chapter, see also these reviews of Western and Eastern military and nuclear technology:

Haslam, Jonathan. *The Soviet Union and the Politics of Nuclear Weapons in Europe, 1969–1987—The Problem of the SS-20* (Basingstoke, 1989).
Podvig, Pavel, ed., *Russian Strategic Nuclear Forces* (Cambridge, MA, 2004).
Prados, John. *The Soviet Estimate: U.S. Intelligence Analysis and Soviet Strategic Forces* (Princeton, NJ, 1986).
Zaloga, Stephen. *The Kremlin's Nuclear Sword: The Rise and Fall of Russia's Strategic Nuclear Forces, 1945–2000*. Washington, DC, 2002.

In the absence of new historiographical work on the development and meaning of Western weapons systems, see the following:

Bundesministerum der Verteidigung, ed. *Weißbücher 1970 bis 1983*. Bonn, 1971 until 1983.
Freedman, Lawrence. *The Evolution of Nuclear Strategy*. Basingstoke 1983; reprint 2003.
Rühl, Lothar. *Mittelstreckenwaffen in Europa—Ihre Bedeutung in Strategie, Rüstungskontrolle und Bündnispolitik*. Baden-Baden, 1987.
Jane's International Defence Review offers detailed information on weapon systems and is now also available online: http://jaa.janes.com.

Chapter 4

NATO's Double-Track Decision and East-West German Relations
Hermann Wentker

The NATO Double-Track Decision of 1979 presented a triple challenge to both West and East Germany. First of all, as members of NATO and the Warsaw Pact respectively, both states were compelled to endorse the official position of their own alliance, even if the extent and mode of participation in the decision-making process was considerably different. The West German government under Chancellor Helmut Schmidt contributed significantly to the decision-making process in NATO. In contrast, the East German leadership was subordinate to Soviet wishes and had to comply with Russian demands. Second, both leaderships experienced social resistance to the NATO Double-Track Decision. Again, each government dealt with this in its own way—a demonstration of the axiomatic distinctions between democracy and dictatorship. The third and most substantial problem for Bonn and East Berlin consisted in reconciling loyalty and allegiance to Washington or Moscow while simultaneously maintaining relations with their German counterpart. Despite all their differences, both German states and their respective social systems had a common language that was used by social groups, individuals, and political leaders to influence those on the other side of the East-West German divide.

The Interests of West and East Germany

The top priority for the Schmidt government was to protect its own security within the Alliance. This is the why the Chancellor had so firmly supported both components of the Double-Track Decision. He certainly would have preferred a reduction of Soviet arms superiority in intermediate-range missiles to an installment of new Western missiles.[1] His ultimate goal may have been the establishment of security by détente, yet Schmidt could not picture the "European peace order" put forth by his predecessor, Chancellor Willy Brandt, and his associate Egon Bahr. Their original idea had been to transform communist societies by recognizing the status quo and gradually increasing East-West contacts. Schmidt did not believe in this approach and pursued a policy of equilibrium, which had the added advantage of being compatible with the requirements of military security.[2]

This approach fitted seamlessly with Schmidt's policy on Germany in general. Being a "sober realist," he sought to achieve real progress for the Germans in the East and West through a process of give and take, especially regarding travel arrangements. Although he accepted the existence of the two Geman states as a reality, for him this did not imply that the German question was solved. But until it was, he urged the two governments to set "irreconcilable differences aside and make practical arrangements for mutual benefits."[3] A major driving force behind this policy was the promotion of national cohesion in times of tension, because, as he had announced in 1974, he also felt "responsible for the fate of the Germans in East Germany and Berlin," even if this called for financial sacrifices.[4]

While Schmidt's motives were ultimately political, those of Erich Honecker, the political leader of East Germany, were primarily financial. The raison d'état of East Germany had two principle demands: loyal allegiance to the Soviet Union (which in return was supposed to provide military protection as well as economic remittances) and delimitation from West Germany. Since the 1970s the Soviet Union had proven unreliable as a supplier of commodities and food. It increased prices within Eastern bloc countries, especially for crude oil. Although increased East-West German contacts counteracted the principle of delimitation, a relationship with West Germany had become increasingly important for Honecker, who had an expensive social-political program to finance. When the Soviet leadership announced in late 1981 that they would cut crude oil deliveries by two million tons the following year, the East German economy became virtually dependent on West Germany. This is illustrated by the two billion deutsche mark (DM) loan granted to East Germany and mediated by Franz Josef Strauss.[5] Thus the East German leaders were relying on a continuation of détente to enable them simultaneously to maintain good relations with the Soviet Union and West Germany. When NATO announced the Double-Track Decision and the Soviets invaded Afghanistan, the delicate balance of East-West German relations was threatened and East Berlin feared adverse reactions.

East-West German Political Developments Before and After the NATO Double-Track Decision (1979–81)

Honecker tried hard to prevent the Double-Track Decision by talking to Schmidt just before the crucial NATO meeting. He was fully aware that by doing so he was acting contrary to the directives laid down by Leonid Brezhnev at the beginning of October 1979, when the latter urged for unity within the Warsaw Pact. In fact, Brezhnev had asked Honecker to abstain from close communication with West Germany. On 28 November 1979, Honecker proposed an urgent meeting with Schmidt, and pleaded with the Danish Foreign Minister Anker Jørgensen to delay a decision within NATO for six months. Although the delay was rejected, a meeting was arranged for 2 December. The Soviet leadership interfered and prevented Honecker from attending an internal German summit. Moscow, suspicious of East Berlin's special relationship with Bonn, did not tolerate such unilateral decisions on the part of the East German government, as these ran counter to its own plan to exert pressure on West Germany.[6]

NATO's Double-Track Decision and the Soviet invasion of Afghanistan narrowed the scope of action for the two German governments. Certainly both tried to continue developing a cooperative relationship, but their leaders operated under different constraints. Schmidt, although frequently critical of the Carter administration, underlined the "necessity of alliance solidarity with the United States." But because of the weight West Germany carried in NATO, Schmidt could act more independently than Honecker, who had far less influence within the Warsaw Pact. For example, Bonn to a degree sought to conduct "business as usual" with socialist countries, especially East Germany, and hence objected to the US call for an economic embargo.[7] Although Schmidt joined the boycott of the Olympic Games in Moscow in 1980, he successfully persuaded the Soviet Union to come to the negotiating table in Geneva during his visit to Moscow from 30 June to 2 July 1980.

For his part, Honecker tried to stall but ultimately had to decide between cooperation with Bonn and allegiance to Moscow. As long as the installation of Western missiles was open to debate, he delayed making a final decision. Honecker saw three options for a way out. First of all, he supported the Soviet position both within the framework of the Warsaw Pact and in the East-West German talks. This was made easier by Moscow's consent to participate in negotiations in Geneva. Second, the East German leadership took advantage of its connections and made efforts approved by the Soviet Union to manipulate the peace movement in West Germany. As the peace movement was growing and the support for the Double-Track Decision in the Social Democratic Party was waning, they felt reassured in taking this approach. Third, Honecker did not tire of stressing to Schmidt that he would make every effort "to ensure the international crisis did not damage relations between [the] two countries."[8]

Both governments therefore continued to come to agreement and to initiate new projects costing millions of deutsche marks, especially in transport (mainly for development and improvement of highways in East Germany). To ensure that West Germany abandoned the resolution for an arms upgrade, the Social Democratic Party needed to withdraw support for the Double-Track Decision but still remain in government.⁹

In 1980 the GDR appeared to haved changed its course in regard to its relationship with West Germany by increasing mandatory exchange rates and through Honecker's other demands made in in Gera on 13 October of that year.¹⁰ This attempt at delimitation was due to the Polish crisis and not to orders from Moscow. Honecker clearly demonstrated a readiness toward further bilateral negotiations in a series of gestures during the winter of 1980–81. His opponents in the Politburo recognized this strategy and tried to denounce him in Moscow. The Soviet leadership did not consider removing him from office, but in August 1981 Brezhnev warned Honecker not to engage too closely with West Germany.¹¹

Schmidt also came under increasing pressure in 1981. The newly elected American president, Ronald Reagan, was insisting that inter-German trade arrangements be abandoned and the US embargo against the Soviet bloc be supported on the international level.¹² In the meantime, the peace movement

Figure 4.1. US President Gerald Ford (right) in conversation with the first secretary of the Central Committee of the SED, East Germany, Erich Honecker on 1 August 1975 at the Conference on Security and Cooperation in Europe (CSCE) in Helsinki, Finland (BArch B 145 Bild-00003774 / Engelbert Reinecke)

had turned into a formidable popular domestic movement in West Germany and was increasingly creating problems for the Social Democratic Party and its policy in support of an arms upgrade. Moreover, former Chancellor Willy Brandt and his associate Egon Bahr launched a "parallel foreign policy" with trips to Moscow and East Berlin: both stuck to the Double-Track Decision, but they were also inclined to sympathize with the Soviet position and to accept that their intentions to negotiate were indeed serious.[13] This made it harder for Schmidt to support the Double-Track Decision and at the same time maintain détente policy with East Germany.

Despite these difficulties, Schmidt and Honecker continued to cooperate with each other. Aided by an interim high in Soviet-American relations at the beginning of the Geneva INF negotiations on 30 November 1981 and during Brezhnev's visit to Bonn, the frequently delayed East-West German summit finally took place. However, the meeting between Honecker and Schmidt on 11–13 December in the Hubertusstock hunting lodge yielded few concrete results. Both politicians were deceiving themselves when they talked about significantly influencing US-Soviet negotiations.[14] Although both were striving toward a positive outcome, their actual ability to sway the two superpowers was negligible. What remains important is the mere fact that this meeting took place. Soon after, on 13 December, geopolitical tensions rose again with the imposition of martial law in Poland.

East-West German Politics and NATO's Double-Track Decision during the Transition from Chancellor Schmidt to Chancellor Kohl (1982–83)

In August 1982, Brezhnev advised Honecker to use "tougher language with Schmidt." A new East-West German summit would be ruled out unless East Germany demonstrated "a firm stance" against West Germany. Honecker recognized the fragility of the Bonn coalition government but made the mistake of assuming that the coalition would last until the next scheduled election in 1984. Everything possible would be done to sustain "the agreed path of influencing the FRG with the purpose of advancing peaceful coexistence, arms limitation, and disarmament, as well as the development of balanced and mutually beneficial bilateral relations." Nonetheless Honecker was willing to postpone his impending visit to Bonn by one year, to 1983.[15] Presumably he hoped to arrive with sufficient time left to prevent the anticipated arms deployment decision in the fall of 1983.

Just a few weeks later Honecker was told about the shaky position of the West German government. The Federal Minister of the Chancellery,

Hans-Juergen Wischnewski, informed him on 13 September of the discord in the Social-Liberal coalition and the likelihood of a change in leadership. According to Wischnewski, the chancellor was in need of "some short-term success. It would be helpful if the relations between the two German states were beneficial in this respect." For example, a concession from Honecker with regard to a reduction of the mandatory exchange rate—which the East German government currently demanded from non-Warsaw Pact citizens on entry into East Germany—would improve Schmidt's chances in his struggle to remain in office. Honecker remained intransigent on this point but was ready to compromise in other areas. Alarmed at the prospect that intermediate-range missiles would be stationed in West Germany, he threatened a deterioration in East-West German relations if the plans were to go through. Neither Schmidt's nor Honecker's expectations were realized.[16] On 1 October 1982, the German Parliament elected CDU Chairman Helmut Kohl as the new chancellor following a motion of no confidence. Parliamentary elections on 13 March 1983 confirmed a new Christian-Liberal coalition.

Kohl's concepts of foreign and East-West German policy hardly differed from those of his predecessor. In his mind, too, NATO was the "core of German *raison d'état*." Even more than Chancellor Schmidt, he demanded unswerving loyalty to NATO and the United States because he was "convinced of the fundamental and identical security interests shared by Germans and Americans across the Atlantic." At the beginning of September 1983 he described the imminent deployment of medium-range weapons as a "bitter" obligation to demonstrate Western unity. For Kohl the second element—the arms control policy—was subordinated to the first, maintaining Western unity. His coalition partner, Hans-Dietrich Genscher, Foreign Affairs Minister and leader of the Liberal Free Democratic Party (FDP), saw this differently: he and his party sympathized with both aspects of the Double-Track Decision.[17] With respect to East-West German relations, the difference between the consecutive chancellors was more a matter of rhetorical emphasis than practical policy. In his second government statement, delivered to the parliament on 4 May 1983, Kohl highlighted more clearly than his predecessor a normative distance to the regime in the GDR. He referred to "the Wall, barbed wire fencing, shooting orders, and harassment of people" as "an attack on humanity." Despite such verbal aggression against the regime, he pushed for the development of East-West German relations and demanded, as had Schmidt, a reduction in the mandatory exchange rate. Equally significant, Kohl upheld Schmidt's invitation to Honecker made at the Hubertusstock hunting lodge in December 1981.[18]

The East German leadership received numerous signals, before and after the governmental change in Bonn, indicating that the new West German government aimed for continuity in bilateral relations. It was nonetheless obvious that "the opportunities for nondeployment of new American medium-range missiles in [West Germany ... diminished] with the election victory of the CDU/CSU."[19] At the same time, the financial situation of East Germany continued to deteriorate rapidly. Besides a reduction in crude oil deliveries, it had to deal with a stoppage of Western credit after late 1981: without additional loans there was a real threat of insolvency. The East German negotiator Alexander Schalck-Golodkowski and the West German conservative CSU politician Franz Josef Strauss arranged for the two billion DM loan from West Germany mentioned previously. Negotiations began in mid-1982 and a final contract was agreed in May and June 1983. Consequently, East Germany's room for acting independently diminished, and the situation was aggravated when the new Communist Party General Secretary Yuri Andropov demanded renewed allegiance from his East German allies. Foreign Affairs Minister Oskar Fischer and Erich Honecker declared themselves in line with the Soviets and stressed their unique position to exert pressure on the West German government in alliance with the peace movement.[20]

Honecker's demonstrations of solidarity with the Soviet position were disingenuous, as Werner Krolikowski of the Politburo reported to Moscow in late March. During a tour of the Leipzig Spring Fair, the General Secretary visited the trade stall of the West German company Mannesmann and "had the audacity to adopt Kohl's demagogic slogan: 'Make peace with fewer weapons.'" Moreover, Honecker was accused of having failed to critically comment on the oncoming arms upgrade, while endorsing the continuation of East-West German cooperation; he even "announced his upcoming visit to West Germany," which he apparently wished to accomplish before the American deployment of medium-range weapons. Krolikowski concluded, "[Honecker] is not convincingly joining our ranks, and he is even less convincing in his attacks on the enemy."[21]

Honecker cancelled his visit to West Germany on 28 April 1983 after speaking with the Soviet Ambassador Pyotr Abrasimov the day before. He demonstrably fulfilled the expectations of the Soviet leadership, but sent Bonn this message: "A postponed visit is not a cancelled visit."[22] His subsequent trip to Moscow on 3–7 May 1983 yielded a public and expected display of alliance solidarity between the Soviet and East German leadership. Andropov stressed the importance of continuing the "struggle against militarization" in the West. However, he did not contradict Honecker when he declared that "a conflict between East and West Germany would not be conducive to a movement opposed to missiles."[23] Thus Honecker could continue to present East-West German relations as building bridges toward peace with Moscow's tacit agreement.

In April at the Karl Marx conference in East Berlin, Honecker had profiled East Germany as a state with thoroughly peaceful intentions: "Peace and again peace is the utmost guiding principle of our policy." All peace-seeking nations should "regardless of different political programs, ideological positions, and religious beliefs work jointly and in union across class barriers and other obstacles to safeguard nations from the catastrophic effects of nuclear war."[24] Later he referred in particular to East-West German cooperation as a "coalition of reason." This was not an attempt at an alternative security and social policy reaching across blocs of interest but a tactically motivated appeal for a union of all peace-seeking forces—with the very notable exception of the independent peace groups in East Germany.[25]

The slogan "coalition of reason" turned out to be particularly apt when public communication with Kohl increased in the fall of 1983. In his letter to the Federal Chancellor, dated 5 October and soon after published in the media, Honecker wrote that "all who wish to prevent humanity's downfall through nuclear catastrophe should join in a coalition of reason." Honecker concluded the letter, written "in the name of the German people," by raising his voice to join those in West Germany who shared with him a common concern for "international security" and called for a "Europe free of nuclear weapons."[26] In his response Kohl defended the NATO position, but he went on to "willingly" adopt Honecker's "chosen wording of a necessary coalition of reason" and continued with this message: "All my efforts and intents will serve to create a breakthrough to this reason in all areas."[27] Kohl was careful not to equate peace with stability and acknowledged that peace would be incomplete without basic freedoms and a guarantee for human rights. However, his response included an endorsement of the "shared responsibility" for peace on the part of the two German states.

The East German government directed its attention not only to the new West German government but also to Kohl's main opposition—the Social Democrats. Formal party relationships were established from November 1982 onward and multiple contacts were cultivated on various levels.[28] In addition, the government built up relations with the Green Party, which had been elected into the West German Parliament in March 1983. Honecker invited a well-known leader of the Green Party, Petra Kelly, along with several other prominent party members to East Berlin in May 1983. He intended to explore common interests and to discuss how these could be exploited to influence policies in West Germany. The visit of Kelly and her companions on 31 October 1983 soon showed that both sides shared only one interest: the rejection of the Western arms upgrade. Other issues raised proved controversial, and Honecker faced fierce criticism by the Green Party for his handling of the East German independent peace groups.[29]

The Green Party delegation avoided manipulation by Honecker and, in an unexpected reversal, had quite a disrupting effect: first of all, it staged provocative performances in East Germany, and second, it openly supported East German peace groups to which they later maintained close personal ties. Immediately after the meeting with Honecker, the delegation met with protagonists of such groups in the home of Rev. Rainer Eppelmann. The meeting with Honecker, widely reported in the East German media, triggered a "downright euphoric optimism" among the East German peace movement to which the regime reacted with numerous arrests.[30] After this, the East German government put a stop to all possible public displays by Green Party members in their country. As contacts and relationships between sections of the Green Party and members of the East German peace movement advanced, the latter became familiar with the Western protest movement. A selective takeover of its culture of protest ensued: East German activists employed provocative and symbolic action and selected additional themes for their protests. Kelly and her associates, such as Gert Bastian, were thus able to pass along to their East German friends their decidedly critical perspectives of the political system in West Germany and its established representatives. This explains the apparent reservations held by large sections of the East German civil rights movement toward the West German political system in 1989–90 when it became clear that the unification of Germany was a possibility.

These connections—to both West German and international peace movements—secured for East German protesters a certain measure of protection from state repression: an open letter to Honecker signed by representatives of peace organizations from around the world in January 1984 led to the release of Baerbel Bohley and Ulrike Poppe, who had been in custody since 12 December 1983.[31] Although the Ministry of State Security (Stasi) employed secret informants in the West German peace movement as well as in the Green Party in order to gain a measure of influence on the political positions taken with respect to East-West German relations, it needs to be recognized that these relations had a momentum of their own. East-West German communication thus assumed a heightened social dimension.

The West German Parliament's Arms Upgrade Resolution and Its Impact on East-West German Relations

In the fall of 1983 it became increasingly clear that the West German parliament would pass a vote in favor of missile deployment. The Politburo of the CPSU had already decided that in such a case operational-tactical missiles were to be transferred to GDR and CSSR territory and cruise missiles placed in the European part of the Soviet Union.[32] However, the Soviet leadership was at a loss about what strategy to pursue politically. Vadim Zagladin, deputy head of the International Liaison Department of the Central Committee of the Communist Party, put the question to Herbert Haeber, head of the East German Socialist Unity Party's division for the West, on 5 October 1983 in Moscow: "What can we do if the Geneva negotiation ends with no results and the deployment of missiles begins? Should we carry on as before, and if not, what should we change?" Zagladin reflected on this question and concluded, "We do not yet have any real idea about what should be done politically."[33] Honecker could assume that Moscow had no political concepts for the future.

Shortly thereafter Haeber made a trip to West Germany. Discussions with numerous government and opposition leaders confirmed what East Berlin had suspected for a long time: the Social Democratic Party would reject the deployment of missiles by a majority vote at its convention in November, whereas the representatives of governmental parties expected the deployment later that month. Honecker also learned the following from Haeber's report: "In all discussions one notices the term 'damage limitation' being used as a central theme." While representatives of the governmental parties did not fear that East-West German relations might be affected, leading members of the SPD were convinced that relations were deteriorating and accused the Kohl government of illusionism.[34]

This information was probably central to Honecker's response to the West German Parliament's arms upgrade resolution of 22 November 1983. He believed he could develop his own strategy with impunity. The first signs of his intentions are visible at the end of October. At the time the primary state newspaper *Neues Deutschland* (New Germany) reprinted a letter written by an East German Protestant Church parish. It asked Honecker in particular for unilateral disarmament. The publication of this letter probably demonstrated a willingness on the part of the government to grant a greater role to citizens who showed interest in international peace. In an interview Honecker granted to the West German *Stern* magazine on 3 November he said that he was prepared for the introduction of new missiles on East German territory as a countermeasure to NATO's deployment, but personally was not "thrilled" about it. Apart from that, he was working toward further cooperation in East-West German relations.[35]

At the meeting of the Socialist Unity Party Central Committee on 25 November 1983, Honecker announced the counterdeployment of operational-tactical missiles in East Germany. Then he added, "Of course, these neces-

Figure 4.2. A poster protesting against the NATO Double-Track Decision in front of a house destroyed during World War II on Fehrbelliner Str.—Schönhauser Allee in East Berlin, 9 June 1985 (ullstein bild—CARO / Page Pijorr)

sary and indispensible measures to prevent a strategic military superiority of the US are not producing cheering and jubilation throughout the land." In contrast to Soviet leaders, he affirmed his set intention for a continuation of international disarmament negotiations and, as for East-West German relations, he was anxious to "control the damage as much as possible."[36] It was no coincidence that Honecker took up the term "damage control," which was broadly used by West German government officials; it was meant as a message to Bonn that they need not fear a deterioration of East-West German relations.

On 18 November 1983, state secretaries in the Federal Chancellery in Bonn came to the conclusion that, in the short term, the arms upgrade would result in a cooling off of East-West German relations, but not become a crisis. The Permanent Representative in East Berlin, Hans Otto Bräutigam, expected only "polemical attacks" and possibly a "reduction in the German-German travel volume." But even that did not happen. Bräutigam reported the following on 25 November: "Honecker's commitment to continued cooperation appears to be serious and shows considerable personal engagement. Given the opaque leadership situation in Moscow, it is striking how far the SED General Secretary is prepared to go out on a limb. He seems to be using his entire political clout to secure continuity of dialogue and cooperation in his own party and vis-à-vis Moscow."[37]

Honecker did not yield to the ensuing Soviet pressure. Dependency on the West German rival was increasing, and he simply could not afford to antagonize Bonn. The chancellor in turn applauded Honecker's statements to the Central Committee, confirmed his own commitment to East-West German dialogue and concluded, "The two states in Germany find themselves, with respect to each other, in a unique association of responsibility toward Europe at large and the German people in particular." Honecker took up the term "association of responsibility" in his subsequent phone conversation with Kohl and emphasized that "realism and reason" should "truly gain the upper hand" in East-West relations despite criticism of Western deployment of nuclear weapons.[38]

East-West German relations took an unexpected upward turn due to the two billion DM loan pledges to East Germany in 1983 and 1984. As of 27 December 1983, young people no longer needed to undertake the mandatory currency exchange when visiting East Germany, and the East-West German border saw antipersonnel devices being dismantled.[39] In 1984 some 48,400 people were allowed to leave East Germany. Honecker personally ordered such permissions to be granted partly as a preemptive move to prevent GDR citizens from occupying embassies.[40] At the same time, this contained an element of deepening détente.

Honecker was anxious to provide East Germany with a profile as a "peace-loving state" and therefore called in a discussion group of SED and SPD experts to deliberate on the possibility of establishing a chemical weapons-free zone.[41] Politically this could work only as long as Moscow followed a confrontational course toward the West. When Gorbachev took office in 1985, Honecker's policies were again in line with Moscow, but East Germany's special role was now lost.

Conclusion

The two German states were able to avoid a deterioration of East-West German relations despite an international political shift toward a hostile global atmosphere and even though room for political maneuvering was considerably restricted. Unlike West Germany, East Germany was a dictatorship that could afford to ignore internal resistance. The regime tried to penetrate the pluralistic structures of West Germany with the aim of preventing missile deployment. The relations between the West German peace movement and the Green Party, however, gathered their own momentum, which led to the strengthening of the independent peace groups in East Germany. This proved to be extremely inconvenient to the East German leadership at the time.

By and large West Germany came out the winner in this dispute. Despite internal opposition, it was able to maintain close ties with the United States without compromising policies on East-West German relations. The East German government, however, could not escape a conflict of interest between Moscow and Bonn as it faced the Double-Track Decision and its consequences. The general mood in East German society, as well as its economic dependency on West Germany, created sufficient incentive for East Germany to engage in a limited conflict with Moscow—a risk that appeared viable as the Soviet government showed weakness and a lack of perspective. Against this background it strove toward closer relations with West Germany although its existential dependency on the Soviet Union remained unchanged.

Hermann Wentker is the director of the Berlin branch of the Institute of Contemporary History Munich-Berlin (IfZ) and professor of modern and contemporary history at the University of Potsdam. His research concentrates on the history of international relations in the nineteenth and twentieth centuries as well as the history of the German Democratic Republic. Selected publications include: *Zerstörung der Großmacht Rußland? Die britischen Kriegsziele im Krimkrieg* (1993), *Justiz in der SBZ/DDR 1945–1953: Transformation und Rolle ihrer zentralen Institutionen* (2001), *Außenpolitik in engen Grenzen: Die DDR im internationalen System 1949–1989* (2007), *Zweiter Kalter Krieg und Friedensbewegung: Der NATO-Doppelbeschluss in deutsch-deutscher und internationaler Perspektive* (coedited with Philipp Gassert and Tim Geiger, 2011); *Die Geschichte der SED: Eine Bestandsaufnahme* (coedited with Jens Gieseke, 2012).

Notes

1. See Tim Geiger's essay in this volume.
2. Helga Haftendorn, *Sicherheit und Entspannung: Zur Außenpolitik der Bundesrepublik Deutschland 1955–1982* (Baden-Baden, 1983), 733–35.
3. Verbal comments made by Günter Gaus about a letter from Schmidt to Honecker, 2 August 1976, in Heinrich Potthoff, *Bonn und Ost-Berlin 1969–1982: Dialog auf höchster Ebene und vertrauliche Kanäle, Darstellung und Dokumente* (Bonn, 1997), 356.
4. Quotation from a conversation between Schmidt and Mittag on 17 April 1980, published in Potthoff, *Bonn und Ost-Berlin 1969–1982*, 507; Hartmut Soell, *Helmut Schmidt: 1969 bis heute, Macht und Verantwortung* (Munich, 2008), 503.
5. Hermann Wentker, *Außenpolitik in engen Grenzen: Die DDR im internationalen System 1949–1989* (Munich, 2007), 398–410, 421–28, 477–86, 500–6.
6. Hermann Wentker, "Zwischen Unterstützung und Ablehnung der sowjetischen Linie," in *Zweiter Kalter Krieg und Friedensbewegung: Der NATO-Doppelbeschluss in deutsch-deutscher und internationaler Perspektive*, ed. Philipp Gassert, Tim Geiger, and Hermann Wentker (Munich, 2011), 138–40.
7. Information delivered by the head of the SED Western Division Herbert Häber about his stay in the Federal Republic on 2–3 August 1980 published in Detlef Nakath and Gerd-Ruediger Stephan, eds., *Die Häber-Protokolle: Schlaglichter der SED-Westpolitik 1973–1985* (Berlin, 1999), 224–25.
8. Conversation between Schmidt and Honecker on 8 May 1980, published in Potthoff, *Bonn und Ost-Berlin 1969–1982*, 516.
9. Wentker, "Zwischen Unterstützung und Ablehnung," 140–42.
10. Honecker demanded recognition of the GDR citizenship, dissolution of the Central Registration Office in Salzgitter, a change of status of the permanent representations into proper embassies, and an agreement on border demarcations along the Elbe river, in the mid-valley line: excerpts from Honecker's speech published in Bundesministerium für Innerdeutsche Beziehungen, ed., *Innerdeutsche Beziehungen: Die Entwicklung der Beziehungen zwischen der Bundesrepublik Deutschland und der Deutschen Demokratischen Republik 1980–1986, Eine Dokumentation* (Bonn, 1986), 77.
11. Notes taken by Werner Krolikowski on 13 November and in December 1980, published in Peter Przybylski, *Tatort Politbüro: Die Akte Honecker* (Berlin, 1990),

340–44, 345–48; notes recorded from memory on the meeting between Breschnew and Honecker on 3 August 1981, published in Hans Hermann Hertle and Konrad Jarausch, eds., *Risse im Bruderbund: Die Gespräche Honecker-Breschnew 1974 bis 1982* (Berlin, 2006), 202.

12. Oliver Bange, "Keeping Détente Alive: East-West German Relations under Helmut Schmidt and Erich Honecker," in *The Crisis of Détente in Europe: From Helsinki to Gorbachev, 1975–1985*, ed. Leopoldo Nuti (London, 2009), 235.
13. Conversation between Egon Bahr, Hermann Axen, and Erich Honecker, 4 September 1981, in Potthoff, *Bonn und Ost-Berlin 1969–1982*, 585–612, see especially 590. Comments on a conversation between Willy Brandt and Leonid I. Breschnew, 30 June 1981, interview with Brandt by the journal *Der Spiegel*, 6 July 1981, in Willy Brandt, Berliner Ausgabe, Vol. 9, *Die Entspannung unzerstörbar machen: Internationale Beziehungen und deutsche Frage 1974–1982*, bearbeitet von Frank Fischer (Bonn, 2003), 319–26, 327–43, see especially 323, 333.
14. Exclusive personal conversation between Schmidt and Honecker, 11 December 1981, published in Potthoff, *Bonn und Ost-Berlin*, 652–671, see especially 660, 661.
15. Notes about the meeting between Honecker and Breshnew, 11 August 1982, published in Hertle and Jarausch, *Risse im Bruderbund*, 249, 254, 255.
16. Notes on a conversation between Honecker and Wischnewski, 13 September 1982, published in Detlef Nakath and Gerd-Rüdiger Stephan, eds., *Von Hubertusstock nach Bonn: Eine dokumentierte Geschichte der deutsch-deutschen Beziehungen auf höchster Ebene 1980–1987* (Berlin, 1995), 82–90, see especially 84, 85.
17. Andreas Rödder, "Bündnissolidarität und Rüstungskontrollpolitik: Die Regierung Kohl-Genscher, der NATO-Doppelbeschluss und die Innenseite der Außenpolitik," in Gassert, Geiger, and Wentker, *Zweiter Kalter Krieg*, 123–36, for quotation see 127–28.
18. Karl-Rudolf Korte, *Deutschlandpolitik in Helmut Kohls Kanzlerschaft: Regierungsstil und Entscheidungen 1982–1989* (Stuttgart, 1998), 107–114, for quotation see 111.
19. Speech delivered by Hermann Axen at a conference of the secretaries responsible for ideological and international issues of the Central Committee of the fraternal parties of socialist countries, 14–15 March 1983, in Stiftung Archiv der Parteien und Massenorganisationen im Bundesarchiv (henceforth SAPMO), DY 30 IV 2/2.035/24, 31–71, see 42.
20. Michael Ploetz and Hans-Peter Müller, *Ferngelenkte Friedensbewegung? DDR und UdSSR im Kampf gegen den NATO-Doppelbeschluss* (Münster, 2004), 161, 165–66.
21. Note written by Werner Krolikowski, 30 March 1980 in Przybylski, *Tatort Politbüro*, 352–55.
22. Hans Otto Bräutigam, *Ständige Vertretung: Meine Jahre in Ost-Berlin* (Hamburg, 2009), 309.
23. Minutes of the offical talks between the party and state delegation of the GDR and the USSR, 3 May 1983 in SAPMO, DY 30/11359 (no pagination); Michael Ploetz, *Wie die Sowjetunion den Kalten Krieg verlor: Von der Nachrüstung zum Mauerfall* (Berlin, 2000), 275.
24. Speech by Honecker, in *Neues Deutschland*, 12 April 1983, 4.
25. Very apt: Benno-Eide Siebs, *Die Außenpolitik der DDR 1976–1989: Strategien und Grenzen* (Paderborn, 1999), 241–42.

26. This document quoted according to *Innerdeutsche Beziehungen*, 154–55.
27. Kohl's words directed at Honecker, 24 October 1983, in *Innerdeutsche Beziehungen*, 158–60.
28. Frank Fischer, *"Im deutschen Interesse": Die Ostpolitik der SPD von 1969 bis 1989* (Husum, 2001), 178–215.
29. Talks of the Green Party Delegation and Honecker, 31 October 1983, published in Heinrich Potthoff, *Die "Koalition der Vernunft": Deutschlandpolitik in den 80er Jahren* (Munich, 1995), 201–23. On the ambitions of the Green Party, and in particular Petra Kelly, with respect to the GDR, see Saskia Richter, *Die Aktivistin: Das Leben der Petra Kelly* (Munich, 2010), 164–73.
30. According to Lukas Beckmann on 7 November 1983 published in Josef Boyer and Helge Heidemeyer, eds., *Die Grünen im Bundestag: Sitzungsprotokolle und Anlagen 1983–1987* (Düsseldorf, 2008), 319.
31. Ulrike Poppe, "'Die Unterstützung, die wir brauchten': Petra Kelly und die Oppositionellen in der DDR," in *Petra Kelly: Eine Erinnerung*, ed. Heinrich-Böll-Stiftung (Berlin, 2007), 70–73.
32. Julij A. Kwizinskij, *Vor dem Sturm: Erinnerungen eines Diplomaten* (Berlin, 1993), 322.
33. Information about a meeting between Haeber with Zagladin, 4–5 October 1983 in Nakath and Stephan, *Die Häber-Protokolle*, 366–69, for quotation see 367.
34. Information about a sojourn in the Federal Republic of Germany by Haeber, 9–16 October, 1983, published in Nakath and Stephan, *Die Häber-Protokolle*, 369–85, for quotation see 371.
35. Wentker, "Zwischen Unterstützung und Ablehnung," 148–50.
36. Honecker's speech from a discussion published in *Neues Deutschland*, 26–27 September 1983, 3.
37. Quoted according to Korte, *Deutschlandpolitik*, 188, 190.
38. Wentker, "Zwischen Unterstützung und Ablehnung," 151.
39. See the documents published in *Innerdeutsche Beziehungen*, 154–56.
40. See Anja Hanisch, *Die DDR im KSZE-Prozess 1972–1975: Zwischen Ostabhängigkeit, Westabgrenzung und Ausreisebewegung* (Munich, 2012), 350–52.
41. Wentker, "Zwischen Unterstützung und Ablehnung," 152–53.

Select Bibliography

Valuable information is provided by the documentations by Potthoff (1997 and 1995). Potthoff publishes documents from West German and East German sources. Nakath's and Stephan's documentations (1995 and 1999) are solely based on documents from the SED archive.

Particularly informative are books by Potthoff (1999) and, for the era of Chancellor Kohl, by Korte. A monography of Helmut Schmidt's policy of Germany is lacking. The second volume of his biography by Soell contains some helpful notes. Wentker gives an important discussion about the attitude of the East German leadership.

Korte, Karl-Rudolf. *Deutschlandpolitik in Helmut Kohls Kanzlerschaft: Regierungsstil und Entscheidungen 1982–1989*. Stuttgart, 1998.

Nakath, Detlef, and Gerd-Rüdiger Stephan. *Von Hubertusstock nach Bonn: Eine dokumentierte Geschichte der deutsch-deutschen Beziehungen auf höchster Ebene 1980–1987.* Berlin, 1995.

———. *Die Häber-Protokolle: Schlaglichter der SED-Westpolitik 1973–1985.* Berlin, 1999.

Potthoff, Heinrich. *"Die Koalition der Vernunft": Deutschlandpolitik in den 80er Jahren.* Munich, 1995.

———. *Bonn und Ost-Berlin 1969–1982: Dialog auf höchster Ebene und vertrauliche Kanäle, Darstellung und Dokumente.* Bonn, 1997.

———. *Im Schatten der Mauer: Deutschlandpolitik 1961 bis 1990.* Berlin, 1999.

Soell, Hartmut. *Helmut Schmidt: 1969 bis heute, Macht und Verantwortung.* Munich, 2008.

Wentker, Hermann. "Zwischen Unterstützung und Ablehnung der sowjetischen Linie: Die DDR, der Doppelbeschluss und die Nachrüstung." In *Zweiter Kalter Krieg und Friedensbewegung: Der NATO-Doppelbeschluss in deutsch-deutscher und internationaler Perspektive*, ed. Philipp Gassert, Tim Geiger, and Hermann Wentker, 137–54. Munich, 2011.

Chapter 5

Political Parties

Jan Hansen

The controversy surrounding the NATO Double-Track Decision not only opened the way for the peace movement to challenge longstanding principles of traditional security policy but also led to the bitter polarization of the West German party system. A grossly simplified picture of the debate would place the Christian Democratic Union (CDU), the Christian Social Union of Bavaria (CSU), and the Free Democratic Party (FDP) in one camp advocating the arms upgrade versus the Green Party in another, with the Social Democratic Party (SPD) somewhere in the middle. However, the real situation was far more complex. Indeed all parties were more or less divided on this issue. Even members of the CDU, CSU, and FDP, who were the staunchest supporters of the transatlantic American alliance, harbored a certain degree of doubt about the reasoning behind the arms upgrade and nuclear deterrence. The SPD party in particular was torn by deep conflict. Chancellor Helmut Schmidt, who had instigated discussions and was a driving force for the Double-Track Decision, faced growing opposition within his party and found it increasingly difficult to depend on a political majority for his own security policy. In contrast, the increasing popularity of the Green Party, which attracted tremendous support from the arms-upgrade protesters, highlighted the difficulties that established parties had in responding to new societal demands.[1]

Signs and Omens

Political parties gave mixed responses in the internal alliance discussions when it became clear that, following the philosophy of the Harmel Report of 1967, NATO would make an offer in its negotiations with the Soviet Union contingent on the threat of an arms upgrade.[2] The conservative Christian CDU/CSU parties and the liberal FDP hardly discussed the issue. Even the nascent green movement was more focused on environmental themes. "Peace" would gradually establish itself only as a second policy pillar. The

Social Democratic Party, in contrast, swiftly stood up and took a controversial position: Egon Bahr's emotional rejection of the neutron bomb in 1977, when he was federal executive director of the SPD, can be read as a symptom of a new sensibility on matters of security.[3] In an early 1979 article published by the influential chairman of the SPD's parliamentary group, Herbert Wehner, in *Die Neue Gesellschaft* (The new society), he vehemently rejects the option of an arms upgrade. Early critical statements from the working groups of the Social Democratic Women and the Young Socialists also mirror a widespread unease with the possible deployment of new nuclear weapons.[4]

The logic of the party conference resolution reflects this skepticism about a possible deployment of arms, even though the SPD seemed to agree with the decision of the allied parties. Closer observation reveals significant differences: whereas the communiqué of the NATO Council of 12 December 1979 speaks of a binding "commitment to deployment"[5] in the event that negotiations with the Soviets failed, the delegates of the SPD party congress in Berlin worded their statement to the effect that there should be no "automatic" deployment.[6] NATO's communiqué mentions "parallel and complementary approaches." In contrast, the SPD decided that proposals about arms control should receive higher priority than those for an arms upgrade. Furthermore the party concluded that in the course of negotiations there should always be the option that delegates could "revise prior decisions when deemed necessary." This was a resolution that left the backdoor open if the SPD considered negotiations were not being conducted with sufficient zeal. This condition pacified internal party conflict yet left the party at odds with official NATO decisions.

"Negotiate and, if need be, arm yourself"

The Social Democrats' decision in Berlin was reached under the leadership of Helmut Schmidt. In a speech in London in 1977, the chancellor had already pointed out the disparities within the so-called gray-zone weapons and suggested that these be addressed in political negotiations.[7] On the basis of a security triad of deterrence, arms control, and power balance, he argued steadfastly for the principle of reaching decisions within the alliance and defended this with the aphorism "negotiate and, if need be, arm yourself."[8] Criticism evolved when international relations suffered a crisis: the prospect of a successful negotiation deteriorated, and then arms deployment became more likely. The situation left large parts of the Social Democratic Party membership more or less in discord with the alliance decision, whereas the vast majority of the conservative Christian CDU/CSU parties and the liberal FDP supported the resolution without reservation, as the double-edged approach corresponded exactly to their policies.

Liberal Party member and Foreign Affairs Minister Hans-Dietrich Genscher supported both aspects of the NATO decision as did Chancellor Schmidt. The emphasis on arms control was particularly important to the Liberal Party's position. Genscher's views did not differ so much in this respect from those of Schmidt, but from the perspective of Helmut Kohl and Franz Josef Strauss they did. The Liberal program for the parliamentary election in 1980 promised to do everything to "enter into serious negotiations and to make the offer to the Warsaw Pact acceptable." The aim would be to "completely renounce the production and deployment of medium-range nuclear weapons on both sides."[9] This marked emphasis on arms control should be understood as a response to criticism from within the ranks of the party. A minority of the Liberals objected to the arms upgrade resolution. In particular William Borm, who was later exposed as an informant for the Ministry for State Security of the German Democratic Republic, called for cooperation with the peace movement, the Green Party, and like-minded Social Democrat followers.[10] His position, however, never gained ground among the majority of the FDP membership as it did in the SPD.

The position of the conservative Christian Democratic Union also came close to that of NATO, but from the opposite end of the political spectrum. Its experts on security matters initially hesitated to back the decision, since major protagonists regarded a direct arms upgrade as more promising than one linked to a negotiated settlement.[11] At its Hamburg convention in 1981 the CDU abided by the thinking of its general secretary, Heiner Geissler, who described the Double-Track Decision as a "roadmap to disarmament";[12] the party passed a resolution that "subscribes to a consistent and timely implementation of both parts of this decision."[13] This firm support by the CDU for the Double-Track Decision needs to be seen in conjunction with the tremendous importance that the party attributed to the Atlantic orientation and with its absolute loyalty to the NATO alliance. Helmut Kohl in particular regarded this orientation as "*the* central declaration of German foreign policy: that we are part of the West, sharing the values of the Western community in the NATO alliance, and, of course, the members of the Alliance of the European Community."[14] In spite of this profound commitment to the NATO Double-Track Decision, the party repeatedly showed a bias more toward accentuating the threat of an arms upgrade than toward compromising in negotiations. Many Christian Democrats saw "no way past the necessary upgrade of the West with modern medium-range weapons."[15] Such reasoning was chiefly determined by a perception of the Soviet Union as an aggressive military power, a view more commonly found in the Christian Union than in other parties. According to Helmut Kohl, peace was "profoundly threatened because the Soviet Union had shifted the power balance between East and West in its favor through accelerated arms production and global aggression."[16]

It would be wrong to assume that security policymakers were completely critical of the peace movement. Even the CDU had members who expressed a certain understanding for the concerns that motivated peace protests.[17] As a representative of the Junge Union (Young Conservatives), Christian Wulff demanded that his party "take into account that many people in this country, both young and old, are experiencing anxiety." And Matthias Wissmann, national chairman of the Junge Union, was concerned that the CDU would be seen exclusively as the "party that does not adequately discuss the disarmament topic." Wulff and Wissmann, who did not fully approve of, but expressed a certain interest in, the demands of the peace movement, remained in the minority. The vast majority displayed an attitude of incomprehension and rejection toward the protesters. Heiner Geissler's polemical statement—the pacifism of the peace movement differed "very little" from the "pacifism of the 1930s," which in turn "made Auschwitz possible"—was remarkable in this respect.[18] Even though party leaders tried hard to deny the peace movement's concerns by accusing it of gullibly believing communist

Figure 5.1. CDU peace conference in the Konrad Adenauer House held under the slogan "Peace with Fewer Weapons" on 3 February 1983 in Bonn (BArch B 145 Bild-F065003-0012 / Engelbert Reineke)

propaganda,[19] all principal parties—the CDU, FDP, and SPD—could not ignore the political views of the peace movement. As a countermove they expounded on the NATO Double-Track Decision and its supposed logic. At the height of the dispute, the federal government published a number of informational brochures to explain its safety policies to the general public.[20] The peace movement forced the established parties to justify their positions and to legitimize the production and deployment of nuclear weapons. Thus, the effect of the extra-parliamentary protests on all parties should not be overlooked. Even the Christian Democrats were not devoid of doubt on the logic of nuclear deterrence, as can be seen by the party's 1981 Berlin Declaration when considering it within the context of mounting social pressure: the declaration states that nuclear deterrence could be dismantled "step by step."[21]

"Come to terms, not to arms"

Criticism of the postulate that nuclear deterrence was indispensable was voiced, at the very latest, on the anniversary of the NATO decision in December 1980. Even though preliminary arms control negotiations had begun two months earlier, Karsten D. Voigt, SPD Member of Parliament, stated on the record that in his view "the objectives pertaining to the arms upgrade of the Berlin Convention are not being fulfilled … and it is necessary … to begin a new discussion about the arms upgrade decision."[22]

Apart from Voigt, it was principally SPD Chairman Willy Brandt and his political ally Egon Bahr who posed the question of whether any new results on arms control were at all likely considering the rapid deterioration of East-West relations.[23] Large numbers of Social Democrats followed this reasoning and expressed increasing criticism of the possible deployment. Formally Voigt supported his position by pointing to an obvious shift in US foreign policy priorities. The Berlin convention of the SPD had indeed made its approval of the NATO decision contingent on the ratification of SALT II (Strategic Arms Limitation Talks) by the US Senate, and President Jimmy Carter flatly refused to ratify this agreement after the Soviet Union invaded Afghanistan. At this point many Social Democrats no longer felt bound by their approval to the arms upgrade. Ronald Reagan, Carter's successor in the White House, also exhibited some reservation toward arms control. This led to growing skepticism about the option of an arms upgrade. It may therefore be said that the majority of the SPD members supported the negotiation aspect of NATO's decision, but had strong reservations about the deployment of Euromissiles.

In terms of content, the Social Democrat's criticism of the arms upgrade was rooted in a grave concern about the future of the détente policies. Support of détente formed the core of the Social Democratic identity and therefore any related policies had great significance for the party. There was a very real fear of an imminent escalation of the nuclear arms race should negotiations fail. Brandt considered the current crisis in East-West relations as having the potential to develop into "the most serious threat to global peace since the end of World War II." All further "escalation of the arms race ... infringes on our security."[24] In his opinion all effort should thus be invested in stopping the arms race. This stronger emphasis on the policy of détente was a nuanced but important distinction between Brandt and Schmidt.

In addition to his keen interest in the arms race, Brandt's political thinking addressed the role of the North-South division. In his 1985 book *Der organisierte Wahnsinn* (Arms and hunger) he proposed a global rethinking of disarmament as a precondition for developmental aid.[25] The combining of disarmament with demands for increased economic support of and cooperation with developing countries, or alternatively for increased spending on social issues, characterized discussions in the Social Democratic sphere.

Given his critical position toward the arms upgrade, Brandt tried to integrate the so-called *Neuen Soziale Bewegungen* (New social movements) into his party. As chairman he sought to win back the support of the peace movement activists for the Social Democratic Party by positioning it as a "party of integration";[26] in this way he differed from Chancellor Schmidt, who rejected the security policies of the protesters and insisted on strict demarcation. It was precisely the relationship between the SPD and the peace movement in general, and the participation of SPD members in the peace movement's protests in particular, that caused deep divisions between Brandt and Schmidt and within the entire membership of the party.

Disarmament

The Green Party and segments of the SPD rejected the arms upgrade regardless of the results of negotiation. The former tank division/battalion commander and later Green Party politician, Gert Bastian, voiced his criticism of the Double-Track Decision in an article printed in the Social Democrat Party bulletin *Vorwärts* (Forward) titled "Before the (arms) Race Gets Out of Control." He argued against the NATO decision "because of the threat of an unavoidable disastrous escalation of the nuclear arms race."[27] Among the opponents to the arms upgrade this criticism of armament dynamics became the argumentative topos employed against the government. This argument also found fertile ground in the SPD. The Baden-Wuerttemberg SPD leader Erhard Eppler argued that apart from US weaponry, the strategic and tactical missiles of Britain and France provided adequate protection, and an arms upgrade was therefore unnecessary.[28] The frequently heard argument of the need for a balance of power was countered by the mayor of Saarbruecken, Oskar Lafontaine, who claimed that NATO did not suffer a medium-range missile disadvantage compared to the Soviet Union.[29]

Unlike the majority of Social Democrats, the Green Party feared that the escalation of the arms race would spin out of control and called for immediate, unilateral, and unconditional disarmament. NATO's action was supposed to exert moral pressure on the Soviet Union and force it to disarm likewise.[30] At the same time, the Green Party was far more critical than Eppler or Lafontaine of Soviet arms production in general, and it included the SS-20s in its demands for disarmament. Its *Friedensmanifest* (Peace manifesto) from 1981 states that the party was "far from regarding the Soviet Union as a haven of peace … [Its] structure and scope is that of a military power capable of conquering."[31] As the Green Party rejected categorically "all new nuclear weapons in Europe," their demand for disarmament was addressed to the Soviet Union as well as to the United States.

Opponents of the arms upgrade were unanimous in their unwavering rejection of nuclear weapons. Eppler viewed the mere existence of such weapons as the chief problem in contemporary security policy and opposed them on moral grounds.[32] Green Party delegates similarly appealed for "a global ban on the storage and production of nuclear, chemical, and biological weapons"[33] at their national convention in Saarbruecken in 1980. The party's peace manifesto also aimed for the denuclearization of the East-West conflict. It was hoped that "the first unilateral disarmament measures" would prepare the way "to our final objective: the peaceful coexistence of all humankind."[34]

The call to veto nuclear weapons was the inevitable consequence of disagreement over the principles supporting the East-West balance of power and theories of deterrence. The outright dismissal of established security doctrines led inexorably to a reexamination of their underlying assumptions. Lafontaine, for example, proposed that the Federal Republic should "withdraw from NATO military organizations."[35] The same plea to leave NATO was put forward by the Green Party, albeit much more forcefully. Rudolf Bahro, a well-known Green politician, justified a demand for both East and West German neutrality, stating that Germans did not wish to be "US-dominated and controlled and protected to death."[36] As the Green Party primarily attributed the nuclear arms race to ideological competition between the superpowers, it postulated surmounting the fundamental logic of bilateral confrontation.

The rejection of traditional concepts of defense led to intensive discussions among the West German parties about alternatives. With their federal program of 1980, the Green Party defined a nonmilitary strategy of "social defense" as an alternative.[37] This presumed that a potential aggressor would be deterred by the organized resistance of peaceful citizens and by general civil disobedience within its own borders. "Social defense" does not pursue a traditional defense of national borders but instead seeks to protect civic structures against outside aggression. This alternative defense strategy was immediately rejected by the other parties and probably marks most clearly the difference between the established political parties and the green movement.

Consequences

Between 1981 and 1982 the protests against the intended deployment of Euromissiles by the Alliance intensified in proportion to the deterioration rate of the Geneva negotiations on the Soviet medium-range missiles. The talks were initially postponed, and when they did finally begin the negotiators made no headway. The proceedings were closely observed in the Federal Republic of Germany and triggered a twofold response: they served to foster either cohesion or dissent within West Germany's parties, and they essentially polarized the political landscape between supporters and opponents of NATO. Put simply, parties could be classified on the basis of whether the arms conflict had a stabilizing or destabilizing effect on them.

Most obviously the debate helped to consolidate the Green Party, which drew an enormous number of supporters from the peace movement. Initially premised on environmental concerns during the late 1970s, the Green Party began addressing the arms race and the topic of peace, thereby achieving a breakthrough that enabled it to win sufficient votes to enter the Bundestag (Parliament) in 1983. This success of what might be called the antiparty party, that is, the antiestablishment party,[38] can be explained not only by the widespread discontent among a segment of society frequently referred to as "alternative" with regard to the established parties, but also by shifting socio-cultural factors. As a fourth faction in Parliament, the Greens distinguished themselves by introducing new topics and themes, in addition to staging unconventional and sometimes sensational performances during the proceedings of the Bonn parliament.[39]

Although the Christian Democratic parties, in contrast to the Green Party, clearly stated that they were in favor of the arms upgrade, the dispute had a consolidating effect on them as well. The parties' security policy was closely tied to the US position and was based on anticommunist principles. This made them, if negotiations failed, the strongest advocates for the arms upgrade even before taking up governmental responsibilities on 1 October 1982. The conservatives achieved impressive results, garnering just under 49 percent of the votes in the general election of 1983. In this sense the controversy surrounding the Double-Track Decision had an integrating and mobilizing effect on the conservative sphere. The CDU's efforts to distance itself from the peace movement contributed to its success and were in line with the political opinion of its supporters.

The Liberal Party managed a superb political balancing act. The dispute within the coalition government about the arms upgrade had demoralized the FDP's alliance with the SPD. But it was a conflict over the federal budget that allowed the Liberal Party to break with the government, and it entered immediately into a new coalition with the CDU/CSU. At the same time the leadership of the party could quell critical voices among its own ranks by emphasizing the importance of arms control.[40] Some of the more socially progressive members quit the Liberal Party in the wake of Günter Verheugen, who resigned his membership in 1982, and crossed the floor to the SPD. However the controversy about the Euromissile deployment never took on the explosive dimensions in the Liberal Party that it had among the

Figure 5.2. SPD election poster for the parliamentary elections in 1983 (BArch Plak 104-PM0357-013)

Social Democrats. This was demonstrated at the Karlsruhe convention in November 1983 when a clear majority confirmed the resolution put forward by Foreign Affairs Minister Genscher and a considerable but not decisive 24 percent of the delegates rejected missile deployment.[41]

While the FDP cleverly avoided internal party dissent, the Social Democrats were bitterly divided on the issue of deployment. At the national convention in Munich in April 1982 Helmut Schmidt for the last time managed to persuade SPD delegates to follow his policies.[42] Yet a party's decision, reached in the autumn of 1982, reflected a change in its own stance on missile deployment in light of the disappointing results from US-Soviet negotiations. It also mirrored the continuously growing opposition within the party to the deployment of missiles.[43] After the loss of government control in September 1982, more and more regional and state levels of the Social Democratic Party voted against the arms upgrade. Noteworthy is that these protests were in no small measure dictated from the party base. The SPD candidate for the chancellorship after the breakup of the Social Democrat-Liberal coalition, Hans-Jochen Vogel, no longer ruled out a rejection of deployment in his election campaign of 1983. It hardly surprised political observers when the SPD at its special party congress in Cologne in November 1983 voted almost unanimously against the arms upgrade with only fourteen votes going the other way.[44]

Criticism of the State and "Self Recognition"

In the fall of 1983, the Geneva talks failed due to the unyielding attitudes of the two superpowers. During an intense debate in Parliament, which lasted for two days and ended with a majority vote in favor of missile deployment,[45] noteworthy events took place in the Bonn government district. Thousands of demonstrators participated in roadblocks, sang songs in front of police barricades, and held public discussions in a forum they dubbed the "parliamentary majority." Seen in historical perspective, such mass protests obviously indicated widespread unease about the decision-making structures of West Germany's parliamentary democracy.

In October 1983 the Green Party had already introduced a bill to undertake a national consultative referendum on the deployment of medium-range missiles, thereby implying that the elected members to Parliament did not represent the will of the majority of the population.[46] In November of the same year, the Party took the matter to the Federal Constitutional Court. In a sophisticated legal argument they accused the government of violating the constitution by supporting the deployment of arms.

Appealing to "resistance" and "civil disobedience" and calling for direct democracy by way of plebiscitary voting were what characterized the grassroots political thinking of the green movement. Contemporary conservative observers saw this as either antipolitical or simply the result of emotional antistate sentiments. The extra-parliamentary state criticism went further than that. It seriously doubted the legitimacy of state action that was regarded by the movement as unsupported by the majority of citizens. Thus the dispute about the arms upgrade reveals an underlying social conflict of major importance with significant historical dimensions.

Ironically the green movement's articulately expressed reservations toward the principles behind the normal functioning of the state, and toward those of the West German political elite, became the prerequisite for its inclusion in that very same system. In as far as the debate led to a loss of trust in the state, even the most vocal critics underwent a certain transformation that Klaus Naumann tried to capture in the notion of *Selbstanerkennung* (self-recognition).[47] For the Green Party and the extra-parliamentary opposition this meant that the conflict with the West German state, the questioning of its structures and mechanisms, and the search for alternatives ensured that over the course of several years, the movement itself became institutionalized and played an integral part of this daily political life. Paradoxically the opposition to a West German party consensus led to a conscious integration into a parliamentary system and normalcy.

Jan Hansen studied history and philosophy at the Humboldt-University Berlin, where he received his PhD in 2014. He is currently a lecturer and research fellow in the Department of History at the Humboldt-University Berlin (History of Western Europe and Transatlantic Relations). Hansen is the author of *Abschied vom Kalten Krieg? Die Sozialdemokraten und der Nachrüstungsstreit (1977–1987)* (2016) and coeditor of *Making Sense of the Americas: How Protest Related to America in the 1980s and Beyond* (2015).

Notes

1. The following discussion does not intend to treat all parties equally as the presentation needs to reflect the fact that the CDU, SPD, FDP, and Green parties had internal disputes of varying degrees of intensity.
2. Andreas Rödder, "Bündnissolidarität und Rüstungskontrollpolitik: Die Regierung Kohl/Genscher, der NATO-Doppelbeschluss und die Innenseite der Außenpolitik," in *Zweiter Kalter Krieg und Friedensbewegung: Der NATO-Doppelbeschluss in deutsch-deutscher und internationaler Perspektive*, ed. Philipp Gassert, Tim Geiger, and Hermann Wentker (Munich, 2011), 123–36; Silke Mende, *"Nicht rechts, nicht links, sondern vorn": Eine Geschichte der Gründungsgrünen* (Munich, 2011), especially

341; Saskia Richter, "Der Protest gegen den NATO-Doppelbeschluss und die Konsolidierung der Partei Die Grünen," in Gassert, Geiger, and Wentker, *Zweiter Kalter Krieg und Friedensbewegung*, 229–45; Jan Hansen, "Making Sense of Détente: German Social Democrats and the Peace Movement in the Early 1980s," *Zeitgeschichte* 40 (2013): 107–21.
3. Egon Bahr, "Ist die Menschheit dabei, verrückt zu werden? Die Neutronenbombe ist ein Symbol der Perversion des Denkens," *Vorwärts*, 21 July 1977, 4; Kristina Spohr Readman, "Germany and the Politics of the Neutron Bomb, 1975–1979," *Diplomacy & Statecraft* 21 (2010): 259–85.
4. Herbert Wehner, "Deutsche Politik auf dem Prüfstand," *Die Neue Gesellschaft* 26, no. 2 (1979): 92–94; "Frauen für den Frieden—Frauen gegen Wettrüsten: Appell sozialdemokratischer Frauen vom 3. Dezember 1979," *Blätter für deutsche und internationale Politik* 25, no. 1 (1980): 117–18; "Resolution des Bundeskongresses der Jungsozialisten vom 26. bis 28. Juni 1981 in Lahnstein," *Blätter für deutsche und internationale Politik* 26, no. 7 (1981): 882–83.
5. "Ministerial Communiqué: Special Meeting of Foreign and Defense Ministers, Brussels (December 12, 1979)," reproduced on the website of the North Atlantic Treaty Organization: www.nato.int/docu/comm/49-95/c791212a.htm; for the historical background, see Kristina Spohr, "Helmut Schmidt and the shaping of Western security in the Late 1970s: The Guadeloupe Summit of 1979," in *International History Review* 37 (2015): 167–92.
6. *Parteitag der Sozialdemokratischen Partei Deutschlands, 3.–7.12.1979 in Berlin, 2. Band: Angenommene und überwiesene Anträge* (Bonn, 1979), 1228–44, see especially 1243.
7. "Politische und wirtschaftliche Aspekte der westlichen Sicherheit," speech delivered by Helmut Schmidt to the International Institute for Strategic Studies in London on 28 October 1977, published in *Bulletin* 112 (1977): 1013–20.
8. Speeches given by Schmidt to his party's convention in Berlin and Munich: *Parteitag der Sozialdemokratischen Partei Deutschlands, 3.–7.12.1979 in Berlin, 1. Band: Protokoll der Verhandlungen* (Bonn, 1979), 157–201; *Parteitag der Sozialdemokratischen Partei Deutschlands, 19.–23.4.1982, in München, 1. Band: Protokoll der Verhandlungen* (Bonn, 1982), 126–65.
9. "Unser Land soll auch morgen liberal sein: Wahlprogramm zur Bundestagswahl 1980 der Freien Demokratischen Partei," decided at the national convention in Freiburg on 7 June 1980, published in Archiv des Liberalismus (henceforth AdL), Druckschriftenbestand, Signatur D1-242: 12.
10. William Borm to Erhard Eppler, 1 April 1981, published in Archiv der sozialen Demokratie (henceforth AdsD), Dep. Erhard Eppler, 1/EEAC000057.
11. See Thomas Risse-Kappen, *Die Krise der Sicherheitspolitik: Neuorientierungen und Entscheidungsprozesse im politischen System der Bundesrepublik Deutschland 1977–1984* (Mayence/Munich, 1988), 90–97, 123–43.
12. *Protokoll des 30. Bundesparteitages der Christlich-Demokratischen Union Deutschlands, 2.–5.11.1981 in Hamburg* (Bonn, 1981), 79.
13. Ibid., 362–63.
14. Quoted in Andreas Rödder, "Bündnissolidarität und Rüstungskontrollpolitik," 126 (original emphasis).

15. Friedrich Zimmermann, "SPD-Politik: Sozialistische Unfähigkeit," *Bayernkurier*, 4 April 1981, 1.
16. Kohl to the CDU convention in Berlin, 1980, *Protokoll des 28. Bundesparteitages der Christlich-Demokratischen Union Deutschlands, 19.–20.5.1980 in Berlin* (Bonn, 1980), 29.
17. *Protokoll des CDU-Parteitages 1981 in Hamburg*, 60, 89.
18. *Verhandlungen des Deutschen Bundestages* (henceforth BT-Protokolle), 10. Wahlperiode, 13. Sitzung, 15 June 1983, 755.
19. Holger Nehring and Benjamin Ziemann, "Do All Paths Lead to Moscow? The NATO Dual-Track Decision and the Peace Movement—A Critique," *Cold War History* 12 (2012): 1–24.
20. For example, see Presse- und Informationsamt der Bundesregierung, ed., *Aspekte der Friedenspolitik: Argumente zum Doppelbeschluss des Nordatlantischen Bündnisses* (Bonn, 1981).
21. "Die Berliner Erklärung des CDU-Bundesausschusses, 10.5.1982," published in *CDU-Dokumentation vom 13.5.1982*, 6.
22. "Protokoll der Fraktionssitzung, 20.1.1981," published in AdsD, SPD-Bundestagsfraktion, IX. Wahlperiode, 2/BTFI000009.
23. For example, see Egon Bahr, "Zehn Thesen über Frieden und Abrüstung," in *Sicherheitspolitik contra Frieden? Ein Forum zur Friedensbewegung*, ed. Hans Apel et al. (Bonn, 1981), 10–17.
24. Willy Brandt, "Die Entspannung unzerstörbar machen: Internationale Beziehungen und deutsche Frage 1974–1982," arranged by Frank Fischer (Bonn, 2003) (Berliner Ausgabe Bd. 9), Document 52: 254–268, see especially 254.
25. Willy Brandt, *Der organisierte Wahnsinn: Wettrüsten und Welthunger* (Cologne, 1985), 22.
26. Willy Brandt, *Die Partei der Freiheit: Willy Brandt und die SPD 1972–1992*, arranged by Karsten Rudolph (Bonn, 2002) (Berliner Ausgabe, Bd. 5), Document 79, 354–363, see 356; for further reading, see Judith Michel, "Dissociation and Cooperation: Willy Brandt, the United States and the New Social Movements," in *Making Sense of the Americas: How Protest Related to America in the 1980s and Beyond*, ed. Jan Hansen, Christian Helm, and Frank Reichherzer (Frankfurt, 2015), 293–310.
27. Gert Bastian, "Bevor der Wettlauf außer Kontrolle great," *Vorwärts*, 18 December 1980, 16–17.
28. Erhard Eppler, "Die Bedrohung hat sich durch die SS-20 nicht erhöht," *Spiegel* interview published in Wilhelm Bittorf, ed., *Nachrüstung: Der Atomkrieg rückt näher* (Reinbek near Hamburg, 1981), 137–46.
29. Oskar Lafontaine, *Angst vor den Freunden: Die Atomwaffenstrategie der Supermächte zerstört die Bündnisse* (Reinbek near Hamburg, 1983), 67.
30. "Strafanzeige des Bundesvorstands der Grünen wegen Vorbereitung eines Angriffskriegs, Bonn, April 1981," in *Entrüstet Euch: Analysen zur atomaren Bedrohung*, ed. Bundesvorstand Die Grünen (Bonn, 1983), 160–65.
31. Bundesvorstand Die Grünen ed., *Friedensmanifest, verabschiedet von der 4. Ordentlichen Bundesversammlung der Grünen, 2.–4.10.1981 in Offenbach* (Bonn, 1981), published in *Archiv Grünes Gedächtnis* (henceforth AGG), SBe 258-1(3), 10–11.
32. Erhard Eppler, *Die tödliche Utopie der Sicherheit* (Reinbek near Hamburg, 1983), 101.

33. *Bundesprogramm der Grünen,* adopted at the national convention, 21–23 March 1980 in Saarbrücken (Bonn, 1980), published in AGG, grün 041-1(1992), 19.
34. *Friedensmanifest der Grünen,* 1981, 17.
35. Lafontaine, *Angst vor den Freunden* (Reinbek near Hamburg, 1983), 81.
36. Rudolf Bahro, *Wahnsinn mit Methode: Über die Logik der Blockkonfrontation, die Friedensbewegung, die Sowjetunion und die DKP* (Berlin, 1982), 68.
37. *Bundesprogramm der Grünen,* 1980, 19.
38. Petra Kelly's use of the term made it popular; see Saskia Richter, *Die Aktivistin* (Munich, 2010), 206–8.
39. Mende, *Geschichte der Gründungsgrünen,* 461–67, 471–76; Helge Heidemeyer, "(Grüne) Bewegung im Parlament: Der Einzug der Grünen in den Deutschen Bundestag und die Veränderungen in Partei und Parlament," *Historische Zeitschrift* 291 (2009): 71–102, see especially 73, 93; Josef Boyer and Helge Heidemeyer, eds., *Die Grünen im Bundestag: Sitzungsprotokolle 1983–1987* (Düsseldorf, 2008), the introduction is excellent; Stephen Milder, "An 'Other American': Petra Kelly and the Power of Green Politics in the United States," in Hansen, Helm, and Reichherzer, *Making Sense of the Americas,* 245–65.
40. Compare to the election promise "Freiheit braucht Mut," adopted at the national convention in Freiburg, 29–30 January 1983 in ADL, Druckschriftenbestand, Signatur D1-250, 15.
41. Andere Richtung "Die Freidemokraten stehen hinter ihrem Vorsitzenden Genscher—und der steht rechts," *Spiegel,* 21 November 1983, 22–23.
42. *Parteitag der Sozialdemokratischen Partei Deutschlands, 19.–23.4.1982, in München, 1. Band: Protokoll der Verhandlungen,* 910.
43. *Aufbruch nach vorn. Bundeskonferenz, 18.–19.11.1982 in Kiel, Politik: Aktuelle Informationen der Sozialdemokratischen Partei Deutschlands* 8 (1982): 22.
44. *Außerordentlicher Parteitag der Sozialdemokratischen Partei Deutschlands, 18.–19.11.1983, in Köln, Protokoll der Verhandlungen und Dokumentarischer Anhang* (Bonn, 1983), 198.
45. *BT-Protokolle,* 36/10, 22.11.1983, 2586.
46. Drucksachen des Deutschen Bundestages, 10/519, 24.10.1983.
47. Klaus Naumann, "Nachrüstung und Selbstanerkennung: Staatsfragen im politisch-intellektuellen Milieu der 'Blätter für deutsche und internationale Politik'," in *Streit um den Staat: Intellektuelle Debatten in der Bundesrepublik 1960–1980,* ed. Dominik Geppert and Jens Hacke (Göttingen, 2008), 269–89, see especially 271.

Select Bibliography

A very good introduction to the armament discussions of the parties is provided by Cooper. The thesis by Weber is recommended as a balanced introduction to the CDU/CSU's internal party discussion. Rödder also summarizes the debates within the CDU/CSU and the Liberal Party in a very readable style. A discussion based on sources from archives about the Double-Track Decision among these parties is lacking to date. The material and sources for the SPD and the Green Party are much more extensive. A reliable account of the Social Democratic discussion can be found in Hansen who examines the debate on the basis of unpublished sources and presents a novel approach on how to historicize the late Cold War. Mende offers a very thorough investigation into the origins of the Green party. Milder gives a good introduction to the discussion about the arms upgrade.

Cooper, Alice Holmes. *Paradoxes of Peace: German Peace Movements since 1945*. Ann Arbor, MI, 1995.

Hansen, Jan. "Making Sense of Détente: German Social Democrats and the Peace Movement in the Early 1980s." *Zeitgeschichte* 40 (2013): 107–21.

———. *Abschied vom Kalten Krieg? Die Sozialdemokraten und der Nachrüstungsstreit (1977–1987)*. Berlin/Boston, 2016.

Mende, Silke. *"Nicht rechts, nicht links, sondern vorn": Eine Geschichte der Gründungsgrünen*. Munich, 2011.

Milder, Stephen. "Between Grassroots Activism and Transnational Aspirations: Anti-Nuclear Protest from the Rhine Valley to the Bundestag." *Historical Social Research* 39 (2014): 191–211.

Rödder, Andreas. "Bündnissolidarität und Rüstungskontrollpolitik: Die Regierung Kohl/Genscher, der NATO-Doppelbeschluss und die Innenseite der Außenpolitik." In *Zweiter Kalter Krieg und Friedensbewegung*, ed. Philipp Gassert, Tim Geiger, and Hermann Wentker, 123–36. Munich, 2011.

Weber, Tim M. *Zwischen Nachrüstung und Abrüstung: Die Nuklearwaffenpolitik der Christlich Demokratischen Union Deutschlands zwischen 1977 und 1989*. Baden-Baden, 1994.

Chapter 6

Eco-pacifism:
The Environmental Movement as a Source for the Peace Movement

Silke Mende and Birgit Metzger

Alongside peace, ecology became the cause for one of the most powerful and influential protest movements in West Germany as it did elsewhere in Western industrialized societies during the early 1970s. In the second half of this decade the civic use of nuclear energy became a focus of domestic political dissent. Environmental issues proved remarkably effective at drawing together diverse groups in the social protest movement. The environmental movement also provided an important realm of experience for the "New Peace Movement" of the late 1970s and early 1980s and furnished significant resources, both human and institutional.

The Environmental Movement of the 1970s: Environmental Conservation Societies and Citizens' Initiatives

For some time contemporary historians have seen the early 1970s as a turning point in global social change.[1] The report, *The Limits to Growth*, published by the Club of Rome in 1972[2] and the first oil crisis in 1973 are two historical milestones that triggered widespread public discussion on the environment and the exploitation of natural resources.[3] New scientific findings, mass media reports on obvious damage to the environment, and a shift in values all helped to create an intellectual atmosphere in which a wider public could critically observe—in a way never before possible—changes in the natural environment caused by industrial society.[4] Existing environmental damage proved, on closer inspection, to be more extensive than previously thought, and the consequences were often difficult to assess due to the complexity of ecological processes. Amid these developments, the former conservation societies were joined by new protest movements, and together they forged a new environmental protection movement. The most striking change was how the hitherto politically conservative and elitist conservation societies reformed and assumed a new, inclusive identity. Their active membership had been quite limited, but these societies transformed into a broad-based environmental protection movement, which regarded itself politically as liberal to moderately left-wing or reformist.[5] The discovery that environmental protection was essentially a political matter and required some form of protest helped to mobilize activists from two interest groups: conservation societies, many of which had existed since the turn of the twentieth century, and citizens' initiatives, which increasingly appeared during the 1970s.

The associations' perspective on nature and environment changed as they gained insight into the complexity of ecological problems.[6] Since the 1950s conservationists had increasingly backed up their aesthetic and moral evaluations with scientific arguments about the environment. This was accompanied by a major reassessment of the subject of ecology to include its global dimension, and of environmental protection to cover numerous areas, ranging from water and air pollution to policies on transportation, energy, and urban ecology. At the same time, the image and the identity of conservationists were reinvented: conservationists searched for new forms of action and protest, sought greater media and public attention, and took on a confrontational stance against the state. The natural conservation and cultural heritage societies had since their very foundation argued that environmental destruction was a symptom of a comprehensive crisis in the industrialized world.[7] Now such perspectives were complemented by ecological-scientific arguments that appealed to not only conservative but also progressive and emancipated citizens. In this way the issues and themes surrounding environmental protection and conservation of resources were introduced to young and open-minded people, and yet remained attractive to traditional and conservative followers. The Bund Naturschutz in Bayern (Union for the Conservation of Nature in Bavaria), founded in 1905, assumed a pioneering position in this process of renewal. It transformed itself in 1975 into the Union for the Environment and Nature Conservation (BUND) with a national membership.[8]

Among the concerns to arise from the 1970s, themes of ecology and environmental protection were taken on by the so-called New Social Movements. These movements were established in the wake of 1968, and the social sciences define them in contrast to labor movements.[9] They developed in the tradition of the "New Left" and student protest movements but display some differences. Supporters were predominately young, middle class, and highly educated with a mostly urban focus.[10] Thematically and ideologically they were characterized by great diversity, although their key commitment to social justice and civil or human rights was by no means new.

These post-1970 citizens' initiatives, or action groups, can be distinguished in both quantitative and qualitative terms from those participating in earlier public protests that dealt with environmental issues.[11] It is estimated that in the middle of the 1970s, about fifteen to twenty thousand citizens' initiatives in West Germany actively pursued specific regional concerns at a local level, although precise numbers on initiatives and their volunteers are difficult to obtain.[12] Environmental topics became increasingly important, with changes in urban development, public transportation, and energy consumption serving as the main objectives.[13] Unlike their predecessors, such initiatives not only directed their protests against specific projects, but also expressed fundamental criticism of various technocratic solutions that fell short of consumers' requirements and therefore failed to confront underlying social problems. Furthermore, activists demanded transparency and participation in the planning process, an indication that they saw themselves as part of the wider protest movement; many, in fact, were closely associated with a nascent social group known as the "alternative milieu."[14] In 1972 the Bundesverband Bürgerinitiativen Umweltschutz or BBU (Association of Citizens' Initiatives for Environmental Protection) was founded and built a network of organizational initiatives. It soon developed into a large umbrella association that became "the undisputed leader of environmental initiatives" during the 1970s.[15]

The Antinuclear Protest

Along with a shift in perspectives and an expanding network of organized activists, it was the "nuclear issue" that pushed the environmental protection movement to considerable prominence from the mid-1970s onward. Protests against nuclear power plants produced the largest protests West Germany had ever seen, with several hundred thousand participants, numbers that would later be surpassed by the protests against the arms upgrade.[16]

The controversy surrounding the civilian use of nuclear energy evolved during the 1970s into the most prominent theme among the members of nongovernmental environmental protection groups. Previously, nuclear energy had been considered a pioneering key technology that promised safe, convenient, and environmentally friendly energy for all. This view was even shared by conservationists at first.[17] This changed with an increased awareness of the relationship between environmental exploitation and economic growth and was reinforced when the federal government of Germany passed a bill that opened the way to an accelerated expansion of nuclear energy. The bill stated that by 1985 nearly half of all electricity generated would come from nuclear power plants. In the early 1970s it was just 5 percent.

The seeds of the protests against nuclear power could also be found in the many local initiatives that challenged specific construction projects. The protests against a nuclear power plant in Wyhl between 1973 and 1976 played a paradigmatic role. Here environmentalists and supporters of the New Left joined local residents, professional farmers, and winemakers.[18] The interests of the protesters were diverse, ranging from socio-economic assertions of autonomy to demands for socially and environmentally sustainable energy production, as well as for a more democratic society. The social and political heterogeneity of the protest group, along with the unconventional forms of protest used—such as the occupation of the construction site in 1975—resulted in huge media attention, far-reaching public support, and a new political dimension.

Nuclear energy symbolically represented the potentially unlimited temporal and spatial negative effects of industrial growth. Antinuclear concerns were not just about the risks to health and the environment but also about the threat posed by inscrutable and hardly regulated large-scale technology—not to mention the feeling that the decision-making processes, which appeared to be heavily influenced by capital interests and government dealings, were not transparent.[19]

The conflict contributed in large measure to "demystify the role of the expert or scientist."[20] Certainly the discussion called for profound knowledge, but at the same time it demonstrated that experts were not neutral or unbiased. Thus the environmental movement began to promote "counter-experts": scientifically trained environmentalists who compiled "critical" expert reports for the movement. Organizations such as The Freiburg Institute for Applied Ecology (Freiburger Öko-Institut) were founded to serve this purpose.

Equally significant and influential during the 1970s were nuclear scientists who switched sides and turned into critics of the governmental program. This trend came to a head in the context of the terrorist threats known as "German Autumn" (Deutscher Herbst) and a debate about "internal security." The most prominent case was Klaus Traube, responsible for the construction of a fast breeder nuclear plant in Kalkar. He combined his concern for environmental protection with a fundamental critique of capitalism and state structures, a strategy that increasingly put state authorities on the offensive. In what came to be known as "the Traube case," the Bundesverfassungsschutz (Federal Office for the Protection of the Constitution) kept the manager and nuclear scientist under surveillance and monitored his conversations during 1975 and 1976. However, his alleged links to terrorists proved unfounded. A nationwide scandal developed over the government's treatment of Traube in that it seemed to confirm for many people that the state was increasingly violating the fundamental rights of individual citizens. In general, the large-scale constructions of nuclear power plants were seen as an important step on the way to a technocratic police state. The link between nuclear power and the state was the theme of a widely read book by futurologist Robert Jungk in 1977. Its title, *The Nuclear State,* became a memorable trope that summed up the criticism of the antinuclear movement.[21] Police violence against demonstrators seemed to confirm suspicions of a looming totalitarian state and helped the environmental protection movement to be seen as a campaign of political resistance acting in self-defense against state authoritarianism. Acts of civil disobedience such as sit-ins, occupations or blockades, and damage to property appeared appropriate and justified in this context.

The conflict over the civilian use of nuclear power came to a climax in the second half of the 1970s with events at the construction site of Wyhl, which became a leading example for the protest movement. It should be noted, however, that the Wyhl protests differed from the large-scale demonstrations later held in Kalkar, Grohnde, and Brokdorf. The latter saw repeated violent clashes between police and demonstrators while the protests in Wyhl have come to be known as widely peaceful. Consequently the protest movement engaged in a controversial discussion about the use of violence.[22] The controversy about nuclear power thus assumed such a prominent position that it split West German society into proponents and opponents. The SPD/FDP-led government still supported nuclear power, viewing it as the technology of the future. However, the general consensus within the established parties had already broken down, and the Green Party, still in its early days of formation, expressed a clear antinuclear political stance.[23]

Critique of the state became emblematic for the environmental movement, and this practice helped to distinguish the current movement from its predecessors. Yet citizens' initiatives and institutionalized environmental protection societies cooperated with government agencies and ministries responsible for environmental concerns. Many environmental projects were sponsored by public funds.[24] The government administration became increasingly defensive about its policies regarding environmental protection, as the critics of the government won the upper hand in this polarized public debate.

In sum, during the 1970s the environmental movement went through a period of politicization in which it linked itself to causes like democracy and citizens' rights, civil and human rights, and the emancipation of women, as well as to the "Third World" movement. The debate about the arms upgrade added a final issue at the end of the decade. This quickly rose to the top position on the West German protest agenda. The cluster of themes around the arms race corresponded well with concerns about environmental protection as well as the nuclear power debate: it constituted another issue in the quest for "survival".

The "New Peace Movement" and Its Relationship to the Environmental Movement

Against the backdrop of global political developments that marked the end of détente and heralded the advent of a "Second Cold War," many Western countries saw the birth of "new" peace movements based on the pacifist traditions of the 1950s and 1960s.[25] One reason for the peace movement's huge success in mobilizing crowds was that it could expand on existing structures and draw on the experiences of prior protest movements. From 1979 on, an especially close tie between peace and environmental movements, apparent in their political attitudes and methods of protest, was established through their shared human resources and institutional structures and their overlapping interests.

Perceptions and Interpretations of Crisis

Both the environmental and peace movements regarded themselves as undertaking a "campaign to secure human survival" during an acute crisis of industrial civilization. The objective was "to avert a global catastrophe for humanity".[26] Within this view, the "threat of nuclear war, which would destroy all life on earth in one blow, and the gradual destruction of nature through unbridled industrialization … were merely two sides of the same kind of social-political-economic growth."[27]

Behind this campaign lay a sense of a fundamental crisis, and its social critique took on a variety of approaches. Slogans like "bring peace to nature" or "eco-pacifism" (Ökopazifismus, or Ökopax for short) evoked diverse evaluations among contemporaries and had various connotations. They followed a tradition of thought that characterizes humans as good and peaceful within the context of nature. Violence and the destruction of the environment are seen as caused by the social conditioning of an unnatural order.

Hence the concept of "nature" became the center of gravity for a utopia: the "gentle, nonviolent, green republic," as demanded by the Green Party during the national elections in 1983.[28] *Ökopax*, or eco-pacifism, signaled the fusion of the environment and peace movements and urged for a utopian "state of peace between man and nature."[29] Here, too, the compatibility and potency of theoretical systems that, in the case of ecology, would allow the integration of innovative scientific methods with holistic concepts of natural history can be seen. Classified as "political ecology," such ideas were widely disseminated.[30]

Another line of thought also made reference to "nature" as a philosophical norm and a form of utopia. It became known as eco-feminism and traced connections between the oppression of women and the exploitation of nature. A variation on this theme was the controversial idea that women are innately connected to nature in an essentialist sense. They, the argument suggests, are therefore peaceful and pro-life as opposed to men, who are alienated from nature and essentially destructive. Women were thus expected to fulfill an important role once the envisioned fundamental social change occurred, and feminism was to achieve this.[31] The American physicist Fritjof Capra argued this case. His book *The Turning Point* (*Wendezeit*) was a West German bestseller in the early 1980s and illustrates the proximity of eco-pacifism and eco-feminism to the New Age movement, which also propagated holistic visions of the world.[32]

Beginning in 1980, environmentalists increasingly voiced their criticism of the military's role in the exploitation of natural resources, environmental pollution, destruction of nature, and damage to health. By pointing out that the same technology fueled nuclear plants and atomic bombs, they challenged the strict distinction between civilian and military uses of nuclear energy.[33] Warnings against a military and an ecological catastrophe were rhetorically merged into a scenario of a disastrous terminal crisis. The German prefix *atom-* came to represent anxiety, whether used in a civilian or a military context. In the meantime, another environmental concern, the forest dieback, a major focus of the West German environmental debate in the 1980s,[34] was rhetorically linked to missile deployment.

Rhetorical devices served polemical purposes by evoking powerful associations. This is illustrated by a certain discourse of victimization that recalls the Holocaust or the bombing of Hiroshima and brings into play parallels between the Nazis' mass murder crimes and the Allied bombing campaigns during World War II.[35] The identical use of slogans in the forest dieback debate demonstrates how intertwined the peace and environmental movements and their perception of crisis had become. Common institutions and protest events reflect the merging of ideas.

Networks

Well before the NATO Double-Track Decision, activists had made efforts to combine a commitment for environmental protection with political aspirations for peace. As early as the 1950s, the Naturfreunde (Friends of Nature), an association with origins in the labor movement, for example, devoted time and effort to make peace a political issue.[36] Another group, the Junge Europäische Föderalisten (JEF, Young European Federalists), affiliated to the Social Democratic Party, followed the same path. Among their members were Roland Vogt and Petra Kelly, who would later become founding members of the Green Party, as well as national chairman Jo Leinen (SPD), who would become Minister of the Environment in Saarland.[37] All three held leading positions in the umbrella Association of Citizens' Initiatives for Environmental Protection (BBU) that became perhaps the most important institutional player in the alliance between the peace and environmental movements. The BBU hosted a joint conference with the Deutsche Friedensgesellschaft—Vereinigte KriegsdienstgegnerInnen (DFG-VK, German Peace Society / United War Resisters) in Kassel in October 1979. The program title was "Ecology and Peace Movements." The BBU also developed plans to draw a map of West Germany with the locations of nuclear missile bases and nuclear power plants. They would illustrate the rather dense network of nuclear sites that covered West Germany and its neighboring countries. On the other hand, it would also allow everyone to locate sites in their own neighborhoods. Other actors executed it at a later stage.[38]

Respect for the other movement's cause was mutual among environmentalists and peace activists: environmental groups commissioned reports and studies on the potential environmental consequences of nuclear war,[39] while peace groups actively supported environmental campaigns.[40]

In addition to members of the two main movements, politicians and Christian groups, especially Protestant ones, joined in the call for environmental protection and peace.[41] Foremost among the political parties, the Green Party, which had emerged from the New Social Movements, achieved its first electoral successes not least because of the perceived environmental and nuclear threat. The program of eco-pacifism (*Ökopax*) influenced this party on many levels.[42] Some members of the Social Democratic Party (SPD) supported the movement, with certain limitations. They participated in discussions about issues and concerns raised by the New Social Movements and began increasingly to oppose Chancellor Helmut Schmidt with respect to environmental and peace issues. Even among the Liberal Party (FDP) and the conservative parties, there were individual members who deviated from

Figure 6.1. Caricature "It's not so bad, one forest dies, another one takes its place" (Horst Haitzinger, Pershingwald, 1983 / Museum of Contemporary History, Bonn)

128 | Silke Mende and Birgit Metzger

Figure 6.2. Poster "Defend yourselves! Against the nuclear threat," a map indicating nuclear installations by the Green Party, 1981 (Archiv Grünes Gedächtnis, Berlin)

party lines and drew a link between peace and environmental protection. After the election success of 1982–83, members of the new conservative Kohl-government, such as Minister of the Interior Friedrich Zimmermann (CSU), started to employ the rhetoric of *Ökopax,* which illustrates how effectively the protesters had introduced their concerns into the political agenda.

When the two movements met, prominent protagonists served as mediators.[43] For example, Lutheran pastor and journalist Jörg Zink worked as a prime advocate not only for the peace movement but also for the environmental movement.[44] Erhard Eppler, former minister of development and leader of the Social Democratic Party in the state of Baden-Württemberg, represented environmental and peace concerns within his party. And outside of the political parties there were other public figures who spoke out for environmental protection and peace. The previously mentioned author of the book *The Nuclear State,* Robert Jungk, linked the threat of a nuclear armed conflict with a "gigantic war against the environment" and advocated "a peace treaty with nature" in a speech delivered at a massive peace demonstration in Bonn.[45] The popular television host and author Hoimar von Dithfurth also constructed argumentative and semantic connections between the environment, the antinuclear movement, and peace.[46] In this way, the peace and environmental movements had a far-reaching impact on society. They encompassed a political spectrum ranging from conservatives to members of the left-wing alternative milieu and included nonhierarchical and autonomous groups.[47]

Forms of Protest and Political Culture

Finally, the political culture, mobilization strategies, and forms of protest mirrored the connection between the environment and peace movements. As mentioned earlier, there were plans to construct a nuclear plant in Wyhl, Baden-Württemberg. The protest movement founded a community college, the Volkshochschule Whyler Wald, which aimed to inform and educate people on nuclear risks and environmental topics. At the beginning of the 1980s the original campaign against nuclear energy was broadened to include the topics of peace and deforestation.[48] Such enlightened strategies of reasoning included counter-experts working principally for the environmental movements. Their methods were gradually copied by a number of experts on security policy from the peace movement.[49] In addition, both movements pursued legal action for their aims and purposes. The environmental movement took the initiative and obtained a successful, if only temporary, court order against the planned nuclear plant in Wyhl. This probably contributed to the plan's ultimate demise.[50] Spectacular claims and court proceedings attracted tremendous media attention and the New Social Movements integrated this efficacious strategy into their political action repertoire. In 1983 the Green Party organized a tribunal in Nuremberg against the proliferation of weapons of mass destruction in East and West and followed a dual strategy:[51] it deliberately made reference to the Nuremberg war crimes trials and emphasized once again a blend of criticism of American policies and questionable historical comparisons. And it drew on familiar formats from the extra-parliamentary protest movement, namely the Vietnam War Crimes Tribunal (1966–67) organized by Bertrand Russell, among others, and the subsequent Russell Tribunals.

The links between environmental and peace movements can be observed in many other forms of action, which, beginning in 1968, were part of a broad repertoire of strategies used by the protest movements. Along with large demonstrations and creative public-oriented activities these strategies also included catchy everyday practices.[52] A peace dove on a blue ground or the symbol for "swords into plowshares" printed on jackets worn by protesters was commonplace as were antinuclear protest buttons and similar materials promoting the women's movement. Adopting publicity strategies in the media tradition of 1968,[53] the New Social Movements managed to create a permanent media presence through spectacular tactics such as invading construction sites. Topics relating to the environment therefore remained an ongoing news item in the popular media throughout the 1970s.[54]

The peace movement may be said to exhibit a more defined style of political action than the environmental movement. The idea established in the 1960s of negotiating rationally to achieve the best results under the given circumstances gave way to a more upfront and visceral way of doing things, which was to confront the public with an alternative, highly charged utopian model that aimed at understanding facts through intuition and emotion. Many forms of action sought to provoke the immediate emotional response of "concern" and included vivid descriptions of apocalyptic nuclear scenarios. Engendering fear was positively attributed with the power of persuasion. This strategy was intended to encourage individuals to join in political action and no longer gave the negative impression of being sensationalist.[55] The environmental movement also employed the emotion of fear from its very inception, and haunting symbolism was part of its ideological expression.[56] Under the influence of the peace movement this aspect was reinforced by the environmental movement, which adopted emphatic forms of symbolic protest that incorporated the smearing of blood or formation of human chains.[57] The protest culture of the environmental movement was thus not only a donor but also a recipient of novel ideas to the peace movement.

Nevertheless, the two movements did not merge but remained distinct in, among other things, appearance and action. Perhaps the most distinguishing attribute early on was the use of violence during protests. Occasionally the peace movement had used blockades or, in isolated cases, even sabotage, but on the whole the campaigns were conducted peacefully according to their pacifist tradition. In contrast, at the beginning of the 1980s some currents of the environmental movement accepted violent confrontations, particularly in association with protests against nuclear energy and huge infrastructural projects such as a new runway in Frankfurt international airport. These campaigns were characterized by substantial confrontations with the police and other authorities, and this particularly turned off conservative and middle-class observers. At the same time these violent protests were the subject of an intensive and ardent debate within the environmental movement itself.[58] The peace movement, however, was generally more successful in maintaining its peaceful image during protests and was considered broadly acceptable.

During this time, some members of the environmental movement tried to model protests after those successfully carried out by the peace activists. They acknowledged the tremendous success that the peace movement enjoyed in mobilizing vast crowds for protests and in obtaining support from various quarters by consensual methods and positive media coverage. Particularly during the debate over the forest dieback, an issue that built a cross-generational and politically nonpartisan consensus, activists tried applying this model.[59] However, in this case a huge mobilization of gatherings or protests failed, perhaps because a clearly defined adversary was absent.

Conclusion

The relationship between the environmental and peace movements was intimate and complex in its dynamics. Initially based on a common membership in the New Social Movements and on the adherence of social groups to an alternative culture during the 1970s, they were able to draw on the experiences of the "1968 generation." At the same time they were both "survival" movements grounded in traditions that went back well before the student movement or the New Left, and this accounts for their appeal in middle-class and conservative circles. Unlike the 1968 movements, they displayed a cross-generational heterodox following that embraced supporters from opposing political camps.

The basis for the cooperation between the environmental and peace movements was the general sense of a crisis caused by a man-made violation of humans and nature that called for change. The two groups countered this grim reality with a postulated utopian vision of a peaceful natural world for all humans. They aroused a pervasive sense of existential threat by depicting horrific visions of catastrophe and voicing emotional outbursts of despair and creating a sense of impending danger that seemed boundless and beyond control. To counter these threats, both movements issued demands, primarily to national government agencies, that referenced German experience and interpretations and, especially in the rearmament debate, sometimes assumed national or even nationalistic tones.[60] At the same time, both the environment and the peace movements had extensive networks, both transregional and transnational.[61]

Institutions and individuals strengthened the alliance on a practical level. These people came not only from the ranks of the protest movements but also from political parties or churches. This turnout reflects the unusually wide social range of both movements.[62] The forms of protest show mutual influences and processes of learning. Elements of their popular and publicity-oriented symbolic strategies illustrate how powerful the alliance between ecology and the peace movement had become in public perception. Initially the environmental movement had a stronger impact on the peace movement, but later on, influences also traveled in the opposite direction. However, the numerous points in common should not obstruct the distinctions between the two movements, as they continued to employ specific and individual forms of protests.

Finally, the question arises as to the endurance and resilience of the alliance between the environment and peace movements. It remains to be seen how the manifold connections between the movements developed after the nuclear conflict was resolved and controversy about the arms upgrade came to an end. As the debate about deforestation also declined, it may be asked whether the fruitful symbiosis had turned into a fight for attention and support.

Silke Mende is assistant professor of contemporary history at the University of Tübingen and "Chercheuse associée" at the Centre d'histoire de Sciences Po, Paris. She is the author of *Nicht rechts, nicht links, sondern vorn: Eine Geschichte der Gründungsgrünen* (2011) and is currently working on a research project on the history of Francophonie and the changing idea of a French modernity in the late nineteenth and early twentieth centuries.

Birgit Metzger is an assistant professor of contemporary history at the Saarland University. She is the author of *"Erst stirbt der Wald, dann Du!" Das Waldsterben als westdeutschens Politikum 1978–1986* (Frankfurt am Main and New York, 2015) and is currently working on a research project on the history of accidents in the French and German military in the twentieth century.

Notes

 1. For example, see Konrad Jarausch, ed., *Das Ende der Zuversicht? Die siebziger Jahre als Geschichte* (Göttingen, 2008); Anselm Doering-Manteuffel and Lutz Raphael, *Nach dem Boom: Perspektiven auf die Zeitgeschichte seit 1970*, 2nd ed. (Göttingen, 2010).
 2. Dennis Meadows et al., eds., *The Limits to Growth: A Report for The Club of Rome's Project on the Predicament of Mankind* (New York, 1972). On this point see Friedemann Hahn, "Von Unsinn bis Untergang: Rezeption des Club of Rome und der Grenzen des Wachstums in der Bundesrepublik der frühen 1970er Jahre," (PhD diss, University of Freiburg, 2006), http://www.freidok.uni-freiburg.de/volltexte/2722/pdf/hahn_friedemann_2006_von_unsinn_bis_untergang.pdf.
 3. For example, Franz-Josef Brüggemeier and Jens Ivo Engels, eds., *Natur und Umwelt in Deutschland nach 1945: Probleme, Wahrnehmungen, Bewegungen und Politik* (Frankfurt am Main, 2005).
 4. Franz-Josef Brüggemeier, *Tschernobyl, 26. April 1986: Die ökologische Herausforderung* (Munich, 1998), 191–216.
 5. Jens Ivo Engels, *Naturpolitik in der Bundesrepublik: Ideenwelt und politische Verhaltensstile in Naturschutz und Umweltbewegung 1950–1980* (Paderborn, 2006); Ute Hasenöhrl, *Zivilgesellschaft und Protest: Eine Geschichte der Naturschutz- und Umweltbewegung in Bayern 1945–1980* (Göttingen, 2010).
 6. On the following points, see Engels, *Naturpolitik*; Hasenöhrl, *Zivilgesellschaft*; Kai F. Hünemörder, *Die Frühgeschichte der globalen Umweltkrise und die Formierung der deutschen Umweltpolitik (1950–1973)* (Stuttgart, 2004).
 7. Raymond H. Dominick, *The Environmental Movement in Germany: Prophets and Pioneers, 1871–1971* (Bloomington, IN, 1992); Willi Oberkrome, *"Deutsche Heimat": Nationale Konzeption und regionale Praxis von Naturschutz, Landschaftsgestaltung und Kulturpolitik in Westfalen-Lippe und Thüringen (1900–1960)* (Paderborn, 2004); Friedemann Schmoll, *Erinnerung an die Natur: Die Geschichte des Naturschutzes im deutschen Kaiserreich* (Frankfurt am Main, 2004).
 8. Hasenöhrl, *Zivilgesellschaft*, 284–307.
 9. Roland Roth and Dieter Rucht, introduction to *Die Sozialen Bewegungen in Deutschland seit 1945: Ein Handbuch*, ed. Roth and Rucht (Frankfurt am Main, 2008), 13–17.
10. Ibid.
11. Frank Uekötter, "Wie neu sind die Neuen Sozialen Bewegungen? Revisionistische Bemerkungen vor dem Hintergrund der umwelthistorischen Forschung," *Mitteilungsblatt des Instituts für soziale Bewegungen* 31 (2004): 115–38.
12. Udo Kempf, "Bürgerinitiativen: Der empirische Befund," in *Bürgerinitiativen und repräsentatives System,* ed. Bernd Guggenberger and Udo Kempf, 2nd. ed. (Opladen, 1984), 296.

13. West Berlin serves as an example: Theodor Ebert, "Konfliktformation im Wandel: Von den Bürgerinitiativen zur Ökologiebewegung," in *Bürgerinitiativen in der Gesellschaft: Politische Dimensionen und Reaktionen*, ed. Otthein Rammstedt (Villingen, 1980), 352–54.
14. Sven Reichardt and Detlef Siegfried, eds., *Das alternative Milieu: Antibürgerlicher Lebensstil und linke Politik in der Bundesrepublik Deutschland und Europa 1968–1983* (Göttingen, 2010). Recently, Sven Reichardt, *Authentizität und Gemeinschaft: Linksalternatives Leben in den siebziger und frühen achtziger Jahren* (Berlin, 2014).
15. Engels, *Naturpolitik*, 332. See also Udo Kempf, "Der Bundesverband Bürgerinitiativen Umweltschutz (BBU)," in Guggenberger and Kempf, *Bürgerinitiative*, 404–23.
16. Roland Roth and Dieter Rucht, "Chronologie von Ereignissen," in Roth and Rucht *Soziale Bewegungen*, 670–93.
17. Hasenöhrl, *Zivilgesellschaft*, 400–61; Joachim Radkau, *Die Ära der Ökologie: Eine Weltgeschichte* (Munich, 2011), especially 411–17.
18. On this point and on the following, see Engels, *Naturpolitik*, 350–76; Bernd A. Rusinek, "Wyhl," in *Deutsche Erinnerungsorte*, ed. Hagen Schulze and Étienne François (Munich, 2001), 2: 652–66; Dieter Rucht, *Von Wyhl nach Gorleben: Bürger gegen Atomprogramm und nukleare Entsorgung* (Munich, 1980).
19. Thomas Dannenbaum "'Atom-Staat' oder 'Unregierbarkeit'? Wahrnehmungsmuster im westdeutschen Atomkonflikt der siebziger Jahre," in Brüggemeier and Engels, *Natur und Umwelt*, 268–86.
20. Albrecht Weisker, "Powered by Emotion? Affektive Aspekte in der westdeutschen Kernenergiegeschichte zwischen Technikvertrauen und Apokalypseangst," in Brüggemeier and Engels, *Natur und Umwelt*, 219.
21. Robert Jungk, *The Nuclear State* (London, 1979). Compare with Dannenbaum, "Atom Staat," 274–76.
22. On political violence in the New Social Movements, see Alexander Sedlmaier, *Consumption and Violence: Radical Protest in Cold-War West Germany* (Ann Arbor, MI, 2014). Recently, on the difficult question of how to research political violence and police violence, see Freia Anders and Alexander Sedlmaier, "The Limits of the Legitimate: The Quarrel over 'Violence' between Autonomist Groups and the German Authorities," in *Writing Political History Today*, ed. Willibald Steinmetz, Heinz-Gerhard Haupt, and Ingrid Gilcher-Holtey (Frankfurt, 2013), 291–316.
23. Silke Mende, *Nicht rechts, nicht links, sondern vorn: Eine Geschichte der Gründungsgrünen* (Munich, 2011).
24. On this point and on the following, see Engels, *Naturpolitik*, 394–98.
25. Holger Nehring, "Politics, Symbols and the Public Sphere: The Protests against Nuclear Weapons in Britain and West Germany, 1958–1963," *Zeithistorische Forschungen/Studies in Contemporary History* 2 (2005): 180–202.
26. Harald Müller, "Ökologiebewegung und Friedensbewegung: Zur Gefährdung des Lebensraumes," in *Die neue Friedensbewegung: Analysen aus der Friedensforschung*, ed. Reiner Steinweg (Frankfurt am Main, 1982), 185.
27. Ibid.
28. Die Grünen, "Diesmal die Grünen: Warum? Ein Aufruf zur Bundestagswahl 1983," adopted by the Federal Assembly in Sindelfingen on 14–15 January 1983, 5.

29. Ulrich Linse, *Ökopax und Anarchie: Eine Geschichte der ökologischen Bewegungen in Deutschland* (Munich, 1986), 57.
30. Ludwig Trepl, *Geschichte der Ökologie: Vom 17. Jahrhundert bis zur Gegenwart* (Frankfurt am Main, 1987).
31. For example, see Maria Mies and Vandana Shiva, *Ökofeminismus: Beiträge zur Praxis und Theorie* (Zurich, 1995); see also Radkau, *Ära der Ökologie*, 282–336.
32. Fritjof Capra, *The Turning Point: Science, Society, and the Rising Culture* (New York, 1982). On this topic see also Pascal Eitler, "'Alternative' Religion: Subjektivierungspraktiken und Politisierungsstrategien im 'New Age' (Westdeutschland, 1970–1990)," in Reichardt and Siegfried, *Das alternative Milieu*, 335–52. On this point see also Reinhild Kreis in this volume.
33. For example, Petra Kelly and Jo Leinen, *Prinzip Leben. Ökopax. Die neue Kraft* (Berlin, 1982).
34. The debate on the dying forests is covered in Roland Schäfer and Birgit Metzger, "Was macht eigentlich das Waldsterben?" in *Umweltgeschichte und Umweltzukunft: Zur gesellschaftlichen Relevanz einer jungen Disziplin*, ed. Patrick Masius et al. (Göttingen, 2009), 201–27; Birgit Metzger, *"Erst stirbt der Wald, dann Du!" Das Waldsterben als westdeutsches Politikum (1978–1986)* (Frankfurt am Main, 2015).
35. See also Tim Warneke, "Aktionsformen und Politikverständnis der Friedensbewegung: Radikaler Humanismus und die Pathosformel des Menschlichen," in Reichardt and Siegfried, *Das alternative Milieu*, 466–67.
36. Hasenöhrl, *Zivilgesellschaft*, 95.
37. Robert Camp, "'Für ein Europa der Regionen: Für eine ökologische europäische Gemeinschaft,' Über die Europapolitikerin Petra Kelly," in *Die Grünen in Europa, Ein Handbuch*, ed. Heinrich-Böll-Stiftung (Münster, 2004), 12–29; Saskia Richter, *Die Aktivistin: Das Leben der Petra Kelly* (Munich, 2010), 72–74.
38. On the planned BBU maps and on the importance of maps for the peace movement generally, see Susanne Schregel, *Der Atomkrieg vor der Wohnungstür: Eine Politikgeschichte der neuen Friedensbewegung in der Bundesrepublik 1970–1985* (Frankfurt am Main, 2011), 80–87. The congress in Kassel is further discussed in ibid., 58–59.
39. Müller, "Ökologiebewegung," 177.
40. For example, see flyer: neuer westeuropäischer Volksmissionsdienst—Friedensdienst, Mönchengladbach, 1982 (Bundesarchiv B_342/ 916).
41. Claudia Lepp, "Zwischen Konfrontation und Kooperation: Kirchen und soziale Bewegungen in der Bundesrepublik (1950–1983)," *Zeithistorische Forschungen/Studies in Contemporary History* 7, no. 3 (2010): 364–85. See also the contribution by Sebastian Kalden and Jan Ole Wiechmann in this volume.
42. On this point and on the following, see the contribution by Jan Hansen in this volume.
43. On this point and on the following, see the contribution by Saskia Richter in this volume.
44. He spoke repeatedly at demonstrations about dying forests and received the prize of the Bundesnaturschutz in 1983.
45. Robert Jungk, "Für den größeren Frieden zwischen Mensch und Natur," in *Friedensdemonstration für Abrüstung und Entspannung in Europa* Bonn 10.10.1981, ed.

Aktion Sühnezeichen Friedensdienste / Aktionsgemeinschaft Dienst für den Frieden (Berlin, 1981), 137–39.
46. Hoimar von Ditfurth, *So lasst uns denn ein Apfelbäumchen pflanzen: Es ist soweit* (Hamburg, 1985).
47. Regarding the peace movement, see Warneke, "Aktionsformen," 446–51.
48. Engels, *Naturpolitik*, 372–74; Ulrich Beller, "Bürgerproteste am Beispiel Wyhl und die Volkshochschule Wyhler Wald," in *Vom Hotzenwald bis Wyhl: Demokratische Traditionen in Baden*, ed. Heiko Haumann (Cologne, 1977), 269–90.
49. Warneke, "Aktionsformen," 461, 466.
50. Engels, *Naturpolitik*, 344–76.
51. Die Grünen Bundesverband, *Nürnberger Tribunal gegen Erstschlags- und Massenvernichtungswaffen in Ost und West 18. bis 20.2.1983 Nürnberg, Meistersingerhalle* (Bonn, 1983).
52. Compare with Schregel, *Atomkrieg*, 226–66; Warneke, "Aktionsformen"; and the contribution by Kathrin Fahlenbrach and Laura Stapane in this volume.
53. Martin Klimke and Joachim Scharloth, ed., *1968: Handbuch zur Kultur- und Mediengeschichte der Studentenbewegung* (Bonn, 2008).
54. See also Fahlenbrach and Stapane in this volume.
55. Compare, for example, with Frank Biess, "Die Sensibilisierung des Subjekts: Angst und 'Neue Subjektivität' in den 1970er Jahren," *Werkstatt Geschichte* 49 (2008): 51–71; Susanne Schregel, "Konjunktur der Angst: 'Politik der Subjektivität'" und 'neue Friedensbewegung,' 1979–1983," in *Angst im Kalten Krieg*, ed. Bernd Greiner, Christian Th. Müller, and Dierk Walter (Hamburg, 2009), 495–520.
56. See also Radkau, *Ära der Ökologie*, 147–52.
57. For example, the action event "Blutspur" (blood trail) by the artist Rolf Schulz from Hamburg against dying forests staged in collaboration with the BBU on 21–22 November 1987 (Archiv des Schwarzwaldvereins, Ordner: Waldsterben/Waldschäden, 1983–87).
58. On the topic of the Startbahn-West, see Sabine Dworog, "Luftverkehrsinfrastruktur: Zur Rolle des Staates bei der Integration eines Flughafens in seine Umwelt," *Saeculum* 58 (2007): 115–49.
59. "Adlige und Autonome," in *TAZ*, 4 October 1983.
60. See also the contribution by Marianne Zepp in this volume.
61. Jan-Henrik Meyer, "'Where do we go from Wyhl?' Transnational Anti-Nuclear Protest targeting European and International Organisations in the 1970s," in *Historical Social Research* 39 (1) (2014).
62. See also the contribution by Christoph Becker-Schaum in this volume.

Select Bibliography

Helpful introductions and general overviews of the history on the environmental movement are published by Brüggemeier, Radkau 2013, and Uekötter.

The history of the environmental movement in Germany is well researched until the middle of the 1970s. Schmoll provides a survey of its predecessors beginning in the late nineteenth century, and Dominick and Chaney describe its development from its origins until the 1970s. The development of the West German nature conservation and environmental protection movement has been written by Engels in his pioneering study. Discussing the regional example of Bavaria, Hasenöhrl offers deep insights. Hünemörder gives an account of the environmental movement and environmental policies in West Germany up to 1973. Goodbody provides a collection of articles discussing historical, cultural, and social aspects of environmentalism in Germany.

Radkau 1983 remains the most important work on the history of nuclear conflict and the antinuclear protest. Another contemporary source relating to discussions at the time is Rucht. Tiggemann's focus rests on problems of nuclear waste and its disposal.

Brüggemeier, Franz-Josef. *Schranken der Natur. Umwelt und Gesellschaft 1750–2013*. Essen, 2014.

Chaney, Sandra. *Nature of the Miracle Years: Conservation in West Germany, 1945–1975*. New York, 2008.

Dominick, Raymond H. *The Environmental Movement in Germany: Prophets and Pioneers, 1871–1971*. Bloomington, 1992.

Engels, Jens Ivo. *Naturpolitik in der Bundesrepublik: Ideenwelt und politische Verhaltensstile in Naturschutz und Umweltbewegung 1950–1980*. Paderborn, 2006.

Goodbody, Axel. *The Culture of German Environmentalism*. New York, 2002.

Hasenöhrl, Ute. *Zivilgesellschaft und Protest: Eine Geschichte der Naturschutz- und Umweltbewegung in Bayern 1945–1980*. Göttingen, 2010.

Hünemörder, Kai F. *Die Frühgeschichte der globalen Umweltkrise und die Formierung der deutschen Umweltpolitik (1950–1973)*. Stuttgart, 2004.

Radkau, Joachim. *Aufstieg und Krise der deutschen Atomwirtschaft 1945–75: Verdrängte Alternativen in der Kerntechnik und der Ursprung der nuklearen Kontroverse*. Reinbek near Hamburg, 1983.

———. *Nature and Power: A Global History of the Environment*. Cambridge, 2008. First published in German as *Natur und Macht* (2002).

———. *The Age of Ecology*. Cambridge, 2013. First published in German as *Die Ära der Ökologie* (2011).

Rucht, Dieter. *Von Wyhl nach Gorleben: Bürger gegen Atomprogramm und nukleare Entsorgung*. Munich, 1980.

Schmoll, Friedemann. *Erinnerung an die Natur: Die Geschichte des Naturschutzes im deutschen Kaiserreich*. Frankfurt am Main, 2004.

Tiggemann, Anselm. *Die "Achillesferse" der Kernenergie in Deutschland: Zur Kernenergiekontroverse und Geschichte der Entsorgung von den Anfängen bis Gorleben 1955 bis 1985*. Lauf, 2004.

Uekötter, Frank. *The Greenest Nation? A New History of German Environmentalism*. Cambridge, MA, 2014.

Chapter 7

Rationality of Fear: The Intellectual Foundations of the Peace Movement

Marianne Zepp

In the fall of 2010, 88-year-old Horst-Eberhard Richter was invited to present his newly published book, *Moral in Zeiten der Krise*[1] (Morality in times of crisis) in Berlin. The chairperson introduced him as the one who had given the peace movement its intellectual and analytical basis, and went on to say that Richter was credited with intellectually binding together psychoanalysis, perspectives on peace, and political protest. The author almost brusquely responded that this was not what it was all about. It was about a common future, social involvement, and a new sense that science carried a political responsibility. Tenaciously he expressed exactly the values that had characterized the actors in the peace movement in the course of the previous decades: social responsibility, normative behavior, and scientific analysis. The following chapter addresses and evaluates this interaction between science, political action, and moral commitment to social issues.

By the mid-1970s as liberalization permeated society and the end of détente seemed imminent, more and more voices were raised against the Cold War ideology of deterrence. The studies on peace and conflict that resulted during this period put the concept of peace in a wider historical context and sought solutions from an international perspective. These became the foundation and provided the intellectual reasoning for a mass movement unique in the post-World War II history of the German Federal Republic.

The movement was marked by three distinct characteristics: first, it attracted intellectuals from different professions and academic disciplines. Second, a number of profoundly different social groups converged in the movement (the political perspectives ranged from communist to nationalistic to environmentalist and from former army personnel to peace activists). Third, participants regarded themselves as part of a social movement that called for the proposal and enforcement of a new policy in regard to the confrontation between the superpowers.

At the height of the Cold War, a conflict and peace theory had already been formulated, mainly by the Norwegian scholar Johan Galtung, which tried to address the shortcomings of the doctrine of deterrence and the arms race from a completely new systemic perspective. At the same time, aggression research, which originated in and was motivated by dealing with the Nazi past, broadened the definition of peace. This research was combined with a specifically German ethic of responsibility that was closely linked to the issue of a critical approach to nationalistic trends within the peace movement. The peace movement furthermore regarded itself as a social movement and thus popularized a new concept of the public sphere, based on individual responsibility as well as collective political action.

Peace Studies as an Alternative to the Logic of Deterrence

During the European crisis about the deployment of medium-range missiles a morally inspired and scientifically justified alternative to the Cold War logic of defense and deterrence became politically acceptable. As early as the late 1960s, scholars of international relations had developed a structural theory of peace that challenged the Cold War order. In 1966, Johan Galtung, in a series of lectures delivered to a Danish radio station, outlined a program for academic peace studies.[2] As director of the Oslo International Peace Research Institute founded in 1959, he became the founding father of European peace studies.[3] By the end of the decade Galtung could count on a number of internationally relevant peace research institutes.[4]

The activities of this Norwegian scholar were groundbreaking for a particular model of peace studies that promoted a new view of society based on a system of transnational relations.[5] Galtung continuously stressed that peace studies are an applied form of research and thus a guideline for behavior. Based on this premise he defined it as goal-oriented.[6] Grounded in normative ethics that matched pacifist ideals, it had "the task to discover conditions to hinder or to foster peace, in a negative sense defined by the absence of war and in a positive sense (integration and cooperation) to provide for peaceful coexistence."[7] This resulted in an integrated model of science able to integrate inter- and multidisciplinary knowledge and experience.[8] In addition, Galtung also called for peace research as an independent association of different academic disciplines to establish new networks and projects within academia.[9]

Galtung's approach was, in his own words, motivated by a rupture from the pacifist movement up to that point. Without challenging the normative basis of the movement he decidedly rejected "military policy as a means of upholding democratic values or as a method of deterrence and military defense."[10] The predominant theory postulated that the only means to maintain peace was the balance of power between military blocks, the acceptance of the arms race with the accompanying threat of a nuclear war, and the destructive potential of unique historic dimensions as a necessary evil. He dismissed this approach and replaced it with his idea of a new "holistic peace."[11] His opposing supranational model relied on international organizations and anticipated a social balance between states.[12] His expanded concept of pacifism included policies of Third World development, that is, he analytically linked the interdependencies between social, economic, and political development. This approach was radical in that it took a "symmetric point of view" that assumed the convergence between East and West. In this way, as early as the 1960s, Galtung's work intellectually prepared the way for a breakthrough beyond the conventional power blocks' approach and the peace movement would rely on this concept during the next two decades.

Responding to criticism that he was ignorant of power politics in society and neglected the interests of political actors, Galtung developed the concept of structural violence. "The 'absence of organized direct violence' corresponds to a negative model of peace—in contrast, getting beyond structural violence enables 'social justice' and a positive model of peace."[13] Contemporaries recognized that this theoretical model was suitable for the aspirations of the peace movements and envisaged a comprehensive social transformation, namely a "change in social structure toward societies based on fundamentally democratic and egalitarian values."[14] Thus Galtung provided a new definition of the concept of peace that not only influenced research but also offered the peace movement an approach that provided the foundation for its social impact.

His concept of peace was furthermore supposed to serve as an analytical tool for conflict situations in order to establish peace research as an integrated discipline within the humanities.[15] In Galtung's view, scientists are political actors. According to his reasoning, normativity and analysis form a synthesis. This kind of thinking was symptomatic of the action-oriented social science in the early 1960s.[16]

His reassessment of military and defense policy led to the realization that armament, together with a previously unknown inherently destructive potential, threatened world peace. This interpretation became a decisive factor in the collective expectation for a new kind of peace order. It paved the way for the linking of criticism of militarism with criticism of armament, and for these to be the decisive components of peace research and catalysts for the peace movement. From the middle of the 1970s independent and nonacademic experts, such as journalists, popularized this line of thinking and contributed significantly to the social impact of the peace movement by publicly questioning military policy decisions and strategic arms analysis from the perspective of peace policy and with the aim of disarmament. This, to a great extent, influenced the establishing of peace research institutions in the Federal Republic of Germany among other Western countries.

Toward a Rearmament Debate

The era of détente during the chancellorship of Willy Brandt had raised hopes that a way out of the Cold War might be found, despite ongoing armament threats. But now there was growing evidence that conventional politics was incapable of overcoming Cold War belligerence.[17]

In the United States, particularly during Nixon's presidency, a theory of "nuclear war fighting capabilities" developed as the basis for international relations. Proponents of this theory within the American administration supported an escalation strategy that sought to dominate the arms race by building up a profound deterrence. All areas of public life, such as politics, military affairs, business, scientific research, and the media were part of this complex. The debacle of the Vietnam War was one of the sources for this US strategic thinking and guided its behavior in the global race between the superpowers. Consequently, efforts were made to make and test feasibility studies of a limited nuclear war. These strategic concepts were in stark contrast to the views of the peace movement.

In West Germany the critical stance toward technology that had been voiced by female and male scientists since the end of World War II became the determining core of identity within the peace movement. Their efforts to inform the public about the dangers of nuclear arms provided an impetus to the nascent peace and conflict studies during the second half of the 1960s.[18] This trend found an echo in the Federal Republic of Germany where leading natural scientists had also been developing a critical ethic of responsibility since the 1950s. Both strands came together and led to a series of initiatives and the founding of several institutions.[19] The Arbeitsgemeinschaft fuer Friedens- und Konfliktforschung (AFK, Association for Peace and Conflict Research) was founded in 1968 and was followed by the establishment of research facilities in Hesse, Hamburg, and Bavaria, which focused on the East-West conflict and were united by the umbrella organization of the Deutschen Gesellschaft für Friedens- und Konfliktforschung (DGFK, German Society for Peace).[20] They followed Galtung's ideas on democratic peace. In addition they adopted the concept of social justice and, since the 1980s, the idea for an ecological transformation of society.[21]

The debate in the growing peace movement about the role of military and armament was at its peak when NATO reached the decision about the arms' upgrade (NATO Double-Track Decision). A joint declaration of scientists, known as the Mainzer Appell (Appeal of Mainz), had an impact on the public discourse.[22] The arguments were principally twofold:[23] the scientists first argued against the conception that a nuclear war could be contained, and second, called for a European peace order built on ethical and moral principles that would overcome the confrontation of the superpowers. Linus Pauling, American chemist and Nobel Peace Prize winner, argued that the heightened complexity of the technology bore an increasing risk of an accidental nuclear attack. The physicist Hans-Peter Dürr perceived "the security policy of the West … to be at crossroads" and turned against the idea that a balance of terror would be sufficient to safeguard world peace. Another physicist, Victor F. Weisskopf, argued with a greater emphasis on moral values and ethical evaluations that the use of nuclear weapons was a crime against humanity.[24] Weisskopf pointed out that to put an end to military thinking one had to rely on a communal European construct, a postwar pan-European agreement that conflict ought to be resolved peacefully. Within European tradition the ideology of the Cold War presented a major obstacle to future peace. According to British historian and peace activist E. P. Thompson, during the Cold War the two concepts of freedom and peace had come to be regarded as mutually exclusive ideological opposites. It took the peace movement to rejoin these two concepts.[25] Thompson also put forward the theory of a "new" Cold War: the military weapons arsenal had grown, material interests had joined together to form a military-industrial complex including research institutions, particularly in the United States.[26] To oppose this scenario he came up with the idea of a neutral and independent Europe.[27] This concept of an autonomous Europe was taken up by the peace movement in the Federal Republic (and somewhat later in the German Democratic Republic) and became part of a specific national discourse of special responsibility deriving from the dealings with National Socialism.

Nationalism in the Peace Movement: Transcending the East-West Confrontation and Assuming Responsibility in Historical Perspective

Postwar German society manifested a specific willingness for peace. This consensus for a peaceful society in both German states, a direct result of the

Figure 7.1. The writer and scholar Robert Jungk during a meeting of the Second European Conference on Nuclear Disarmament in the International Congress Centre, Berlin, on 9 May 1983 (ullstein bild / Rieth)

World War II experience, had been propagated by the elites as a national identity trait since 1945. Maintaining peace after 1949 had thus become an integrating ideological element for both states. This had two results: first, both states distinguished themselves from the militarism of National Socialism in their official rhetoric, and second, both states used this peace rhetoric to define their perception of their idea of a nation state by competing ideologically within the framework of the Cold War.[28] Very early on, segments of West German society, particularly the pacifist groups, were concerned that the confrontation between the two military blocks threatened Germany as a whole.[29] The protests of the 1950s against the rearmament policy of Chancellor Adenauer tied this to the idea of German national unity. Initiatives such as the *Paulskirchenbewegung* (Paul's Church Movement) cofounded by Gustav Heinemann, later president of the Federal Republic of Germany, were the first organized attempts by a movement supported by politicians and intellectuals to raise political awareness and at the same time make an impact on the parliamentary system.[30] All of these initiatives rejected communism and held fast to the paradigm of German reunification.[31]

This was a point of departure for the peace movement. Peter Brandt, a historian, and Detlef Lehnert, a political scientist, used a geostrategic argument in the West German debate by pointing out that both German states were located "at the demarcation line of confrontation."[32] From this perspective, they argued that West German society had followed Western models of nation-state building with a bourgeois-democratic development and thus "... facilitated its being a political nation with a value-oriented sense of identity."[33] This characterized the culture of peace in Germany: a national discourse of commitment and victimization and an emphasis on a value-oriented sense of responsibility, derived from historical experiences with National Socialism.

Since the 1960s the newly reestablished discipline of psychoanalysis in West Germany had inspired the peace movement. Alexander Mitscherlich had done the groundwork for this move intellectually (although he was not involved with the peace movement). His treatise "Die Unfähigkeit zu trauern" (Inability to mourn) became a diagnostic tool for the acquisition of self and a new imperative of contemporary society at the time.[34] It was gradually associated more and more with a deeply ingrained postulate in German discourse regarding the duty to remember the past. Implicitly this was considered a prerequisite for achieving lasting peace in society.[35]

In the 1970s, Horst-Eberhard Richter politicized this approach and applied it to family and group therapy.[36] At the same time he brought psychoanalysis into the service of democratizing society. His vantage point was the psychological disposition of the Germans after the end of National Socialism. Taking up the findings of research on aggression, he applied these to the peace movement and warned against "identifying with the aggressor."[37] He argued for a more humane society and against projections of an enemy image. Richter collaborated in research initiatives of the peace movement and supported its political campaigns together with scientists to place the movement on the political stage, albeit with little success, as he admitted himself.[38]

Politically the discourse on the geo-strategic position of Germany merged with a new contextualization of the "unresolved German question,"[39] that is, the possibility of national reunification. While the official policy of détente and the accompanying "policy of small steps," called for a harmonization of relations with the Eastern bloc and especially with East Germany, the argument that both German states were equally threatened by nuclear missiles served as a (moral) basis for another bloc-bridging approach by the peace movement. The resolution passed by the superpowers to deploy medium-range missiles on German territory brought principles of German sovereignty into question. Germany was seen primarily as a battlefield for an exchange of nuclear strikes between the superpowers. The right wings of the CDU and FDP parties were accused of being "vassals to the leadership of the US."[40] Ideas of a "third way" based on the Scandinavian model to bring about a peace settlement by gradually harmonizing relations and Austria's neutrality policy were elements that tried to bring about a European peace order. Proponents of such nonalignment theories emphasized "the particular and historically motivated commitment to anti-fascist and anti-militarist principles … carried the special responsibility to seek policy initiatives for a new European peace partnership beyond the East-West confrontation."[41]

Thomas Jäger,[42] in contrast, saw the peace movement as a nationalistic movement grounded in ideas of nationhood or the people.[43] This meant that the concept of a German nation would be reified as a single actor within a divided country. National sovereignty was socially constructed through ethnicity as "an enactment of a national essence battling against foreign influences."[44] This theory of two occupied German states would eventually result in a national and anti-imperialist struggle nourished from a regionalist perspective. Only "mass protests" from "below" would open the possibility for disarmament. Jäger diagnosed certain shared ideas with the New Right in regard to an ethnic-German focus by attributing equal value to "peace and national self-determination" and elevated the sovereignty of the German people above or next to sovereignty of a German nation-state. Furthermore such ideas presupposed that a certain social homogeneity would mean that particularistic interests and national differences would cease to exist. At the same time the moral integrity of this way of thinking was compromised by the German dealings with its past: "national shame and national megalomania join in a new German mission: to bring peace to the world."[45]

The historian Dan Diner undertook a contemporary analysis of a supposed nationalism within the peace movement. He described how a historical consciousness and strategic thinking within the peace movement determined the question of nation.[46] By putting at stake the very foundations of the prevailing European security system, a national perspective gained ground. Diner distinguished between the pragmatic critique of the security system and a new formulation of German cultural identity. This protest charged the issue of peace with a "latent historical consciousness."[47] These patterns of interpretation were based on the repression of the historical causes that led to Germany's division, in that Germany was seen as colonized by occupying powers, and was strengthened by the concept of national belonging based on national-territorial elements. The adoption of a new national identity was furthermore backed up by anti-Western and anti-American resentments. It implied that principles of Western democracy would be neglected and the impact of German imperialism ignored. Diner thus objected to a national discourse about security policies that sought to extinguish political bloc alliances and questioned the existing postwar European order. He urged the peace movement to cultivate a reflective and critical stance toward itself.[48]

Other voices also advised caution in the debate about national unity and called for openness toward other policy options. The fact that there was no political authority to speak for a united Germany was ignored and the real situation of the two German states was disregarded.[49]

The German peace movement was characterized by three distinct traits: first, a nationalism grounded in concern over the military nuclear threat posed to both German states; second, the aspiration to overcome German division; and third, a rhetoric of responsibility derived from generally consenting to maintain peace in the postwar era. Any tendency toward aggressive nationalism within the movement was counteracted by a culture of self-reflection, critical and analytical thought, as well as a search for democratic legitimacy.

The Peace Movement as a Political Movement

"[It] is obvious that political parties and large organizations concerned with tactical calculations are generally unable to organize or be representative in processes of social learning the way that social movements can."[50] This self-definition as a social movement placed the participants in the peace movement in opposition to institutions and established party politics.

The more popular the peace movement became, the greater the risk that it would be conflated with social protest and political opposition groups legitimized through the diffuse notion of a "mass movement."[51] Activists prepared a strategy to form an "active mass movement" by putting the emphasis on self-empowering elements. Initial efforts were made in the early 1980s: the first major public manifestation was a mass demonstration in Bonn, at the Bonner Hofgarten in October 1981, rallying about 300,000 people. The Koordinationsrat (Counsel for Coordination) comprised some thirty organizations, nearly all of which had been working at the local, grassroots level since the early 1980s. In October 1983 they succeeded in mobilizing half a million people.[52] The Krefelder Appell (Krefeld Appeal) was signed by five million people.[53]

Two elements characterize the peace movement: an alternative order of peace and a unique German national approach motivated by different perspectives on dealing with the past. How are these characteristic features to be classified in the context of postwar history? Sociologist and political scientist Ulrike C. Wasmuht describes in a contemporary analysis the conditions that led to the formation of the peace movement. In her analysis she identifies a structural reason for the emergence of social movements: in a situation of crisis, large sections of the population realize that political institutions are failing to respond or take appropriate measures. Wasmuht diagnoses a normative value-based change in the collective consciousness. Thus, peace activists claimed to speak on behalf of the collective but did not act in accordance to collective behavior. She identifies the following indicators of a social movement:[54] public awareness, relatively undeveloped organization structures, criticism of the status quo, the experience of an existential crisis in a particular historical setting, an impulse for dynamic social change, and a process of sustained learning among a large part of the population. She thus argues strongly that without the careful consideration of all these social contexts the dynamics of a movement cannot be understood.[55]

From a historical perspective, one may read Wasmuht's argumentation as an attempt to legitimize the political viability of the movement. Political scientist Joachim Raschke points out that the very concept of a "movement" still held negative connotations in the Federal Republic of Germany during the 1970s: it recalled National Socialism and its self-designation as a "movement," and it brought to mind numerous instances of state repression in response to the rise of popular movements since 1789.[56] Prerequisite to a new assessment of the concept was the appearance of a new postwar generation and the student movement. Yet the peace movement was essentially a movement willing to express criticism while maintaining distance from established politics and policy institutions, and it strove toward political and social empowerment. Until today there is an ongoing debate among scholars as to whether the movement threatened or inspired democracy in the Federal Republic of Germany. Benjamin Ziemann defines it as a social movement that differed from the pacifism of the period between the world wars and up until 1945, which he characterizes as follows: a closed social caste of personalities from the middle class with strong ideological commitment, and, after 1945, a movement that was able to mobilize large crowds.[57] The historian Jost Dülffer rejects the application of the term "peace movement" in his description of the forms of resistance against the rearmament and nuclear armament during the 1950s in the Federal Republic of Germany. His concept of movement demarcates the place of political action, in other words, a movement happens outside of institutionalized politics: "A political or social movement can be defined as a collective effort by nonestablished and noninstitutionalized groups to change society or to prevent such change." There needs to be continuity in this process of mobilization or permanent cohesion. And in this respect one may well argue that during the 1950s there had only been "a trend that lacked a base," which considerably differentiated it from the movement during the 1970s and 1980s.[58]

Yet some authors even find totalitarian attributes in the social movements. A movement's moral appeals to transcendental authorities and its implicit assumption of an unquestionable truth can be countered with accusations of irrationalism and of emotional manipulation (as in the use of "scare tactics").[59] Recent historical research has in the meantime concluded that the concept of peace, and especially collectively formulated peace expectations, depend on context and normative dichotomies between victim and perpetrator, and these are tied to semantic strategies that tend to obfuscate rather than reveal hidden ambiguities and contradictions.[60] This holds true for the peace movement of the late 1970s and early 1980s. It was closely associated with ethical and normative standards, hero worship, and dramatic emotions. Certain public speakers, for example, took the liberty to represent the movement as if they embodied it. They thus converted the issue of representation into acts of self-empowerment.[61]

As a counterpart, academic peace studies took on the role of a reflective sounding board for the movement. These scholars were dedicated to making the peace movement politically viable.[62] In matters of security analysis, they urged time and again to engage Realpolitik. Ulrich Albrecht, a professor of peace and conflict studies at the Otto Suhr Institute for Political Sciences at the Free University of Berlin, for example, proposed "the integration" of the peace movement's strategies "into everyday politics." Furthermore, he argued that "the option of German neutrality," a much-used figure of speech in the discourse about nationality, needed to be tied to a demand for arms reduction and a policy of détente and he strongly argued that this "concept to preserve peace" was "far closer to the spirit of the law [referring to the Basic Law prohibiting an aggressive or preventive war and demanding international cooperation to safeguard peaceful relations] ... than nuclear armament."[63] The "enlightenment"[64] that the scholars were able to offer to the movement focused on three issues: the arms control debate, unilateral disarmament, and defensive models of armament as an alternative to a continuous nuclear arms race. Connected with these approaches was the goal to prevent a further militarization of society.[65]

Dieter Senghaas,[66] who deserves praise for drawing attention to the interdependencies between international relations and development policy as well as conflict resolution and peace studies, received broad scientific recognition within Germany. He pointed out that peace studies did not merely respond to military decisions but could actively articulate a critique that "was irrefutable in the face of empirical scientific findings."[67] He noted that protagonists of the peace movement were able to unite political action and scientific findings. Galtung's theoretical call for normative motivated action was thus converted into real political action. In sum, even if one concedes that the peace movement used a holistic approach with no ambiguities, contradictions, or disagreement about objectives, the question of the degree of political competence and influence that it exerted remains unanswered. However, it is significant that with the help of science, initiatives, and projects, scholars were able to put forward proposals and alternatives that are still valid today.

Conclusion

Without the postwar German consensus to maintain peace, the peace movement of the 1970s and 1980s would have been unthinkable. In particular, counter-experts popularized developing ideas about an international order of peace that bridged Cold War ideological polarization. The buildup of nuclear arms was seen as threatening, especially on the part of the United States. This concern was accompanied by the discourse reinforcing a collective sense of fear. Discourse about national victimization were revitalized and demands for more national sovereignty increased. A surge in intellectual democratization starting in the late 1960s changed the nature of the peace movement to that of political self-empowerment. This made it an important factor in the democratization of postwar Germany.

Marianne Zepp received her MA at the Johannes-Gutenberg-University of Mainz in history, sociology, and German literature and her PhD at the Technical University, Berlin, in contemporary history in 2006. Her research focuses on contemporary history, politics of memory, European and international development of democracy, as well as gender politics. She is the author of *Redefining Germany: Reeducation, Staatsbürgerschaft und Frauenpolitik im US-amerikanisch besetzten Nachkriegsdeutschland* (2007); "Weiblichkeit als politisches Argument. Frieden und Demokratie im Übergang zu einer deutschen Nachkriegsgesellschaft," in *Frieden durch Demokratie. Genese, Wirkung und Kritik eines Deutungsmusters,* ed. Jost Dülffer and Gottfried Niedhart (2011), 187–205. Zepp worked with the Heinrich-Böll-Foundation for over fifteen years in Berlin as a program director for Contemporary History and Democratic Development before joining the foundation's Tel Aviv office as a program director for Israeli-German relations and relations with Europe in 2011. In 2016 she resumed her former position in Berlin.

Notes

1. Horst-Eberhard Richter, *Moral in Zeiten der Krise* (Frankfurt am Main, 2010).
2. Johan Galtung, *Modelle zum Frieden: Methoden und Ziele der Friedensforschung*

(Wuppertal, 1972). Corinna Hauswedell, *Friedenswissenschaften im Kalten Krieg: Friedensforschung und friedenswissenschaftliche Initiativen in der Bundesrepublik Deutschland in den achtziger Jahren* (Baden-Baden, 1997), 50–51.
3. Lutz Mez, Einleitung to *Modelle zum Frieden: Methoden und Ziele der Friedensforschung,* by Johan Galtung (Wuppertal,1972), 7.
4. Ibid.
5. Benjamin Ziemann, ed., *Perspektiven der Historischen Friedensforschung* (Essen, 2002), 15.
6. Johan Galtung, "Ziel und Mittel der Friedensforschung," in *Modelle,* 29; Johan Galtung, "Friedensforschung," in *Friedensforschung,* ed. Ekkehart Krippendorff, (Cologne and Berlin, 1968), 519–36.
7. Krippendorff, ed., *Friedensforschung,* 527.
8. Ibid., 529.
9. Ibid., 530
10. Lutz Mez, Einleitung, 12. With the self-professed claim to critically deal with the military strategy of the state as a peace researcher, he went beyond the traditional pacifism position that had developed as a counter-movement to the national militarism of the nineteenth and early twentieth centuries and that had always rejected military measures because of their violence and brutality (Jeffrey Verhey, "Die Geschichtsschreibung des Pazifismus und die Friedensbewegung," in Ziemann, *Perspektiven,* 273).
11. Johan Galtung, "Modelle zur Verteilung militärischer und nichtmilitärischer Gewalt," in *Modelle,* 51–61.
12. Johan Galtung, "Supranationale Friedensmodelle," in *Modelle,* 75–87.
13. Mez, Einleitung, 17. For a critical discussion of structural violence see Ziemann, *Perspektiven,* 22.
14. Mez, Einleitung, 19.
15. Ziemann refers to the inherent sociopolitical implications in the concept of structural violence, the imperative for a new image of society, and the definitional problems with extending the term. Ziemann, *Perspektiven,* 20.
16. Hauswedell discusses a parallel development in the natural sciences that is also discussed in the following as well as ideas in the social sciences. Hauswedell, *Friedenswissenschaften,* 49.
17. Dieter Senghaas, "Der Frieden und seine Erforschung," *Blätter für deutsche und internationale Politik* 12 (2010).
18. Lawrence S. Wittner, *Towards Nuclear Abolition: A History of World Nuclear Disarmament Movement, 1971 to the Present,* vol. 3: The Struggle against the Bomb (Stanford, CA, 2003).
19. According to Carl Friedrich von Weizäcker in his 1961 speech delivered on the occasion of the award for the Friedenspreis des Deutschen Buchhandels: "Bedingungen des Friedens im technischen Zeitalter."
20. Hauswedell, *Friedenswissenschaften,* 49.
21. See the contribution by Silke Mende and Brigitte Metzger in this volume.
22. The first congress of scientists from the field of natural sciences took place in Mainz during July 1983. The title of the congress had been "Verantwortung für den Frie-

den: Naturwissenschaftler warnen vor neuer Atomrüstung" or "Responsibility for Peace: Scientists Warn about Renewed Nuclear Armament."
23. Hans-Peter Dürr, *Verantwortung für den Frieden: Naturwissenschaftler warnen vor neuer Atomrüstung* (Mainz, 2–3 July 1983) (Hamburg, 1983),18.
24. Victor F. Weisskopf, "Europa trägt Verantwortung," in Dürr, *Verantwortung*, 32.
25. E. P. Thompson, *Beyond the Cold War* (London, 1982).
26. Ibid., 17.
27. E. P. Thompson, "Appeal for European Nuclear Disarmament" (founding statement of European Nuclear Disarmament [END]), 1980.
28. Jost Dülffer, "Die Protestbewegungen gegen Wiederbewaffnung 1951–55 und atomare Aufrüstung 1957/58 in der Bundesrepublik Deutschland: Ein Vergleich," in *Im Zeichen der Gewalt: Frieden und Krieg im 19. und 20. Jahrhundert*, ed. Jost Dülffer (Cologne, 2003), 205; Marianne Zepp, "Weiblichkeit als politisches Argument: Frieden und Demokratie im Übergang zu einer deutschen Nachkriegsgesellschaft," in *Frieden durch Demokratie: Genese, Wirkung und Kritik eines Deutungsmusters*, ed. Jost Dülffer and Gottfried Niedhart (Essen, 2011), 204–5.
29. Dülffer already observed a conjunction between the national question and the concept of peace right after the founding of the two German states in 1949.
30. For example the Gesamtdeutsche Volkspartei founded by Gustav Heinemann and Helene Wessel.
31. Dülffer, "Protestbewegungen," 210.
32. Peter Brandt and Detlef Lehnert, "Die 'Deutsche Frage' in der europäischen Geschichte und Gegenwart," in *Deutsche Fragen: Europäische Antworten*, ed. Ulrich Albrecht et al. Schriftenreihe des AK atomwaffenfreies Europa e.V., Bd. 2. (Berlin, 1983), 19–41.
33. Ibid.
34. Alexander and Margarete (Nielsen-) Mitscherlich, *Die Unfähigkeit zu trauern: Grundlagen kollektiven Verhaltens* (Munich, 1967).
35. Ulrike Jureit and Christian Schneider, *Gefühlte Opfer: Illusionen der Vergangenheitsbewältigung* (Stuttgart, 2010), 110–11.
36. Horst-Eberhard Richter, *Patient Familie: Entstehung, Struktur und Therapie von Konflikten in Ehe und Familie* (Hamburg, 1970).
37. "Engagierte Analysen," interview Horst-Eberhadt Richters with Elena Pasca, 1 February 2005, http://www.psychanalyse.lu/articles/RichterInterview.htm.
38. Hauswedell, *Friedenswissenschaften*, 198–99. More popular was the approach taken by Margarete Mitscherlich. She carried the theory of aggression into the women's peace movement. In her book *Die friedfertige Frau* [The peaceful sex] (Frankfurt am Main, 1985), she combined results from recent aggression research with feminist positions and asked women to change their behavior. The book was very successful but also controversial. The author was accused of taking an identitary position.
39. Ulrich Albrecht et al., eds., *Deutsche Fragen: Europäische Antworten* (Schriftenreihe des AK atomwaffenfreies Europa e.V., Bd. 2.) (Berlin, 1983).
40. Albrecht et al., preface to *Deutsche Fragen*, 7.
41. Brandt and Lehnert, "Die 'Deutsche Frage',", in Albrecht et al, *Deutsche Fragen*, 38.
42. Professor for International Relations and Foreign Policy, Universität Köln.

43. Thomas Jäger, "Unvermuteter Nationalismus—friedensbewegter Nationalismus?" *Vorgänge* 25 (1986): Heft 6, 82–93.
44. Ibid., 84.
45. Ibid., 89.
46. Dan Diner, "Die 'nationale Frage' in der Friedensbewegung: Ursprünge und Tendenzen," in *Die neue Friedensbewegung: Analysen aus der Friedensforschung*, ed. Reiner Steinweg (Frankfurt am Main, 1982), 86–112.
47. Ibid., 88.
48. Holger Nehring and Benjamin Ziemann, "Führen alle Wege nach Moskau? Der NATO-Doppelbeschluss und die Friedensbewegung. Eine Kritik," *Vierteljahreshefte für Zeitgeschichte* 59 (2010): 81–99.
49. Günter Gaus also warns against "German-German rainbow chasing cloud shenanigans." His thoughts about illusions, irrationalism, and idealistic fanaticism can be found in "Wir dürfen an den Einflusssphären in Europa nicht rühren," in Albrecht et al, *Deutsche Fragen* 67–75.
50. Andreas Buro, "Kann die 'neue' von der 'alten' Friedensbewegung lernen?" in *Die neue Friedensbewegung: Analysen aus der Friedensforschung* (Friedensanalysen 16) (Frankfurt am Main, 1982), 407.
51. Again, it is Gaus who, while pleading for rationality in all matters of peace, points out that it is ultimately the government and its agencies that carry the responsibility for decisive action. Günter Gaus, "Einflusssphären in Europa [Spheres of influence in Europe], in Albrecht et al, *Deutsche Fragen* 68.
52. See also the contribution by Kathrin Fahlenbrach and Laura Stapane in this volume.
53. Christoph Becker-Schaum deals with the institutions of the peace movement in this volume.
54. Ulrike C. Wasmuht, *Friedensbewegungen der 80er Jahre: Zur Analyse ihrer strukturellen und aktuellen Entstehungsbedingungen in der BRD und den Vereinigten Staaten von Amerika nach 1945. Ein Vergleich* (Gießen, 1987), 22–23.
55. Ibid., 31.
56. Joachim Raschke, *Soziale Bewegungen: Ein historisch-systematischer Grundriss* (Frankfurt am Main, 1985), 13.
57. Ziemann, *Perspektiven*, 23.
58. Dülffer, "Protestbewegungen," 205; Nehring and Ziemann, "Führen alle Wege," 98.
59. The emotional history of the peace movement is beyond the scope of this paper. For this topic see Bernd Greiner, Christian T. Müller, and Dierk Walter, eds., *Angst im Kalten Krieg* (Hamburg, 2009).
60. Ziemann, *Perspektiven*, 25.
61. A case in point is when Anton-Andreas Guha began his speech by saying that he would accept "a vague representation … for the Peace Movement" by talking publicly. Guha's ideas, including his criticism of the security policy and the decision reached in Brussels, are to be found in Sozialdemokratische Partei Deutschlands, ed., *Sicherheitspolitk contra Frieden? Ein Forum zur Friedensbewegung* (Berlin and Bonn, 1981).
62. Peter Schlotter, ed., *Die neue Friedensbewegung: Analysen aus der Friedensforschung* (Friedensanalysen Bd. 16) (Frankfurt am Main, 1982). Einführung, 9–12. Peter

Schlotter "Zur Zukunft der Friedensbewegung: Rahmenbedingungen alternativer Politik," in Steinweg, *Die Neue Friedensbewegung,* 16–33.
63. Ulrich Albrecht, "Neutralismus und Disengagement: Ist Blockfreiheit eine Alternative für die Bundesrepublik?" in: Albrecht et al, *Deutsche Fragen,* 98.
64. See Stephan Tiedtke, "Wider den kurzen Atem: Thesen zur sicherheitspoltischen Strategie der Friedensbewegung," in Schlotter, *Friedensbewegung,* 35.
65. Ibid., 34–53.
66. Dieter Senghaas is a social scientist and peace researcher born in 1940. Between 1972 and 1978 he was head of a research group at the Hessian Foundation for Peace and Conflict Studies. Since 1978 he has been a professor at the University of Bremen.
67. Senghaas, *Der Frieden,* 88.

Select Bibliography

Hauswedell offers a presentation on the development and establishment of peace research and peace studies. Wasmuth compares the peace movement in West Germany and the United States at the later stages and provides a categorization based on structural characteristics of social movements. An interpretation of the analysis by Galtung can be found in Krippendorf and Galtung. Ziemann is the first to offers a proper historical perspective on the peace movement and Gassert summarizes recent research.

Dülffer, Jost, and Gottfried Niedhart, eds. *Frieden durch Demokratie: Genese, Wirkung und Kritik eines Deutungsmusters.* Essen, 2011.

Gassert, Philipp, Tim Geiger, and Hermann Wentker, eds. *Zweiter Kalter Krieg und Friedensbewegung: Der Nato-Doppelbeschluss in deutsch-deutscher und internationaler Perspektive.* Munich, 2011.

Galtung, Johan. *Modelle zum Frieden: Methoden und Ziele der Friedensforschung.* Wuppertal, 1972.

Hauswedell, Corinna. *Friedenswissenschaften im Kalten Krieg: Friedensforschung und friedenswissenschaftliche Initiativen in der Bundesrepublik Deutschland in den achtziger Jahren.* Baden-Baden, 1997.

Krippendorff, Ekkehart, ed. *Friedensforschung.* Cologne and Berlin, 1968.

Wasmuth, Ulrike C. *Friedensbewegungen der 80er Jahre: Zur Analyse ihrer strukturellen und aktuellen Entstehungsbedingungen in der BRD und den Vereinigten Staaten von Amerika nach 1945. Ein Vergleich.* Gießen, 1987.

Ziemann, Benjamin, ed. *Perspektiven der Historischen Friedensforschung.* Essen 2002.

Chapter 8

The Institutional Organization of the Peace Movement

Christoph Becker-Schaum

The peace movement was not an organization in the traditional sense. There were no members, no board, no statutes, and no ledger. It was a movement encompassing organizations of different kinds, working within various domains, and allowing for different levels of involvement. Formal membership was not required; those who took an interest were welcome to participate without further commitment. Although there was no board of directors, there were those who took on responsibility and there were rules to be followed—only in this sense did the peace movement resemble an institutional organization. Tracing its history reveals the organizational requirements of the peace movement, the largest political movement in the Federal Republic of Germany.

The Organizational Network of the Peace Movement

When the German parliament sanctioned the deployment of Pershing II and cruise missiles in November 1983 there was hardly any city in West Germany that did not have at least one grassroots action group for peace. The total number in the entire country is estimated to have been between four and five thousand,[1] an order of magnitude that seems plausible only when one considers that the thirty organizations then comprising the peace movement's Coordinating Committee could muster the support of up to 3,100 local and regional action groups, and that no less than 1,900 action groups had signed the call for a peace demonstration in Bonn in June 1982.[2] The surprisingly large number of action groups countrywide indicates a first peculiarity of the peace movement. The increasing support for the movement did not result in the growth of individual groups but rather in the set-up of new groups. It worked like a pyramid sales scheme and led, for example, to no less than sixty local groups participating in a blockade protest in the university town of Münster in October 1983. In other parts of the country the network of interlinked action groups was far less dense.

Such examples do not yield a realistic estimate of the number of people actually involved. Methods to determine the number of participants in the peace movement vary: one may distinguish between active members and sympathizers,[3] or differentiate among participants willing to sign a proclamation, those ready to participate in a demonstration, and those prepared to get involved in a campaign of civil disobedience.[4] Signing a proclamation required less commitment than taking part in a demonstration. Taking part in a blockade protest of a missile site involved the risk of being arrested, charged, and sentenced by a court, and participants were often asked to attend a training session to prepare for the event. Such commitment requires careful consideration. The figures available express different levels of commitment and willingness to take risks. Some eight hundred persons were taken into custody at Mutlangen in the first six weeks after the deployment of the Pershing II for taking part in a nonviolent protest demonstration,[5] but about 400,000 persons attended a mass demonstration in Bonn on 10 June 1982[6] and the number of those who signed the Krefeld Appeal was more than ten times this figure.[7]

Opinion polls offer information on active members of the peace movement in contrast to sympathizers. They are based primarily on self-assessments of respondents. In 1983 more than three million people were recorded as active members. Four years later, during the national election in 1987, political scientist Franz Urban Pappi estimated a "hard core" of at least 1.8 million active supporters of the peace movement.[8] Approximately 1.3 million people took to the streets in November 1983 to protest against the deployment decision by the German parliament. They were certainly aware that the majority of the West German population was sympathetic to their cause: depending on the survey, anywhere up to 75 percent of the voting population was opposed to the stationing of new medium-range missiles within their country's borders.[9] This was the peak moment in the mobilization of citizens on behalf of the peace movement. Taken together, the reported numbers of activists in attendance at peace demonstrations suggest the unusual breadth of the movement's social anchoring. The figures are linked to each other in a very pragmatic way. Without the dense network of grassroots action groups for peace with their information desks in pedestrian zones, at markets, and in front of town halls, no signatures could have been collected. And without their publicity efforts, there would not have been 400,000 people at the demonstration in Bonn. The four to five thousand action groups made up the local institutional base of the peace movement. Yet, despite a widely shared claim that they worked on grassroots democratic principles, there is little known to date about individual local groups and initiatives.[10]

Much more attention has been directed toward the peace movement's Coordinating Committee. It initially represented twenty-one organizations. This grew to twenty-six, then thirty, and later contracted to twenty-seven. The Coordinating Committee's member organizations were nominated for the first time at the Action Conference on 4 April 1982 in Bonn. They were responsible for the organizational and political preparation of the mass peace demonstration scheduled for 10 June 1982 in the same city. The peace movement's Action Conferences were open to everybody. There was no delegate system. Thus the conferences did not necessarily represent the opinion of the majority of the supporters, but they better reflected the growing appeal of such a nationwide grassroots meeting. The first five Action Conferences were staged between February 1982 and April 1983 and were attended by some 600 to 850 people. The number of participants soared at the following meeting in November 1983 to 1,500 and in February 1984 shrank to 1,300, before retracting to approximately 800 at subsequent events.[11] Between 1982 and 1989, thirteen Action Conferences were held, at first in the capital Bonn and later (from the third one onward) in Cologne. The Coordinating Committee had an Executive Committee of six members, also nominated at the Action Conferences. Formally the six-member Executive Committee was requested by the Action Conference to assume the day-to-day management of its activities. All members of the Coordinating Committee and the Executive Committee were thus representatives of organizations and associations operating nationally.

Apart from the national Coordinating Committee with its permanent office in Bonn, there were a number of regional networks,[12] some of which also maintained offices (e.g., the Peace Office Hanover). These were not only in big cities but also in rural areas (e.g., in the town of Kastellaun in Hunsrück). On the one hand, regional agencies had a pivotal role in information exchanges between the Executive Committee, Coordinating Committee, and local action groups. On the other hand, the fact that there were so many regional peace groups reflects a grassroots democratic view of politics shared by the movement's members, many of whom harbored a profound distrust of centralized decision-making structures, including the Coordinating Committee, and of the media interest that such large offices attracted.[13] One example of this skepticism is found in a brochure published on 10 June 1982 by the Tübingen Association for Peace Education on the occasion of the Bonn demonstration held the same day that stated, "There is no central organizing body for the peace movement … The peace movement is a decentralized grassroots movement."[14] This assessment notwithstanding, it should be

Formen der Willensbildung und Entscheidungsfindung in der Friedensbewegung

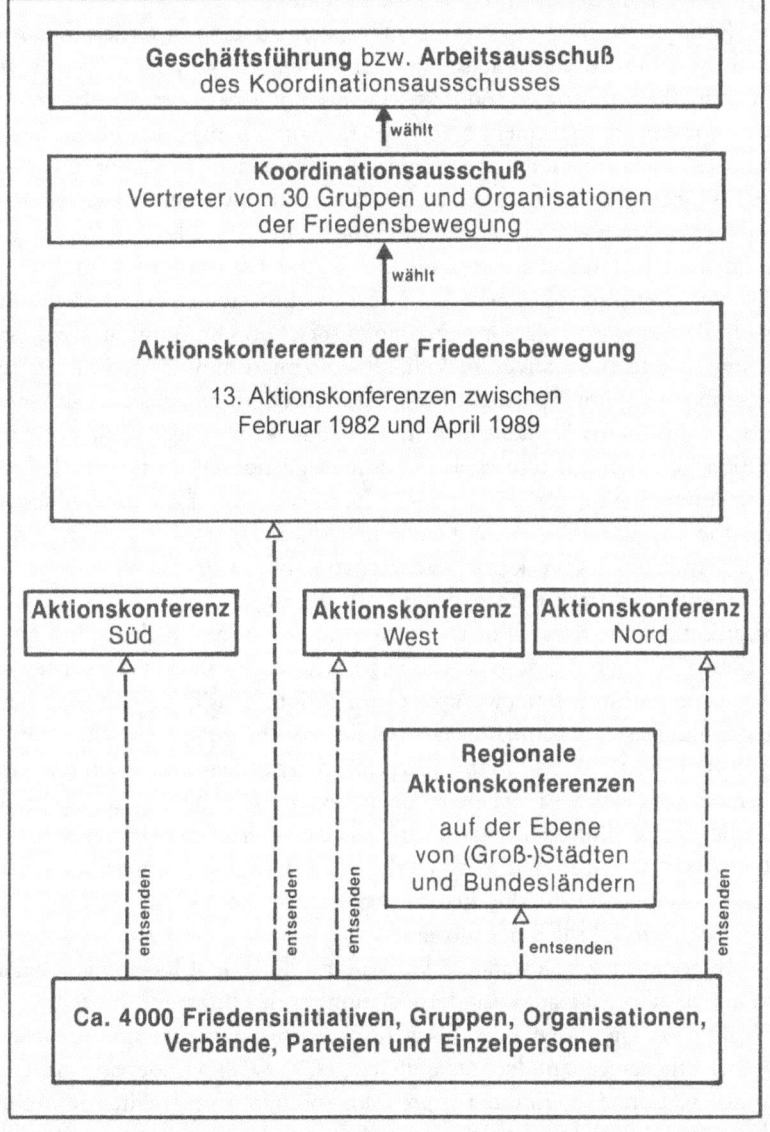

Figure 8.1. Forms of interest aggregation and decision-making in the peace movement (Adapted from Thomas Leif, *Die professionelle Bewegung: Die Friedensbewegung von innen* [Bonn, 1985].)

said that all the major demonstrations were in fact organized with the help of the Coordinating Committee. The triad of grassroots initiatives, regional networks, and central coordination made up the (far from tension-free) institutional framework of the peace movement.

In the 1980s the peace movement was defined less by a vertical hierarchy than by its horizontal dimension: its truly remarkable political and social breadth. The unrestricted cooperation and—not always easy—collaboration within the peace movement among participants as diverse as liberal Christians, feminists, members of the alternative movement and labor unions, as well as Liberals, Social Democrats, Socialists, and Communists was a singular and extraordinarily significant event in the history of the Federal Republic of Germany. The Green Party, founded in 1979–80, was a further addition to this heterogeneous movement.[15] This cooperation stood in marked contrast to the 1970s when collaboration among social opposition groups was prevented by numerous forces, including the dogmatism of the radical left and its numerous splinter parties, the alienation brought on by the self-imposed exile of the alternative movement from mainstream society, militancy from sections of urban subcultures, as well as the vigilance reflected in the Radicals Decree banning supposed "enemies of the constitution" from the civil service and the impact of Red Army Fraction (RAF) terrorism.[16] The peace movement represented a break from the stagnation of the 1970s.

Considered from the perspective of the peace movement's institutional organization, the breadth of the movement was a real challenge insofar as it forced individual groups to cooperate with each other in a balanced relationship within a framework of coordination. Sensitivity to other views and willingness to assimilate were two sides of the same coin. The political groups of the 1970s had found such receptivity difficult. Just as the vertical hierarchy of the peace movement guaranteed the legitimacy of key decisions, the horizontal dimension was not merely a matter of practical expediency. The overall political credibility of the peace movement was at stake. The key words here are the dominance of particular groups and the control or remote-control of the peace movement.[17]

In addition to the standard vertical and horizontal hierarchies characteristic of all organizations and associations, a third dimension needs to be taken into account: dynamics. Social organizations swimming in the currents of social movements undergo major changes. They tend to develop great enthusiasm, a drive to criticize the prevailing politics, and a desire to promote their increasingly radical objectives, and they end up coming across as completely transformed organizations. Simultaneously new organizations, subgroups within the current organization as well as competing organizations, are set up and they establish new objectives and mobilize new supporters.

After pursuing these objectives over a period of months or years, the momentum dissipates, groups break up, and some sort of normality returns. The peace movement was a movement in this dynamic sense. In political discourse today, "social movement" has become a self-designation of groups perceiving themselves to be in radical opposition to the political system.[18] This definition of a social movement does not apply to the peace movement of the 1980s. According to Franz Urban Pappi's analysis, it was distinguished by its pluralistic and evolving character.[19]

Finally it should be pointed out that the time factor and major events had an influence on shaping the institutional structure and dynamics of the peace movement. The NATO Double-Track Decision of 12 December 1979 created an ideal situation for mobilizing mass protests because the deployment was not to take place until four years after the decision was reached.[20] On the other hand, fixating on the prevention of deployment presented a strategic risk. What if the deployment of new American medium-range missiles could not be prevented? In this respect, insistence on the so-called minimal consensus (the agreement that the one common cause was the prevention of deployment) led to a political impasse. A radicalization of the goals and the creative expansion of forms of protest was the peace movement's defense against possible failure.

The Establishment of the Peace Movement (1975–81)

Andrei S. Markovits and Philip S. Gorski discern four phases in the development of the peace movement.[21] The first phase ends in 1979 and was shaped on the one hand by the emergence of new peace movement organizations, namely the Aktionsgemeinschaft Dienst für den Frieden (AGDF, Action Committee Service for Peace), the Aktion Sühnezeichen/Friedensdienste (ASF, Action Reconciliation Service for Peace), both Christian organizations, and the Komitee für Frieden, Abrüstung, und Zusammenarbeit, (KOFAZ, Committee for Peace, Disarmament, and Cooperation) with strong links to the Deutsche Kommunistische Partei (DKP, German Communist Party), and on the other hand by the "first appearance of autonomous and grassroots social associations in the new peace movement."[22] AGDF, ASF, and KOFAZ thus had the advantage of being first on the ground. In the second phase, stretching from the NATO Double-Track Decision to the mass demonstrations of 1981, the social composition of the peace movement took shape: participants included former conservatives like Alfred Mechtersheimer and Gert Bastian, as well as *Ökopax* (the ecology and peace alliance) of the Bundesverband Bürgerinitiativen Umweltschutz (BBU, Association of Citizens' Initiatives for Environmental Protection), the Green Party, numerous Christian organizations, the left wing of the Social Democratic Party (SPD), the DKP, and finally "independent" or "autonomous" grassroots organizations.[23] The authors differentiate between the third and fourth phase of the peace movement with the change having occurred in the summer of 1983. This date seems critical as it marks the beginning of "independent" and "autonomous" groups planning their own "resistance operations" against the missile deployment, a move said to have threatened the unity and effectiveness of the peace movement.[24]

This outline is indeed helpful. However, there is presumably a connection between the institutional formation of the movement and its practical politics and thus a three-part division of phases is more convincing. The first phase would then describe the formation of the peace movement beginning in 1975, the second would deal with the mass demonstrations of 1981 and 1982, and a third phase would cover the onset of decentralization in the summer of 1983 with a pronounced shift of protest actions to missile deployment sites.

The balance between the various groups and currents within the peace movement was a prerequisite for its success. There are a number of indications that these conditions were in place before the NATO Double-Track Decision was taken. The major changes were caused by: (1) a new receptiveness of the environmental movement toward the objectives of the peace movement, (2) the hesitant willingness of the Christian peace movement to cooperate with communist organizations, (3) the cooperation of communist organizations within a framework of the German Communist Party (DKP) alliance policy, and (4) the search by the newly founded Green Party for suitable alliance partners that would make it more attractive to disaffected supporters of the Social Democratic Party of Germany.

The receptiveness of the BBU to the objectives of the peace movement was closely linked to the personal commitment of Roland Vogt, member of the BBU's executive board. The BBU and its president, Hans-Helmuth Wüstenhagen, had at an early stage pointed out the connection between nuclear power plants and the production of weapons-grade plutonium. Yet the linkage between civilian and military uses of nuclear energy remained a difficult topic. A proposal by Vogt in 1975 to stage the Easter march close to the nuclear reactor site in Wyhl in order to address openly the relationship between civil and military uses of nuclear power was declined by local citizens' groups. They feared being associated with left-wing factions. In 1978 the BBU initiated a task group against civilian and military uses of nuclear facilities and passed a resolution to "offer resistance to military as well as civilian nuclear facilities in the future."[25] In October 1979 BBU and the Deutsche Friedensgesellschaft—Vereinigte KriegsdienstgegnerInnen (DFG-VK, German Peace Society—United War Resisters) jointly organized a congress entitled "Ecology and Peace Movement," which indicated the beginning of an organizational cooperation between the two movements.[26] This cooperation was not unanimously supported by BBU members. A BBU chairman, Hans Günter Schumacher, was a civilian employee of the armed forces and under considerable pressure. He justified his decision not to stand for reelection in 1980 by saying that he could not support the recent developments within the BBU ecology and peace section.[27] There was also resistance from the antimilitaristic left, which refused for some time to add the rejection of nuclear power plants to the list of demands at the Easter marches.[28]

BBU Chairman Schumacher's reservations were due not only to his personal situation as shown by the general ambivalence of the Christian peace movement. Volkmar Deile, managing director of ASF, wrote a personal statement commenting that the Berlin blockade, the Berlin Wall, the violent suppressions of the Hungarian uprising, and the Prague Spring were reasons for the prevalence of anticommunism among open-minded Christian communities, despite the threat to mankind from a military arms race of insane dimensions. It was the real-life consequences of the Soviet Union's policy and its participation in the arms race that nourished anticommunist sentiments. The deadlock in the work for peace caused by prevailing anticommunism could therefore be broken only by open criticism of the Soviet Union. If the movement wanted to break free of its present restrictions, it would have to be allowed to denounce the "misdirected developments in the Soviet Union." "This is not the end of cooperation with communists in peace work," Deile said, "but a beginning, with clear-cut conditions."[29]

One of the lessons learned in the 1970s was that the German Communist Party (DKP) would not form alliances with organizations that had criticized it as openly as Volkmar Deile did in the example above. A change in strategy altered this pattern. The "concept [by the Ministry for State Security of East Germany] for politically active measures to promote the peace movement in West Germany" made specific recommendations about conspiratorial action with regard to a number of groups within the West German peace movement and also referred to the DKP's alliance strategy. The paper stressed an important point: "The content and structural diversity of the peace movement needs be taken into account." This was elaborated as follows: "It can be assumed that slogans, reasoning, and arguments put forth by alternative peace groups are substantively and rhetorically sound."[30] This flexible approach toward other organizations was, in the opinion of the authors, strategically advantageous for the DKP. "The development of different groups within the broad political spectrum of the peace movements offers the DKP favorable grounds for successful alliances."[31]

The new strategic concept was thus in line with the parameters of KOFAZ, which sought to influence the West German public toward a favorable view of Soviet positions in the CSCE process by enlisting the help of well-known public figures.[32] Party strategists considered that showing willingness to cooperate with other political currents in the context of the peace movement was not only expedient in respect to a prevention of the deployment of Pershing II and cruise missiles, but it was also desirable for the forthcoming federal election. The election in 1983 proved to be a debacle in the history of the DKP, since it won only 0.2 percent of the votes. Instead, it was the Green Party that was seen as the party of the environmental and peace movements, and so it entered parliament for the first time.

It is all the more remarkable that the Green Party participated in the communist-controlled Krefeld Initiative, the organization of which was in the hands of the Deutsche Friedensunion (DFU, German Peace Union),[33] a follow-up organization of the outlawed Communist Party of Germany. In fact, technically speaking, it was not the Green Party but Petra Kelly as an individual who joined it. But at the time Kelly was one of the three elected co-spokespersons. She informed the party committees—the Federal Executive Board and Bundeshauptausschuss (BHA, Federal Committee)—after the fact. The Green Party's minutes suggest that the rest of the leaders were not pleased about its chairperson's unilateral decision.[34] However, the Federal Executive Board and the Federal Committee subsequently supported her unanimously and even endorsed her future dealings with the Krefeld Initiative at the same time pointing to the exemplary significance of the BBU's cooperation "with all the forces of the peace movement in Germany."[35] The minutes of the Federal Executive Board meeting of 11 January 1981 included an item on the agenda about peace policy with respect to the Social Democratic Party (SPD) as its principle target group, one-sided support for the Krefeld Appeal would have been counterproductive.[36] Yet, within the Green Party, Kelly's accession to the Krefeld Initiative remained controversial, much to her irritation. The Green Party supported the call of the Russell Peace Foundation, which was aimed at the United States and simultaneously at the Soviet Union, with far more enthusiasm. Kelly demanded equal recognition for both initiatives and did not wish to see one singled out to the detriment of the other. She also warned against a hasty labeling of the Krefeld Initiative as a communist-controlled endeavor and emphasized how Gert Bastian influenced the adopted resolutions. Meanwhile the federal government claimed that membership in the Krefeld Initiative put Kelly and

Bastian in the communist camp.[37] Kelly and Bastian left the Krefeld Initiative in January 1984.

All four cases demonstrate a growing willingness to cross ideological borders. In each case this was in the political interest of the association, and was confined to the pursuit of specific objectives. There was no newly found mutual sympathy at play when, beginning in the 1980s, representatives of organizations from a plethora of bodies gathered to take on the task of coordinating and controlling mass demonstrations for the peace movement.

The Mass Demonstrations of the Peace Movement (1981–82)

The era of mass demonstrations and the history of the Coordinating Committee began with the Protestant Church Congress in Hamburg. On the last day of this event, 19 June 1981, Volkmar Deile of the ASF and Ulrich Frey of the AGDF met with representatives of twenty other organizations—a mix of Christian, ecological, pacifist, and communist groups—to discuss the planned demonstration and rally in Bonn on 10 October 1981.[38] At this meeting the final wording of the call for the demonstration was agreed upon, after preapproval from several of the participants involved. Further, it was agreed that on 13 July and 27 August 1981 there would be preparatory meetings with the local peace advocacy groups in Bonn. Ninety-five representatives attended the first meeting; and "340 organizations and groups that had signed up for the call as of that date"[39] were invited to the second meeting. The entire responsibility for the organization, financial support, and content remained exclusively with the ASF and the AGDF, and the inclusion of the remaining 340 organizations and groups was aimed at ensuring the support of the entire "breadth of the peace movement."[40] Thus there were two levels of participation: first, the two organizations responsible along with an inner-circle of another twenty organizations that prepared all necessary steps; and second, the bulk of the hundreds of local action groups that made up the entire spectrum of the peace movement. Some groups regarded this structure as hierarchical and voiced criticism. Those with more radical demands felt excluded.[41] The entire effort was geared toward launching the demonstration on 10 October 1981 and a consecutive rally in the Hofgarten in Bonn. Afterward this, the confederation would be dissolved.

The consultations in the inner-circle were resumed shortly after the demonstration, however. Ulrich Frey recalled, "At that time we were urged to continue, to push on and to coordinate the peace movement. We rejected this idea because we did not want to impede the development of a broad popular movement. We then … recognized that it was necessary to meet for informal discussions among the circle of groups from October 10 and thus resumed these breakfast meetings."[42] The advantage of a breakfast meeting was its unrestrained character, which allowed for an informal exchange. This was, however, also a drawback. There was no transparency about agreements and the formal legitimacy of the meeting remained unclear. Legitimacy was achieved in the process, as no political camp was dominant and thus all parties aspired to find consensus,[43] a classic example of output legitimacy. Smaller independent groups and initiatives within the peace movement, however, looked upon this with suspicion and felt excluded, while more powerful organizations, many of which were associated with the Social Democratic Party, were present at the breakfast talks.[44]

The final arrangement made by AGDF and ASF was an invitation to an Action Conference scheduled for 6–7 February 1982 in Bonn, which had been initialized in the breakfast talks. This Action Conference elected a Coordinating Committee and an Executive Committee to provide the lacking organizational legitimacy to the movement. From the independent initiatives' point of view, however, nothing had changed, since the participants of the breakfast talks and the Coordinating Committee were practically identical. The overall structure of the peace movement remained the same as it had been during the time of the breakfast talks and the two preparatory meetings for the demonstration of 10 October 1981. The Action Conference served primarily as a forum for the exchange of ideas and had little to do with political resolutions or programs. The organizational and financial responsibility assumed by the ASF and AGDF in October 1981 now passed to the Coordinating Committee.

The first Coordinating Committee comprised the following organizations: Arbeitsgemeinschaft Katholischer Hochschul- und Studentengemeinden (Union of Catholic Higher Education and Student Organizations), Bundeskongress Autonomer Friedensinitiativen (BAF, Federal Congress of Autonomous Peace Initiatives), the Bundeskongress Entwicklungspolitischer Aktionsgruppen (BUKO, Federal Congress of Development Policy Action Groups), BBU, DFG-VK, Demokratische Sozialisten (DS, Democratic Socialists), Deutsche Jungdemokraten (German Young Democrats), Evangelische Studentengemeinden (ESG, Protestant Student Communities), Föderation gewaltfreier Aktionsgruppen (FÖGA, Federation of Nonviolent Action Groups), Frauen für den Frieden (Women for Peace), the Green Party, KOFAZ, Konferenz der Landesschülervertretungen (Conference of the State Student Unions), Russell Initiatives, Sozialistische Deutsche Arbeiterjugend (SDAJ, Socialist German Workers Youth), Sozialistische Jugend Deutschlands—Die Falken (SJD, Socialist Youth of Germany—the Falcons), and Vereinigte Deutsche Studentenschaften (VDS, United German Student Bodies).[45] Also among the founding members were the Christian ASF, AGDF, Ohne Rüstung Leben (ORL, Living without Arms), and the Young Socialists, but these four organizations did not support the demonstration at the NATO-summit in Bonn and thus withdrew from the Coordinating Committee.[46] Even without the Christian peace initiatives and the Young Socialists, the communist organizations were not in a dominant position. Rather, Günter Bannas's commentary in the conservative newspaper *Frankfurter Allgemeine Zeitung* about the subsequent Coordinating Committee holds true: "It is generally said that the DKP with its apparatus does not control the peace movement, but on the contrary that the other groups make use of the DKP apparatus for their own purposes."[47]

The original Executive Committee consisted of Tissy Bruns (VDS), Peter Grohmann (ESG), Jo Leinen (BBU), Klaus Mannhardt (DFG-VK), Eva Quistorp (Women for Peace), and Werner Rätz (BUKO). Two of its members belonged to groups affiliated with the German communist parties, the other four members decidedly not. However, these numbers are beside the point when we look at the actual procedures of the Coordinating Committee and Executive Committee. The essential factor remained the determination to find consensus among the committees. Eva Quistorp, who had already attended the first meeting of the Hamburg Church Congress and would serve on the Executive Committee until 1986, described the function of the committee to be the task of "thinking ahead" and of searching for "compromise" and "potential solutions."[48]

The Decentralization of the Peace Movement (1983–86)

The activities of the first Coordinating Committee ended with the demonstration on 10 June 1982. Volkmar Deile and Ulrich Frey once again took the initiative to resume talks about future projects. The Coordinating Committee grew gradually to twenty-six members and finally to thirty as new organizations were invited to attend meetings. The Executive Committee remained the same, apart from the fact that the ASF took the place of the ESG. Preparations followed the same pattern as in the previous year, and the Action Conference convened on 16–17 April 1983 to discuss in workshops the autumn campaigns for the same year.[49] The Action Conference decided to arrange "parallel public meetings to promote peace in Bonn and in southern and northern Germany," and split responsibilities for the first time, a move that had been particularly requested by representatives from the independent peace initiatives. The Coordinating Committee and Executive Committee

Figure 8.2. Poster Menschen- und Aktionskette für Frieden & Arbeit von Duisburg nach Hasselbach 20 Oktober 1984 (Human chain for peace & work from Duisburg to Hasselbach, 20 October 1984) (BArch Plak 007-021-040)

remained responsible for Bonn, but regional assemblies took on responsibility for public gatherings in the south and the north of the Federal Republic.[50]

Decentralization became the hallmark of the weeks of demonstrating in the fall of 1983.[51] The emphasis rested on various forms of direct action: long human chains stretching across the Swabian Alps, around the Department of Defense in Bonn, and a US military base in Bremerhaven. Blockades in front of the Pershing II base in Mutlangen and other acts of civil disobedience required much more detailed preparation and a more active role from all participants than did mass demonstrations. Klaus Vack, who was in charge of organizing a so-called blockade of celebrities that included dedicated writers like Heinrich Böll and Günter Grass in September 1983, revealed some twenty-five years later the efforts necessary in planning the event.[52] Groups of several hundred experienced activists had each, as it were, adopted a handful of celebrities for a few hours. This enabled public figures to participate in such protests.

The same decentralized strategies applied from 1984 on to protests at sites destined for the deployment of cruise missiles in Hasselbach in the Hunsrück region and in equal measure to actions intended to hinder military maneuvers in the Fulda Gap. Responsibility rested with local groups and regional associations that had no representation in the Coordinating Committee. This decentralization of protests resulted in a certain detachment of the Coordinating Committee and its members from the base of peace initiatives.[53] This detachment of the upper echelons of the movement from the grassroots is specifically illustrated in events that took place at Wüschheim/Hasselbach,[54] a depot for ninety-six cruise missiles that were supposed to be stationed in Germany. On 20 October 1985, a record-breaking human chain stretched the entire distance from Hasselbach to Duisburg. One year later, Hasselbach became the venue of the last major peace rally before the cruise missiles were withdrawn and scrapped in 1988. Approximately 200,000 people attended the demonstration in Hasselbach on 11 October 1986. The Coordinating Committee's resolution for the demonstration included a statement that said the local peace group had to approve any protest action that involved civil disobedience.

Conclusion

The institutional organization of the peace movement was directly dependent on the willingness of the groups within the various political factions to cooperate fairly, and this collaboration in turn was subject to the willingness of the various organizations to accommodate opposition movements in the communist countries of Central and Eastern Europe. It was nevertheless possible to work within the parameters established by a minimal consensus until November 1983, when the German parliament reached a decision about deployment. Until then, the entire strategy of the peace movement was aimed at a revision of the West German opinion about the NATO Double-Track Decision. Afterward the strategy of the peace movement shifted to the sites where a deployment of intermediate-range nuclear missile was intended. The Coordinating Committee was ill prepared for this shift as its role of representing political currents within the peace movement far outweighed its function as a parliament for the interests of local and regional peace initiatives.

Christoph Becker-Schaum is Research Associate at the Leibniz Center of Contemporary History in Potsdam. He has previously taught courses on European parties and party systems at the Otto-Suhr-Institute of Political Science at the Free University of Berlin. His publications include *Arnold Herrmann Ludwig Heeren: Ein Beitrag zur Geschichte der Geschichtswissenschaft zwischen Aufklärung und Historismus* (1993); "Von der Protestbewegung zur demokratischen Alternative: Die Grünen Hessen 1979–2004," in *Hessen. 60 Jahre Demokratie. Beiträge zum Landesjubiläum,* ed. Helmut Berding and Klaus Eiler (2006), 151–87.

Notes

1. Ulrike Wasmuht, *Friedensbewegungen der 80er Jahre. Zur Analyse ihrer strukturellen und aktuellen Entstehungsbedingungen in der Bundesrepublik Deutschland und den Vereinigten Staaten von Amerika nach 1945: Ein Vergleich* (Gießen, 1987), 171; Thomas Leif, "Entscheidungsstrukturen in der westdeutschen Friedensbewegung," *Leviathan* no. 4 (1989): 554; Ulrich Frey, "Erfahrungen der Friedensbewegung mit dem Staat Bundesrepublik Deutschland," *Die neue Gesellschaft* no. 1 (1984): 30.
2. The number of supporting peace advocacy groups is documented in Koordinierungsausschuß der Friedensorganisationen, ed., *Aufstehen! Für den Frieden, Friedensdemonstration anläßlich der NATO-Gipfelkonferenz in Bonn am 10. 6. 1982* (Bornheim, 1982), 33. A table with details about the organizational subdivisions of members of the Coordinating Committee is to be found in Rüdiger Schmitt, *Die Friedensbewegung in der Bundesrepublik Deutschland: Ursachen und Bedingungen der Mobilisierung einer neuen sozialen Bewegung* (Opladen, 1990), 104.
3. Schmitt, *Friedensbewegung,* 70–78.
4. Roland Roth, "Das politische Handlungsrepertoire der neuen sozialen Bewegungen: Eine Skizze," in *Jahrbuch* 1987, ed. Komitee für Grundrechte und Demokratie (Sensbachtal, 1988), 285–86.
5. Michael Schmid, "Vor 25 Jahren: 'Prominentenblockade' am Pershing-Depot in Mutlangen," http://www.lebenshaus-alb.de/magazin/005236.html.

6. Thomas Leif, *Die professionelle Bewegung: Friedensbewegung von innen* (Bonn, 1985), 82, states 450,000 participants. Hans Günter Brauch, *Die Raketen kommen! Vom NATO-Doppelbeschluss bis zur Stationierung* (Cologne, 1983), 172, gives a number between 350,000 and 400,000.
 7. Udo Baron, Kalter Krieg, and Heißer Frieden, *Der Einfluss der SED und ihrer westdeutschen Verbündeten auf die Partei 'Die Grünen'* (Münster, 2003), 98–99.
 8. Frey, "Erfahrungen," 30. Franz Urban Pappi, "Neue soziale Bewegungen und Wahlverhalten in der Bundesrepublik," in *Wahlen und Wähler: Analysen aus Anlaß der Bundestagswahlen 1987*, ed. Max Kaase and Hans-Dieter Klingemann (Opladen, 1990), 163.
 9. All polling organizations surveyed citizens in 1983 asking about opinions on the deployment of new medium-range missiles. All but one recorded a clear objection, with disapproval rates of up to 78 percent. The Allensbach Institute for Demoskopie constitutes the exception since it is the only one to publish an approval of the deployment by German citizens; however this study was commissioned by the federal government. "Hier Mehrheit, dort Minderheit: Umfragen der Meinungsforscher zum Nato-Doppelbeschluß und ihre Widersprüche," *Der Spiegel* 35 (1983): 28–29. Other surveys that document a broad consensus of rejection are to be found in Leif, *Die professionelle Bewegung*, 13–14. See also Bruce Russett and Donald R. Deluca, "Theater Nuclear Forces: Public Opinion in Western Europe," *Political Science Quarterly* 98 (1983): 179–96.
10. The most detailed information with local relevance is provided by Susanne Schregel, *Der Atomkrieg vor der Wohnungstür: Eine Politikgeschichte der neuen Friedensbewegung in der Bundesrepublik 1970–1985* (Frankfurt am Main and New York, 2011).
11. Leif, *Die professionelle Bewegung*, 166, 178, 183, 191, 203, 210, 227, 241.
12. See figure 8.2.
13. Interview with Roland Vogt, excerpts recorded in Leif, *Die professionelle Bewegung*, 284.
14. Uli Jäger and Michael Schmid-Vöhringer, *"Wir werden nicht Ruhe geben …": Die Friedensbewegung in der Bundesrepublik Deutschland 1945–1982, Geschichte, Dokumente, Perspektiven* (Tübingen, 1982), 42.
15. On the subject of the national parties and the Green Party, see the contribution by Jan Hansen in this volume.
16. Hans-Ulrich Wehler, *Deutsche Gesellschaftsgeschichte: Bundesrepublik und DDR 1949–1990* (Munich, 2008), 317–21.
17. Hans-Peter Müller and Michael Plötz, *Ferngesteuerte Friedensbewegung? DDR und UdSSR im Kampf gegen den NATO-Doppelbeschluß* (Münster, 2004).
18. Roland Roth, *Demokratie von unten: Neue soziale Bewegungen auf dem Wege zur politischen Institution* (Cologne, 1994).
19. Pappi, "Neue soziale Bewegungen," 149.
20. The point in question was that the development and production of missiles required time. The contract for the supply of the Pershing II missile was concluded in February 1979, nine months before the NATO Double-Track Decision was reached. Brauch, *Die Raketen kommen*, 134.
21. Andrei S. Markovits and Philip S. Gorski, *The German Left: Red, Green, and Beyond* (New York, 1993), 99–106.

22. Ibid., 101.
23. Ibid., 102–4.
24. Ibid., 105–6.
25. Cited in Wolfgang Beer, "Ökologie- und Friedensbewegung: Fazit einer Wechselwirkung mit Open-end," in *antimilitarismus information* 7 (1979): iv–99.
26. See also the contribution by Silke Mende and Brigitte Metzger in this volume.
27. Markus Kaczor, "Der Bundesverband Bürgerinitiativen Umweltschutz: Geschichte einer Bewegungsorganisation unter dem Aspekt des Ziel- und Strategiewandels," Master's thesis, Universität Hamburg 1986, 78–79 in *Archiv Grünes Gedächtnis* (henceforth *AGG*), Bestand A—Dieter Rucht, Sign. 9.
28. Kaczor, "Der Bundesverband," 81. Roland Vogt repeated his call for action unsuccessfully at the meeting of the peace movement on 6–7 February 1982; Leif, *Die professionelle Bewegung*, 168. "Ich habe darauf hingewirkt, dass Ökologiebewegung und Friedensbewegung zusammenkommen," interview with Roland Vogt in Heinrich-Böll-Stiftung, *Grünes Gedächtnis 2012*, 10–31.
29. Volkmar Deile, "Gibt es für Christen eine Bedrohung aus dem Osten?" *antimilitarismus information* 9 (1979): iv, 116–119.
30. A concept for political measures to actively promote the peace movement in West Germany, 1–2 *AGG*, Bestand A—Cornelia Brinkmann, temp. sign. 12.
31. Ibid., 6. The concept with regard to its contextual significance is further discussed by Carlo Jordan, Armin Mitter, and Stefan Wolle, *Die Grünen der Bundesrepublik in der politischen Strategie der SED-Führung (Zwischenbericht)* (Berlin, 1994), 9–12 in *AGG*, Bestand B.II.2, sign. 216.
32. Baron, *Kalter Krieg*, 43–52.
33. Ibid., 86–110.
34. Petra Kelly, "Krefelder Dokumentation und persönliche Erklärung," 29–30 June 1981 in *AGG*, Bestand B.I.1, sign. 513.
35. NN., "Der nächste Kongreß der Grünen," *Die Unabhängigen* 49, 6 December 1980.
36. *AGG*, Bestand B.I.1, sign. 513.
37. Hans Apel et al., *Sicherheitspolitik contra Frieden? Ein Forum zur Friedensbewegung* (Berlin and Bonn, 1981), 29–33.
38. Leif, *Die professionelle Bewegung*, 59–67.
39. Ibid., 61.
40. Frey, interview, cited in ibid., 61.
41. Ibid., 60.
42. Frey, cited in ibid., 61.
43. Leif, "Entscheidungsstrukturen," 545.
44. Leif, *Die professionelle Bewegung*, 66–67.
45. Koordinierungsausschuß der Friedensorganisationen, ed., *Aufstehn! Für den Frieden: Friedensdemonstration anläßlich der NATO-Gipfelkonferenz in Bonn am 10.6.1982* (Bornheim, 1982), 157–58.
46. Leif, *Die professionelle Bewegung*, 68.
47. Thomas Leif, *Die strategische (Ohn-) Macht der Friedensbewegung: Kommunikations- und Entscheidungsstrukturen in den achtziger Jahren* (Opladen, 1990), 95–96.
48. Cited in Leif, *Die professionelle Bewegung*, 272.
49. Ibid., 62–65, 199.

50. Ibid., 88.
51. Tim Warneke, "Aktionsformen und Politikverständnis der Friedensbewegung: Radikaler Humanismus und die Pathosformel des Menschlichen," in *Das Alternative Milieu: Antibürgerlicher Lebensstil und linke Politik in der Bundesrepublik Deutschland und Europa 1968–1983*, ed. Sven Reichardt and Detlef Siegfried (Göttingen, 2010), 445–72.
52. Klaus Vack, "Prominentenblockade," http://www.lebenshaus-alb.de/magazin/005237.html. The topic of the celebrities' blockade is also taken up in the contribution by Kathrin Fahlenbrach and Laura Stapane in this volume.
53. On this point, see also the contribution by Susanne Schregel in this volume.
54. Schregel, *Der Atomkrieg vor der Wohnungstür*, 124–29.

Select Bibliography

The principal author is Leif, who published a study on the organization of the peace movement in 1985. He later expanded his essay into a dissertation on the capability of the peace movement to develop strategies. Four other dissertations supplement his work: Wasmuht compares the dynamics of the American and the West German peace movement, Schmitt applies American resource mobilization theory to the German peace movement, Baron analyzes communist organizations in the peace movement and the attempts by the German Democratic Republic to instrumentalize the newly founded Green Party, and finally there is the recent dissertation by Schregel about the peace movement in relation to neighborhoods. The German peace movement does not only build on experiences from the American movement, the periodization used in the chapter here is informed by Andrei S. Markovits and Philip S. Gorski and their analysis of the German peace movement presented in their book on the transformation of the German Left. Also instructive is chapter 5 of *Paradoxes of Peace: German Peace Movements since 1945* by Alice Holmes Cooper who follows the organizational innovation of the peace movement in the 1980s. Among contemporary political and sociological writers, Schaub and Schlaga and Hesse should all be consulted. Buro, a first-hand and well-informed witness to the peace movement, has written a relevant contribution to the recent handbook on social movements in Germany.

Baron, Udo. *Kalter Krieg und heißer Frieden: Der Einfluss der SED und ihrer westdeutschen Verbündeten auf die Partei 'Die Grünen'*. Münster, 2003.
Buro, Andreas. "Friedensbewegung," in *Die sozialen Bewegungen in Deutschland seit 1945*, ed. Roland Roth and Dieter Rucht, 267–91. Frankfurt am Main and New York, 2008.
Cooper, Alice Holmes. *Paradoxes of Peace: German Peace Movements since 1945*. Ann Arbor, MI, 1996.
Hesse, Dagmar. "The West German Peace Movement: A Socio-Political Study." *Millennium: Journal of International Studies* 14, no. 1 (1985): 1–21.
Leif, Thomas. *Die professionelle Bewegung: Friedensbewegung von innen*. Bonn, 1985.
———. *Die strategische (Ohn-) Macht der Friedensbewegung. Kommunikations- und Entscheidungsstrukturen in den achtziger Jahren*. Opladen, 1990.

Markovits, Andrei S., and Philip S. Gorski. *The German Left: Red, Green, and Beyond.* New York, 1993.

Schaub, Annette, and Rüdiger Schlaga. "Verbände, Gruppen und Initiativen der westdeutschen Friedensbewegung." *Friedensanalysen* 16 (1982): 377–400.

Schmitt, Rüdiger. *Die Friedensbewegung in der Bundesrepublik Deutschland: Ursachen und Bedingungen einer neuen sozialen Bewegung.* Opladen, 1990.

Schregel, Susanne. *Der Atomkrieg vor der Wohnungstür: Eine Politikgeschichte der neuen Friedensbewegung in der Bundesrepublik 1970–1985.* Frankfurt am Main and New York, 2011.

Wasmuht, Ulrike. *Friedensbewegungen der 80er Jahre. Zur Analyse ihrer strukturellen und aktuellen Entstehungsbedingungen in der Bundesrepublik Deutschland und den Vereinigten Staaten: Ein Vergleich.* Gießen, 1987.

Chapter 9

The Spaces and Places of the Peace Movement

Susanne Schregel

Helmut wir kommen, wenn's sein muß auch geschwommen!
(Helmut, we're coming, even if we have to swim!)[1]

Under a clear blue autumn sky, hand in hand, flowers, songs, a 108-km-long Festival of Peace, a human chain in loops and tangles, colorful and diverse, vivid and creative, winding through dense housing, across town squares, waves building up and swirling around cars and buses, meandering across to the four-lane highway, finally spilling over onto the neighboring stubble fields: a vibrant ribbon as a living symbol.[2]

Resistance against the arms race has grown considerably in the course of the past year and has led to numerous regional activities. The Easter march no longer took place just in one or two big cities like it had in the 1950s, it was organized almost everywhere throughout West Germany. The fight for nuclear weapon-free zones has also spread countrywide, starting with activities in small towns and big cities in the north as well as the south. In the meantime, a number of different forms of protest against the continuous arms buildup have been developed regionally. An hour of silence is regularly held in an increasing number of locations in the Federal Republic. Many different kinds of vigils are being kept. The idea of peace camps ... has taken root here as well. Boycotts, blockades, and similar forms of protest against armament have become daily events.[3]

These three excerpts serve to spotlight the history of the peace movement: Hundreds of thousands of participants flocked to a mass demonstration in Bonn on 10 October 1981. Among the crowd, the crew of the *Disarmament* addressed Chancellor Helmut Schmidt with the slogan cited above. The poetic description in the second quotation refers to the 108-km-long human chain from Stuttgart to Neu-Ulm that activists formed in the autumn of 1983. Holding hands, countless people protested jointly against the deployment of new medium-range missiles in West Germany. Finally, the third citation illustrates the widespread unfolding of local events across the country, with numerous protests "for peace."

In fact, many of the political actions carried out by the peace movement were deliberately arranged spatially: agents of the peace movement assembled in specific, often symbolically charged places, such as the West German capital of Bonn, their local town hall, or in front of military installations and bunkers. In demonstrations protesters employed forms of action that intentionally manipulated space. For instance, they positioned their bodies in protest marches, in human chains, or in silent vigils.[4] The debate about NATO's Double-Track Decision was, as a consequence, not limited to geopolitical boundaries, but from the beginning had a wider territorial orientation. Peace activists explicitly involved a spatial dimension in practical action and in finding a political self-definition: actors in the peace movement articulated common political positions and demands in specific places and with the help of particular spatial arrangements or deliberate spatial strategies. This chapter discusses the 1980s peace movement's use of space, place, and spatial strategies.[5]

Political Action between Center and Periphery

A look at the spatial orientation of the many activities devoted to peace reveals that protests were located on different levels of the spatial scale with both centralizing and decentralizing tendencies. The great mass demonstrations of the peace movement attracted considerable media and public attention. As well as being protest *events,* these mass demonstrations simultaneously created symbolic *spaces* that could, in principle, be shared by all activists and had an integrating effect. The demonstration staged on the occasion of the German Protestant Church Congress in Hamburg in June 1981 ("Be afraid, nuclear death threatens us all!") with a hundred thousand participants and a great deal of publicity marked a significant breakthrough for a new protest movement directed against the deployment of Pershing II and Ground-Launched Cruise Missiles.[6] Even today, the mass demonstrations in the Hofgarten in Bonn on 10 October 1981, 10 June 1982, and 22 October 1983, and, on the same day as the latter, the human chain from Stuttgart to Neu-Ulm, share a place in public memory.[7]

Alongside such centralizing events, peace movement activists also sought to ground their activities "for peace" in locally oriented and decentralized contexts. This appreciation of the intimate, small-scale, and "concrete" moment derived from the so-called New Social Movements and the alternative politics of the 1970s. Even before the global political situation had become more hostile with the onset of the crises in Iran and Afghanistan, popular interpretations of alternative politics had placed a value on personal experience and "concreteness," close social environments and decentralization as key elements of political action.[8] The rise after 1980 of numerous peace groups at the regional and local levels in the contexts of local government, home, and work provided the organizational know-how to realize these ambitions in the field of peace politics.[9] The appreciation of grassroots political action was further promoted by the advent of alternative local networks, infrastructure, media, and local history workshops. Additionally, the organizational form of "peace weeks" brought together activists and paved the way for the local coordinating networks of the peace movement.[10] Thus it is interesting to note how, in a debate focused at first sight on defending geopolitical boundaries and the confrontation of "East" and "West," small-scale policy below the level of the nation-state grew in importance.[11] This was true for all strands of the politically heterogeneous movement. But even though these activities were often framed as "municipal" or "local," it is equally important to stress that the peace movement's political activities were embedded in far more complex relationships. Actual practices and patterns of interpretation referring to the local domain frequently evolved out of transnational transfer processes.[12] They drew on the experience of foreign peace activists and related consistently to locations outside West Germany. Nevertheless, to address these practices as being "locally oriented" helps to underline that the activists of the peace movement had very particular reasons for wishing to operate within a small-scale political arena.

Sites of Military Importance

The meaning of spaces, places, and spatial strategies in the practical context of the peace movement is best demonstrated with the help of examples. Incidents involving opposition to the military for instance show how demands for peace found a concrete local focus.

On sites of military importance, peace movement activists carried on a pointed debate over the role of the military, and in particular over the "arms race." Sites housing (atomic) weapons, military installations, and other locations considered relevant to the armed forces became the focus of a general debate about defense policy and its costs. Many places of local or regional importance were put on the political map as a result of the peace movement's protests.

The controversy about NATO's Double-Track Decision and the planned deployment of new nuclear missiles prompted, from 1980 onward, a heightened public interest in the location of the nuclear arsenal already located in West Germany. This involved the Pershing IA missiles, planned to be partially replaced by the Pershing II, Nike anti-aircraft missiles, short-range Lance missiles, and nuclear-chargeable howitzers and fighter aircraft. In addition there were sites for the storage of nuclear warheads as well as other installations necessary for a nuclear defense infrastructure. For reasons of national security, the number and precise location of such military sites was not officially announced. Beginning in 1981, a wave of publications dealing with military installations in the Federal Republic was produced to sate the increasing public curiosity.[13] Committed to the goal of providing "concrete" and locally relevant argumentation, peace activists tried to conduct studies or "military analysis from below" to find out about military sites in their own communities and to make sure locals knew about them. Protagonists felt that informing citizens of illegitimately withheld knowledge about military installations, suspected storage sites for nuclear munitions, and other places of military importance would provide proof that the military had penetrated the very center of their communities. The activists aimed at making a seemingly anonymous concept like the "arms race" take concrete form in everyday life and hoped this would make it politically assailable.[14]

Stationierungsorte (deployment sites) was the name given to the storage facilities for the Pershing II and cruise missiles as foreseen by the NATO Double-Track Decision. These attracted particular attention and public debate in the context of the peace movement. The 56th US Field Artillery Brigade units in Heilbronn, Schwäbisch Gmünd, and Neu-Ulm took charge of a total of 108 Pershing II missiles. Depots were located at the Heilbronn "Waldheide," in Neu-Ulm, and in Mutlangen near Schwäbisch Gmünd. Quick reaction alert positions were located in the "Waldheide" and in the "Lehmgrube" south of Neu-Ulm.[15] All ninety-six cruise missiles destined for the Federal Republic of Germany were to be placed at a site close to Hasselbach/Wüschheim in the Hunsrück.[16]

Mutlangen became the paradigmatic image of a *Stationierungsort*. Many of the protests and blockades against Pershing II missiles were concentrated on this location.[17] The protests focused on particular themes and were logistically supported by a permanent group of activists who managed to attract a great deal of media interest. For instance, a so-called "celebrity blockade" produced notable images of the fenced military terrain on 1–3 September 1983.[18] Thus Mutlangen became an important symbolic location for the peace movement, although the site served primarily as a training ground for soldiers and was not necessarily a critical staging area for the use of the Pershing II missiles.[19]

Highlighting Mutlangen as a place of protest as well as a place of militarization invoked parallels with already symbolically charged locations. For example, a photo depicts some demonstrators in front of the Pershing depot site's principle gate, across which a banner announces "Pershing macht frei" (Pershing makes you free). The slogan is framed on either side by crosses, in the background barbed wire can be seen on both sides of the banner. This reference to the infamous Nazi concentration camp slogan "Arbeit macht frei" (work makes you free) and the composition of the photograph present Mutlangen as an analogous site, capable of similar (evil) destruction.[20] Furthermore, the German "deployment sites" formed part of a symbolic ensemble, which included foreign locations or counterparts—especially Greenham Common in Great Britain and Comiso in Italy.[21]

In addition to these symbolically charged national "deployment sites," political protests for peace took place in a number of other military locations. Particularly noteworthy are the demonstrations and blockades in Großengstingen in the Swabian Alps (28 July–12 August 1982), the decentralized follow-up events on the third anniversary of the NATO Double-Track Decision (12 December 1982) at numerous military sites in West Germany, as well as the women's Peace Camp in the Hunsrück.[22]

Figure 9.1. Demonstrators in front of the US military base in Mutlangen holding a banner with the inscription "Pershing macht frei" (Pershing makes you free) (Hans Günter Lambertz / Haus der Geschichte, BaWü, DLG 0449/053)

Spaces and Places of Potential Destruction

Spatial factors also contributed to the peace movement's search to find a common definition with respect to imminent dangers. Thus the debate about the consequences of armament and war was also carried out in the locations of possible destruction. As likely targets of enemy strikes, military installations were one example. Peace activists also addressed the destructive potential of a nuclear war referring to spaces such as the (nuclear) shelter, the fictional spaces of nuclear war scenarios, and the human body itself—as the actual and foremost locus of nuclear annihilation.

Shelters had already been important sites for the peace movement in the debates about rearmament during the 1950s and 1960s.[23] At the beginning of the 1980s, criticism of civil defense measures flourished again within the West German peace movement, having been stimulated by the UK Civil Defense opposition and by debates about a new threat of war after the Soviet invasion of Afghanistan.[24] Activists loudly criticized (nuclear) shelters as concrete places of war preparation that fostered a false hope of survival and created the impression that conducting a nuclear war was indeed feasible. In fact, shelters were practically useless, activists insisted: they offered no effective protection for the population and no prospects for survival after a nuclear war. In any event, there were only enough public shelters for a fraction of the population. At the same time, the construction of private bunkers was criticized as being socially elitist and exclusionary.[25] Besides local civil defense measures, the civil defense opposition also directed its criticism to the government bunker in the Ahr valley.[26] This shelter was said to serve the survival needs of a small elite at the expense of the general population. Labeled the "VIP bunker" or "celebrity bunker,"[27] the shelter complex fueled a debate about social justice and inequality in a nuclear war.[28]

Even fictitious sites of destruction assumed political relevance in the peace movement. Gudrun Pausewang's novel *Die letzten Kinder von Schewenborn* (The Last Children of Schewenborn) is a well-known example.[29] There were also fictitious stories about the effects of a nuclear war on actual towns and regions. A small town, Hattenbach in the eastern part of Hesse, experienced sudden fame and became a special "place of the peace movement" after an award-winning documentary series by CBS television presented the village as the first atomic victim of a Soviet military push through the so-called Fulda Gap.[30] Peace activists also wrote short scenarios aimed at alerting citizens to the dangers of a nuclear war by describing the effects on the immediate environment. Such scenarios portrayed in a few pages the fate of the writer's own city or local region after a nuclear strike, vividly detailing the suffering and death of the local population.[31] In this debate over possible nuclear destruction, peace activists frequently invoked memories of the local destruction suffered during World War II.[32]

The most immediately tangible, quite literally incarnate location where a nuclear war would enfold was the human body. Many of the peace movement's forms of action addressed the burning, radiation, or "liquidation" of the body.[33] Practices such as forming a human carpet or enacting a "die-in," in which corpses appeared to have been dropped and left lying inert, created nightmarish spectacles that confronted urban passersby in the middle of their daily routines.[34] Human formations created temporary and symbolic spaces of potential destruction and were used as a political tool to express divergent political objectives in a public arena.

Counter-Places of Peace

Not least, the creation of "places of peace" makes obvious the extent to which political strategies of the peace movement deliberately entailed spatial aspects. This example demonstrates that spaces and places were used not only to articulate and illustrate political statements: activists within the peace movement went a step further by implementing specific spatial strategies to effectuate political change in "counter-places" of their own making. Dystopian spatial formations of bodies and scenarios depicting the threat of nuclear war were, for instance, clearly intended to evoke emotional reactions such as fear and concern in order to motivate political action. Human bodies were also used to create symbolic formations associated with positive qualities—such as rallies, human chains, and circles of silence—which aimed at encouraging certain guiding principles such as solidarity, communality, and alternative forms of sociality, and should thereby develop new options for social change.[35] The designation of nuclear weapon-free zones as "places of peace" was another form of space-based political action. Small or even tiny "nuclear weapon-free zones" were declared in freely chosen locations, for instance in roads, houses, schools, churches, and other sites. This practice was another move to anchor opposition to arms policy in everyday life and, in the home environment of citizens, to promote political ambitions such as the creation of a nuclear weapon-free Europe or a nuclear weapon-free world.[36]

In the Federal Republic of Germany, a number of locally elected governmental bodies also developed urban peace policies. These initiatives were not identical with those of the peace movement but were inspired by the latter.[37] In accordance with movements in other countries, for instance the Netherlands and the United Kingdom,[38] peace groups and politicians lobbied local councils to address peace politics and announce peace policy statements.

Figure 9.2. Rally outside the US military base in Mutlangen on 3 September 1983 including a child's stroller that has been declared a "nuclear weapon-free zone" (ullstein bild / Rieth)

Numerous local authorities established "nuclear weapon-free zones."[39] In addition, elected local representatives attempted to develop the outlines of a "communal peace agenda" and to strengthen it with the help of institutional structures. In the early 1980s, for example, city representatives convened in meetings to discuss communal peace policy under the slogan "Cities for Peace," and made plans for municipal peace projects.[40]

In the context of nuclear weapon-free zones and the growing involvement of local authorities in peace politics, one could discern a trend toward "glocalization." This term suggests a process of globalization that is in no way a negation or annihilation of idiosyncratic local characteristics. On the contrary, it stresses that diverse local conditions provide the catalyst for globalization, and highlights that local characteristics can evolve out of globalizing processes.[41] Thus, although nuclear weapon-free zones evolved within the context of a normative orientation toward local political action, their spatial relationships were, in practical terms, far more complex. The practice of declaring nuclear weapon-free zones was transferred transnationally, primarily from various British localities, to the Federal Republic of Germany. Furthermore, activists often justified the concept of nuclear weapon-free zones in neighborhoods or communities with reference to a spread of these zones in many other countries.⁴² Nuclear weapon-free zone declarations in communities could result in attempts to pass this form of political practice on to twin towns or sister cities in other nations, or lead to efforts to establish new contacts with potential partner cities at the city council level. Partnership ties between West German communities and those in the German Democratic Republic (which became politically viable after 1986)⁴³ could to some extent be traced to such practices of communal peace policy.

Another initiative that fell on fertile ground in the Federal Republic and received increasing support after the mid-1980s demonstrates the unique relationship between "local" and "global" forms of action in the context of political efforts for disarmament and peace. First presented by the Mayor of Hiroshima on 24 June 1982 at the Second UN General Assembly Special Session on Disarmament in New York, an international program designed to promote solidarity among cities was announced with the objective of eliminating all nuclear weapons ("Program to Promote the Solidarity of Cities toward the Total Abolition of Nuclear Weapons"). In this case, the cooperation between cities was intended to employ local action in an international context to change global structures.⁴⁴ The first congress of German cities united in the program for intercity solidarity took place in Hanover in January 1987. The conference passed a declaration stressing that "municipal authorities could help create the conditions that would assist more and more people to become aware of the possibility of advancing peaceful development in the world and foster conditions of non-violent social relations, … thereby opening up prospects for a world without weapons." To achieve this aim, the declaration suggested several practical steps. Besides local initiatives for international cooperation such as twin town partnerships, it proposed municipal peace education programs for children, youth, and adults, and suggested addressing the issue of war and peace in the municipal cultural policy.⁴⁵

Conclusion

Since the end of the Cold War and the withdrawal of most of the nuclear weapons from Germany, the places and spaces of the peace movement are primarily a matter of commemorative culture. Ephemeral arrangements of human bodies at certain locations, like the peace movement's silent circles in inner cities or like human chains, survive only in written records and visual sources. Only sporadically might a careful observer find an occasional relic of a nuclear weapon-free zone such as a sign or sticker. Some remains of civil defense installations do still exist and have recently been rediscovered by bunker societies as Cold War *lieux de mémoire*. As a subject of the politics of history, however, they still are rather marginal, as the example of the governmental bunker shows.[46] The vast majority of military sites made problematic by the peace movement have lost their significance, without many deliberate measures having been made so far to memorialize the nuclear confrontation to which they are connected. Looking at Cold War memory and its political landscapes, the peace movement itself appears to have become part of contemporary history, although its historical character is still uncertain. A debate on the commemorative culture with respect to the places and spaces of the peace movement seems to have hardly begun in the Federal Republic of Germany.

Susanne Schregel is a EURIAS Junior Fellow at The Institute for Advanced Studies in the Humanities (IASH) at the University of Edinburgh and Postdoctoral Research Fellow in the a.r.t.e.s. Graduate School for the Humanities Cologne, research group "Transformations of Knowledge." Prior to that, she was Postdoctoral Fellow at the German Historical Institute London (Research Scholarship) and Research Fellow at the IKKM (Internationales Kolleg für Kulturtechnikforschung und Medienphilosophie), Bauhaus University Weimar. She holds a PhD in history from the Technical University of Darmstadt. Her main research interests are in the history of social movements and political protest, the history of spatial-political interrelations and the intersections between social history, political history and the history of knowledge. Selected publications include *Der Atomkrieg vor der Wohnungstür. Eine Politikgeschichte der neuen Friedensbewegung in der Bundesrepublik, 1970–1985* (2011); "Global Micropolitics: Toward a Transnational History of Grassroots Nuclear-Free Zones," in *Nuclear Threats, Nuclear Fear and the Cold War of the 1980s,* ed. Eckart Conze, Martin Klimke, and Jeremy Varon (2016), 206–26; "'Dann sage ich, brich das Gesetz.' Recht und Protest im Streit um den NATO-Doppelbeschluss," in *Ordnung und Protest. Eine gesamtdeutsche Protestgeschichte von 1949 bis heute,* ed. Martin Löhnig, Mareike Preisner, and Thomas Schlemmer (2015), 133–147; "Nuclear War and the City. Perspectives on Municipal Interventions in Defence (Great Britain, New Zealand, West Germany, USA, 1980–1985)," in *Urban History* 42 (2015): 564–83.

Notes

1. Gerd Jahnke and Kersten v. Rosen, "Zurück von Bonn …," *Informationen Ohne Rüstung Leben,* Arbeitskreis von Pro Ökumene 4, no. 18 (1981): 2.
2. "Wir fanden's toll," *Süddeutsche Herbstpost,* Aktionsbüro Herbst '83 der Friedensbewegung in Süddeutschland 1, no. 6 (1983): 1 (Württembergische Landesbibliothek Stuttgart).

3. Konrad Lübbert, "Gewaltfreie Aktionen an militärischen Standorten," in *Christen für die Abrüstung.* Informationsmaterial 3, no. 1 (1983): 49 (Württembergische Landesbibliothek Stuttgart).
 4. On this point, see also the contribution by Kathrin Fahlenbrach and Laura Stapane in this volume.
 5. Recent research increasingly acknowledges that spatial factors play a major role in the constitution and development of social movements. Javier Auyero, "Spaces and Places as Sites and Objects of Politics," in *The Oxford Handbook of Contextual Political Analysis,* ed. Robert E. Goodin and Charles Tilly (New York, 2006), 564–78; Byron A. Miller, *Geography and Social Movements: Comparing Antinuclear Activism in the Boston Area* (Minneapolis, MN, 2000).
 6. On this point, see also the contribution by Sebastian Kalden and Jan Ole Wiechmann in this volume.
 7. Aktion Sühnezeichen/Friedensdienste/Aktionsgemeinschaft Dienst für den Frieden, Bonn 10.10.1981. *Friedensdemonstration für Abrüstung und Entspannung in Europa* (Bornheim-Merten, 1981); Koordinierungsausschuß der Friedensorganisationen, ed., *Aufstehn! Für den Frieden. Friedensdemonstration anläßlich der NATO-Gipfelkonferenz in Bonn am 10.6.1982* (Bornheim-Merten, 1982); DFG-VK Baden-Württemberg and Christian Herz, eds., *Die Menschenkette: Ein Rückblick,* 2nd ed. (Karlsruhe, 1984); Rüdiger Schmitt, *Die Friedensbewegung in der Bundesrepublik Deutschland: Ursachen und Bedingungen der Mobilisierung einer neuen sozialen Bewegung* (Opladen, 1990), 14. See also the contribution by Kathrin Fahlenbrach and Laura Stapane in this volume.
 8. In contrast, Thomas Leif argues that the peace movement was not characterized by pluralistic and decentralized organizational structures. In fact, "centralized decision-making" prevailed in the nationally active Coordinating Committee of the peace movement. The description of the peace movement as a grassroots democracy, therefore, had to be considered a myth. Thomas Leif, "Die Friedensbewegung zu Beginn der achtziger Jahre: Themen und Strategien," *Aus Politik und Zeitgeschichte* B26 (1989): 28–40. In my opinion, the establishment of a central coordinating committee does not contradict the pursuit of decentralization and localized political action.
 9. Schmitt, *Die Friedensbewegung,* 159–64; Leif, "Die Friedensbewegung," 34–35.
 10. Schmitt, *Die Friedensbewegung,* 117–37; Sven Reichardt and Detlef Siegfried, "Das Alternative Milieu: Konturen einer Lebensform," in *Das Alternative Milieu: Antibürgerlicher Lebensstil und linke Politik in der Bundesrepublik Deutschland und Europa 1968–1983,* ed. Sven Reichardt and Detlef Siegfried (Göttingen, 2010), 9–24; Sven Reichardt, *Authentizität und Gemeinschaft: Linksalternatives Leben in den siebziger und frühen achtziger Jahren* (Berlin, 2014); Detlef Siegfried, "Die Rückkehr des Subjekts: Gesellschaftlicher Wandel und neue Geschichtsbewegung um 1980," in *Geschichte und Geschichtsvermittlung: Festschrift für Karl Heinrich Pohl,* ed. Olaf Hartung and Katja Köhr (Bielefeld, 2008), 125–46.
 11. See, for instance, Günther Gugel and Uli Jäger, "Kommunale Friedensarbeit," in *Handbuch Kommunale Friedensarbeit,* ed. Günther Gugel and Uli Jäger (Tübingen, 1988), 8–20.
 12. On the subject of such transnational transfer processes, see also the section in this chapter, "Counter-Places of Peace."

13. For example Wolf Perdelwitz, "Atom-Rampe Deutschland: Wie die Bundesrepublik mit Atomwaffen vollgestopft wird, wo sie versteckt sind und welche Gefahr uns dadurch droht," in *Der Stern*, 19 February 1981, 26–34 and 218; Burkhard Luber, *Bedrohungsatlas Bundesrepublik Deutschland* (Wuppertal, 1982); Die Friedensliste NRW, *Militärland BRD: Atomwaffen, C-Waffen und militärische Anlagen* (Düsseldorf, 1985); Alfred Mechtersheimer and Peter Barth, *Militarisierungsatlas der Bundesrepublik: Streitkräfte, Waffen und Standorte, Kosten und Risiken* (Darmstadt and Neuwied, 1986); William M. Arkin and Richard W. Fieldhouse, *"Nuclear battlefields": Der Atomwaffen-Report*, trans. Wolfgang Biermann et al. (Frankfurt am Main, 1986); Burkhard Luber/Arbeits- und Forschungsstelle Militär, Ökologie und Planung (MÖP) e.V. and Die Grünen Bundesvorstand, eds., *Militäratlas von Flensburg bis Dresden: 3.000 Daten zur Militarisierung der BRD und DDR* (Bonn, 1986). See also Oliver Bange's chapter in this volume.

14. Practical guides for instance were Ulrich Albrecht, "Wie man sein lokales Kernwaffenlager findet," in *Kündigt den Nachrüstungsbeschluß! Argumente für die Friedensbewegung*, ed. Ulrich Albrecht (Frankfurt am Main, 1982), 169–75; Karl-Klaus Rabe, "Wie man Atomwaffen-Standorte erkennen kann und welche Ansatzpunkte für Aktionen es dort gibt," in *Keine neuen Atomwaffen in der Bundesrepublik: Aktionshandbuch 3 zur bundesweiten Friedenswoche Frieden schaffen ohne Waffen*, ed. Aktion Sühnezeichen/Friedensdienste (Bornheim-Merten, 1982), 173–79.

15. Bernd Holtwick, "'Flexible response.' Der NATO-Doppelbeschluss und seine Umsetzung in Baden-Württemberg," in *Zerreißprobe Frieden: Baden-Württemberg und der NATO-Doppelbeschluss*, ed. Haus der Geschichte Baden-Württemberg (Stuttgart, 2004), 11–13.

16. Matthias Kagerbauer, "Die Friedensbewegung in Rheinland-Pfalz: Der Hunsrück als Zentrum des Protests gegen die Nachrüstung," MA thesis, Johannes-Gutenberg-Universität Mainz, 2008, 63–64; Bundesminister der Verteidigung, *Marschflugkörper im Hunsrück: Eine Bürgerinformation* (Bonn, 1986).

17. However, other sites had also been publicly discussed, in particular Heilbronn after a fatal accident involving a Pershing II in early 1985. Cf. Erhard Jöst, ed., "Die Heilbronner Waldheide als Pershing-Standort," http://www.stadtarchiv-heilbronn.de/stadtgeschichte/unterricht/bausteine/waldheide/; Uli Jäger, "Heilbronn: Eine Stadt wehrt sich gegen Atomraketen," in *Zwischen Atomraketen und Waffenschmieden: Fallstudien über Möglichkeiten und Grenzen kommunaler Friedensarbeit in Baden-Württemberg*, ed. Uli Jäger, Günther Gugel, Michael Schmid-Vöhringer, and Christiane Vetter (Tübingen, 1988), 19–42.

18. On this point, see also the contribution by Kathrin Fahlenbrach and Laura Stapane in this volume.

19. Sabrina Müller has written about the situation in Mutlangen: "'Frieden schaffen ohne Waffen': Der gewaltlose Widerstand gegen die Nachrüstung," in Haus der Geschichte Baden-Württemberg (ed.), *Zerreißprobe Frieden*, 26–29; Manfred Laduch, Heino Schütte, and Reinhard Wagenblast, eds., *Mutlanger Heide: Ein Ort macht Geschichte* (Schwäbisch Gmünd, 1990); Volker Nick, Volker Scheub, and Christof Then, *Mutlangen 1983–1987: Die Stationierung der Pershing II und die Kampagne Ziviler Ungehorsam bis zur Abrüstung* (Stuttgart, 1993).

20. References to the Nazi period in the peace movement are discussed by Andrea Humphreys, "'Ein atomares Auschwitz': Die Lehren der Geschichte und der Streit um die Nachrüstung," *Grünes Gedächtnis* (2008): 39–62; Eckart Conze, "Modernitätsskepsis und die Utopie der Sicherheit: NATO-Nachrüstung und Friedensbewegung in der Geschichte der Bundesrepublik," *Zeithistorische Forschungen/Studies in Contemporary History* 7, no. 2 (2010), http://www.zeithistorische-forschungen.de/16126041-Conze-2-2010, section 9.
21. Other sites were Molesworth (Great Britain), Florennes (Belgium), and Woendsrecht (Netherlands).
22. Joachim Lenk, *Soldaten, Sprengköpfe und scharfe Munition: Militär am Einödstandort Engstingen 1939 bis 1993* (Münsingen, 2006), 190–207; Peter E. Quint, *Civil Disobedience and the German Courts: The Pershing Missile Protests in Comparative Perspective* (London, 2008), 12–16; "Frieden schaffen ohne Waffen: Rundbrief 12.12.1982" (Württembergische Landesbibliothek Stuttgart); Christiane Leidinger, "Frauenwiderstandscamps in Reckershausen im Hunsrück von 1983 bis 1993," *wissenschaft & frieden* no. 2 (2010), http://www.wissenschaft-und-frieden.de/seite.php?artikelID=1620.
23. Nicholas J. Steneck, "Eine verschüttete Nation? Zivilschutzbunker in der Bundesrepublik Deutschland, 1950–1965," in *Bunker: Kriegsort, Zuflucht, Erinnerungsraum*, ed. Inge Marszolek and Marc Buggeln (Frankfurt am Main and New York, 2008), 75–88; Malte Thießen, "Von der 'Heimstätte' zum Denkmal: Bunker als städtische Erinnerungsorte—das Beispiel Hamburgs," in Marszolek and Buggeln (eds.), *Bunker*, 52–4. On civil defense, see also the chapter by Claudia Kemper in this volume.
24. James Stafford, "'Stay at Home'. The Politics of Nuclear Civil Defence, 1968–83," *Twentieth Century British History* 23, no. 3 (2012): 383–407.
25. See, for instance, "'Zivile Verteidigung' = Vorbereitung für den Krieg," *Diskofo: Diskussionsforum für Zivildienstleistende* 12, no. 40 (August 1981); *Friedenskooperative: Materialien für friedenspolitische Basisarbeit*, special issue "Civil defense" (Bonn, March 1985).
26. The building complex was known officially as "Ausweichsitz der Verfassungsorgane des Bundes im Krisen- und Verteidigungsfall zur Wahrung von deren Funktionsfähigkeit." See also Ralf Schäfer, Bundesamt für Bauwesen und Raumordnung and Stiftung Haus der Geschichte der Bundesrepublik Deutschland, eds., *Der Regierungsbunker* (Tübingen, 2006).
27. Die Grünen, *Abrüstungswettlauf/Wehrt Euch! Gegen die atomare Bedrohung: Nukleare Lagekarte* (1981), Sign. 3482 (Stationierungsorte von Atomwaffen), Petra-Kelly-Archiv, Archiv Grünes Gedächtnis, Berlin.
28. The debate about the (nuclear) shelter is summarized by Susanne Schregel, *Der Atomkrieg vor der Wohnungstür: Eine Politikgeschichte der neuen Friedensbewegung in der Bundesrepublik, 1970–1985* (Frankfurt am Main and New York, 2011), 185–225.
29. Gudrun Pausewang, *Die letzten Kinder von Schewenborn oder … sieht so unsere Zukunft aus?* (Ravensburg, 1983). See also the contribution by Philipp Baur in this volume.
30. "'Fulda Gap, the First Battle of the Next War.' Untersuchung zur Militarisierung Osthessens," *Materialien*, 1 and 2 October 1983, 97–110 (Archiv aktiv, Hamburg);

Wilhelm Bittorf, "Ich sag' dem Schwein nicht, wann es stirbt," *Der Spiegel*, 1 March 1982, 105–8; general information is provided by Torsten Halsey, "Hessen—Schauplatz für den Dritten Weltkrieg," in *Amerikaner in Hessen: Eine besondere Beziehung im Wandel der Zeit*, ed. Gundula Bavendamm (Hanau, 2008), 207–27.

31. Ulmer Ärzte-Initiative, Volker Brethfeld et al., eds., *Tausend Grad Celsius: Das Ulm-Szenario für einen Atomkrieg* (Darmstadt and Neuwied, 1983); Karin Fischer and Wilfried Porwol, "Ein Atomkriegsszenario," in *zivilcourage* 7, no. 1 (1981): 24–25; Arbeitsgruppe "Friedenswoche Leutkirch," ed., *Atomkrieg über Leutkirch, Kurzstudie* (Leutkirch, 1983). See also the contribution by Philipp Baur in this volume.
32. Jörg Arnold, "'Kassel 1943 mahnt …' Zur Genealogie der Angst im Kalten Krieg," in *Angst im Kalten Krieg*, ed. Bernd Greiner, Christian Th. Müller, and Dierk Walter (Hamburg, 2009), 465–94.
33. A process associated with the neutron bomb that results in the dissolution of organic tissue.
34. On this point, see also the contribution by Kathrin Fahlenbrach and Laura Stapane in this volume.
35. Thomas Balistier describes numerous forms of political action for peace: *Straßenprotest: Formen oppositioneller Politik in der Bundesrepublik Deutschland zwischen 1979 und 1989* (Münster, 1996).
36. Susanne Schregel, "Global Micropolitics: Toward a Transnational History of Grassroots Nuclear-Free Zones," in *Nuclear Threats, Nuclear Fear and the Cold War of the 1980s*, ed. Eckart Conze, Martin Klimke, and Jeremy Varon (New York, 2016), 206–26.
37. On municipal peace policies in a transnational context, see Susanne Schregel, "Nuclear War and the City. Perspectives on Municipal Interventions in Defence (Great Britain, New Zealand, West Germany, USA, 1980–1985)," in *Urban History* 42 (2015): 564–83.
38. David Regan, *The New City Republics: Municipal Intervention in Defence*, Institute for European Defence and Strategic Studies, Occasional paper no. 30 (London, 1987); Dion van den Berg, "Kommunale Friedenspolitik in den Niederlanden," in Gugel and Jäger, eds., *Kommunale Friedensarbeit*, 210–18.
39. Initially the ASF and DFG-VK spread information about such initiatives in 1983–84 with the help of "Informationsdienst der Kampagne für atomwaffenfreie Städte und Regionen"; from 1985 onward this service was extended as a journal for communal peace action in general. See also Klaus Mannhardt and Die Friedensliste, *Stützpunkte für den Krieg—oder Orte des Friedens? Für kommunale und regionale Friedensarbeit. Gegen Militarisierung* (Bonn, 1985); Knut Krusewitz, Gertrud Schilling, Gerald Flinner, and Die Grünen Hessen, eds., *Militarisierung, Friedensarbeit und kommunale Gegenwehr* (Frankfurt am Main, 1985).
40. Rainer M. Türmer, "Gemeinden für den Frieden," in Gugel and Jäger, eds., *Kommunale Friedensarbeit*, 197–203.
41. Roland Robertson, "Glocalization: Time-Space and Homogeneity-Heterogeneity," in *Global Modernities*, ed. Mike Featherstone et al. (London, 1995), 25–44.
42. Schregel, *Der Atomkrieg*, 267–74 and 306–10.
43. On the general history of sister city partnerships between localities in the German Federal Republic and those in the German Democratic Republic, see Nicole-

Annette Pawlow, *Innerdeutsche Städtepartnerschaften: Entwicklung, Praxis, Möglichkeiten* (Berlin, 1990).
44. The initiative is still active, today with the name "Mayors for Peace." A listing of participating towns and mayors in Germany may be found at http://www.mayorsforpeace.de. The list comprises the following entries: 1983: 1 city; 1984: 13; 1985: 26; 1986: 29; 1987: 21; 1988: 3; 1989: 1. In 2004, the initiative experienced a noticeable revival, with a worldwide membership of 7,114 subscribers on 1 August 2016.
45. "Abschlußerklärung der Konferenz der deutschen 'Solidaritätsstädte' on January 15–16, 1987 (Hannover)," in Gugel and Jäger, eds., *Kommunale Friedensarbeit*, 200–201.
46. Jürgen Reiche, "Streng geheim?! Ein Museum im 'Atombunker der Bundesregierung,'" in *Von Berlin nach Weimar: Kunstgeschichte und Museum*, ed. Michael Bollé (Munich, 2003), 126–33.

Select Bibliography

Miller's work on the American peace movement is of fundamental theoretical and methodological importance. The study of the Boston area shows how geography, space, and spatial scales may gain relevance for social movements' analyses and practical strategies. Referring to this and other studies, I have published a history of the peace movement in the Federal Republic of Germany following its spaces, places, and space-oriented strategies (Schregel 2011). The study covers military installations and nuclear shelters, as well as nuclear war scenarios, human formations, and nuclear weapon-free zones. Additionally, my recent journal article focuses on urban peace policies from a transnational point of view (Schregel 2015). With a rather regional focus, an anthology based on an exhibition to commemorate the twenty-fifth anniversary of the NATO Double-Track Decision at the House of History of Baden-Württemberg contains numerous articles about arms "upgrades" in Baden-Württemberg and events on the "deployment sites" Neu-Ulm, Heilbronn, and Schwäbisch-Gmünd (including Mutlangen). This publication can also be read as one of the first concrete contributions to a debate about the significance of the peace movement's places and spaces for German commemorative culture and politics of history. Kagerbauer wrote a master's thesis (also available online) that examines the controversy over the NATO Double-Track Decision in Rhineland-Palatinate from the perspective of regional history, with a special focus on the debate about defense in the German region of Hunsrück. Arnold has compiled a local study on memories of war and their importance for the peace movement, drawing especially on the example of the air war conducted over the city of Kassel during World War II. The article also discusses aspects of the arms debate and the peace movement of the 1950s.

Arnold, Jörg. "'Kassel 1943 mahnt …' Zur Genealogie der Angst im Kalten Krieg," in *Angst im Kalten Krieg*, ed. Bernd Greiner, Christian Th. Müller, and Dierk Walter, 465–94. Hamburg, 2009.
Haus der Geschichte Baden-Württemberg, ed. *Zerreißprobe Frieden: Baden-Württemberg und der NATO-Doppelbeschluss*, exh. cat. Stuttgart, 2004.

Kagerbauer, Matthias. "Die Friedensbewegung in Rheinland-Pfalz. Der Hunsrück als Zentrum des Protests gegen die Nachrüstung." MA thesis, Johannes-Gutenberg-Universität Mainz, 2008. http://pydna.de/?page_id=369.

Miller, Byron A. *Geography and Social Movements: Comparing Antinuclear Activism in the Boston Area.* Minneapolis, MN, 2000.

Schregel, Susanne. *Der Atomkrieg vor der Wohnungstür. Eine Politikgeschichte der neuen Friedensbewegung in der Bundesrepublik (1970–1985).* Frankfurt am Main and New York, 2011.

———. "Nuclear War and the City. Perspectives on Municipal Interventions in Defence (Great Britain, New Zealand, West Germany, USA, 1980–1985)," in *Urban History* 42 (2015): 564–83.

Chapter 10

The Protagonists of the Peace Movement

Saskia Richter

The peace movement was a social movement comprised of diverse individuals devoted to a common cause with a common collective identity and typically organized on democratic grassroots principles, with self-organization, through a Coordinating Committee. As such, it took a skeptical view of political leaders. However, notwithstanding its grassroots-inspired structures of decision-making, there were key players who succeeded in developing particularly high public profiles with regard to certain issues. For the purpose of introducing such "protagonists" of the peace movement and their celebrity status,[1] the movement is divided here into the following social and political groups: Christians, politically independent participants, left-wing or groups that East Germany secretly supported within the spectrum of the Komitee für Frieden, Abrüstung, und Zusammenarbeit (KOFAZ, Committee for Peace, Disarmament, and Cooperation),[2] Social Democrats, Green Party/alternative, and other groups. This discussion focuses on representatives who took on formal as well as informal leadership positions.

One starting point of the peace movement, besides the 1981 Protestant Church Congress in Hamburg, was the autumn demonstrations in various Western European capitals, including one in the Hofgarten in Bonn on 10 October 1981.[3] Aktion Sühnezeichen/Friedensdienste (ASF, Action Reconciliation Service for Peace) announced that some 300,000 people had come together on this day.[4] It was "one of the largest, most impressive, and best-organized demonstrations in the history of West Germany."[5] According to the organizers Heinrich and Annemarie Böll (1917–85 and 1910–2004, respectively), Gert Bastian (1923–92), Robert Jungk (1913–94), Dorothee Sölle (1929–2003), and others, the demonstration was not directed solely against the United States. Participants called instead for a comprehensive mutual disarmament process.[6] Many organizations such as the Gustav Heinemann-Initiative took part and called on its members to join the peace rally.[7]

Principal Witness and Key Actor Gert Bastian

The Krefeld Appeal, a political manifesto that called on the government of the Federal Republic of Germany to withdraw its consent to deploy Pershing II and cruise missiles in Central Europe, preceded the autumn demonstrations of 1981. Its principle author—a key witness and participant in the peace movement—was Gert Bastian,[8] a former general in the West German Armed Forces who had asked the incumbent Minister of Defense, Hans Apel (1932–2011), for early retirement in opposition to the NATO Double-Track Decision. He then actively courted media attention voicing his opposition and publicly declaring that the introduction and deployment of new intermediate-range missiles in Central Europe was a mistake. In July 1980 he was one of several individuals (including Petra Kelly, Christoph Strässer, Martin Niemöller, Helmut Ridder, and others) who initiated the Krefeld Appeal.

The Krefeld Appeal represented a minimal consensus among different opposition groups within the peace movement. By 1983 it had been signed by more than four million people. It stated, "The participants of the talks in Krefeld on 15 and 16 November 1980 make this joint appeal ... to the federal government: withdraw the approval of the deployment of Pershing II and cruise missiles in Central Europe and take up a position within the Alliance that allays any fears that our country is preparing for a new nuclear arms race that primarily threatens Europeans."[9] The first signatories were Bastian, Petra Kelly (1947–92), and the physicist Karl Bechert (1901–81), who died shortly after,[10] as well as the theologian Martin Niemöller (1892–84), Helmut Ridder (1919–2007), Gösta von Uexküll (1909–93), and Joseph Weber (1908–85).

The media engaged in an ongoing debate at the time about the authorship of the text and whether the writer represented interests of the German Democratic Republic or the Soviet Union. In a letter to the editor of the *Süddeutsche Zeitung* (18 July 1981), Gert Bastian proclaimed himself the author. There are other statements claiming that the Deutsche Friedensunion had been the author, or that all initiators had written it together, which is quite implausible.[11] However, within the peace movement and especially among supporters of the Green Party, the Krefelder Appeal remained controversial. Large segments of groups that backed peace policies were against the organizational and possibly communist background of the initiative. The government of West Germany sought especially to exploit this situation by questioning the credibility of the appeal and the Ministry of Defense eyed the activities of its former army general with "growing concern."[12] Bastian himself sought to calm the discussion: "The Soviet SS-4 and SS-5 missiles have been directed at Western Europe for more than twenty years … NATO's previously calm response was certainly well-founded … It is plain that the USSR … could have turned Western Europe into a terrain of nuclear debris."[13] He did not believe, however, that the Kremlin was capable of such ludicrous and cynical action.

At the rally of the mass demonstration for peace in Bonn on 10 October 1981, Bastian addressed the leaders in the East and West as those who "abuse their power and accumulate ever more weapons, rather than solve the problems of mankind with nonviolence."[14] First and foremost he addressed his own government. Bastian distinguished between the SS-20 armament and the arms upgrade of Pershing missiles. In April of the same year in Groningen, Bastian had already pointed out "significant changes in the West's thinking about nuclear warfare."[15] About a year later, on 10 June 1982, he delivered another speech at a main rally in Bonn.[16] There he defended the German peace movement against allegations that they were communist controlled.

The Groups of the Peace Movement

The following groups and initiatives were represented at the Bonn peace demonstrations and the Coordinating Committee of the Peace Movement: the Aktion Sühnezeichen/Friedensdienste (ASF, The Action Reconciliation Service for Peace), Aktionsgemeinschaft Dienst für den Frieden (AGDF, Action Committee Service for Peace), the Ohne Rüstung Leben (ORL, Living without Arms), Evangelische Studentengemeinde (Protestant Student Parish Organization), the Pax-Christi-Gruppen (Pax Christi [peace of Christ] Groups), and the Initiative Kirche von unten (IKvu, Initiative Church from Below). The theologian and pacifist Dorothee Sölle perhaps best represented the perspective of the Christian groups.[17]

Among the independent groups may be counted the Bundeskonferenz Unabhängiger Friedensgruppen (BUF, Federal Conference of Independent Peace Groups), the Föderation gewaltfreier Aktionsgruppen (FÖGA, Federation of Nonviolent Action Groups), Anstiftung der Frauen für den Frieden (Initiative Women for Peace), the Komitee für Grundrechte und Demokratie (Committee for Basic Rights and Democracy), and the Bundeskongress entwicklungspolitischer Aktionsgruppen (BUKO, Federal Congress of Developmental Action Groups). Eva Quistorp (b. 1945) represented Women for Peace on the Coordination Committee of the Peace Movement.[18] At that time she was less well-known to the general public than Petra Kelly, but she was a driving force in bringing together supporting organizations and creating networks on behalf of the movement.[19]

More groups made up the political spectrum of the Left and KOFAZ than can be discussed here. Members of KOFAZ included Martha Buschmann of the DKP (the German Communist Party), Klaus Mannhardt of the Deutschen Friedensgesellschaft (German Peace Society), Horst Trapp of the Deutschen Friedensunion (German Peace Union), Christoph Straesser of the Jungdemokraten (Young Democrats), and peace researcher Gerhard Kade (1931–95), whose contributions will be discussed in further detail below.[20]

Among the established parties, the protest against the NATO Double-Track Decision was primarily articulated by the German Social Democrats.[21] Their party was faced with great turmoil during its shift from initiator of the NATO Double-Track Decision under Chancellor Schmidt's government to its opponent. The party was faced with a difficult initiation test; it could opt only to oppose the upgrade of arms by yielding government responsibilities. Helmut Schmidt lost his chancellorship through a constructive vote of no confidence against the CDU party leader Helmut Kohl.[22] Willy Brandt (1913–92), Erhard Eppler (b. 1926), and Oskar Lafontaine (b. 1943) then took on leading roles as critics of the arms upgrade.

Right from the start the Green Party and the so-called alternative groups formed a strong network within the peace movement. The Green Party envisaged a nonviolent society and lobbied for dissolution of all military blocs. Important protagonists of the Green Party were also figureheads of the peace movement: Petra Kelly and her partner, Gert Bastian. Kelly and Bastian were media celebrities and could be seen as leading figures within these movements although their positions and actions were not without controversy. The German Democratic Republic civil rights activists Bärbel Bohley (1945–2010) and Rudolf Bahro (1935–1997) constituted a subdivision of the "alternatives" from a transnational perspective.[23]

Finally, political scientist Thomas Leif has categorized the remaining groups: Bundesverband Bürgerinitiativen Umweltschutz (BBU, Association of Citizens' Initiatives for Environmental Protection), the Liberalen Demokraten (LD, Liberal Democrats), the Jungdemokraten (Young Democrats), and the Demokratischen Sozialisten (DS, Democratic Socialists).[24] As an example of a nondogmatic socialist, the activist and office secretary Klaus Vack (b. 1935) is discussed, along with a group of artists and journalists, including Joseph Beuys, Heinrich and Annemarie Böll, Robert Jungk, and Franz Alt (b. 1938).

The Peace Movement Activists

The Theologian: Dorothee Sölle

Dorothee Sölle (1929–2003) was born into a German academic family by the name Nipperdey. She studied philosophy and ancient languages in Freiburg and Cologne before switching to German literature and theology in 1951. Three years later she married the painter Dietrich Sölle. After obtaining her Ph.D. in literature, she went on to become an internationally active academic. She concentrated on the horrors of Auschwitz and posed the question, Where was God during the time of the Nazi regime in Germany?

Her engagement with crimes committed under National Socialism and during World War II led her to the peace movement: Sölle called for worldwide disarmament and felt Germany should begin this process unilaterally. Known for this position, she took part in sit-ins staged in front of the US military base in Mutlangen and participated in other protests.[25] Like many activists, she was convicted of attempted coercion by the authorities.[26] Sölle's positions were radical. She emphasized her female gender and always sought to support those in society who are most vulnerable: "Dear brothers and sisters, I speak to you as a woman who comes from one of the richest countries on earth. It is a country with a bloody past, stinking of gas."[27]

Like many of her fellow activists, Sölle rejected a separation between political and private aspects of life. She thought in terms of categories of relationships, friendship and love, and demanded equal rights for men and women. Whenever she was accused of arguing emotionally, she replied: "I think this is the most stupid male-biased accusation that anyone can possibly make. Because I enjoy … expressing my emotions; you cannot deny emotions as if they were illegitimate children … If we deny our emotions, we deny ourselves."[28]

The Organizer: Eva Quistorp

Peace activist Eva Quistorp, born in 1945, is a founding member of the Green Party. Her father was an active member of the Bekennende Kirche (Confessional Church) during the era of the Nazi regime, and she grew up in a vicarage before studying German and Protestant theology. In 1965 Quistorp moved to West Berlin, where three years later, after having done volunteer work, she began studying politics at the Otto Suhr Institute of the Free University.[29] At times she lived in the home of Brigitte and Helmut Gollwitzer. Both were authoritative figures in the 1968 movement, and by 1980 they would join the group of activists who founded the Green Party.

In the 1970s Eva Quistorp worked in the milieu of the New Social Movements. She traveled to Latin America, where she developed her views on gender politics and women's rights.[30] Like other founding members of the Green Party, she took an active part in the antinuclear movement demonstrations in Gorleben in 1977. This event was a meeting of many very different political perspectives, social backgrounds, and views on life. One integrating force, however, was the "common cause," which was "united against nuclear waste, united against the Castor [transports]." Looking back on the event, Quistorp concluded that "a wonderful process came out of this."[31]

In 1980 Eva Quistorp cofounded the groups Women for Peace and Initiative Women for Peace. At a later date she became a member of the Coordinating Committee for the organization of nationwide peace protests.[32] In retrospect she outlined her task in the following way: "In the Coordination Committee we had a certain amount of power to make decisions; namely we decided who would speak at the large demonstrations, how to organize the (event). And we had to keep the alliance together. But the peace movement also shared characteristics of the alternative movement: there was a tremendous amount of decentralized activities from below."[33]

The German Democratic Republic and Its Peace Researcher: Gerhard Kade

The German Democratic Republic was very interested in preventing the arms upgrade, although it could not oppose NATO in its own right.[34] The government therefore took informal action by sending out undercover agents to West Germany. Although the thesis about a remote-controlled peace movement is not sustainable, it is nevertheless true that agents acted on behalf of the Ministry for State Security, and that they had a central role in the development of strategies and arguments against the arms upgrade.[35] One of these informal agents was Gerhard Kade.

KOFAZ was the central organization that connected the West German peace movement with the DKP and the SED (Socialist Unity Party). Gerhard Kade headed the organization after the mid-1970s.[36] Kade was also a secret employee of the Ministry for State Security of the GDR under the code name "Super." According to Markus Wolf, chief of the General Intelligence Administration, the organization Generals for Peace (Generäle für den Frieden) was annually supported with 100,000 deutsche marks.[37] Kade was its initiator and unofficially managed the organization.[38] It is assumed that Kade exercised influence on Gert Bastian, whom he managed to recruit as a general for the initiative.[39] Kade quite possibly wrote certain passages of the book *Generals for Peace*.

Ecology and Peace in the Social Democratic Party of Germany: Erhard Eppler

Erhard Eppler (b. 1926) started trying to reform the SPD in the early 1970s. He intended to develop the organization into an ecologically oriented party.[40] However, his local branch of the SPD in Baden-Württemberg resisted this move. Eppler was unable to prevent the Green Party from entering into the regional state parliament after they obtained 5.6 percent of the vote in the elections of March 1980. Thus the Green Party effectively became a political rival to the social democratic movement.

At the same time Eppler participated in the ecology movement as well as the peace movement.[41] He decidedly opposed NATO's arms upgrade and argued against the positions of his fellow party member and head of government Chancellor Helmut Schmidt. The topic of his speech on 10 October 1981 in Bonn was titled "How is disarmament politically possible? From preventing the arms upgrade to a mutual process of disarmament." Eppler wanted to play the same role for the SPD that the Green Party played in parliament: that is, being a link between the peace movement and his party or perhaps parliament at large. His resistance toward the official party line was not successful: in 1982 he had to leave the executive party committee. However, in 1984, after the arms upgrade had been implemented and the election had been lost, he was able to return.

The Figurehead: Petra Kelly

Petra Kelly was the most prominent figure of the peace movement in the early 1980s.[42] She originally held party membership in the SPD but registered as a member of the Green Party when it was founded. For instance, Kelly was the top candidate on the list for the first election to the European Parliament in 1979 and was on the electoral lists for the national election in 1980. Kelly's name was also on the electoral lists for the Bavarian state election in 1982. She introduced the concept of the "anti-party" party, stressing that green politics was a politics of social movements. As a politician of the Green Party, Kelly wanted to represent the interests of the "New Social Movements" in parliament.[43]

In the peace movement Kelly took up important positions in matters of antinuclear policies and the roles to be played by women in the peace movement. She justified certain political positions with reference to her own life, such as mourning for her sister Grace who had died of cancer and her interest in the effects of radiation in medical and military technology or in civil use. This enabled her to assume a central position, reflecting diverse trends of the founding members of the Green Party by combining private and public aspects of her life with serious politics and open protest.

Kelly was able to boost her informal position because Green Party policies were from the group's inception a politics of "movement"—*Bewegungspolitik*—that brought issues, symbols, forms and participants of the ecological, peace, feminist, and Third World movements into the German parliament. The protest against the NATO Double-Track Decision contributed considerably to anchor the Green Party organization within the social movements to the extent that in the general election of 1983 it successfully entered parliament.[44] Petra Kelly had been the leading candidate and was a gifted communicator who eloquently addressed the public and captured media attention.[45]

Figure 10.1. Petra Kelly (Green Party, Die Grünen) blocking access to a missile depot of the US military base in Mutlangen on 1 September 1983. She is wearing a steel helmet decorated with cut flowers (ullstein bild / Krewitt)

The Civil Rights Activist: Bärbel Bohley

Bärbel Bohley (1945–2010) lived as a qualified artist in the German Democratic Republic.[46] Since the early 1980s she fought for freedom of opinion, expression, and travel. In 1985 she cofounded the Initiative for Peace and Human Rights. Bohley was arrested in 1983 for "communication with the intent of treason" (spying). Her arrest ended after six weeks because of international protests on her behalf. She cofounded the New Forum in 1989, which led to the demise of East Germany, as the German weekly paper *Die Zeit* stated in the headline to her obituary in 2010.[47]

An independent peace movement behind the Berlin wall arose in the early 1980s. Bohley actively initiated this movement. Together with Katja Havemann, the widow of the East German dissident Robert Havemann, she founded the SED-opposition group Frauen für den Frieden (Women for Peace) in 1982.[48] In doing so, she openly turned against the existing regime and attracted the increased attention of state security (Stasi), which monitored her work from then on. Bohley was arrested jointly with Ulrike Poppe and detained in Hohenschönhausen, East Berlin. She was later deported without trial to West Germany but voluntarily returned to East Germany in August 1988.[49]

The Party Theorist: Rudolf Bahro

Rudolf Bahro (1935–97) was a member of the Sozialistische Einheitspartei Deutschlands (SED, Socialist Unity Party) when he published his book *Die Alternative* (The Alternative) in 1977. It is a critique of the political and economic system of the GDR from a Marxist-communist point of view. The publication pushed him toward the political sidelines of the state and into the focus of international attention. The West German journal *Der Spiegel* published an advance copy of the book, after Bahro had been accused by the Ministry of State Security of carrying out "intelligence work" and was arrested. At the same time the SED expelled him from the party.

The book helped mobilize international supporters, who demanded his release from custody. As an author, Bahro received numerous awards. In 1979 the GDR finally yielded to public pressure and released him from prison. Afterward he went into exile in West Germany, where he cofounded the Green Party in 1980 and became a representative of ecological socialism. Bahro also published another book, *Elements of a New Policy: The Relationship between Ecology and Socialism* in 1980. Within a brief three years, he took fundamental steps in his academic career. He obtained a doctorate at the University of Hanover and was qualified as university lecturer in 1983.

Bahro advocated within the Green Party and on an international level in the European Nuclear Disarmament (END) to support calls for a nuclear-free Europe.[50] He supported a position of political non-alignment and called on East and West Germany to disarm: "It has now been generally accepted that the logic of the arms race will be broken only if a force arises that lies beyond the power of competition of the two industrial systems and which recognizes that industrialization can no longer be seen as a silver bullet to achieve freedom and social justice."[51]

The Socialist: Klaus Vack

Klaus Vack (b. 1935) participated since the 1950s in the emerging peace movement in West Germany. He was a founding member of the Sozialistisches Büro (Socialist Bureau), which became the principal organization and information center of the "undogmatic left" in Germany.[52] Within the Socialist Bureau, Vack became a passionate leader. He was a chief organizer of the Easter marches and early on denounced nuclear weapons and poison gas depots.[53] In Mutlangen he demonstrated together with Annemarie and Heinrich Böll, Petra Kelly, and Gert Bastian. In 1986 he labeled the blocking of the US military and Pershing II missiles base in Baden-Württemberg an act of civil disobedience.[54]

Vack established lines of communication between protesters and sympathizers. He commented that protesters at the military base in Mutlangen "enact[ed] an elementary and direct form of democracy on the street."[55] He remained loyal to grassroots elements within the peace movement despite his prominence in the movement. In 1980 Vack and his wife, Hanne Vack, were among the founding members of the Committee for Basic Rights and Democracy, for which they worked until 1998.[56] The couple was honored with the Fritz Bauer Prize of the Humanist Union in 1996.

The Artist: Joseph Beuys

Joseph Beuys (1921–86) was an artist and the enfant terrible of the green movement. Beuys demonstrated against the destruction of forests and announced in 1982 at the world art exhibition *Documenta 7* in Kassel that he would plant seven thousand oaks in the city.[57] He sang a song entitled "Sonne statt Reagan" (Sun instead of Reagan), as the German word for rain is *Regen,* nearly identical to the last name of the former US President Ronald Reagan.[58] The song became a hit among the protest movements and remains anchored in German collective memory. His entire life was shaped by his experiences serving in World War II, when the plane he was traveling with

Figure 10.2. Record cover: "Sonne statt Reagan" (Sun instead of Reagan) the eponymous single by Joseph Beuys, 1982 (VG Bild-Kunst)

crashed in the Crimea. He said that later he had been warmed by a coat, his wounds tended with fat. Both materials play a central role in his oeuvre.

Beuys took an active interest in politics and the policy decisions of the Federal Republic of Germany. In 1967 he founded the German Student Party, prompted by a demonstration against Mohammad Reza Pahlavi's visit to Germany (known in the West as the Shah of Iran). On the occasion of the art exhibition *Documenta 5* in 1972, Beuys called for direct democracy by popular referendum and positioned himself on the liberal-left wing of a changing Federal Republic of Germany under the Chancellorship of Willy Brandt in the 1970s. He supported performance art and democratized the prevalent concept of art in general. Everyone should be able to become an artist. Likewise, anyone should be allowed to succeed in politics.

The Writer and His Wife: Heinrich and Annemarie Böll

Heinrich Böll (1917–85) was born into a family of artists. In 1942 he married Annemarie. After World War II, he began his literary activity and soon wrote narratives influenced by his war experiences. Both he and his wife became activists in the peace movement. Böll was awarded the Georg Büchner Prize of the German Academy for Language and Literature in 1967. In 1970 he became president of the German PEN center, and in 1971 he became president of the International PEN center. Böll was awarded the Nobel Prize for Literature in 1972.

Heinrich Böll spoke in Bonn at the 1981 demonstration against the NATO Double-Track Decision. In September 1983 he joined a celebrity blockade with his wife Annemarie at the US military base in Mutlangen.[59] He also spoke in October of that same year at the peace rally in the *Hofgarten* in Bonn. As an intellectual, Böll warned of the consequences of resurgence in German national confidence. He constantly pointed to the guilt of his country and the responsibility for National Socialism and World War II. In his work and in his speeches he was a confident pacifist. Furthermore, he called for humane treatment of the Red Army Fraction (RAF) terrorists,[60] which alienated conservative groups in the Federal Republic. His commitment to such causes made him a reliable and respected representative of the political left.

The Journalists: Robert Jungk and Franz Alt

The dedication of many journalists to the ideals of the peace movement should not be underestimated. Two examples are Robert Jungk and Franz Alt.[61] Son of a Berlin family of actors, Jungk (1913–94) studied in Paris at the Sorbonne, as well as in Prague and Zurich. In 1934 he was expatriated by the Nazis. Jungk came to prominence as an international journalist and futurist.[62] His book, *Tomorrow is Already Here,* brought him sudden fame in 1952.

Another of his books, *The Millennium Man: From the Future Workshops of our Society* (1973), contributed substantially to the ecology movement. Shortly after the report *The Limits to Growth* was published by the Club of Rome, Jungk drew attention to the shortcomings of industrialization, including problems with engineering and corresponding social harm and cultural degradation. At the time, soft technology and decentralization suggested a way forward. In the context of the antinuclear movement his book *The Nuclear State* (1977) had a great impact.

Jungk had already embraced the intellectual milieu of the peace movement before the protests against the NATO Double-Track Decision began.

In the early 1980s he developed ideas for alternative ways of living that matched the aspirations of political protest in this decade and accorded well with the foundation of the Green Party. In his speeches at peace movement events Jungk focused on the issues of ecology and peace.

Franz Alt (b. 1938) belongs to a later generation of journalists. After World War II he studied and graduated with a doctoral thesis on Chancellor Konrad Adenauer. As a political journalist he initially joined the conservative Christian Democratic Union before transforming into the voice of the ecology movement and becoming the guru of the West German peace movement.[63] His book *Peace is Possible: The Policy of the Sermon on the Mount* (1983) sold a million copies. Alt formulated arguments for the peace movement similar to those of Jungk. He also provided a prominent name and a face to the movement, as he had been a television celebrity since the initial broadcast of his political program "Report Baden-Baden" in 1972.

Conclusion

What may be concluded after looking at fourteen portraits of the peace movement's protagonists from East and West Germany? Although the sketchy data on life and biographies do not cover the entire range of actors and protests against the NATO Double-Track Decision, the celebrity descriptions provided here help shed light on individual facets and individual focal points of the movement.

As a former general, Gert Bastian was a principal witness of the peace movement. His role as an activist is particularly significant because he was involved in the wording of the Krefeld Appeal that embodied the minimal consensus resolution. Bastian's background furthermore furnished him with expertise and credibility. Then there were the prominent women who gave a voice to the peace movement, stressing the importance of emotions, trust, and humanitarian concerns when it comes to policy considerations: Theologian Dorothee Sölle, organizer Eva Quistorp, and the early figurehead of the Green Party, Petra Kelly, all integrated aspects of feminism into their work as well, including their demands for disarmament in the East as well as the West.

Bärbel Bohley and Rudolf Bahro were civil rights activists in East Germany who envisaged alternative ways of social living. Both were arrested. While Bahro was expatriated to West Germany, Bohley remained in the GDR and continued her work corresponding with the West German peace movement. Bahro cofounded the Green Party in1980. Gerhard Kade was a peace researcher, who worked in West Germany on behalf of the East German state security. Kade supported numerous peace-political organizations, including the Generals for Peace, for which he recruited Gert Bastian. Kade was funded and worked on behalf of the Stasi and was able to advance to an influential position in the early 1980s.

In the ranks of the SPD, Erhard Eppler became a well-known advocate of peace policies. Despite his prominence he made few friends in his party because of his criticism of the SPD Chancellor Helmut Schmidt and his position on the NATO Double-Track Decision. Eppler also failed in his efforts to prevent the Green Party from becoming an independent political force. Hanne and Klaus Vack were independent activists in the peace movement who participated side by side with Annemarie and Heinrich Böll in the blockades at Mutlangen. They exchanged information with local activists and helped create networks. The artist Joseph Beuys, and the journalists and writers Franz Alt and Robert Jungk were all instrumental to the peace movement in contributing important ideas and in articulating arguments.

It might be said of all activists mentioned that their individual commitment made them the mouthpiece for certain groups within the movement, even though each was prominent in his or her own right. All were well connected to elites and to local grassroots activists. With such connections, these activists helped organize protests against the arms upgrade. Through their words and actions, they either directly called upon large segments of the population to protest or they provided inspiration by articulating their personal resistance against such measures as the Double-Track Decision.

Saskia Richter was an assistant professor in political science at the University of Hildesheim. She received her PhD from the University of Göttingen and the Free University of Berlin with a biography on Petra Kelly. Her research explored the foundational period of the Green Party and its internal leadership structures, as well as protest, social movements, and democratic participation. Her publications include, among others, *Die Aktivistin: Das Leben der Petra Kelly* (2010).

Notes

1. In 2013 Dieter Rucht introduced the term *key figure*. See Dieter Rucht, "Schlüsselfiguren statt Führer: Zur (Selbst-)Steuerung sozialer Bewegungen," *Forschungsjournal Soziale Bewegungen. Analysen zu Demokratie und Zivilgesellschaft* 26 (2013): 32–43.
2. "Committee for Peace, Disarmament, and Cooperation was founded in Bad Godesberg on 7 December 1974. As a nonregistered association, the organization had neither a statute nor supervisory body. Reputedly it maintained close contact with the SED and communist groups in the FRG." Udo Baron, "Die verführte Friedensbewegung," *Die politische Meinung* 407 (2003): 56–58.

3. Wilfried von Bredow, "Zusammensetzung und Ziele der Friedensbewegung in der Bundesrepublik Deutschland," *Aus Politik und Zeitgeschichte* (hereafter, *APuZ*) 24 (1982): 7; Ulrich Frey, "Die Friedensbewegung im Westen in den achtziger Jahren," *Friedensforum* no. 2 (2008): 33–35. On this point see also the contribution by Kathrin Fahlenbrach and Laura Stapane in this volume.
4. Flyer from Aktion Sühnezeichen/Friedensdienste, Bonn, 10 October 1981, Archiv Grünes Gedächtnis (henceforth AGG), Petra Kelly Archive (henceforth PKA) 3430.
5. Von Bredow, "Zusammensetzung und Ziele," 8.
6. Flyer from Aktion Sühnezeichen/Friedensdienste, Bonn 10 October 1981, AGG, PKA 3430.
7. Gustav Heinemann-Initiative, newsletter no. 10, 3 October 1981, AGG, PKA 3430.
8. Saskia Richter, "Gert Bastian: Seitenwechsel für den Frieden?" in *Seiteneinsteiger: Unkonventionelle Politiker-Karrieren in der Parteiendemokratie*, ed. Robert Lorenz and Matthias Micus (Wiesbaden, 2009), 410–30.
9. Karlheinz Lipp, Reinhold Lütgemeier-Davin, and Holger Nehring, eds., *Frieden und Friedensbewegung in Deutschland 1892–1992* (Essen, 2010).
10. Wilhelm Wegner, "Vorbilder. Karl Bechert gilt als Vater der Antiatombewegung in Deutschland," *Chrismon* 2 (2012).
11. Saskia Richter, "Gert Bastian: Seitenwechsel für den Frieden?" in Lorenz and Matthias Micus, *Seiteneinsteiger*, 418.
12. Ministry of Defense Secretary of State Willfried Penner quoted in newspaper article "Ex-General macht Sowjetpropaganda!" (Former General Proliferates Soviet Propaganda), *Bild am Sonntag*, 15 February 1981.
13. Gert Bastian, *Frieden schaffen! Gedanken zur Sicherheitspolitik* (Munich, 1983), 96–97.
14. Gert Bastian, "Wer Pershing sagt, muß keineswegs SS-20 sagen," in *Bonn Oct. 10, 1981: Friedensdemonstration für Abrüstung und Entspannung in Europa. Reden, Fotos ...*, ed. Aktion Sühnezeichen/Friedensdienste; Aktionsgemeinschaft Dienst für den Frieden (Bornheim, 1981), 149.
15. Gert Bastian, "Die SS-20 eignet sich nicht als Erstschlag-Waffe," *Blätter für deutsche und internationale Politik* 7 (1981): 783.
16. Lecture by Gert Bastian, 10 June 1982, AGG, PKA 984.
17. "Gestorben: Dorothee Sölle," *Der Spiegel*, 4 May 2003.
18. The role of women in the peace movement is also discussed by Reinhild Kreis in this volume.
19. Andreas Buro, "Friedensbewegung," in *Die sozialen Bewegungen in Deutschland seit 1945. Ein Handbuch*, ed. Roland Roth and Dieter Rucht (Frankfurt am Main, 2007), 278–81.
20. Dirk Banse and Michael Behrendt, "Der Stasi-Maulwurf von Bonn," *Die Welt*, 28 April 2004.
21. The chapter by Jan Hansen in this volume also discusses the Peace Movement, and therefore I omit a discussion of Brandt and Lafontaine at this point.
22. Friedhelm Boll and Jan Hansen, "Doppelbeschluss und Nachrüstung als innerparteiliches Problem der SPD," in *Zweiter Kalter Krieg und Friedensbewegung: Der NATO-Doppelbeschluss in deutsch-deutscher und internationaler Perspektive*, ed. Philipp Gassert, Tim Geiger, and Hermann Wentker (Munich, 2011), 203–28.

23. See also the contribution by Rainer Eckert in this volume.
24. For more on this and other group categories, see Thomas Leif, *Die professionelle Bewegung: Friedensbewegung von innen* (Bonn, 1985), 53.
25. Mechthild Müser, "Was hast Du getan, wird der Engel mich fragen," Zum 80. Geburtstag der Theologin Dorothee Sölle, *Bayern 2*, 27 September 2009 (radio transcript).
26. "Dorothee Sölle vor dem Amtsgericht in Schwäbisch Gmünd," in Lipp, Lütgemeier-Davin and Nehring, *Frieden und Friedensbewegung*, 7. "Friedensbewegung der achtziger Jahre in den beiden deutschen Staaten sowie nach der Wiedervereinigung," in Lipp, Lütgemeier-Davin, and Nehring, *Frieden und Friedensbewegung*, 379.
27. Quoted in Müser, "Was hast du getan," 9.
28. Ibid.
29. Interview with Eva Quistorp, "Die Seele der Grünen," in *Grünes Gedächtnis 2010*, ed. Heinrich Böll Stiftung (Berlin, 2010), 13.
30. Ibid., 15–18.
31. Ibid., 18.
32. Joachim Raschke, *Die Grünen: Wie sie wurden, was sie sind* (Köln, 1993), 114.
33. Interview with Eva Quistorp, "Die Seele der Grünen," 28.
34. Hermann Wentker, "Zwischen Unterstützung und Ablehnung der sowjetischen Linie: Die DDR, der Doppelbeschluss und die Nachrüstung," in Gassert, Geiger, and Wentker, *Zweiter Kalter Krieg*, 137–54. See also the contribution by Hermann Wentker in this volume.
35. Holger Nehring and Benjamin Ziemann, "Führen alle Wege nach Moskau? Der NATO-Doppelbeschluss und die Friedensbewegung, eine Kritik," *Vierteljahreshefte für Zeitgeschichte* 59, no. 1 (2011): 81–100.
36. Udo Baron, *Kalter Krieg und heißer Frieden: Der Einfluss der SED und ihrer westdeutschen Verbündeten auf die Partei "Die Grünen"* (Münster, 2003), 43–44.
37. Markus Wolf, *Spionagechef im geheimen Krieg: Erinnerungen* (Munich, 1997), 343.
38. "Pankows 'nützliche Idioten'? Die westdeutsche Friedensbewegung und der Einfluss des Ministeriums für Staatssicherheit," http://www.daserste.de/planspiel/allround_dyn~uid,y5338dmbh2a1brtz~cm.asp.
39. Dirk Banse and Michael Behrendt, "Der Stasi-Maulwurf von Bonn," *Die Welt*, 28 April 2004.
40. Erhard Eppler, "Warum denn nicht mit den Grünen?" *Der Spiegel* 32 (1978): 21–23.
41. Proposal for the schedule of the final rally on 10 October 1981, AGG, PKA 3430.
42. Saskia Richter, *Die Aktivistin: Das Leben der Petra Kelly* (Munich, 2010).
43. Interview with Petra Kelly, "Wir sind die Antipartei-Partei," *Der Spiegel*, 14 June 1982.
44. Saskia Richter, "Der Protest gegen den NATO-Doppelbeschluss und die Konsolidierung der Partei *Die Grünen* zwischen 1979 und 1983," in Gassert, Geiger, and Wentker, *Zweiter Kalter Krieg*, 229–45.
45. For example, Marion Schreiber, "Immer nur bei anderen gut," *Der Spiegel*, 3 October 1983.
46. http://www.baerbelbohley.de/dossier.php. See also the contribution by Rainer Eckert in this volume.
47. Robert Ide, "Bärbel Bohley lebte für die Freiheit," *Tagesspiegel*, 11 September 2010.

48. Ibid.
49. Gedenkstätte Berlin-Hohenschönhausen, Bärbel Bohley, http://www.stiftung-hsh .de/page.php?cat_id=CAT_181&con_id=CON_1358&page_id=724&subcat_id= CAT_181&recentcat=CAT_165&back=1&special=0&html=0.
50. Guntolf Herzberg and Kurt Seifert, *Rudolf Bahro: Glaube an der Veränderbare. Eine Biografie* (Berlin, 2002), 359–61.
51. Rudolf Bahro, "Ein Netz von erheblicher Spannkraft," *Der Spiegel,* 13 December 1982.
52. Michael Schmid, "Jahrzehntelang unermüdlich für Frieden und Gerechtigkeit: Klaus Vack ist 70 geworden," http://frilahd.twoday.net/stories/755038.
53. Wilhelm Bittorf, "Giftgas ging, Unrecht bleibt," *Der Spiegel,* 29 October 1990.
54. Klaus Vack, "Ziviler Ungehorsam in Mutlangen, October 5, 1986," AGG, PKA 2220.
55. Ibid., 9.
56. Elke Steven, "Hanne und Klaus Vack verabschieden sich vom Komitee für Grundrechte," *Friedensforum* 1 (1999), http://www.friedenskooperative.de/ff/ff99/1-10 .htm.
57. Rudolf Schmitz, "Überforderung als Prinzip," *Deutschlandradio Kultur,* 23 January 2006.
58. Bernhard Schulz, "Joseph Beuys: Der prophetische Künstler," *Tagesspiegel,* 23 January 2011.
59. See also the contribution by Kathrin Fahlenbrach and Laura Stapane in this volume.
60. "Heinrich Böll: Ein 'anderer' Deutscher. Zum 25. Todestag," *3Sat,* 16 July 2005.
61. See also the contribution by Marianne Zepp in this volume.
62. "Robert Jungk, der Mann, der die Zukunft entdeckte," *Die Zeit,* 5 May 1961.
63. Ulrich Schwarz, "Als Franz Alt schwanger wurde ...," *Der Spiegel,* 13 May 1985.

Select Bibliography

The literature on the subject is based on contemporary publications and on portraits and biographies that were published in retrospect. Von Bredow has written on the social and political background of the peace movement. Schmid's essay follows on von Bredow, describing the social structure and driving forces and critical moments for peace activists. Leif provides a description of the groups and organizations that made up the Coordinating Committee of the peace movement.

Surprisingly little has been written about the most important protagonist of the peace movement: Gert Bastian. Schwarzer provides some information. An essay by Richter is an attempt to give a more precise explanation with respect to the peace movement. Wind has published a biography on Dorothee Sölle. The life and death of Petra Kelly got a sensitive report by her close friend Sara Parkin. For an academic biography see Richter. For additional academic treatment, see Bevan (2001) and Milder (2010). A perspective on both the life and the oeuvre of the artist and activist Joseph Beuys is provided by De Domizio Durini. Herzberg and Seifert, two companions of Rudolf Bahro, have written a biography of their colleague. Vormweg writes about Heinrich Böll, and for information on Erhard Eppler, there is a recently published biography by Faerber-Husemann written from the perspective of the SPD.

Bevan, Ruth A. "Petra Kelly: The *Other* Green." *New Political Science* 23, no. 2 (2001): 181–202.
von Bredow, Wilfried. "Zusammensetzung und Ziele der Friedensbewegung in der Bundesrepublik Deutschland." *Aus Politik und Zeitgeschichte* 24 (19 June 1982): 3–13.
De Domizio Durini, Lucrezia. *The Felt Hat: Joseph Beuys, a Life Told.* Rome, 1992.
Faerber-Husemann, Renate. *Der Querdenker: Erhard Eppler, Eine Biografie.* Bonn, 2010.
Grey, Mary. "Diversity, Harmony and in the End, Justice: Remembering Dorothee Soelle." *Feminist Theology* 13, no. 3 (2005): 343–57.
Herzberg, Guntolf, and Kurt Seifert. *Rudolf Bahro: Glaube an das Veränderbare. Eine Biografie.* Berlin, 2002.
Leif, Thomas. *Die professionelle Bewegung: Friedensbewegung von innen.* Bonn, 1985.
Milder, Stephen. "Thinking Globally, Acting (Trans-)Locally: Petra Kelly and the Transnational Roots of West German Green Politics." *Central European History* 43, no. 2 (2010): 301–26.
Parkin, Sara. *The Life and Death of Petra Kelly.* London, 1994.
Reid, James H. *Heinrich Böll: A German for His Time.* Oxford and New York, 1988.
Richter, Saskia. "Gert Bastian: Seitenwechsel für den Frieden?" in *Seiteneinsteiger: Unkonventionelle Politiker-Karrieren in der Parteiendemokratie,* ed. Robert Lorenz and Matthias Micus, 410–30. Wiesbaden, 2009.
———. *Die Aktivistin: Das Leben der Petra Kelly.* Munich, 2010.
Schmid, Günther. "Zur Soziologie der Friedensbewegung und des Jugendprotestes." *Aus Politik und Zeitgeschichte* 24 (19 June 1982): 15–30.
Schwarzer, Alice. *Eine tödliche Liebe: Petra Kelly und Gert Bastian.* Cologne, 1993.
Vormweg, Heinrich. *Der andere Deutsche: Heinrich Böll. Eine Biografie.* Cologne, 2000.
Wind, Renate. *Dorothee Sölle: Rebellin und Mystikerin.* Stuttgart, 2008.

Chapter 11

The Independent Peace Movement in East Germany

Rainer Eckert

Discussion of contemporary German history frequently takes as a given that when Germans lived under a dictatorship, they predominantly, if not exclusively, demonstrated conformity, obedience, and submission. However, a closer inspection of the Nazi period and the communist dictatorship shows a different picture.[1] The anticommunist opposition in the German Democratic Republic (GDR) included an independent peace movement, which first developed under the protection of Protestant churches. This movement later took on a political character and played a decisive role in the fall of the communist regime.[2] The year 1989 illustrates—for example, the meeting of the Gruppen Konkret für den Frieden VII (Groups for Peace, Here and Now VII) in February in Greifswald—how other opposition organizations, such as human rights and environmental groups, took the place of the peace movement. Ultimately this process gave way to the emergence of political opposition parties and movements that both intellectually and with regard to their membership grew out of the peace movement.

Of particular interest is the Catholic Church's attitude on this point. Catholicism was a minority faith in East Germany and existed in a kind of diaspora situation after the end of World War II and the dictatorship of the Socialist Unity Party of Germany (SED). The church thus kept its distance from discussions about the socio-political aspects of independent peace cooperation while focusing on establishing cross-border ties with the Vatican.[3] It was not until 1983 that the Berlin Conference of Bishops criticized the international arms race and the military instruction (*Wehrunterricht*) received in schools and other educational training institutions of East Germany. Irrespective of these institutional constraints, however, many lay Catholics joined Protestant groups and were particularly committed to the ecumenical peace movement of the 1980s.

The Spectrum of Peace Efforts

The peace movement in the Soviet Occupation Zone (SBZ) and subsequently in the German Democratic Republic needs to be distinguished from the peace efforts initiated and supported by the SED and its allies, including parties pretending to be independent and other dependent organizations that were designed to serve official interests. Members of those organizations also included a sizeable group of established theologians, especially at East German universities, which included the Weißenseer Arbeitskreis (Weissenseer Working Group) in East Berlin, the Christliche Friedenskonferenz (CFK, Christian Peace Conference) and parts of the Protestant establishment. Indeed many supporters of this state-sponsored church policy worked simultaneously for the secret police of the Ministry of State Security. This fact continued to evoke bitter memories in the Protestant church after German unification and has still not been thoroughly investigated today. For their part, the SED considered members of the independent peace groups to be "hostile-negative," which is to say "subversive," Western agents. On this basis, cooperation between the two sides was obviously out of the question and was never seriously considered.

Within the spectrum of peace initiatives in the broadest sense of the term, however, one needs to include the state administration's peace policy, or more precisely that of the SED. It was a fundamental problem for the state party to declare on the one hand that socialism was an integral part of the peace process and vice versa, while simultaneously arguing for a "just war," that is, a "struggle against imperialism." The SED always considered the "struggle for peace" equivalent to fighting for its sovereignty against outside forces and to maintaining or increasing its hold on legitimate power inside the country. It regarded the Peace Council of the GDR (Friedensrat der DDR) and the World Peace Council as the tools to implement these aims.

In this context it should be pointed out that there was also a struggle about the "official" church and Protestant peace policies. The SED pressured all Protestant churches to represent the government's views on peace policy toward West Germany and all foreign powers.[4] Thus the peace activities of the Protestant establishment began immediately after the liberation from National Socialism within the Evangelische Kirche in Deutschland (EKD, Protestant Church in Germany) and extended until 1969, to be continued in the Bund der Evangelischen Kirchen der DDR (BEK, Federation of Protestant Churches in East Germany).[5]

Swords into Plowshares: The Development of the Independent Peace and Civil Rights Movement

After the aggression of the Warsaw Pact countries toward Czechoslovakia on 21 August 1968, a dissident citizens' or civil rights movement started to develop in the early 1970s. Members consisted of employees of the Protestant churches, people who had lost their jobs due to political pressure, intellectuals, artists, and members of marginalized youth groups. Apart from a commitment to peace and disarmament, the opposition relied in large part on East Germany's official recognition of human rights at the Helsinki Conference on Security and Cooperation in Europe (CSCE) in 1975. The civil rights movement of the late 1970s and 1980s was closely associated with this peace movement, whose focal points were to be found in social diaconal—or "open"—work, such as that performed by young people in regional centers in places like Jena, Rudolstadt, and Halle-Neustadt from 1971 onward. This strategy allowed for discussions about the establishment of a social peace service. Annual peace seminars, for example, began in 1973 in Königswalde, a small town of about six hundred inhabitants close to Zwickau. Here mostly young people gathered twice a year to talk about human rights and peacekeeping. Participants were thus encouraged to discuss critical issues not covered in East German media. Protests were voiced against East German military education at schools, and activists tried to establish ties with members of the West German and Western European peace movements. Peace groups of the Protestant churches formed by young parish members played a major role, as did church schools, educational training centers, and the Evangelische Studentengemeinden (ESG, Protestant Students Communities), jointly working for peace.[6] Especially the ESG, but also the Jungmännerwerk (Young Men's Association) and the Katholische Studentengemeinden (Catholic Student Communities), hosted events that promoted free speech, although it should be added that spying by the secret police could not be avoided. In any case, these groups presented platforms for discourses on religion, philosophy, and history, as well as current issues; these included integrity of creation and the question of whether and to what extent a Christian should partake in an atheist state's military service.

Young Christians in particular were influenced and shaped by events that began in the mid-1970s and provoked critical thinking and various forms of protest. One of those pivotal events was the self-immolation of Protestant Minister Oskar Brüsewitz on 18 August 1976 in Zeitz. Enacted as a protest against communist youth policy, the suicide of this martyr brought about several important developments. First, it mobilized followers to criticize the strategy of certain church leaders of creating a "church within socialism"[7] and to take a more clearly defined moral stand on social issues. Second, his protest drew attention to the fate of East German youth. Such public awareness would soon fuel the momentum of the peace movement as further protests were staged against the "military education" enforced in East German schools (a measure introduced by the SED in 1978 to help ensure the militarization of a communist dictatorship) and against NATO's Double-Track Decision in late 1979 (which was also opposed by the West German peace movement). The independent, as opposed to the state-sponsored, peace movement in East Germany had now established its center in the movement "Swords into Plowshares" (from Isaiah 2:3–4, also Micah 4:3). The Saxon State youth pastor Harald Bretschneider had chosen the image, taken from a sculpture in front of the UN building in New York designed by the Soviet sculptor Evgeniy Vuchetich, and it became the symbol for peace in the following decades.[8] This icon appeared immune to SED manipulation but alluded at the same time to profound Christian values. It quickly became popular, especially among the young, and became even more famous when the theologian Friedrich Schorlemmer had a blacksmith forge a symbolic sword into a plowshare in June 1983 at a church convention in Wittenberg.[9]

In the years following 1979 the peace movement in East Germany enjoyed a growth spurt. Up to this point only select Protestant youth congregations and working groups had participated in peace efforts. This changed when the nature of this peace work became public ("open work") and ever more groups were drawn into systematically discussing issues pertaining to peace. At the same time the number of conscientious objectors increased, as did the number of *Bausoldaten* (conscripts allowed do their military service by working on construction projects). It was only to be expected that the SED would feel challenged by the developments under the peace symbol of the Protestant church and accuse its leaders of being "hostile-negative elements" who supported the aspirations of the "class enemy" and undermined the defense capability of East Germany, thus ultimately jeopardizing peace. Repression set in not only against those who carried the emblems of "Swords into Plowshares" in schools and universities but also against apprentices in all domains. Young Christians had to remove their badges from parkas and jackets and were "guided by the police," in other words, registered by the police and punished for violating "socialist norms." Many teachers or police officers simply removed the badges by force, but other badge wearers were expelled from school or dismissed from universities. In some cases, the police beat young people on the street who had been identified as adolescent independent peace activists.

Figure 11.1. Der Wittenberger Friedenskreis (The Wittenberg Peace Group) invited the participants of a church convention on 24 September 1983, to a meeting at the Lutherhof. Approximately 2,000 mostly young people gathered in an ancient monastery after sunset to watch a blacksmith forge a sword into a plowshare (epd-bild / Bernd Bohm).

When the State Youth-instigated counter-movement called "Der Friede muss bewaffnet sein" (Peace must be armed) had little success, the SED pressured the Protestant churches and their leadership. Although certain members of the churches repeatedly protested against government blackmail, the church leaders withdrew their support for the movement that they had backed for so long. Thus the Saxon Synod declared in a letter dated 24 March 1982 that it could no longer protect young Christians from the consequences of their independent peace statements.[10]

Make Peace without Weapons

In the early 1980s there were independently operating groups within church structures, such as the Pankow peace group and the Friedrichsfelder peace circle, both named after districts in Berlin. In 1980, the Protestant churches initiated a first Peace Decade under the motto "Frieden schaffen ohne Waffen" (Make peace without weapons). The decade was intended to be a period of intense peace efforts and it lasted until 1989 when the Berlin wall fell. A similar initiative in Dresden was proposed in 1981 for a program of "social peace service" that was to replace military service. These and similar activities increased noticeably throughout the 1980s and had a mobilizing effect. This holds particularly true for the Berlin Appeal "Frieden schaffen ohne Waffen," written by East Berlin's Pastor Rainer Eppelmann and prominent dissident Robert Havemann in 1982, and the Dresden Peace Forum of the same year. Unlike many West German intellectuals who in the Krefeld Appeal in November 1980 focused their protest on the NATO Double-Track Decision, these East German authors grounded their reasoning on two premises: they linked a secure peace in Europe with the resolution of the hitherto unresolved German question, that is, the partition of Germany, and demanded German political self-determination as well as the dissolution of both German states from their respective military alliances.[11] This brought the theme of Germany's division onto the agenda. Furthermore the authors, like many other public figures signing the Appeal, emphasized that any consideration of peace was closely interconnected to the granting of democratic rights and civil liberties in East Germany. The SED was thus challenged at its very center.

Groups that adopted the Berlin Appeal's demands were glad for the opportunity to incorporate elements and patterns of religious arguments into their protests against the dictatorship and its militaristic objectives as this offered at least some protection against political persecution. Apart from the Peace Decades and church-sponsored initiatives, the work of Frauen für

Figure 11.2. East German civil rights activist Bärbel Bohley holding a banner declaring "We hunger for disarmament. Fasting for Life" at an event named Fasting for Peace in the East Berlin Redeemer Church in August 1983 (Roland Jahn / Gustav Havemann Gesellschaft, Berlin).

den Frieden (Women for Peace), the *Frieden konkret* (Peace, here and now) seminars, the Environmental Library at the Zion Church in East Berlin, the Green-ecological network Arche (Ark), and the Freundeskreis Wehrdiensttotalverweigerer (Friends of Conscientious Objectors to Military Service) were responsible for attracting public attention and creating an increasing interconnectedness among the various peace efforts. The *Frieden konkret* seminars were especially active and developed into an annually held coordination meeting of peace groups in opposition to the SED regime. At this time there were approximately a hundred consolidated and independently functioning associations, with peace groups existing in nearly all cities of East Germany, that could mobilize supporters, for example, in the Protestant student communities or church schools. The Aktionskreis Halle (AKH, Action Group of Halle) was the most important association of the Catholic Church.

Peace Contacts across the Border

The support from the West—and particularly from West Germany—for the independent peace movement was small and confined to certain public figures, a few groups of expatriates from East Germany, and a few church parishes. Particularly memorable was the meeting on 31 October 1983 between SED General Secretary Erich Honecker and seven West German politicians of the Green Party in East Berlin, at which Petra Kelly wore a T-shirt with the slogan "Swords into Plowshares." Lukas Beckmann from the Green Party handed Honecker a "personal peace treaty," a document originally drafted by the churches of Mecklenburg and Saxony. The SED politician finally ratified the following points: a reduction of enemy images and negative stereotypes and abdication of reciprocal violence.[12] The dictator, however, refused to sign an obligation to initiate a process of disarmament in his own country. Instead, he ordered the release from custody of an East German peace movement activist on the following day. But this did little to relax the situation in East Germany, because only a few days later a communal attempt by the Green Party members in collaboration with East German opposition to deliver disarmament appeals to the US and USSR embassies was stopped by state security. Coordinated joint protests between East-West remained an exception despite West German peace initiatives repeatedly drawing attention to the situation in East Germany.

Although East German peace activists defined their goals and strategies for action partly in relation to the West German disarmament movement, the two sides had little in common, since the movement in the West was primarily directed against NATO's nuclear weapons while East German activists called for bilateral or general disarmament, given the omnipresence of Soviet troops in their country. The Western peace activists showed little understanding of the importance of democratization in the Soviet bloc or interest in opening a discussion about German unification for the sake of peace.[13] On this point the peace movement in East Germany was frequently more realistic and also less affected by anti-Americanism than some quarters in the West. Nonetheless, groups of the independent peace movement in East Germany were interested in being acknowledged in the West as this promised a measure of protection against political persecution. It should be kept in mind that many Christians participating in the peace movement in both the East and the West had direct cross-border contacts, especially in twin parishes, and thus learned to understand different views and perspectives. What effect this had on the peace movement in the two German states is, as of now, still largely unknown. The same applies to individual contacts in West or East Germany with Central Europe, where relations with Charter 77 in Czechoslovakia and the Polish opposition were most obviously fruitful.

Official Peace Policy

The SED leadership faced two problems after the NATO Double-Track Decision of 1979 and the reduction in Soviet oil deliveries in 1982, a measure taken by the USSR to help offset its economic difficulties: on the one hand, SED leaders wanted to stay loyal to Moscow and maintain its alliance, and on the other, their country was becoming increasingly dependent on the West economically. Therefore East Germany needed, at least on the face of it, to continue a policy of détente. The political leverage it could gain from the policies of the Soviet Union was at the same time extremely limited, and so it sought to strengthen the peace movement in the Federal Republic of Germany while preventing Bonn from committing to an arms upgrade. Erich Honecker in East Berlin may subjectively have been quite serious in his commitment to peace and against a nuclear war, but his two-fold dilemma intensified after the decision by the West German Bundestag on 22 November 1983 to ratify and, if necessary, implement the NATO Double-Track Treaty.[14]

The first problem was the principle of "peaceful coexistence" adopted from the Soviet Union, which in the changing circumstances of the 1980s led to increasing ideological "contortions."[15] For one thing, the ultimate goal of the establishment of a universal communist system remained a utopian objective. At the same time, a military confrontation was ruled out and peace elevated to a supreme good, regardless of the existing social order. Yet "class struggle" and fighting "aggressive imperialism" remained essential ingredients of state ideology. In order to reconcile these opposing goals, vague descriptions of an association of "people of different social status, political position and general ideological conviction from all countries and regions of the world" were being offered as the official doctrine.[16]

In the eyes of the SED leadership the independent peace activists in their country were not members of a peace movement but representatives of a "hostile-negative force" remote-controlled by the West. The East German state party thus tried to curb the independent peace movement in the second half of the 1980s by representing its own organizations as the true instigators of disarmament efforts. In September 1987 at the peace march in commemoration of Olof Palme, this approach resulted in representatives from both the official and the oppositional peace movements showing up at the event. At the same time the party leadership also pressured the Protestant churches to oppose the unofficial peace groups. Even if the SED did not fundamentally alter its methods, it reacted with increasing sensitivity to the Western opinion on its rule and governmental practices. Erich Honecker's visit as party Secretary General to the West German capital in September this same year certainly played a role in this area. The secret police meanwhile kept harassing activists of the independent peace movement such as Bärbel Bohley, Roland Jahn, and Ulrike Poppe. This did not prevent regional peace meetings from taking place but resulted at times in individual members of the opposition resigning and defecting to the Federal Republic of Germany. However, there was a marked tendency for groups such as the Arbeitskreis Solidarische Kirche (Working Group Church Solidarity) and Kirche von unten (Church from Below) to maintain a distance from the Protestant establishment by staging their own alternative church conventions. Over the years a great diversity of opposition groups emerged, and these were joined by groups openly committed to the recovery and conservation of the badly damaged environment as well as to human rights issues.

The Peace Movement in the Second Half of the 1980s

The development of an opposition with a twofold political concept that linked international military détente with internal democratization[17] gained momentum in 1987 when the Konziliare Prozess für Gerechtigkeit, Frieden, und Bewahrung der Schöpfung (Congregational Process for Justice, Peace, and Integrity of Creation) drew on a proposition for a peace council first put forward by Dietrich Bonhoeffer in 1934. The Sixth Assembly of the World Council of Churches in Vancouver in 1983 seized on this idea, and starting in 1988 (under the motto "A Hope Learns to Walk") Catholics worldwide joined ecumenical gatherings. Of utmost significance was that the third session of the Ecumenical Assembly in Dresden in April 1989 decided to publish twelve "resolution texts" that pointed to substantial "cancerous defects" in the society of East Germany.[18] The list included the SED's and government's complete and total claim to domination and power with respect to politics and economics, but also to society at large and in relation to individual people. Citizens found themselves treated exclusively as objects of state administration and not as individuals collaborating with the leadership in a critical manner. Resulting tensions between rulers and the ruled would ultimately threaten not only inner peace but also peace in the common "European house." In effect, this conciliar process enacted by the ecumenical assemblies took the communist rulers at their word, and created a predicament for a repressive SED regime that helped erode its legitimization. From this point of view, Peter Maser's observation is right that in its final stages the peace work of the BEK (at least partly) liberated itself from the constraints of East German state structures.[19]

What helped further a critical attitude toward the state in the later years of the peace movement were a series of Protestant church conventions organized not by official church leaders but by parish members, particularly in East Berlin and Leipzig. Finally the opposition group Initiative Frieden und Menschenrechte (Initiative for Peace and Human Rights), founded between 1985 and 1986, took a crucial step forward by leaving the umbrella of the Protestant churches at the beginning of 1989. By demanding a public role, it was able to discard the self-imposed constraints to act only in private or on church premises and contributed to East Germany's dictatorship stumbling day after day toward its demise through a peaceful revolution. The prayers for peace, which had been performed for years at St Nicholas Church in Leipzig, turned out to have more than symbolic significance: they saw fruition in the city's peaceful demonstration of seventy thousand people on 9 October 1989. The transformation from independent groups in the peace movement to political opposition groups would become the foremost condition for the successful revolution that achieved freedom and German unity.

Conclusion

The East German opposition, including the principal leaders of the independent peace movement, did not recognize until very late the possibility of a revolutionary transformation of the outmoded power system run by the SED. Even after their catastrophic results in the first free parliamentary elections in decades on 18 March 1990 (with the exception of the newly formed East German Social Democratic Party, which, however, also failed to achieve its lofty predictions), many civil rights and peace activists still believed that the prospective unification would generate fundamental changes in the "old" West Germany, which they could influence. One hope was that both German states would leave their respective military blocs and achieve a demilitarized united Germany. Another was the vision of a German unification process that was inextricably tied to a European unification process. At the same time, participants only grasped rather slowly how inseparably East Germany's existence as a state had been connected to the dictatorial regime of the state party.

In this context the independent peace movement rapidly lost influence as many of its representatives joined different opposition groups and became increasingly active in a wider variety of political parties. The highly militarized communist dictatorship, along with its entire military apparatus, melted away, and soon afterward the Soviet or Russian troops withdrew from their strongholds in the East and left a now united Germany. The independent peace movement had lost its frame of reference and objectives. Today it has become part of a pan-German movement for peaceful conflict resolution. Eastern Germany is characterized by a continuation of the Peace Decades of the Protestant Church. Nowadays they have nowhere near the political importance or experience the same level of participation that they had achieved in East Germany, but this also applies to the church and its work in general. The independent peace movement of East Germany was thus in its specific form unique and a product of the second German dictatorship. Under new and democratic conditions the struggle for disarmament and peace almost inevitably would need to find new forms.

Yet, the independent peace movement as a whole did have an impact beyond the 1989 revolution and shaped the process of German reunification albeit in an indirect manner.[20] Two ministers of the first freely elected East German government, Rainer Eppelmann and Markus Meckel, had been *Bausoldaten,* and many other political actors had previously participated in the independent peace movement. The experience they gained in the peace movement helped them assimilate the democratic process and nurtured their principles of nonviolence and open controversy. The legacy of the peace movement was felt not least by the representatives of the democratic forces in the Round Table conferences, and its experiences were incorporated into a draft constitution for a democratic East German state, which never came about. Although it was neither realistic nor desirable to hope for such a political entity, a suitable coat of arms would have been the emblem "Swords into Plowshares" depicted on the national black-red-gold background as an apt memorial to a peaceful revolution.

Rainer Eckert is the former director of the Zeitgeschichtliches Forum Leipzig der Stiftung Haus der Geschichte der Bundesrepublik Deutschland and professor at the Institute for Cultural Studies at the University Leipzig. He is the recipient of the 2008 Constitutional Medal in recognition for his contributions on behalf of the liberal-democratic development in the state of Saxony and the 2009 recipient of the Federal Cross of Merit with Ribbon of the Federal Republic of Germany. He is the author of numerous publications on contemporary German history and politics of memory.

Notes

1. On this debate with regard to East Germany see, for example, Ilko-Sascha Kowalczuk, "Von der Freiheit, Ich zu sagen: Widerständiges Verhalten in der DDR," in *Zwischen Selbstbehauptung und Anpassung: Formen des Widerstandes in der DDR*, ed. Ulrike Poppe, Rainer Eckert, and Ilko-Sascha Kowalczuk (Berlin, 1995), 90; Rainer Eckert, "Widerstand und Opposition in der DDR: Siebzehn Thesen," *Zeitschrift Geschichtswissenschaft, Berlin* 44 (1996): 1, 52.
2. Peter Maser, "Selbständigkeit, Einheit und innerer Zusammenhang der Friedensbewegung in der DDR," in *Raketenpower um Europa: Das sowjetische SS 20-Abenteuer und die Friedensbewegung*, ed. Jürgen Maruhn and Manfred Wilke (Munich, 2001), 164. For a brief outline of the problem, see Hubertus Knabe, "Unabhängige Friedensbewegung," in *Lexikon Opposition und Widerstand in der SED-Diktatur*, ed. Hans-Joachim Veen et al. (Berlin and Munich 2000), 141–43.
3. Ehrhart Neubert, *Opposition in der DDR 1949–1989* (Berlin 1997), 468–69.
4. On this and on the Protestant opposition in East Germany in general, see Neubert, *Opposition*.
5. According to Peter Maser, these can structured in a first (the peace efforts in the EKD), second (engagements in the BEK and its surroundings), and finally a third phase (cooperation as well as differentiation between church and independent groups). For an overview of this process see Maser, *Selbstständigkeit*, 162–96, or more generally, Bernd Eisenfeld, *Kriegsdienstverweigerung in der DDR, ein Friedensdienst? Genesis, Befragung, Analyse, Dokumente* (Frankfurt am Main 1978).
6. Neubert, *Opposition*, 463–70.
7. Helmut Müller-Enbergs, Wolfgang Stock, and Marco Wiesner, "Das Fanal: Das Opfer des Pfarrers Brüsewitz aus Rippicha und die evangelische Kirche. Münster 1999," in *Das Signal von Zeitz: Reaktionen der Kirche, des Staates und der Medien auf die Selbstverbrennung von Oskar Brüsewitz. Eine Dokumentation*, ed. Harald Schultze (Leipzig, 1993).
8. Rainer Eckert and Kornelia Lobmeier, *Schwerter zu Pflugscharen: Geschichte eines Symbols* (Bonn, 2007).
9. Ibid., 6–11.
10. Ibid., 20.
11. See also the contributions of Hermann Wentker and Saskia Richter in this volume.
12. Eckert and Lobmeier, *Schwerter*, 22. See also Hermann Wentker in this volume.

13. Maser, *Selbstständigkeit*, 188.
14. See also Hermann Wentker in this volume.
15. See also the cumbersome elaborations in Waltraud Böhme and Gert-Joachim Glaessner, *Kleines Politisches Wörterbuch*, 7th edition (East Berlin, 1988) on the following terms: *Frieden, Friedensbewegung, Friedensprogramme der UdSSR, Friedensrat der DDR, Friedliche Koexistenz und Weltfriedensrat* (285–92, 295–98, 1080–81).
16. *Kleines Politisches Wörterbuch*, 288.
17. Neubert, *Opposition*, 558.
18. Maser, *Selbstständigkeit*, 182.
19. Ibid., 184.
20. Eckert/Lobmeier, *Schwerter*, 44–45.

Select Bibliography

Neubert published the authoritative work on the history of resistance and opposition in East Germany. This includes a description of the Protestant church members' activities and the peace movement. More recent discussions on the peace movement were published by journalists in West Germany and are to be found in Buescher, Wensierski, and Wolschner. Ehring and Dallwitz offer a general review of the early years of West Germany. Bickhardt provides a preliminary summary depiction of East Germany's peace movement by an East German dissident living in the Federal Republic of Germany. Knabe has written a well-informed and accurate description of the development of the peace movement in East Germany. Kukutz provides an analysis of the peace movement with first-hand knowledge. The West German church historian Maser presents a well-informed overall account of the events with a particular emphasis on the peace movement in the Protestant churches and their relationship to the independent peace movement.

Bretschneider and Pohl also offer a brief general outline with special reference to the ecumenical peace group in Dresden-Johannstadt. For information about the emblematic "Swords into Plowshares" and its origin and significance, see Eckert and Lobmeier and Eckert. Silomon gives a well-researched analysis of the peace-political work of the Protestant churches in East Germany, including the organization and important objectives of the peace decades at the time of their inception, entitled "Swords into Plowshares."

Bickhardt, Stephan. *Spuren: Zur Geschichte der Friedensbewegung in der DDR.* Berlin, 1988.
Bretschneider, Harald, and Johannes Pohl. "Die Friedensbewegung in der DDR." In *Wie schmeckte die DDR? Wege zu einer Kultur des Erinnerns*, ed. Joachim Klose, 335–52. Leipzig, 2010.
Büscher, Wolfgang, Peter Wensierski, and Klaus Wolschner, eds. *Friedensbewegung in der DDR. Texte 1978–1982.* Hattingen, 1982.
Eckert, Rainer. "Schwerter zu Pflugscharen." In *Erinnerungsorte der DDR*, ed. Martin Sabrow, 503–15. Munich 2009.
Eckert, Rainer, and Kornelia Lobmeier. *Schwerter zu Pflugscharen: Geschichte eines Symbols.* Bonn, 2007.
Ehring, Klaus, and Martin Dallwitz. *Schwerter zu Pflugscharen: Friedensbewegung in der DDR.* Reinbek near Hamburg, 1982.

Knabe, Hubertus. "Unabhängige Friedensbewegung." In *Lexikon Opposition und Widerstand in der SED-Diktatur,* ed. Hans-Joachim Veen, et al., 141–43. Berlin, 2000.

Kukutz, Irena. "Die Bewegung 'Frauen für den Frieden' als Teil der unabhängigen Friedensbewegung der DDR." In *Materialien der Enquete-Kommission "Aufarbeitung von Geschichte und Folgen der SED-Diktatur in Deutschland",* ed. Deutscher Bundestag, 7 vol., 2:1285–1408. Baden-Baden 1995.

Maser, Peter. "Selbständigkeit, Einheit und innerer Zusammenhang der Friedensbewegung in der DDR." In *Raketenpower um Europa: Das sowjetische SS 20-Abenteuer und die Friedensbewegung,* ed. Jürgen Maruhn and Manfred Wilkeeds, 162–96. Munich 2001.

Neubert, Ehrhart. *Geschichte der Opposition in der DDR 1949–1989.* Berlin 1997.

Silomon, Anke. *"Schwerter zu Pflugscharen" und die DDR: Die Friedensarbeit der evangelischen Kirchen in der DDR im Rahmen der Friedensdekaden 1980 bis 1982.* Göttingen, 1999.

Chapter 12

Visual and Media Strategies of the Peace Movement

Kathrin Fahlenbrach and Laura Stapane

When in the fall of 1983 some 1.3 million West German citizens responded to a call by the peace movement to protest the implementation of the NATO Double-Track Decision, the event was extensively covered and documented by the national media and press.[1] Television images of mass demonstrations in Hamburg, Bonn, West Berlin, Stuttgart, and Neu-Ulm were broadcast to West German households between 15 and 22 October 1983, a week of protest action that culminated in a "People's Assembly for Peace."[2] United in protest against the deployment of the new US Pershing II and cruise missiles in West Germany, people from all over the country gathered to demonstrate peacefully while the mass media covered the events. The evening news reported, "The desire for peace sent protestors to Bonn today. Early this morning thousands trekked from railway stations and parking lots to one of several rallying points in the Federal Republic."[3]

Under the spotlight of tremendous media attention, the Hofgarten in Bonn hosted the central rally with prominent speakers such as Green Party politician Petra Kelly, SPD leader and former chancellor Willy Brandt, and Nobel Prize winner and writer Heinrich Böll; meanwhile Hamburg and West Berlin also witnessed gatherings of opponents to the arms buildup. Lines of marchers, approaching a common point from various directions in "star formations," converged at the Rathausmarkt in the Hanseatic city and at Schoeneberg town hall in the western part of Berlin, calling for peaceful "renegotiations" instead of "an arms upgrade"; they nonviolently demonstrated for disarmament in both the East and West.[4] In addition, approximately 200,000 activists formed a 108-kilometer-long human chain stretching along the Bundesstrasse 10, symbolically linking the European headquarters of the US Armed Forces in Stuttgart and Wiley Barracks in Neu-Ulm, where, according to information obtained by the peace movement, American Pershing II missiles would be deployed.[5] Through such symbolic actions, along with the inclusion of celebrities at its events, the peace movement managed to leverage media attention and mobilize sympathizers and activists across various age and social groups. Also contributing to the movement's success in mass mobilization was its ability to draw upon expressive forms of protest rooted in the empathic protest habitus of alternative culture.

The peace movement's effective use of symbolism in rallying its supporters was a result of a protest culture that had been evolving since the 1960s. This protest culture was anchored in the habits and philosophies of an alternative lifestyle that viewed the personal as the political.[6] The visual aspect of peace demonstrations—which comprised everything from posters to human chains to staged enactments like "die-ins"—distilled collective core values and expressed latent anxiety. They efficiently manifested socio-political conflict in affective ways to coax sympathizers into supporting demands such as "Stop the NATO Double-Track Decision" and "No to Arms Upgrading."

Protest Habitus and Expressive Codes of Demonstration

Protests against the deployment of nuclear weapons were commonplace in West German society throughout the 1980s, and, with their strong emphasis on visual symbolism, the events lent themselves to impressive documentation in press photos and film footage. And, of course, it was not just images from Bonn dominating evening news broadcasts and print media in the years 1981 to 1984. Elsewhere hundreds of thousands of participants flocked to events initiated by the peace movement. Whether these were demonstrations, human chains, marching "star formations," sit-ins, "mother-and-child-demonstrations," celebrity blockades (such as the one in Mutlangen in September 1983),[7] symbolic "mass die-ins" as a reminder of nuclear war victims,[8] or large-scale peace festivals, such as Artists for Peace,[9] all events appear very similar when captured on camera. The photos and film footage depict a social cross-section of different generations: children playing, young parents, dancing teenagers, middle-aged men and women, as well as senior citizens, all united in their common determination to demonstrate against the decision to deploy US Pershing II and cruise missiles in the Federal Republic of Germany. Unlike the protests of the student movement during the late 1960s and early 1970s, the peace demonstrations of the 1980s drew upon a far-reaching fear—that of nuclear annihilation—which mobilized people of all ages. It was a conflict that gripped large parts of German society across generational and denominational boundaries.[10]

However, it should be noted that the alternative milieu that developed in the context of the student protests during the late 1960s constituted the active base of the peace movement. The core of this social milieu, referred to as the New Social Movements, can be identified as the so-called "self-fulfillment milieu," which combined political motives of identity with socio-political goals.[11] Characteristic of this type of political identity was a focus on holistic values: self-fulfillment in this context was not seen exclusively as a form of individual hedonism but rather as a prerequisite for tolerance, equality, and the coexistence of pluralistic forms of social life. Such post-materialist values were established after the late 1960s in the context of protest movements to provide guidelines for a social milieu in which lifestyle simultaneously expressed ideals and political convictions.[12] At the very heart of this lifestyle was an anti-authoritarian ideal of the creative, emotional, and spiritual fulfillment of the individual. Correspondingly, followers of this creed developed new expectations of politics. Politics was no longer to follow a traditional internal systemic logic that would, in its quest to retain power, become increasingly "blind" to basic human needs, particularly to issues of environmental and social sustainability. Instead, policymaking should counterbalance the negative impact of postindustrial modernization that individuals suffered from during their lives and that they feared: these might include social and emotional alienation, social inequalities, or the destruction of natural habitats. The peace movement, just like the ecology movement, the new women's movement, or the gay liberation movement, pursued themes and objectives pertaining to questions of personal political identity.[13]

The expression of collective anxieties and needs in an empathetic protest habitus was an outgrowth of the alternative milieu from the late 1960s. Thus, while the protest habitus incorporated values, motives, and worldviews as central components of collective protest identities, it also empowered individuals to address specific political desires. And it was especially through the visual culture inherited by the alternative milieu that individuals could express their views: for instance through body language, idioms and manners, dress, and music.[14]

This visual culture also influenced the public image of protests: protest campaigns in the peace movement were not only equipped with conventional political trappings and symbols (such as the red flag or the raised fist of the labor movement), but also with complex visual, verbal, and musical codes, as well as symbolic forms of action, that expressed habitual beliefs and lifestyles throughout the ranks of participants. The mobilization of public interest and media coverage thus always had two essential functions during the early 1980s: forms of protest and protest events were geared to instrumentally influencing public opinion, and they were simultaneously modes of expression that would mobilize and generate personal commitment from members and sympathizers. Mobilization was directed inward as much as outward. The former provided an opportunity for collective self-assurance and strengthened individual commitment to the movement. The latter put pressure on decision-makers, or rather, members of the government.

Aesthetics of Posters and the Expressive Pathos of Protest

Indicative of the high importance attributed to individualism and self-determination in this alternative milieu was the visual code of authenticity, exemplified in the "do-it-yourself aesthetic" that validated individual rebellion. The peace movement managed to distance itself in this way from professionally produced glossy advertisements of conventional politicians. Moreover, the aesthetics of do-it-yourself appealed not only to political but also to moral and emotional values. "Anti-professionalism" and "authenticity" were thus proof of political credibility and moral integrity.

This was particularly evident in the protest posters of the peace movement during the 1980s. For example, a poster, advertising a demonstration in Bonn on 13 June 1983 shows a protesting crowd breaking through a wall of surrounding nuclear warheads. The slogan states, "Scrap Nuclear Missiles—Take the First Step."[15] Typical of the code of authenticity and *Sponti* (the European name for the spontaneous protest milieu) is the collage technique that emphasizes a "do-it-yourself" quality. Designed like a cartoon, the poster turns the nuclear threat, which may have appeared rather abstract to many, into a simple visual construct that is charged with pathos in a number of ways: a peace-loving community of activists and citizens is confronted by military aggression in the form of weapons. Military and warfare are metonymically abbreviated through the display of (nuclear) weapons and the break in a wall of missile warheads is not only an expression of opposition to military power, but also an act of collective liberation. The poster thus depicts a vision of a large community ridding itself of a restrictive and threatening military power. Here the pathos formula (Aby Warburg) of the protest is visualized, that of a superior humanity in contrast to the purely instrumental and technocratic military logic.[16]

Moreover these posters took on the aesthetics of the student movement. For instance, another poster is divided in half, the appeal "Pershing II—Cruise Missiles. No!" is on the left and the profile of a group of protesters kicking and punching an oversized nuclear warhead is on the right.[17] The warhead has been pushed to the extreme right edge of the poster and is about to topple over. Drawn in a comic book style often found in alternative newspapers, protest posters, and record covers of the late 1960s, the poster contrasts the humanity of the protesters with "cold" technology.[18] A call to participate in the 15–22 October 1983 protests in Bonn uses a poster with a visual scenario in which a large group of protesters collectively defeat the forces of arms. The evocative imagery again utilizes the pacifist pathos formula of protest as the community's power, and human values are opposed to the destructive power of the military.

A third poster, an appeal to join a national day of action on 20 October 1984 in South Germany, combines several of the movement's protest formulas and symbols. The slogan reads, "There is still time to turn back: stop the insanity of armament. NO to Pershing II and cruise missiles."[19] The poster shows a human chain in the shape of the peace symbol. Two nuclear weapons are depicted at the top and two crowds of protesters are converging on it from both sides of the peace symbol. The depicted groups are unquestionably a community of protesting activists with unified posters and slogans. Furthermore antagonistic symbols of the enemy are added in the imagery of weapons, military helmets, and the Daimler-Benz star representing in this case the German armament industry. Impersonal symbolic forms are contrasted with protesting human figures. Similar to the posters described above, the picture is drawn in a comic book style that represents the protesting crowd as a cross-section of a multicultural community comprising members of different ages, denominations, and social backgrounds. The variety of persons underlines core values of the alternative milieu such as individuality, self-determination, and cultural diversity. Hence, in its expressive aesthetics, this poster also defines the empathic protest habitus in contrast to an instrumental rationality of economic and military agency.

Visual Symbols and Images of Protest

Visual symbols were essential elements for expressing protest.[20] These were firmly fixed in the alternative protest milieu and hence expressed a habitual and ideological proximity between the peace movement and environmental movements as well as various Christian groups.[21] Peace symbols, sunflowers, and rainbows could be found on posters, flags, clothing items, as were such religious symbols as doves and the imagery of swords into plowshares.[22] Colors also played a special role. Participants of a church convention in Hanover in June 1983 wore or carried purple scarves with the motto "Turn back to life—The time has come to say 'no'—with no ifs, whens, or buts—to weapons of mass destruction," which became the hallmark of nonviolent protest.[23] This resulted in iconic press photos showing a purple sea of Christian believers protesting peacefully.[24]

On protest marches demonstrators frequently carried homemade papier-mâché Pershing missiles or dummy weapons of all kinds.[25] Some carried

Figure 12.1. Poster "Scrap Nuclear Missiles," "Pershing II—Cruise Missiles. No!" (Netzwerk Friedenskooperative / Stuttgart, Wurttemberg State Library)

US images, such as a Ronald Reagan mask or a Mickey Mouse doll, and homemade "Schießburger"[26] hamburgers decorated with US flags and filled with missile dummies of all kinds. These were commonplace among protests rallies in all West German cities.

Another close look at the posters reveals a surprisingly precise representation of weapons systems and accurate tagging on maps and graphs of deployment locations and missile launching platforms.[27] To a certain degree this precision reflects a high level of professionalism and expert knowledge on the part of peace movement activists. Such images and graphs also suggest that the peace movement wished to inform supporters and opponents alike in the best possible way about upcoming developments and future scenarios.

Images of devastation were key elements in the peace movement's visual antiwar rhetoric. Mushroom clouds, weapons, skulls, destroyed German cities, and victims (mainly women and children) of prior wars figured prominently in demonstration posters and other forms of mass media.[28] This apocalyptical topos was coupled with fear, threat, and a desire for security, and it proved a valuable tool in the struggle for media attention. It also served to mobilize new supporters in the face of a supposed imminent disaster. For example, on 21 November 1983, during a speech on the NATO Double-Track Decision delivered by Chancellor Helmut Kohl, deputies of the Green Party held up protest posters in Parliament that represented images of National Socialism's victims.[29] In a follow-up debate, one day later, Petra Kelly displayed a poster on the speaker's desk that read, "Do you really want to say you knew nothing?" Other deputies of her party did the same.[30]

Images of the Japanese cities destroyed by nuclear bombs at the end of World War II, Hiroshima and Nagasaki, also belonged to the peace movement's repertoire of visual symbols. Likewise, images from Vietnam played a role. A prominent example is the iconic photograph by Eddie Adams that documents the shooting of a Vietcong by a Vietnamese officer in 1968.[31] It became a symbol for the protest against the war in Vietnam and against other forms of political and social repression. The picture was reproduced on millions of placards and posters, was carried at demonstrations, and put on the walls of people's rooms. By their interaction, mass media and protest activists established this picture in the collective memory of Western publics.

The peace movement, like the student movement, used the documentary power of photographs not only to deter war but also to mobilize moral and emotional opposition. By assembling a sequence of war images from different time periods, the destructive power and inhumanity of war assumed a universal, timeless quality. Moreover, these images ultimately morphed into an apocalyptic vision of the world, implying that thanks to the "overkill" level of armament production, weapons would soon reduce the world to rubble, leaving behind famine, sickness, and mass murder among the survivors.[32]

Media Protest as Performance

The body has always been the most important means of communicating protests.[33] When people come together at mass rallies or during social upheavals and revolutions, as well as in isolated and sporadic street demonstrations, their physical presence always makes discontent and opposition of social groups publicly visible and turns events into a collective performance. The individual and the collective body merge in this performance of protest. The aspirations as well as the objectives are displayed on both levels (individual and collective) in an expressive performance of physical action. Public protests are performative in several ways:[34] the very act of joining together in a public space creates a symbolic collective body.[35] In a sense, the action of mobilizing public visibility in the form of a collective body represents in itself a political statement.[36] When expressive functions of protest receive increasing significance, protests will change format. Thus, centrally organized and ritualized rallies and demonstrations are complemented by spontaneous demonstrations and more expressive forms of action such as human blockades, sit-ins, chains, and marches.[37]

The message of the peace movement in the 1980s was then spread not only through posters and banners, but also by the actions of the demonstrators themselves who transmitted messages through their performances.[38] Protesters made practical use of their bodies, for example, in front of US military bases and embassies in the Federal Republic of Germany to block access routes; on a more symbolic level, they also staged events like mass die-ins, echoing the victims of past wars, in order to draw attention to the possible consequences of the arms upgrade of nuclear weapons in the FRG. On 22 October 1983 in Bonn, protesters participating in an Action Week formed a 15-kilometer-long star at the American embassy in Bad Godesberg and playacted a mass die-in at five minutes to midnight.[39] At the end of the human chain stretching from Stuttgart to the city of Neu-Ulm, there was a similar event where hundreds of protesters enacted a mass die-in in front of the US Wiley Barracks. It was exactly symbolic performances such as these that were selected by news editors to accompany television reports in a spectacular fashion.

Enhancing the performative nature of peace protests were sound effects—such as car horns, loud whistles, drumming, banging of metal pots, and ringing church bells—which served to attract attention and reinforce the

Figure 12.2. Protesters form a 108-kilometer-long human chain along Bundesstrasse 10 between Stuttgart and Neu-Ulm protesting against the deployment of new nuclear weapons in the Federal Republic of Germany on 22 October 1983. Recorded near Lonsee (Picture-Alliance)

Figure 12.3. Protesters beginning to perform a mass die-in in front of the US military base Wiley Barracks in Neu-Ulm to express opposition to the deployment of new nuclear weapons in the Federal Republic of Germany on 22 October 1983 (Picture-Alliance)

message. On an event poster of the Coordinating Committee for Bonn it was explained that the noise should make protesters' voices "unmistakably heard."[40] The racket was to remind the incumbent government of Helmut Kohl in no uncertain terms that a large part of the population did not wish to follow the official path of West Germany's military and defense policy. On the other end of the auditory spectrum, however, collective silence was also a mode of protest. For example, a silent vigil was held along a demarcation line of a no-protest zone surrounding the Federal Chancellery in Bonn to commemorate the victims of Hiroshima and Nagasaki at 6:55 PM on 21 October 1983.[41]

Examples like these show an intimate association in the protest culture of the peace movement between a performance of the human body and its depiction in the mass media. Like other social movements, the peace movement had realized at an early stage that its protest would be effective only when it was considered newsworthy by the media and broadcasted.[42] Demonstrations like those described above served as spectacular events, well suited to the media's interests. They visually conveyed abstract and complex protest concerns to a wide-ranging audience through acts of performance: news reports and footage showed the protesters either as a collective group or as individual actors in a physical performance of body or bodies, thus making their message visible and tangible even to detached onlookers."

Nonviolent self-presentation was in this respect of crucial importance. Through their forms of action, activists generally emphasized fundamental pacifist beliefs, dismissed violence, and upheld humanist values such as communal spirit, citizenship, and altruism. In nonviolent actions such as sit-ins, human chains, and symbolic mass die-ins, they displayed the human body as a superior symbol of "humanity" to the media's eye. During protests, activists frequently succeeded in presenting themselves as victims of police violence and the state as an aggressive opponent.[43]

Since noble ideals such as nonviolence, a communal spirit, and personal self-fulfillment consistently characterized their actions, activists managed to successfully influence the popular media's portrayal of them. This can largely be seen in the response of the press reporting on Action Week in the autumn of 1983. Right across the entire spectrum of the West German media one could see images of dancing, singing, and laughing demonstrators who peacefully opposed the decision of the Bundestag and NATO to deploy new nuclear weapons on West German territory and who still sought to prevent this decision at the last minute.[44]

In many of these press photos it can be seen that the protests of the peace movement courted the media, hoping that it would document and disseminate its message. For example, a press picture published by the political magazine *Der Spiegel* shows a number of activists blocking the access route to the West German Ministry of Defense by sitting in the entry. The front-row protesters present a long banner to the cameras that states, "We are blocking the Ministry from slaughtering mankind."[45] This picture reveals a strong visual and linguistic polarization between activists as "defenders of peace" and the state, visibly represented by police officers in the background, accused of being a "human butcher."[46] In the sense of "action mobilization,"[47] a collective body of protesters was visually turned into a particularly pertinent argument: while those specifically addressed in the protest, that is to say, the staff of the Ministry of Defense, are not visible at all, or perhaps only by a surrogate agency in the form of the police in the background of the photo, the visual focus rests on the united community of activists. The enacted message of their collective presence was effectively highlighted by the close-up shot of the accusatory banner.

The visual-rhetorical polarization between a human body and a missile, also seen as having a "body," was a recurring topos not only depicted on protest posters (as previously discussed) but also presented during public protests to the eyes of the media cameras. During demonstrations protestors would symbolically carry, surround, and destroy nuclear warheads made of cardboard. They thus formed part of a ritualized and symbolic resistance against an elusive enemy.

Personalization of Protest

Another strategy to capture visual media attention was to give a personal face to public protest by drawing in prominent personalities. Next to activists such as Petra Kelly and Gert Bastian, the leftist German writer and Nobel Prize laureate for literature Heinrich Böll was an important advocate.[48] He supported the movement and gave it a face by his participation in demonstrations and blockades. By showing his support publicly he helped the movement to obtain sympathy and support, even from those of the bourgeois milieu.[49]

In particular the nonviolent blockade in the late summer of 1983 of the Pershing II missile depot in Mutlangen became a media event that was characterized by the presence of celebrity supporters. During long preparations, the activists chose 1 September 1983 as an appropriately symbolic date for their "antiwar day," since it recalled the anniversary of the German invasion of Poland.[50] Having already set up a peace camp in Mutlangen several weeks earlier, and having seen various selective blockades fail to draw media attention, organizers this time established a celebrity camp with well-known intellectuals like Petra Kelly, Heinrich Böll, Günter Grass, and Walter Jens, which made the event newsworthy.

Two images continue to shape public perception and memories of this event: one is a smiling Petra Kelly wearing a military helmet decorated with flowers. The other shows writer Böll and Bastian along with Oskar Lafontaine and other celebrities surrounded by a large community of protesting activists.

Kelly's portrait represents in an almost prototypical way the peace movement's strategy of symbolic appropriation and reinterpretation of military insignia. The military function of the helmet is ironically foiled in this instance by the floral decoration on the helmet, a traditional symbol of peace: flowers stand for an idealized utopian concept of "nature"[51] among the followers of the alternative milieu and represent "life" as compared to the destructive principle of war. As Kelly was a symbol of the movement, it was fitting that the photo of Kelly's headgear was to become an iconic image of protest that elicits expressive identification.

Another famous photo of the celebrity camp, taken of Böll surrounded by fellow-activists at five o'clock in the morning, could in retrospect also be seen as a positive image of identification—but on closer inspection it appears to be more of a visual deconstruction of the movement. Both the origin and context of the photo support this hypothesis. In his painstaking research and

Figure 12.4. Heinrich Böll, surrounded by Oskar Lafontaine, Annemarie Böll, Gert Bastian, Petra Kelly, and others, on the occasion of the "celebrity blockade" directed against the deployment of medium-range missiles at the US military base in Mutlangen in 1983 (Barbara Klemm / Deutsches Historisches Museum, Berlin)

image analysis, author Fabio Crivellari shows how this picture, taken by the photographer Barbara Klemm, represents an anti-image of the movement.[52] Klemm took the shot on behalf of the daily conservative paper *Frankfurter Allgemeine Zeitung* (FAZ), which used the photo as a symbol in its journalistic campaign against the peace activists. In the eyes of FAZ's editors, the revealing insight rests in the picture's quasi-religious iconography: on the left-hand side Heinrich Böll sits somewhat elevated on a stool in the pose of a thinking man. In the dark night he is illuminated by the lights of camera crews and closely surrounded by activists squatting on the ground. With his raised seating position and illuminated figure in the classic chiaroscuro manner, he assumes the aura of a prophet surrounded by his devoted disciples. Missing in the iconography are the usual peace symbols. The conservative paper used the image to portray the peace movement as a communist-infiltrated and unrealistic community of faithful believers and to illustrate the danger that could be caused by misled, gullible innocents who do not grasp the necessary need for military security of the Federal Republic of Germany and its allies.[53]

Both photos of the same event thus convey different messages and employ divergent strategies. They illustrate vividly the difference between self-representation and third-party visual representation of the movement.

Conclusion

This brief review of the peace movement's visual strategies for mobilizing mass media attention shows that these directly derive from forms of protest established since the student protest movement. They were a legacy of an environment of protest among people belonging to a nonconformist, left-wing section of society. Their symbolism and expressive rituals of protest shared particular visual characteristics with the environmental and the antinuclear movement. Above all, in its forms of protest, the peace movement turned the human body into a potent symbol of the habitual values of this alternative social environment. Its actions also emphasized values of individuality, self-determination, nonviolence, as well as concern for a wider cultural citizenship within the Christian tradition (based on such ideals as altruism and charity). The dove of peace and the symbol of swords into plowshares served as important images.

The successfully established fusion of different core values and symbolic worlds in the public media obviously contributed significantly to the peace movement's success in obtaining its key objectives and created a consensus across various social classes and groups.

Kathrin Fahlenbrach is a professor at the Institute for Media and Communication at the University of Hamburg. Part of her research focuses on the role of visual communication for the construction of collective identities in protest movements, exploring the cognitive and emotional effects of pictures, symbols, nonverbal codes and the visual representation and framing of crisis and conflicts. She is the author of *Protestinszenierungen: Kollektive Identitäten und visuelle Kommunikation in Protestbewegungen* (2002) and *Audiovisuelle Metaphern: Zur Körper- und Affektästhetik in Film und Fernsehen* (2010), as well as most recently, the editor of *Embodied Metaphors in Film, Television, and Video Games: Cognitive Approaches* (2016) and coeditor of *Protest Cultures: A Companion* (2016). She is also the coeditor of the publication series "Protest, Culture, and Society" with Berghahn Books (New York and Oxford, since 2008).

Laura Stapane studied art history, media studies, as well as political science at the University of Oldenburg, where she received her M.A. She subsequently worked at the KHI (Kunsthistorisches Institut) in Florence and the German Historical Institute (GHI) in Washington, DC, as well as the Heidelberg Center for American Studies (HCA) at the University of Heidelberg as a research fellow and project coordinator where she was responsible for the coordination of "The Civil Rights Struggle, African-American GIs, and Germany" (www.aacvr-germany.org) as well as for "The Nuclear Crisis" (www.nuclearcrisis.org) project. She is currently a Senior Creative Consultant at *the peak lab.*

Notes

1. The number counts on participants fluctuate. According to official data provided by the Ministry of the Interior, some half a million people participated nationwide in demonstrations of the peace movement, whereas the organizers claim to have mobilized some 1.3 million followers.
2. Poster, "Volksversammlung für den Frieden," Württembergische Landesbibliothek Stuttgart, Document Centre for Unconventional Literature, poster collection, 1983 G, Friedensbewegung X, Mappe 1 (henceforth DfuL); the program of the event in Bonn was printed on a poster "Aktionswoche vom 15.–22.10.83 in Bonn," ibid., Plakatsammlung, 1983 G, Friedensbewegung X, Mappe 1. ibid., Plakatsammlung, 1983 G, Friedensbewegung X, Mappe 1.
3. *Tagesschau,* 22 November 1983, http://www.myvideo.de/watch/5333376/Tagesschau_22_10_83_P1_2.
4. *Tagesschau,* 22 November 1983. Reports on the number of participants vary again between 190,000 (official count) and 300,000 (unofficial count).

5. Ibid. For photographic images of the human chain from Stuttgart to Neu-Ulm, see also http://www.udo-leuschner.de/nachruestung/831022.htm.
6. Tim Warneke discusses the framing of protest forms by the peace movement in an emphatic, left-wing alternative political manner: "Aktionsformen und Politikverständnis der Friedensbewegung: Radikaler Humanismus und die Pathosformel des Menschlichen," in *Das Alternative Milieu: Antibürgerlicher Lebensstil und linke Politik in der Bundesrepublik Deutschland und Europa 1968–1983*, ed. Sven Reichhardt and Detlef Siegfried (Göttingen, 2010), 445–72.
7. In Mutlangen there was a three-day blockade of the US military base at Schwäbisch Gmünd during 1–9 March 1983.
8. Activists initiated inter alia on 15 October 1983 a symbolic mass death outside the headquarters of US forces in Heidelberg. See the photo collection of Udo Leuschner, http://www.udo-leuschner.de/nachruestung/index.htm.
9. One of the biggest and most successful events of the "Artists for Peace" series, staged by the organizers of the Krefeld Appeal took place on 9 November 1982 in Bochum's Ruhr stadium with approximately 200,000 participants. A massive PR campaign had been advertising this event and more than two hundred national and international artists participated. See Martin Klimke and Laura Stapane, "From Artists for Peace to the Green Caterpillar: Cultural Activism and Electoral Politics in 1980s West Germany," in *Nuclear Threats, Nuclear Fear and the Cold War of the 1980s*, ed. Eckart Conze, Martin Klimke, and Jeremy Varon (New York, 2016).
10. On the topic of the role of churches, see the contribution by Jan Ole Wiechmann and Sebastian Kalden in this volume.
11. Gerhard Schulze, *Die Erlebnisgesellschaft: Kultursoziologie der Gegenwart*, 6th ed. (FrankfurtMain, 1992/1996); Kai-Uwe Hellmann, *Systemtheorie und Neue Soziale Bewegungen: Identitätsprobleme in der Risikogesellschaft* (Opladen, 1996). The turn toward post-materialist values has first been observed by Ronald Inglehart, *The Silent Revolution: Changing Values and Political Styles among Western Publics* (Princeton, NJ, 1977).
12. The values, lifestyles, and ideologies of the alternative milieu that evolved after the late 1960s have been explored in detail by Sven Reichardt, *Linksalternatives Leben in den siebziger und frühen achtziger Jahren* (Berlin, 2013).
13. This topic is discussed in more detail by Hellmann, *Systemtheorie*; Roland Roth and Dieter Rucht, eds., *Die sozialen Bewegungen in Deutschland seit 1945: Ein Handbuch* (Frankfurt am Main, 2008).
14. The social conduct in the student movement is discussed by Joachim Scharloth, *1968: Eine Kommunikationsgeschichte* (Paderborn, 2011); for a discussion of rebellious styles of clothing at the end of the 1960s, see Kathrin Fahlenbrach, *Protestinszenierungen: Visuelle Kommunikation und kollektive Identitäten in Protestbewegungen* (Wiesbaden, 2002), 199–202; musical codes in the social environment of the student movement is analyzed in Beate Kutschke, ed., *Musikkulturen in der Revolte* (Stuttgart, 2008); the development of expressive forms of protest habitus within the student movement is extensively covered by Fahlenbrach, *Protestinszenierung*.
15. Poster, "Atomraketen verschrotten!" DfuL, Plakatsammlung, 1983 G, Friedensbewegung X, Mappe 1.

16. With reference to the Jewish roots of the term, Warneke reveals that the concept of "people" in the peace movement carries romantic connotations and tends to be used in morally appealing rhetoric. Warneke, *Aktionsformen*, 1–35
17. Poster, "Pershing II—Cruise Missiles. Nein!" DfuL, Plakatsammlung, 1983 G, Friedensbewegung X, Mappe 1.
18. This style was developed in the alternative scene by popular artist Gerhard Seyfried, who designed campaign posters for the Green Party in Berlin. On this point, see Kathrin Fahlenbrach, "Die Grünen: Neue Farbenlehre der Politik," in *Das Jahrhundert der Bilder, 1949 bis heute,* ed. Gerhard Paul (Bonn, 2008), 2:474–81.
19. Poster, "Noch ist es Zeit zur Umkehr: Stoppt den Rüstungswahnsinn. NEIN zu Pershing II und Cruise Missiles!" DfuL, Plakatsammlung, E86 Friedensbewegung X, Mappe 2.
20. The use of pictures, visual symbols, and moving images in protest has been studied, e.g., by Todd Gitlin, *The Whole World is Watching: Mass Media and the Making and Unmaking of the New Left* (Berkeley, CA, 1977/2003); Kathrin Fahlenbrach, *Protestinszenierungen: Visuelle Kommunikation und kollektive Identitäten in Protestbewegungen* (Wiesbaden, 2002); John W. Delicath, and Kevin M. DeLuca, "Image Events, the Public Sphere, and Argumentative Practice: The Case of Radical Environmental Groups," *Argumentation* 17 (2003): 315–33. Alice Mattoni, *Media Practices and Protest Politics: How Precarious Workers Mobilize* (Farnham, 2012); Antigoni Memou, *Photography and Social Movements: From Globalization of the Movement (1968) to the Movement against Mobilization (2001)* (Manchester, 2013); Nicole Doerr, Simon Teune, and Alice Mattoni, eds., *Advances in the Visual Analysis of Social Movements* (Bingley, 2013); Priska Daphi, Anja Le, and Peter Ullrich, "Images of Surveillance: The Contested and the Embedded Visual Language of Anti-Surveillance Protests," in Doerr, Mattoni, and Teune, *Advances in the Visual Analysis of Social Movements,* 54–80; Kathrin Fahlenbrach, Erling Sivertsen, and Rolf Werenskjold, eds. *Media and Revolt: Performances and Strategies from the 1960s to the Present* (Oxford and New York, 2014); Peter Ludes, Winfried Nöth, and Kathrin Fahlenbrach, eds., "Critical Visual Theory," special issue, *Triple C: Communication, Capitalism & Critique; Journal for a Global Sustainable Information Society* 12, no. 1 (2014); Kathrin Fahlenbrach, "Images and Imagery of Protest," in *Protest-Cultures: A Companion,* ed. Kathrin Fahlenbrach, Martin Klimke, and Joachim Scharloth (New York and Oxford, forthcoming).
21. The proximity between the peace movement and environmental movement is discussed by Silke Mende and Birgit Metzger in this volume.
22. See also image in Illustration Section II from Rainer Eckert's contribution in this volume.
23. On this point, see the chapter by Sebastian Kalden and Jan Ole Wiechmann in this volume.
24. The purple-colored church scarves also triggered controversy. One instance occurred on 22 October 1983 when fifteen scarf-wearing members of the Green Party were arrested within the no-protest zone of the Parliament. Schily (Green Party) vehemently condemned this action by the Bundestag. Compare to the minutes of the 36th session of the Deutsche Bundestag, 22 November 1983, 2510; and Bilddatenbank des Bundesarchivs: B 145 picture-00047579.

25. The peace demonstration in Bonn on 22 October 1983 in the Hofgarten was accompanied by a dummy missile. See picture archive of AP Images: 8310221240.
26. The papier-mâché "Schießburger" (this is a pun on the English word cheeseburger and the German word *schiess(en)*, to shoot) was part of a demonstration by antinuclear activists on the Muensterplatz in Bonn on 4 April 1981. Its picture may be found in the archive ullstein bild: 00775200.
27. See also Benjamin Ziemann, "The Code of Protest in the West German Peace Movement 1945–1990," *Contemporary European History* 17 (2008): 248.
28. See ibid., 250–52.
29. Minutes of the 35th Session of the Deutsche Bundestag, 21 November 1983, 2330.
30. Underneath the text the poster featured the symbol of US Air Force 50th Tactical Fighter Wing stationed in Hahn (Hunsrück), a bat-like eagle in front of what could be interpreted as the mushroom cloud of an exploding atomic bomb. Minutes of the 36th session of the Deutsche Bundestag, 22 November 1983, 2520; see also Petra Kelly, *Mit dem Herzen Denken: Texte für eine glaubwürdige Politik* (Munich, 1990), 24–36.
31. This photo is discussed as a press icon, e.g., by Robert Hariman and John Louis Lucaites, *No Caption needed: Iconic Photographs, Public Culture, and Liberal Democracy* (Chicago, 2007).
32. Nuclear doomsday scenarios are also discussed by Philipp Baur in this volume.
33. Compare to Andrea Pabst, "Bodies and Bodily Protest: A Plea for a 'Thinking through the Body' in Social Movement Research," in *Between the Avant Garde and the Everyday: Subversive Politics in Europe, 1958 to the Present*, ed. Timothy S. Brown and Lorena Anton (New York and Oxford, 2011), 191–200.
34. Following Christoph Wulf, we conceive performative action as follows: "Social action is defined as *performance*, speaking as a *performative act* and *performative action* is a more general category which subsumes both aspects" (Soziales Handeln wird als *performance*, Sprechen als *performatives Handeln* und *Performativität* als ein abgeleiteter, diese Zusammenhänge übergreifend thematisierender Begriff verstanden). *Performances* are characterized as "situations of performance," which involve a present or specific audience. See Christoph Wulf, *Zur Genese des Sozialen Mimesis, Performativität, Ritual* (Bielefeld, 2005), 12.
35. This has been demonstrated, e.g., by John W. Delicath and Kevin M. DeLuca, "Image Events, the Public Sphere, and Argumentative Practice: The Case of Radical Environmental Groups," *Argumentation* (2003): 17.
36. While "consensus mobilization" serves to support protests with arguments, action mobilization has "the primary intention of rendering a person's body for the purpose of protests. Action mobilization is enacted in the public domain, on the streets and in view of the cameras: it is a display of the mobilization potential engendered by physical presence" (vorrangig darum, den Körper für den Protest zur Verfügung zu stellen. Action spielt sich überwiegend in der Öffentlichkeit ab, auf der Straße, vor den Kameras: Präsentation des Mobilisierungspotentials durch Anwesenheit). Hellmann, *Systemtheorie*, 239.
37. Regarding street protest, see Bernd Jürgen Warneke, ed., *Massenmedium Straße: Zur Kulturgeschichte der Demonstration* (Frankfurt am Main, 1991); Kathrin Fah-

lenbrach, "Protest-Räume. Medien-Räume. Zur rituellen Topologie der Straße als Protest-Raum," in *Straße als kultureller Aktionsraum: Interdisziplinäre Betrachtungen des Straßenraums an der Schnittstelle zwischen Theorie und Praxis,* ed. Sandra Maria Geschke (Wiesbaden, 2008), 98–111; Tina Askanius, "Protest Movements and Spectacles of Death: From Urban Places to Video Spaces," in Doerr, Mattoni, and Teune, *Advances in the Visual Analysis of Social Movements,* 105–33; Delicath and DeLuca, "Image Events, the Public Sphere, and Argumentative Practice," 17.
38. Compare Gerhard Spörl, "Wenn es 'heiß' wird: Das Programm der Friedensbewegung," *Die Zeit* 41, 7 October 1983.
39. *Tagesschau,* 22 October 1983, http://www.myvideo.de/watch/5333376/Tagesschau_22_10_83_P1_2.
40. Poster "Aktionswoche vom 15.–22.10.83 in Bonn," incl. the program of the Action Week, DfuL, Plakatsammlung, 1983 G, Friedensbewegung X, Mappe 1.
41. Spörl, "Wenn es 'heiß' wird."
42. The interaction between protest movements and mass media is also discussed by Todd Gitlin, *The Whole World is Watching: Mass Media in the Making and Unmaking of the Left* (Berkeley, CA, 1980); Dieter Rucht, "The Quadruple 'A': Media Strategies of Protest Movements since the 1960s," in *Cyber Protest: New Media, Citizens and Social Movements,* ed. Wim van de Donk, Brian D. Loader, Paul G. Nixon, and Dieter Rucht (London and New York, 2004), 29–57; Fahlenbrach, *Protestinszenierung*; Alice Mattoni, *Media Practices and Protest Politics: How Precarious Workers Mobilize* (Farnham, 2012); Kathrin Fahlenbrach, Erling Sivertsen, and Rolf Werenskjold, eds., *Media and Revolt: Performances and Strategies from the 1960s to the Present* (Oxford and New York, 2014); Bart Cammaerts, Alice Mattoni, and Patrick McCurdy, eds., *Mediation and Protest Movements* (Bristol, 2013); Simon Cottle and Libby Lester, eds., *Transnational Protest and the Media* (New York, 2011); Nicole Doerr and Alice Mattoni, "Public Spaces and Alternative Media Practices in Europe: The Case of the EuroMayDay Parade against Precarity," in Fahlenbrach, Sivertsen, and Werenskjold, *Media and Revolt,* 386–405.
43. The role of the police is also discussed by Michael Sturm in this volume.
44. For instance, Heinrich Böll thanked the protesters at the start of the main rally in Bonn for their nonviolence.
45. *Der Spiegel* 43, 24 October 1983, 19. On the staging of press photos by the peace movement, see the contribution by Susanne Schregel in this volume.
46. The role of the police in demonstrations is also discussed by Michael Sturm in this volume.
47. "Action mobilization concerns the transformation of consensus into action." Bert Klandermans, "Framing Collective Action," in *Framing Collective Action in Media and Revolt: Strategies and Performances from the 1960s to the Present,* ed. Kathrin Fahlenbrach, Erling Sivertsen, and Rolf Werenskjold (New York and Oxford, forthcoming), 46.
48. From 1970 to 1974, Böll was the first president of the German PEN-Club, and then of the International PEN-Club. Hence he had been an internationally well-known, politically engaged writer. In 1972 he publicly sympathized with the RAF-terrorist Ulrike Meinhof, which produced a political scandal in Germany and demonstrated again his strong leftist conviction.

49. See also the contribution by Saskia Richter in this volume.
50. Fabio Crivellari discusses the symbolic action in Mutlangen at length in "Blockade: Friedensbewegung zwischen Melancholie und Ironie," in *Das Jahrhundert der Bilder: 1949 bis heute,* ed. Gerhard Paul (Göttingen, 2008), 2:482–89.
51. Ideological aspects of the term "nature," as employed in the alternative milieu, are also covered in the chapter by Silke Mende and Birgit Metzger in this volume.
52. Crivellari, "Blockade," 487.
53. Ibid. For reporting in the West German print media in general, see "Eine Bewegung, über die nicht berichtet wird, findet nicht statt: Das Bild der Friedensbewegung in bundesdeutschen und britischen Zeitungen," in *Linksalternative Milieus und Soziale Bewegungen in den 1970er Jahren,* ed. Cordia Baumann, Sebastian Gehring, and Nicolas Büchse (Heidelberg, 2011), 133–59.

Select Bibliography

Fahlenbrach examines the expressive visual protest of the student movement in mass media of the late 1960s. Doerr, Mattoni, and Teune author the first encompassing volume on recent methods and approaches to visual analysis of protest communication.

The changing relationship between the new social movements and the media is among other topics examined by Gitlin. He highlights processes of marginalization and radicalization of student protests in the representation of the American media. Rucht develops a systematic model distinguishing four different types of mass media mobilization strategies employed by social movements. Cammaerts, Mattoni, and McCurdy offer, in their approach to *mediation* of protest, a helpful method of analyzing the manifold and collective dynamic in protest communication, including not only activists, but also audiences and different users of protest communication in mass media and on the internet. The volume published by Fahlenbrach, Sivertsen, and Werenskjold presents current case studies that discuss the interaction between protest movements and mass media with special emphasis on Framing's approach to the subject.

Ziemann provides a discussion of the peace movement's visual strategy. His research covers approximately 600 posters, all published by the German peace movement between 1945 and the 1990s on various occasions. Klimke and Stapane describe the media strategy of the peace movement and the Green Party with the help of two examples, namely events by Artists for Peace (Künstler für den Frieden) and the "Green Caterpillar."

Cammaerts, Bart, Alice Mattoni, and Patrick McCurdy, eds. *Mediation and Protest Movements.* Bristol, 2013.
Doerr, Nicole, Simon Teune, Alice Mattoni, eds. *Advances in the Visual Analysis of Social Movements.* Bingley, 2013.
Fahlenbrach, Kathrin. *Protestinszenierungen: Visuelle Kommunikation und kollektive Identitäten in Protestbewegungen.* Wiesbaden, 2002.
Fahlenbrach, Kathrin, Erling Sivertsen, and Rolf Werenskjold, eds. *Media and Revolt: Strategies and Performances from the 1960s to the Present.* New York and Oxford, 2014.
Gitlin, Todd. *The Whole World is Watching: Mass Media in the Making and Unmaking of the Left.* Berkeley, CA, 1980.

Klimke, Martin, and Laura Stapane, "From Artists for Peace to the Green Caterpillar: Cultural Activism and Electoral Politics in 1980s West Germany," in *Nuclear Threats, Nuclear Fear and the Cold War of the 1980s,* ed. Eckart Conze, Martin Klimke, and Jeremy Varon. New York, 2016.

Rucht, Dieter. "The Quadruple 'A': Media Strategies of Protest Movements since the 1960s," in *Cyber Protest: New Media, Citizens and Social Movements,* ed. Wim van de Donk, Brian D. Loader, Paul G. Nixon, and Dieter Rucht, 29–57. London and New York, 2004.

Ziemann, Benjamin. "The Code of Protest in the West German Peace Movement 1945–1990." *Contemporary European History* 17, no. 2 (2008): 237–61.

Chapter 13

The Churches

Sebastian Kalden and Jan Ole Wiechmann

The two principle Christian churches constituted one of the most responsive environments for debates on peace and security policy in the Federal Republic of Germany around 1980. Processes of social change had already posed challenges to both Protestantism and Catholicism in the 1960s and 1970s. Individualization, pluralization, and secularization led to a "reorientation of the religious,"[1] and this resulted in alternative ways of offering spiritual and practical guidance.

The churches maintained a high social significance at the time of the new peace movement. As integral institutions, together they represented more than 85 percent of the population and provided a platform for the exchange of views on security policy.[2] This important social role was performed not only in parishes, dioceses, the regional churches, and the churches' governing bodies, but also in associations, action groups, and academies, as well as at church conventions.

The intense ecclesiastical discussions during the nuclear crisis represented a specific expression of overall social development. They paradigmatically show that church and religious history cannot be divorced from general political and social history as they are closely interdependent. Considering the close relationship between religious and political identities, it should be noted that politics and religion ought not be considered as two entirely autonomous domains in society.[3] It is therefore important for any analysis of peace and security policy debates in the churches around 1980 to take into account the complex relationship of the churches on the one hand and the political, social, and socio-cultural environment on the other.

Debates about Peace and Security in the Protestant Churches

Toward the end of the 1970s a new phase in the debate on security policy in the Protestant Church was introduced with a controversy between the initiatives Ohne Rüstung Leben (ORL, Living without Arms) and Sicherung des Friedens (Securing Peace).

A union within the region of Württemberg going by the name Living without Arms addressed the public with its agenda and a call "To all Christians" in 1978. They proposed that each Christian personally pledge him/herself to a written pacifist commitment, which deliberately drew on an antimilitarism program adopted by the World Council of Churches in 1975: "I am willing to live without the protection of military armament and I also promise to campaign in our society for peace developed politically without weapons."[4] Living without Arms enjoyed considerable success and publicity, especially after the NATO Double-Track Decision had been reached in 1979. Nationwide about a hundred regional groups were founded and some 24,300 people had signed the pledge by November 1983.[5]

An intense engagement with Living without Arms in West German Protestantism resulted in the establishment of an action group called Securing Peace. This congregation, among them some prominent Protestant Christians, published a statement "To Protestant Christians!" in July 1980, which was explicitly intended as a response to the pacifist program of Living without Arms. To secure peace, this new group deemed it necessary to use armed force for the "protection of life, fundamental human rights, and freedom." The initiative rejected the interpretation of biblical statements as specific security instructions. Even in the nuclear age the state was accorded "administrative power in the sense of an emergency decree from God."[6]

Both texts highlight the breadth of discussions about peace in the Protestant churches during the 1980s. Against the backdrop of social contention in the wake of NATO's Double-Track Decision, this dispute between the groups Living without Arms and Securing Peace was reflected in numerous media reports as well as at conferences and in publications.

Helping to facilitate Christian discussions about peace and to fuel the peace movement as a whole in the late 1970s and early 1980s were the Pentecost Festivals of the Peace Services, held annually since 1974 in the Lower Franconian Friesenhausen and from 1978 onward in Beienrode (Lower Saxony).

Of particular importance was the Seventh Pentecost Festival in 1980, where the conception of a first nationwide Peace Week under the motto "Create Peace without Weapons" (*Frieden schaffen ohne Waffen*) was integrated into the program of some 3,600 participants. The organizers of Action Reconciliation Service for Peace (ASF) and of Action Committee Service for Peace (AGDF) spearheaded this effort. They had already begun to increase their focus on the global implications of armament in the 1970s. In the 1980s they made a conscious effort to position themselves in relation to the emerging new peace movement and its mobilizing campaign. The Pentecost Festival provided them with the opportunity to reach out to large numbers of sympathizers. The event functioned in this way as a meeting point and as a multiplier.

Many ideas for activities in Peace Week had been imported from Dutch concepts developed by the Interchurch Peace Council (IKV) in the 1970s. At the end of the decade a growing number of various regional and local activities followed the Dutch model by organizing vigils, study groups, discussions, and festivities for peace.[7]

Throughout the country about 350 Peace Weeks were finally set up between 16 and 22 November 1980. The great positive response by Christians, citizens groups, political parties, labor unions, women's groups, senior citizens groups, peace services, disarmament action groups, and Third World groups ensured that the initiative "Create Peace without Weapons" became an important part of the new peace movement. Although the Peace Weeks displayed a decentralized character, ASF and AGDF acted as organizational catalysts and also provided important impetus for programmatic development.[8]

The special role of Christians in Peace Weeks was reflected in the figures pertaining to participation: in 1981 a total of 93.3 percent of all Peace Weeks included participating church groups; about a quarter of all organizers were exclusively Christian.[9] The increasing number in 1981, when some three to four thousand Peace Weeks (about ten times as many as in the previous year) took place, is closely associated with the fact that thirteen out of seventeen regional Protestant churches adopted this form of action. In this respect, West German church leaders emulated their partner churches in the GDR, where the "Federation of Evangelical Churches" started organizing longer events— "peace decades"—in 1980.[10] The expansion of the Peace Week activities in the Federal Republic of Germany was intimately connected to a leap forward of the new peace movement into a mass movement in 1981. The Christian organizations had been instrumental to a high degree in this process.

The 1981 Church Congress as Catalyst to a Resolution: "No without Any Yes"

The tremendous mobilization achievements of the Christian peace movement were clear to see at the Protestant Church Congress in Hamburg in 1981. This massive event made publically visible the renaissance that the Protestant Church had experienced in the issues of peace and security. It was also a prime example not only of the way in which church conferences at the time were platforms for critical reasoning or for protests against armament,

Figure 13.1. Cover "The New Peace Movement—Protesting against Armor," 15 June 1981 (DER SPIEGEL 25/1981)

but also of how the Church was a powerful "coordination and cooperation agency" for the new peace movement as a whole.[11]

Apart from the official Church Congress program, which carried the controversial motto "Don't fear!" (*Fürchte Dich nicht!*)[12] that evoked numerous high-profile public debates about what peace meant, the great peace demonstration on 20 June 1981 acquired special significance. With an estimated seventy to a hundred thousand protesters, it was the first major visual exclamation mark of the Christian as well as the general peace movement of the 1980s. In total more than 180 groups and organizations joined a call to reject the NATO Double-Track Decision and propagated "resistance against nuclear folly as a condition for the survival of mankind."[13]

The Church Congress in Hamburg revealed the sheer volume of activists that subsequent demonstrations for peace would be able to generate. It also played a pivotal role for the further development of the organization format and intellectual substance of the new peace movement. The organizations Action Reconciliation and the Dutch IKV were able to advance the planning process for a major demonstration on 10 October 1981 to be staged in Bonn. A coalition between Christian and non-Christian groups agreed upon a common call and yielded all responsibility to the ASF and the AGDF.[14] The preparation and implementation of this demonstration in Bonn by Christian action groups engendered structures that determined the overall peace protests in Germany in the following years. This included the "breakfast meeting" as a precursor of the Coordination Committee of the peace movement, as well as the introduction of action conferences following all mass events. The Hamburg Church Congress was thus far more than a "midwife for the subsequent mass demonstrations."[15]

Finally the social tensions regarding peace and security policy also reached the level of the Protestant Church leadership. Especially in 1981 and 1982 the arms issue provoked a fundamental dispute about the nature of the relationship between faith and politics in a nuclear age.

The point of departure for this controversy was the EKD memorandum "Preserve, Promote, and Renew Peace," which was published in October 1981. Particularly controversial proved to be a reference to the "Heidelberg Theses" of 1959, compiled by an Protestant commission that was not universally approved and barely represented a fragile consensus within the Protestant Church. Although the memorandum condemned the arms race and proclaimed an urgent need to overcome the concept of a deterrence system, it maintained that the Church had to concede that "participation in efforts to secure a peace in freedom with the help of nuclear weapons, continued to be a legitimate line of action for Christians."[16] The ambivalence expressed in these statements outlined a position of a "yes and no" that prevailed in the Council of the EKD since the 1950s. It rejected the use of nuclear weapons, while it continued to tolerate nuclear deterrence as a political war prevention strategy.

In response to this ambiguous "yes and no," the Moderamen—the governing body—of the Reformed Alliance[17] declared explicitly a "no without any yes" to mass destruction in June 1982.[18] It was very clear that the position of the Reformed Church was a matter of religious denomination or a question of a *status confessionis,* because it concerned "a commitment to or a denial of the Gospel." The unconditional "no" aimed therefore at the interface of Christian beliefs and specific political security requirements.

With this deliberate demarcation of the positions of the EKD's memorandum, a potential break between the Lutheran and Uniting churches, which brought together Lutheran and Calvinist traditions on the one side and the Reformed churches on the other side, seemed possible. A schism was avoided, but fundamental and irreconcilable differences were certainly evident.

This theologically as well as politically motivated "no" exerted a profound impact on the new peace movement and especially influenced the protest vocabulary of its Christian following. This became particularly evident at the Protestant Church Congress in June 1983 when the debate about peace reached a climax in the Protestant churches.

Although various demonstration events for peace were staged, it was without any doubt the campaign "Return to Life: The Time Has Come—For a No without Any Yes to Weapons of Mass Destruction" that received the greatest media coverage in the Church Congress.[19] The motto of this peace campaign, which deliberately borrowed from the statement of the Re-

Figure 13.2. Participants of the German Lutheran Church Congress in June 1983 displaying violet scarves imprinted with the motto "Return to Life: The Time Has Come—For a No without Any Yes to Weapons of Mass Destruction" (epd-bild / Norbert Neetz)

formed Alliance, had been printed on ninety thousand purple scarves. They remained a symbol of nonviolent peace protest well after the Church Congress was over. These items of clothing were particularly noticeable during the great rally of the campaign on 11 June and at the closing service, and thus became a visual metaphor for the reality that the Church Congress was taken over by violet.[20]

Upheavals in the Catholic Church during the Nuclear Crisis

It is remarkable that the Catholic debates about peace in the 1980s also took place on such a large scale. The 1950s protests against German rearmament generally and a nuclear armament of the Bundeswehr in particular and the subsequent protests of the Easter March movement of the 1960s had been dominated by conflict in the Protestant churches. However, with the onset of discussion about the NATO Double-Track Decision, an intense peace and political security controversy was conducted in the domain of the Catholic Church. The peace movement had gradually generated a climate in which the hitherto monolithic positions on peace gave way to greater internal pluralism.[21]

At the beginning of the 1980s, there had been attempts to stifle the controversial debate at its inception. For instance the Zentralkomitee der deutschen Katholiken (ZdK, Central Committee of German Catholics) adopted a resolution in November 1981 that unilaterally blamed the Soviet Union, confirmed the toleration of deterrence, and endorsed, in its position as the sole governing body of German churches, explicitly the NATO Double-Track Decision.[22] Against a background of general social conflict over the nuclear crisis, such responses proved to be no longer universally acceptable to all Catholics.

The Central Committee was therefore unable to prevent, among other things, groups such as the German section of Pax Christi, the Federation of German Catholic Youth (BDKJ, Bund der Deutschen Katholischen Jugend) or the Initiative Church from Below (IKvu, Initiative Kirche von unten) from revealing the "end of the consensus" on security policy in Western German Catholicism.[23] Pax Christi began addressing the problem of armament in 1977, and its decision to create a commission on "Disarmament and Security" proved to be a particularly forward-looking measure. In November 1980, the assembly of committee delegates adopted a draft resolution, "Disarmament and Security—Platform of Pax Christi," which can be considered a key document for the discussion on peace and security in Catholic circles and elsewhere in Germany.[24] However, for a long time Pax Christi did not take a clear stance with respect to the NATO Double-Track Decision. In November 1981, when the demand that "in no case should the West introduce new medium-range nuclear weapons" reached a quorum for the first time, the Catholic initiative had definitively arrived in the new peace movement.[25]

The Federation of German Catholic Youth (BDKJ) had also been addressing issues of peace and security since the late 1970s. The umbrella organization of the Catholic Youth voted in 1980 to focus on "peace and justice," as did the Association of Evangelical Lutheran Youth (Arbeitsgemeinschaft evangelischer Jugend) and the Protestant Student Congregation (ESG, Evangelischen Studentengemeinden). The circumstances in 1981 were described by taking "pole positions" that called for taking a new direction in peace and security policy. The member associations of the BDKJ were also asked to address issues of peace and theology, development as well as disarmament policy.[26] The BDKJ participated in numerous ways in discussions about the new peace movement and it also emphasized its own views. In 1982 the BDKJ, for example, organized a peace camp at the Düsseldorf Catholic Church Congress, which underlined the growing strength of the opponents to the NATO Double-Track Decision within the pluralistic umbrella organization. Finally, in 1983, the General Assembly of BDKJ called for a complete stop to the deployment of US medium-range missiles. These developments show a clear shift in position for both Pax Christi and the BDKJ during the nuclear crisis.

By contrast, the Catholic reform oriented Initiative Church from Below (IKvu) from its inception in 1980 insisted on opposing the NATO Double-Track Decision and became even more involved in the secular peace movement. In addition to its central demands for fundamental changes in the operating structures of the church, the topic peace became a "second pillar" of the reform movement during the early 1980s.[27] On the occasion of the 1982 Catholic Congress in Düsseldorf the IKvu organized a major peace demonstration in joint association with the Protestant Action Reconciliation Service for Peace (ASF) and the Dutch Interchurch Peace Council (IKV). It was the first time Catholics were able to offer the media a clear message against the intended deployment of American nuclear missiles and for a nuclear-free Europe.[28] The number of participants, approximately forty thousand, was relatively low but generally the official Catholic and the "Catholics Below" Congress demonstrated a progressive removal of the taboos surrounding the discussions of peace and security policy within the Catholic Church in 1982.

These developments in society at large and in particular among the laiety in Western German Catholicism increased pressure on the leading church bodies to comment on the contentious theme of peace. Especially German bishops were challenged by activities of their counterparts in other states, notably in the United States and in the GDR. In autumn 1982, a second draft of a pastoral letter by the US Bishops Conference titled "The Challenge of Peace" received widespread reception in West Germany and was intensively discussed. The final text was adopted by the bishops at their plenary assembly in Chicago on 4 May 1983. Its sweeping calls to reduce the system of deterrence made it a key document for all peace discussions in the Catholic Church and beyond.[29] With a joint pastoral letter dated 1 January 1983, the Catholic bishops in the GDR also abandoned their hesitation and political restraint and decidedly voiced their opinion on matters pertaining to the politics of their own state.[30]

The German Bishops Conference finally published a pastoral letter under the title "Justice Creates Peace" in April 1983.[31] Although the letter voiced no explicit opinion on the NATO Double-Track Decision, the political journal *Der Spiegel* commented, "[s]o many progressive [statements], all at once" had not been expected.[32] Above all, it was the moral questioning of military deterrence, based on strict criteria—for example, that conventional as well as nuclear weapons may exist only for providing deterrence, and may not increase the risk of war—that helped the Catholic Church within the ranks of its leadership "to gradually reach a level of discussion already attained by the Protestant churches."[33] The declaration of the bishops was in many respects closer to positions taken by Pax Christi, the BDKJ, and IKvu rather than the Central Committee. This was ultimately indicative of the social conditions in which the peace and security policy debate was conducted in parishes throughout West Germany.

Among the well-known public figures of the peace movement, the Protestants could count Helmut Gollwitzer, Heinrich Albertz, Dorothee Sölle, and Erhard Eppler. There were also some prominent personalities from the Catholic Church, which bolstered credibility and made the protests more attractive to the masses. In this respect Franz Alt received the largest response and public attention as a self-professed devout Catholic, journalist, and member of the conservative party CDU. The huge sales figures of his book, *Peace is Possible* (*Frieden ist möglich*) published in 1983, point to an enormous social response to Christian ideas or concepts about peace. Above all, the middle class related to the reasoning and developed awareness of the demands of the peace movement.[34]

Franz Alt's bestseller carried the programmatic subtitle "The Policy of the Sermon on the Mount." With evocative, mostly simple words, the television presenter argued against a separation between religion and politics in the nuclear age. Alt countered the argument supporting the benefit of the system of deterrence in a "period of grace" with the direct political message of the biblical messages "love thy enemy" and "turn the other cheek." Consequently, he categorically rejected the proposed NATO arms production and emphatically urged policymakers to make a radical change of direction: "The Sermon on the Mount or the end of history."[35]

Interdenominational Aspects of the Christian Peace Debate: Forms of Organization and Action

The hesitant departure of the Catholic Church from the Cold War[36] paradigm showed that the divisions within the Christian discussion on peace did not follow denominational lines. Generally there were pointed differences between church committees and organizational levels, as well as between individual parishes and local groups.

Particularly between 1982 and 1984, the Christian peace movement developed into an interdenominational movement. Not only was a lively exchange of views institutionalized, but also large meetings and protests were jointly organized, as were calls for interdenominational peace weeks. A nationwide collaboration among organizations was necessary to set up the Widerstandstag (Day of Resistance) during the peace movement's roster of activities in the fall of 1983, and its success demonstrated the strength of the Coordination Committee. In the early 1980s there existed an acute awareness throughout the Christian peace movement that, given the global threat provoked by nuclear weapons, denominational and national differences had to be bridged. Interdenominational collaboration also occurred at the level of church leadership; several joint statements about peace were released in the early 1980s.

Regarding the actual implementation of peace work, there seems to have been hardly any denominational barriers. Instead, certain forms of action characterized the Christian peace movement as a whole. The nationwide Peace Week in 1980 showed the first signs of the Christian potential for the development of new forms of protest in the peace movement with a range of "colorful" and "imaginative" activities. There were not only lectures, discussions, exhibitions, information stands, services, torchlight processions, and street demonstrations, but also cultural events, peace festivals, theater and film screenings, alternative city tours, role playing, relay races, and children's programs.[37] Organizers almost universally acknowledged the principle of nonviolence as a consequence of religious and political beliefs, often with reference to Mahatma Gandhi or Martin Luther King, Jr. Silent vigils and fasting thus denoted typical Christian forms of civil disobedience. The Christian peace movement's social value change, conceptions of alternative lifestyles, and fusion of personal faith and political accountability manifested a unique "spirituality of resistance," as noted by Dorothee Sölle.

Key Aspects of Ecclesiastical Peace Discussions

While the NATO Double-Track Decision dominated ecclesiastical debates on security policy, this was not the sole concern. The entire system of nuclear deterrence in the East-West conflict was under consideration.

On the one hand, action groups such as Sicherung des Friedens (Securing Peace), the council of the EKD, the German Bishops Conference, and the Central Committee of German Catholics temporarily extended the so-called period of grace of deterrence with different degrees of reservation. The strict criteria to the granting of this provisional extension were aimed primarily at preventing war. On the other hand, the Christian peace movement had, at least since 1983, concluded that it was necessary to express an unconditional "no," not just on the NATO Double-Track Decision but on the production, deployment, and use of all nuclear weapons. "The spirit, logic, and practice of deterrence"[38] posed a greater risk, in the judgment of the Christian peace groups, than the opponent behind the Iron Curtain. The religiously motivated rejection of enemy stereotyping and bogeyman rhetoric apparent in political speeches against anticommunism and anti-Americanism was based on a skeptical view of the nuclear model of international relations.

The central objectives of the Christian peace movement were as follows: sustained relations of détente with Eastern European countries, nuclear-free zones, a conversion to defensive weapons systems, and an armaments policy of unilateral and calculated disarmament implemented in successive steps (gradualism) toward a nonviolent "social defense" method. Contrary to common fears, these demands to dismantle the "mutual assured destruction" did not result in ideas for a neutralist reunified Germany.

The Christian peace groups called for a fundamental reversal in the overall thinking on peace and security policy. To offer alternatives to existing strategies, they resorted to several approaches, which aimed at a policy capable of bringing together secular reason and Christian faith.[39] Particularly powerful was the concept of "security partnership" or "common security," part of which reverted explicitly to Carl Friedrich von Weizsaecker's concept roughly translated as "love thy enemies in an intelligent way." Other important conceptual input for "common security" came from Egon Bahr and the Palme Report.[40] Ideas from the domain of the ecumenical movement, and particularly of the Protestant Churches in the GDR, were also discussed and reviewed. In as much as there had been a substantive transfer of ideas from peace actors in the West to those in the East, in this instance there was a reversal of transfer.[41]

The core idea of this concept of "common security" claimed that peace and security could no longer exist at odds in a nuclear age with increasing global interdependence, but only in cooperation. This meant that the security policy of the East-West conflict always had to consider the needs of the opposing side and could no longer be based on categories of military demarcation, defense, and deterrence.

Taking an even broader perspective well beyond defense issues between NATO and the Warsaw Pact, "common security" could secure global security for all humans. It was for this reason that Christian peace initiatives underlined persistent problems in the north-south divide, and in particular the "Third World." An unquestionable success of the Christian peace movement rests in having produced increasingly official church statements that reflected concrete political thinking along with biblical notions of peace. The movement sensitized the churches' membership to the political need for a comprehensive understanding of peace and security, as the biblical concept "shalom" suggested.

Christian Protest in Transition

The ecumenical movement increasingly fixed its attention on peace and disarmament issues after the mid-1970s. The fifth Assembly of the World Council of Churches in Nairobi had already contributed substantially to the international peace discussion, but the following General Assembly in Vancouver in the summer of 1983 saw a breakthrough for its transnational and interdenominational institutionalization in a worldwide ecumenical movement.

This assembly initially returned to the clear-cut wording of the Amsterdam Assembly in 1948, which was drafted under the immediate responses to World War II: "War is contrary to the will of God." The General Assembly in 1983 developed this statement conceptually. It rejected unconditionally all use, production, and deployment of nuclear weapons, which it identified as a crime against humanity.[42] The Vancouver resolution received a mixed response in various parts of the world. However, it helped initiate the "Conciliar Process of Mutual Commitment to Justice, Peace, and the Integrity of Creation." The goal of its comprehensive agenda, with its commentary on peace policy together with social, ethical, and environmental considerations, was supposed to lead to a council of peace. The full force of this declaration unfolded finally at the 1985 Protestant Church Congress in Düsseldorf.[43] It ensured that peace and disarmament issues became permanent topics on the churches' agenda—and would attract public attention. The Christian peace movement's work in the Federal Republic of Germany henceforth no longer initiated high-profile mass demonstrations but continued in a quieter, programmatic interaction on all levels of church and society. Ultimately it may be concluded that the peace movement's minority following during the first half of the 1980s became the mainstream in all churches.[44]

Sebastian Kalden studied history, church history, as well as peace and conflict studies at the University of Marburg, where he wrote his dissertation on the transnational relations of the Christian peace movement in Western Europe after the NATO Double-Track Decision. He is currently a project manager at the Mecklenburger AnStiftung in Wismar.

Jan Ole Wiechmann studied history, religion, and German at the University of Marburg, where he worked on his dissertation project on security concepts in the Christian peace movement in the Federal Republic of Germany, 1977–1984. From 2008–2009 he was a contributing researcher of the independent commission of historians tasked to explore the history of the Federal Republic of Germany's Foreign Office. He is currently a teacher at the Johann-Heinrich-Voss school in Eutin.

Notes

1. *Säkularisierung und Neuformierung des Religiösen: Gesellschaft und Religion in der zweiten Hälfte des 20. Jahrhunderts, Archiv für Sozialgeschichte* 51 (2011).
2. Helmut Zander, *Die Christen und die Friedensbewegungen in beiden deutschen Staaten: Beiträge zu einem Vergleich für die Jahre 1978–1987* (Berlin [West], 1989), 37, gives a percentage of 43.5 for Catholic and 42.8 for Protestant citizens in the Federal Republic in 1980.
3. Uta Andrea Balbier, "'Sag: Wie hast Du's mit der Religion?' Das Verhältnis von Religion und Politik als Gretchenfrage der Zeitgeschichte," *H-Soz-u-Kult,* 10 November 2009, http://hsozkult.geschichte.hu-berlin.de/forum/2009-11-001.
4. Ohne Rüstung Leben, "Der Aufruf 'An alle Christen' 1978," in *Ohne Rüstung Leben* (Gütersloh, 1981), 20.
5. Good insight about the developments of the action group Ohne Rüstung Leben can be found in the occasional "information" newsletter sent by the group to its supporters since 1978.
6. "Sicherung des Friedens: An die evangelischen Christen!" in Eberhard Stammler, ed., *Sicherung des Friedens: Eine christliche Verpflichtung* (Stuttgart, 1980), 12–13.
7. Leon Wecke and Ben Schennink, "Die 'neue' Friedensbewegung in den Niederlanden," in *Die neue Friedensbewegung: Analysen aus der Friedensforschung,* ed. Reiner Steinweg (Frankfurt am Main, 1982), 16:299–300.

8. The action guide much in use: Aktion Sühnezeichen/Friedensdienst (henceforth ASF), ed., *Frieden schaffen ohne Waffen: Aktionshandbuch 1* (Berlin, 1980).
9. An evaluation of the nationwide Peace Week in November 1981 can be found in Eva Michels, "Auswertung der 2. bundesweiten Friedenswochen 'Frieden schaffen ohne Waffen' 15.–21.11.1981," April 1982, Evangelisches Zentralarchiv Berlin (henceforth EZA), record 97/865, 4.
10. Anke Silomon, *"Schwerter zu Pflugscharen" und die DDR: Die Friedensarbeit der evangelischen Kirchen in der DDR im Rahmen der Friedensdekaden 1980 bis 1982* (Göttingen, 1999).
11. Rüdiger Schmitt, *Die Friedensbewegung in der Bundesrepublik: Ursachen und Bedingungen der Mobilisierung einer neuen sozialen Bewegung* (Opladen, 1990), 152.
12. This expression refers to Luke 2:10 "And the angel said to them, 'Fear not, for behold, I bring you good news of great joy that will be for all the people.'" It is written in the same theological language as in the awkward phrase "No Without Any Yes".
13. Call to the peace demonstration on 20 June 1981 on occasion of the Nineteenth Evangelical Church Congress, "Aufruf zur Friedensdemonstration am 20.6. aus Anlass des 19. Ev. Kirchentag," in *Ansätze* 4 (1981): 37–38.
14. Volkmar Deile and Ulrich Frey, "Wie es zur Demonstration vom 10.10.1981 in Bonn kam," in ASF/AGDF, eds., *Bonn 10.10.1981: Friedensdemonstration für Abrüstung und Entspannung in Europa. Reden, Fotos …* (Bornheim-Merten, 1981), 13–20.
15. Volkmar Deile, "Frieden: Zwischen Sintflut und Regenbogen: Ein herausragendes Thema bei Kirchentagen seit 1967," in *Fest des Glaubens: Forum der Welt. 60 Jahre Deutscher Evangelischer Kirchentag*, ed. Rüdiger Runge and Ellen Ueberschär (Gütersloh, 2009), 30–40, 34.
16. Kirchenkanzlei der Evangelischen Kirche in Deutschland, ed., *Frieden wahren, fördern und erneuern: Eine Denkschrift der Evangelischen Kirche in Deutschland* (Gütersloh, 1981), 58.
17. Ibid., 103.
18. Moderamen des Reformierten Bundes, "Das Bekenntnis zu Jesus Christus und die Friedensverantwortung der Kirche, 12.6.1982," *Kirchliches Jahrbuch*, 108/109 (1981/82): 103–5. Impetus for this explanation came in 1979 when a handout about nuclear weapons was published by the Dutch Reformed Church.
19. AGDF et al., "Umkehr zum Leben: Aufruf zu einer Kampagne während des Kirchentages in Hannover im Juni 1983," *epd-Dokumentation* 25 (1983): 31–33.
20. Ulrich Frey, "Kirchentag als Friedensdemonstration: Einschätzung aus der Sicht der Friedensbewegung," in *Jugend auf dem Kirchentag: Eine empirische Analyse von Andreas Feige, Ingrid Lukatis und Wolfgang Lukatis,* ed. Tilman Schmieder and Klaus Schuhmacher (Stuttgart, 1984), 241–42.
21. A perceptive contemporary view came from Volkmar Deile, "Versuch eines Jahresüberblicks 1982 über die Aktivitäten und Entwicklungen der Aktion Sühnezeichen/Friedensdienste," 3 February 1983, in *EZA* 97/93.
22. Vollversammlung des Zentralkomitees der deutschen Katholiken, "Zur aktuellen Friedensdiskussion, 14.11.1981," in *Herder-Korrespondenz* 35 (1981): 624–30.
23. Thomas Risse-Kappen, "Das Ende der Geschlossenheit: Die Friedensdiskussion in der katholischen Kirche der Bundesrepublik," in *Friedensforschung, Kirche und kirch-*

liche Friedensbewegungen, ed. Hanne-Margret Birckenbach (Frankfurt am Main, 1983), 152–66.
24. Pax Christi, *Abrüstung und Sicherheit: Plattform der Pax Christi* (Frankfurt am Main, 1981).
25. Resolution adopted by the assembly of the Pax Christi delegates on the deployment of intermediate-range missiles in Europe at Rothenfels, 7 November 1981, Bischöfliches Diözesan-Archiv Aachen, record Ala Pax Christi, file 73.
26. Bund der Deutschen Katholischen Jugend, "'Frieden und Gerechtigkeit' Schwerpunktthema von der Hauptversammlung des BDKJ 1981 in Altenberg beschlossen: Startpositionen," *BDKJ-Informationsdienst* 10 (1981): 115–18.
27. "Pazifismus '81: 'Selig sind die Friedfertigen,'" *Der Spiegel,* 15 June 1981, 25.
28. "'Kehrt um—entrüstet Euch!' Aufruf zur Demonstration anlässlich des Katholikentages am 4.9.1982 in Düsseldorf," *Blätter für deutsche und internationale Politik* 8 (1982): 1018–19.
29. United States Conference of Catholic Bishops, *The Challenge of Peace: God's Promise and Our Response; A Pastoral Letter on War and Peace by the National Conference of Catholic Bishops* (Washington, DC, 1983).
30. Joint pastoral letter by the Catholic bishops of the Democratic Republic of Germany on World Peace Day 1983 on 1 January 1983, in *Herausforderung Frieden,* ed. Pax Christi (Frankfurt am Main, 1983), 177–83.
31. Sekretariat der Deutschen Bischofskonferenz, ed., *Deutsche Bischofskonferenz: Gerechtigkeit schafft Frieden, April 18, 1983* (Bonn, 1983).
32. "So gelaufen," *Der Spiegel,* 25 April 1983, 17.
33. Risse-Kappen, "Ende der Geschlossenheit," 164, 165n22.
34. Eckart Conze, *Die Suche nach Sicherheit: Eine Geschichte der Bundesrepublik Deutschland von 1949 bis in die Gegenwart* (Munich, 2009), 541–42; and Andreas Wirsching, *Abschied vom Provisorium: Geschichte der Bundesrepublik Deutschland 1982–1990* (Munich, 2006), 92–93.
35. Franz Alt, *Frieden ist möglich: Die Politik der Bergpredigt* (Munich, 1983), 105.
36. Quotation following Lutz Lemhöfer, "Zögernder Aufbruch aus dem Kalten Krieg: Die katholische Kirche und die bundesdeutsche 'neue Friedensbewegung,'" in *Die neue Friedensbewegung: Analysen aus der Friedensforschung,* ed. Reiner Steinweg (Frankfurt am Main, 1982), 245–57.
37. Inter alia Volkmar Deile, "Die erste bundesweite Friedenswoche 1980: Ergebnisse und Perspektiven aus der Sicht der Initiatoren, 15.6.1981," in *EZA* 97/863.
38. The rejection of "the spirit, logic, and practice of deterrence" was initially put forward by the Federation of Evangelical Churches in the GDR and subsequently often taken up by Christian groups in the West. Compare to inter alia Joachim Garstecki, "Friedensbewegung und Politik," in *Deutsche Vergangenheiten: Eine gemeinsame Herausforderung. Der schwierige Umgang mit der doppelten Nachkriegsgeschichte,* ed. Christoph Klessmann, Hans Michelwitz, and Günter Wichert (Berlin, 1999), 277–85, esp. 282–83.
39. The following is extensivly discussed by Jan Ole Wiechmann, "Der Streit um die Bergpredigt: Säkulare Vernunft und religiöser Glaube in der christlichen Friedensbewegung der Bundesrepublik Deutschland (1977–1984)," in *Archiv für Sozialgeschichte* 51 (2011): 343–74.

40. Report of the Independent Commission on Disarmament and Security Issues, *Common Security: A Programme for Disarmament* (London, 1982).
41. Garstecki, "Friedensbewegung," 282n37.
42. David Gill, ed., *Gathered for Life: Official Report, VI Assembly World Council of Churches, Vancouver, Canada, 24 July–10 August 1983* (Geneva, 1983), 136.
43. Katharina Kunter, *Erfüllte Hoffnungen und zerbrochene Träume: Evangelische Kirchen in Deutschland im Spannungsfeld von Demokratie und Sozialismus 1980–1993* (Göttingen, 2006), 106–7.
44. An apt perspective on Protestantism is provided by Wolf-Dieter Hauschild, "Evangelische Kirche in der Bundesrepublik Deutschland zwischen 1961 und 1979," in Siegfried Hermle, Claudia Lepp, and Harry Oelke, eds., *Umbrüche: Der deutsche Protestantismus und die sozialen Bewegungen in den 1960er und 70er Jahren* (Göttingen, 2007), 74.

Select Bibliography

Zander continues to provide a good overview of the Christian peace discussions during the nuclear crisis. While it lacks a single, clearly defined perspective, a growing number of publications have in recent years contributed to innovative analytical approaches. Among these, Gerster and Wiechmann should be mentioned. Another important contribution is the volume published by Stadtland, which covers the Christian peace debates in the Federal Republic, the GDR, and in the ecumenical movement. An extended perspective is offered in the special issue of the journal *Zeithistorischen Forschungen* on religion in the Federal Republic of Germany. It contributes to a scientific debate about the current religious-historical situation, with Lepp's essay addressing the relationship between the churches and the new social movements.

Gerster, Daniel. *Friedensdialoge im Kalten Krieg: Eine Geschichte der Katholiken in der Bundesrepublik, 1957–1983.* Frankfurt am Main and New York, 2012.
Stadtland, Helke, ed. *"Friede auf Erden": Religiöse Semantiken und Konzepte des Friedens im 20. Jahrhundert.* Essen, 2009.
Wiechmann, Jan Ole. "Der Streit um die Bergpredigt: Säkulare Vernunft und religiöser Glaube in der christlichen Friedensbewegung der Bundesrepublik Deutschland (1977–1984)." *Archiv für Sozialgeschichte* 51 (2011): 343–74.
Zander, Helmut. *Die Christen und die Friedensbewegungen in beiden deutschen Staaten: Beiträge zu einem Vergleich für die Jahre 1978–1987.* Berlin [West], 1989.

Chapter 14

Trade Unions

Dietmar Süss

At the end of August 1983 trade union leaders and representatives of the peace movement met by invitation of the journal *Trade Union Monthly* to exchange views. The intention was to use the following months to draw up plans for a *Friedensherbst* (Autumn of Peace). Many individual trade unions, most prominently the IG Metall trade union, and youth organizations joined forces for the "World Peace Weeks." A variety of events were set up in workplaces, before the mass demonstration on 19 October in Bonn. The culmination of the campaign was a doomsday clock event called "5 Minutes to Midnight" that took place on 5 October when the Deutscher Gewerkschaftbund (DGB, Confederation of German Trade Union) called on its members to join in a five-minute break to protest "against nuclear missiles in the West and East" and for "Peace through Disarmament."

The Confederation of German Trade Unions already had some experience in the peace policy debate. Its reaction to the NATO Double-Track Decision, however, had been relatively muted. The umbrella organization even failed to mention this topic in its discussion of issues relating to the general election in 1980. Indeed it was only in 1981 that the DGB saw it fit to approve, for the first time, a resolution of its National Youth Committee, which demanded "[a]n immediate start to negotiations on arms limitation in Europe, without setting preconditions and with the goal to allow no further deployment of nuclear weapons in the East or West."[1]

The talks between trade unions and representatives of the peace movement did not commence in an atmosphere of intimate fellowship. On the contrary, Hermann Rappe, chairman of IG Chemie-Papier-Keramic, used every opportunity to sharply attack his counterparts in the peace movement. He recalled with considerable pride the longstanding history and tradition of the trade unions' struggle for peace and disarmament, while expressing resentment toward the newcomers to the cause. Right in the middle of a conversation with prominent environmentalist Jo Leinen,[2] who was also a fellow member of the Social Democratic Party of Germany (SPD), and with leading peace activist Volkmar Deile[3] during a meeting in Berlin, Rappe lost patience and shouted, "That's all we need! After more than a century of struggle to say we've lost our competence in peace politics. Well, we are man enough to claim we've got more than enough competence!"[4]

What triggered this outburst? Why did leading trade union officials in 1983 find it so difficult to cooperate with peace activists? And what caused the trade unions, despite initial hesitation, to eventually form part of the peace movement? Four factors are central to answering these questions: first of all, the different organizational cultures and social interpretations in the "old" and the new social movements, second a growing generational conflict within the trade unions and the DGB, third the differing views among the trade unions, and, fourth, the shaping power, reactivation, and transformation of anticommunism. The "peace" debates touched the very core of trade union identity and self-perception. Both of these concepts were intimately linked to the structural economic and social changes in the 1980s, the use of novel forms of protest, and new political actors. Moreover, the development of the relationship between trade unions and the peace movement highlights a social conflict that has been so far rarely addressed in the history of the peace movement: the workplace as a micro-political arena.

The Trade Unions and New Social Movements

In trade union rhetoric it was ceremoniously repeated that the movement had always been a peace movement in its own right, campaigning against the rearmament since the 1950s and joining in the Easter March movement.[5] However, the leadership saw itself primarily as serving the interests of workers, who, at least in the perception of leading trade unionists in the early 1980s, feared losing their jobs more than they feared a nuclear war. Yet this was only one reason for the apparent reluctance of the older trade unionists, who had been socialized in a social democratic tradition. Another can be found in the gulf between old and new social movements.

Trade unionists like Hermann Rappe did not think much of "movements." For them "organization" seemed the only way to ensure a "promising long-term impact on politics in a parliamentary democracy."[6] This revealed a fundamental skepticism about the nature of decision-making in the peace movement, whose internal processes offered a substantially different culture of discussion, negotiation, and formation. These challenged some of the more authoritarian-/patriarchal-minded trade unionists, who considered these methods completely preposterous. For the old-school trade unionists, "organization" towered above everything, and the perception that the various committees of the peace movement showed no clear decision-making structures—no chairmen, secretaries, and authorized representatives—probably contributed significantly to the organizational and cultural remoteness between trade unionists and a peace movement committed to grassroots democracy.

Among trade unions and throughout the DGB these demarcation lines had been drawn early on, well before the peace movement was established and irrespective of political and strategic orientations.[7] Trade union boss Eugen Loderer (IG Metall), for example, observed the incipient antinuclear movement and the growing number of citizens' initiatives with reservation. In particular he was alarmed about their claim to have the right to question and reject government decisions and to claim a legitimacy he felt should not be held by an extra-parliamentary body. In addition, these groups seemed to him both politically and behaviorally suspect. Loderer did not relate to the manners and exuberant dress styles of the "Green" environmental movement.[8] And he was by no means the only one among the (male) top officials of the DGB when he recorded in his memoirs, "In my opinion the Parliament was no grassroots assembly. There are fixed rules or accepted forms of behavior and a Parliament requires a certain kind of dignity. Gimmicky clothes and a good deal of slapstick" did not contribute to policymaking. It was precisely these linguistically and symbolically mediated distinctions that exacerbated initial talks considerably—and the difficulties in dealing with them by no means rested exclusively on the side of the trade unions. In certain circles within the peace movement trade unionists were in turn initially seen as alien and, if not a threat to the movement as such, then certainly an ally to be approached with great caution. Within the movement there was a worry of being "swallowed up" by the trade unions' apparatus or, given the close proximity of the trade unions to Social Democracy, to be "nationalized" at the expense or loss of the special "vitality, creativity, and openness" of the extra-parliamentary movement.

Arms Production and the Trade Union's "Labor for Peace"

The trade union debates about "peace" and "disarmament" touched on specific concerns of the peace movement that went well beyond protests against the NATO Double-Track Decision: a demand for the restructuring of defense, changing production from military to civilian goods (known as conversion), and certain debates about "alternatives in production" and job security. The IG-Metall Jugend (IG Metall Youth) had already raised an appeal in 1971 that stated the DGB should commit to a "development of production plans" to restructure West German arms manufacturers to make "civilian products."⁹ Since the mid- and late 1970s this debate had received new impetus, thanks to rising unemployment and growing economic difficulties. In 1976 several chairmen of workers' councils argued for a relaxation of export restrictions of military technology to crisis areas in order to secure jobs in difficult times. This caused intense debates about the significance of the defense industry for the "German Model."

Against this background, the IG Metall board created a "discussion forum for military technology and jobs," which included members of workers' councils from major arms manufactories. They were asked for their thoughts on a trade union model of "active peace policy" on the shop floor, especially in enterprises producing ethically questionable items. These discussions revolved not only around the ethical dimension of "alternative kinds of work," but also on the question of whether conversion would contribute to job security. Faced with rising unemployment, the councils explored this defense conversion initiative as a possible solution.

IG Metall was the driving force behind the debate about "alternative production" and took the lead in linking the criticism of military spending with a demand for "humane" and "new" types of work. Industrial research think tanks affiliated to the trade union argued that ultimately the armament industry did not create jobs in times of a faltering economy but on the contrary their production methods threatened secure jobs due to rationalization policies. In addition, defense spending did not have a positive effect on the labor market. Government subsidies granted to military research prevented "human" progress, as such resources would not be channeled toward more pressing problems such as environmental protection, food and energy supply, and consumption issues. In sum, arms production endangered the qualitative growth of the economy, accelerated inflation, and prevented the development of innovative technologies.¹⁰

The topic made it for the first time onto the front page of *Gewerkschafter* (The Trade Unionist), the official journal of IG Metall where even non-experts were able to present their projections for the design of future workstations. First reports from members' study groups in arms factories (e.g., the aviation and aerospace company Messerschmitt-Boelkow-Blohm) were also published, which outlined proposals for restructuring "their" corporations and the accompanying difficulties in the immediate implementation in everyday operations. Large companies, such as the shipbuilder Blohm & Voss in Hamburg had, despite initial hesitation on behalf of the employers, initiated working groups to look into converting to manufacture alternative, new, and nonmilitary products while keeping a lookout for new markets. About a dozen businesses set up such company groups that treated the issues of conversion and "peace policy" with respect to their immediate labor processes. For example, they calculated the real costs of the construction of frigates for Turkey, which had been funded by government subsidies, and demonstrated that the funds could have been used to build merchant ships instead, or to modernize the outdated production facilities.[11]

The trade union-sponsored "peace studies" of the Hans-Böckler-Stiftung (Hans Böckler Foundation) provided funding for empirical research on conversion and thus generated expertise that proved essential in disputes within and beyond companies.[12] There is a good amount of evidence that these ongoing debates on arms exports and military production since the 1970s paved the way for closer ties between the trade unionists and the peace movement, precisely because of discussions that merged "work" and "disarmament."

It should, however, be noted that the demands for "alternative modes of production" were never undisputed. A key event was a protest in 1981 by shipyard workers in Kiel. They staged a demonstration against a submarine export to Chile, and therefore turned against their own trade union leadership.[13] This example shows that although "conversion" may have been theoretically convincing, in practice it proved controversial. The demand for a change in production threatened perhaps the essence of entrepreneurship, and failed to inspire massive enthusiasm among employees faced with incipient mass unemployment.[14]

In a 1982 meeting with several leaders of the peace movement, including Petra Kelly and Gert Bastian, the chair of the Cologne DGB Women's Committee, Claudia Woermann-Adam, warned that many employees had initially felt threatened by the demand for conversion. The trade union base only slowly began to discuss the interdependence between the arms race and social welfare cuts.[15] Gunnar Matthiesen from the Committee for Peace Disarmament and Cooperation (KOFAZ), when speaking about motivation to support the peace movement said, "Hardly anyone ever joined the peace movement because of a concern for 'social' issues; it was actual 'fear for their lives' that pushed people to a commitment. And this had never before been a matter for the trade unions. They usually focused on wage policy and an expansion of welfare benefits."[16]

Forms of Protest and the Trade Unions' Convergence with the Peace Movement

The difficulties between old and new social movements also pertained to the new forms of protest used by the peace movement, which exploded the trade unions' rigid rules of action. For the unions, collective protest took place in the form of a strike or a march, as on 1 May. Forming a human chain or building a blockade were not acceptable. The New Social Movement, however, found it hard to limit its forms of expression in this way. Especially the question of what kind of protest against the deployment of missiles was legitimate, or even necessary, was a central point of contention within the trade unions. In particular, they considered a political, and therefore in Germany illegal, strike, or even a general strike against the NATO Double-Track Decision. This controversy was not just about an "active policy for peace" but touched on the fundamental relationship between the state and trade unions in the 1980s and on the significance of a parliamentary majority in favor of the Double-Track Decision and a workforce involved in extra-parliamentary protests.

Especially in IG Metall and its youth organizations there were those who seriously considered a political strike, given the apocalyptic threat posed by the arms race. Some certainly felt the democratic foundations of the Federal Republic were endangered by the deployment of the Euromissiles. The trade union leadership categorically rejected these demands and ruled out further discussions in July 1983.[17] Although a political strike may have inspired revolutionary imaginations in some quarters, it took other forms of collective protest to demonstrate a convergence among the different generations of social movements.

A petition, "Peace through Disarmament," was started on Antiwar Day on 1 September 1981 and continued a form of protest initiated by the Krefeld Appeal, irrespective of political objectives.[18] The DGB employed forms of protest that it had used before in strikes: a "5 Minutes to Midnight" doomsday event in 1983 and a five-minute stoppage in factories and offices as a reminder to negotiators in Geneva. Trade union representatives and leaders were familiar with this kind of protest and had made sure beforehand that public employers would tolerate such action.[19] In all actuality, it did not constitute a particularly dangerous form of protest, despite an attempt by some employers to prevent such workplace interruptions with reference to their "political character."[20] The degree to which the trade union's assessment of collective forms of action had changed within a few years can be seen in the internal conflict over the legitimacy of sit-ins in front of military installations. At the beginning of the 1980s these had been received in leading trade union circles with serious misgivings. Trade union officials, versed in strike methods, had little experience with such forms of civil disobedience, and there was no longer sympathy for "wildcat strikes" outside official trade union guidelines, as there had been 1969.

Skepticism about deliberate violations had by no means disappeared by the mid-1980s. Nonetheless the IG Metall newspaper *metall* reported in

Figure 14.1. A poster "Give Peace a Chance! Antiwar Day 1981, DGB-Youth North Rhine-Westphalia" (DGB Jugend NRW / Stuttgart, Wuerttemberg State Library)

early January 1984 on the conduct of the police in Mutlangen with some anger: "The peace is gone. The so-called soft attitude of the police in Mutlangen belongs to the past …" Ernst Eisenmann, regional head of Stuttgart's IG Metall condemned emphatically recent police attacks. In a speech delivered on 10 December, he demanded that the trade unions and the peace movement should not be divided, but should move closer together.[21] It was primarily younger trade union officials and stewards who called on solidarity within the peace movement, defended the legality of alternative forms of protests, denounced "excessive" government responses, and now saw themselves standing side by side with the activists of the peace movement. They consequently altered the form and language of trade union protests. This might at first sight have appeared somewhat threatening to the trade union leadership. However, the challenge posed by the peace movement was probably far less serious than the threat caused by the controversy over the "New Left," as this movement had been challenging the fundamental identity of the trade unions since the early 1970s.

A number of reasons played a role in the gradual convergence of the trade unions and the peace movement: the learning curve in forms of protest culture was just as important as the political shift witnessed at the beginning of Chancellor Kohl's conservative government. Now the trade union was no longer restrained in verbally attacking "insane defense systems" and "social cuts" as they no longer had to worry about undermining the authority of their own comrades in power. This was probably a considerable incentive for many trade unionists to take less notice of their cultural and political differences with the peace movement and to concentrate on the similarities. The debates in the trade union youth organizations contributed to making the list of demands by the peace movement ever more present on the agenda of major trade union meetings, and thus they initiated a change of focus in the interpretation of trade union policy: the 1970s optimism in progress had been increasingly lost and replaced, apart from the nuclear threat, by a number of other topics such as a young generation growing up with "no prospects," the fear of rationalization, mass unemployment, and a struggle, new at the time, to maintain social political aspects of the welfare system, all of which placed the trade unions in opposition to the Kohl government. Especially younger trade unionists thought about the nuclear threat, a possible showdown between the superpowers, and debates over a "crisis of the welfare state" with some trepidation, and in this situation the distinction between "new" and "old" social movements became permeable. The conflict with the peace movement was then partly a generational matter that was primarily settled by the youth organizations in the trade unions. And the unions ultimately benefited from the new vitality.

Although one ought to bear in mind that within the overall trade union movement individual trade unions showed varying degrees of preparedness to enter political conflict, there was, at the very least among the leading trade union officials in the early 1980s, a prevailing feeling that "only" the trade unions represented a social movement. Indeed it was precisely this self-image that appeared to be threatened by the peace mobilization. IG Metall trade union leader Loderer thus announced the trade union's own plans for 1 September, an Antiwar Day, which not only adhered to the tradition of the organization's antifascist efforts but also emphasized the leading role of the trade unions as an institutionalized peace movement. The relationship between the peace movement and trade unions rested on organizational matters and also raised issues relating to history and identity. The trade unions drew on this tradition and they increasingly linked the threat of a nuclear apocalypse with the horrors of World War II.[22]

The Antiwar Day initiated by the trade unions was symbolically the "correct" day to commemorate the war with the petition "Peace through Disarmament." It was a trade union internal attempt to top the controversial Krefeld Appeal, which was highly disputed within the ranks of the DGB because of the communist involvement, with an official trade union-generated peace initiative.[23] The significance of this campaign rested however less in the total number of signatures than in the trade unions' compulsion to clarify its relationship with the peace movement, which had needed to be addressed since 1981/1982. The signature campaign was part of the trade unions' arduous efforts to find their own language and forms of protest, which for many trade unionists remained unusual, because many, especially among IG Mining (IG-Bergbau) and IG Chemistry (IG-Chemie), still vigorously supported the policy of former Chancellor Helmut Schmidt to implement the NATO Double-Track Decision. An alliance with a movement that criticized this part of a Social Democratic government policy could hardly be taken for granted.

Even more seriously contested was the possible collaboration with "communists," that is, the German Communist Party (DKP) and/or its affiliated organizations. Collaboration was considered not only a political stupidity but also a fall from grace by the trade union, as any form of cooperation might play into the hands of the forces from the "East" and their one-sided demands. The principal of the main board of IG Chemie-Papier-Keramik Wolfgang Schultze condemned all those who had signed the Appeal of Krefeld. "In this instance, everybody must watch out that he does not enter, against best intentions, into an agreement with, so to speak, friends of peace, who … oppose solely or principally the US and NATO, and who do not mention the defense policy of the Soviets at all or only in passing."[24] This

Figure 14.2. A Poster "We want to live! No more nuclear missiles in Central Europe. Peace Walk of the trade union IG Metall and Initiative Ludwigsburg Days for Peace (Initiative Ludwigsburger Friedenstage) for Disarmament in East and West," 09/25/1983 (IG Metall Ludwigsburg / Stuttgart, Wuerttemberg State Library)

elaboration on "political naivety" formed part of a repertoire of terms and expressions that distinguished between the supposedly "realistic" members in the trade unions and the occasionally "naive" peace activists, some of whom, however, could also be found in the ranks of the DGB.[25]

It cannot be claimed that the trade union movement shared a unified position because representatives of the DGB's youth organizations and especially the influential IG Metall loudly voiced their criticism of the policies espoused by the NATO Double-Track Decision and Chancellor Schmidt's government, while the IG Chemie-Papier-Keramik and others, remained distant to parts of the peace movement, not least with respect to the "alliance issue."

The decision of the DGB executive board, which had banned its youth organization in early July from helping to organize the mass demonstration of the peace movement at the Hofgarten in Bonn on 10 October 1981 (individual participation was unaffected), can be understood only against a background of the currently revitalized but otherwise longstanding anticommunist political battles from the early days of West Germany. These received, in the context of a policy of détente, their own dynamic. An outright rejection of the DKP, just like attempts to build up "official" trade union contacts with East Germany on an inter-German level, formed part of the efforts to find a measured and realistic political response to the old anticommunist rhetoric of the 1950s and to adapt strategies to the changing conditions of a Germany with two states.

The DGB certainly reached its decision while considering strategic issues such as how powerful labor trade unions should form alliances with alternative networks, and how such participation should be structured and classified. In another sense the problem also revolved around the relationship to the rather limited number of West German communists who participated in the peace movement, constituting only one group among many. In any case, the DGB youth were tremendously disappointed about the form and outcome of this decision. Protest stirred up also in numerous IG Metall district organizations. On the IG Metall main board, Georg Benz, as executive director responsible for youth and education, did not wish to miss the opportunity to deliver a speech as "trade union secretary and member of the Social Democratic Party" at this rally. Benz had given rise to the impression that the IG Metall would support the demonstration. The IG Metall board vehemently opposed this idea. Nonetheless Benz stuck with his decision to speak as a "private citizen."

This conflict was, on the one hand, a matter of trade union discipline, and on the other, it touched on the nature of the alliance formed with different currents of the "old" and "new" left. Many IG Metall trade union executives suspected that a fair number of young activists were also active in trade union youth education, where they operated, allegedly creating "mischief" and propagating their political views. From these quarters of the trade union came repeated calls to tolerate the Communist Party and radical anticapitalist and pro-Soviet statements advocating greater dialogue instead of segregation from various left movements outside the Social Democrats' sphere. On the occasion of the Antiwar Day on 1 September 1979, DGB chairman Heinz Oskar Vetter was booed by a section of the audience during his speech when he mentioned that the Hitler-Stalin pact had been a prerequisite for the outbreak of World War II. This was only one of many indications for the growing impact of agile alliances close to the DKP.[26] The debate about the history of National Socialism and the role of communist and reformist trade unions in the twentieth century was a key historical and political battle in which sympathizers with the East stressed that the left-wing socialist and communist heritage was a legitimate part of trade union history, and criticized the "Social Democratic" willingness to adapt to capitalism, both in the past and present.[27]

Without knowledge of this history it is impossible to understand why a controversy about possible alliances and partnerships with communists erupted within the context of the debate on the NATO Double-Track Decision: it affected the very core of the trade union's identity and was not merely a matter commented upon by politically interested parties on the outside. The debate was also about the trade unions' relationship to parliamentary democracy, their internal discipline and "unity" of organizational culture, and the historical-political analysis of the GDR and the struggle for a new anticapitalist self-image of trade unions as a countervailing force to the "System"—positions that had a positive resonance and were important issues of political education.[28] Thus the trade unions' controversies about the relationship with the "East" and how to respond to communists generally continued to demarcate lines of conflict until the mid 1980s.

This included foremost the support of Polish colleagues and especially Solidarność (Solidarity) within the trade unions' own sphere of détente. For, in the wake of the social-liberal diplomacy of détente, the DGB had for quite some time provided "silent support" for beleaguered trade union colleagues and assisted in the development of an independent nongovernmental organization. On 13 December 1981, when martial law was imposed in Poland, the trade union initiated numerous campaigns protesting against the arrest of many trade union officials and against the Polish military dictatorship.[29] This unique form of inter-trade union détente policy, which pertained to the essential demand for the legitimacy of strike action and trade union rights, shaped trade union peace initiatives, particularly during the years 1982/83, which invariably kept one eye on Poland. A demand for "peace and disarmament" in this sense did not "exclusively" mean criticism of the arms upgrade but also pertained to a lack of workers' rights.

Readers found little in the bulletins of the DKP on support campaigns with Solidarność. Trade union members affiliated with the DKP sought to avoid tension in workplaces and local cartels, and preferred not to engage in conflict at any cost. They strenuously claimed to act as "true" and reliable representatives of trade union policies. In fact, more than anything else it was the workplace that was to become the central location for the trade unions' peace policy. Coincidently, these were also the places where, depending on the region and in varying degrees, DKP-affiliated trade union organizations were active and at times certainly quite loud and generated their own initiatives. In large companies, like BMW or the defense company Krauss-Maffei, the DKP site groups called for the DGB's mass demonstrations and also actively supported the campaign "5 Minutes to Midnight." This strategy pursued "unity" and not "division" and it seemed quite natural that the DKP strongly supported the DGB's call for demonstrations by mobilizing its own ranks.[30]

Conclusion

The peak of the trade union activities in the peace movement receded soon after the numerous political campaigns of 1983. Other issues came to dominate the trade union's daily agenda: for instance, an intense debate about the supposed "crisis of the trade unions," which had, in the words of Ralf Dahrendorf, "transformed trade unions into defensive organizations of social groups in decline" that were oblivious to the pressing problems of the day. Having undergone a laborious adaptation and learning process with respect to the dynamic "new" social movements, as represented by the environmental movement, leading trade union officials insisted they would not miss the opportunity, as they had with the peace movement. They stressed their competence in addressing ecological and economic matters within an organization willing to learn and their ability to push policies. With rising unemployment rates and hard political confrontations taking center stage during the 1980s, the issues of the peace movement lost importance. To sum up, we may note that the previously existing gulf between certain parts of the trade unions and the peace movement had narrowed by the early 1980s, when the issue of "survival anxiety" about a nuclear war could be reinterpreted as a threat to an utter breakdown of the welfare state and when a commitment to peace was not about "just simply" preventing war but also securing one's own material existence.

Dietmar Süss is a professor of modern and contemporary history at the University of Augsburg. His research focuses on the history of violence, the history of labor, social movements, and contemporary history of religion. He he has published widely on the Third Reich, World War II, and themes in postwar German history, including *Kumpel und Genossen: Arbeiterschaft, Betrieb und Sozialdemokratie in der bayerischen Montanindustrie 1945–1976* (2003); *Das 'Dritte Reich': Eine Einführung* (coedited with Winfried Süss, 2008); and *Death from the Skies: How the British and Germans Endured Aerial Destruction in World War II* (2014).

Notes

1. Lorenz Knorr, *Geschichte der Friedensbewegung in der Bundesrepublik* (Cologne, 1984), 224–25. See also Holger Negring, *Politics of Security: The British and West German Protests against Nuclear Weapons and the Early Cold War 1945–1970* (Oxford, 2013). I would like to thank Knud Andresen for his extremely helpful comments.
2. At the time Leinen was chairman of the Bundesverbandes Bürgerinitiativen Umweltschutz (Association of Citizens' Initiatives for Environmental Protection).
3. Deile was acting chairman of Aktion Sühnezeichen/Friedensdienst (ASF, Action Reconciliation Service for Peace).
4. Hermann Rappe, "Es geht um die Bündnisfrage: Ein Gespräch über das Verhältnis von Gewerkschaften und Friedensbewegung zwischen Volkmar Deile, Jo Leinen, Leonhard Mahlein und Hermann Rappe," *Gewerkschaftliche Monatshefte* 9 (1983): 619.
5. Knud Andresen, "Zwischen Protest und Mitarbeit: Die widersprüchlichen Potentiale gewerkschaftlicher Friedenspolitik 1950–1955," in *Alternativen zur Wiederbewaffnung. Friedenskonzeptionen in Westdeutschland 1945–1955*, ed. Detlef Bald and Wolfram Wette (Essen, 2008), 53–70.
6. Rappe, "Es geht um die Bündnisfrage," 624.
7. For a general overview, see Wolfgang Schröder, "Gewerkschaften als soziale Bewegung: Soziale Bewegung in den Gewerkschaften in den Siebzigerjahren," *Archiv für Sozialgeschichte* 44 (2004): 243–67.
8. Quotation from Klaus Kempter, *Eugen Loderer und die IG Metall: Biografie eines Gewerkschafters* (Filderstadt, 2003), 415.
9. IG-Metall Vorstand, ed., *Protokoll des 10. ordentlichen Gewerkschaftstages der IG Metall* (Frankfurt, 1971), 2:190; following Stefan Strutz, *Der fremde Freund: IG-Metall und Friedensbewegung vom NATO-Doppelbeschluss bis zum Bosnienkrieg* (Frankfurt am Main, 1997), 34–43.
10. Armin Wöhrle, "Gewerkschaften und Friedensbewegung," *Blätter für deutsche und internationale Politik* 26 (1981): 1448–49.
11. "Konversion und alternative Produktion," *Der Gewerkschafter* 1 (1984).
12. Inter alia: Innovations- und Beratungsstelle der IG Metall in Hamburg, ed., *Ins Bild gerückt: Alternative Produktion* (Hamburg, 1986); Jörg Huffschmied, "Rüstungskonversion als Verbindung friedenspolitischer und sozialökonomischer Interessen," *WSI-Mitteilungen,* 36 (1983): 371–85.

13. Strutz, *Der fremde Freund*, 37.
14. Ibid, 43.
15. "Wo steht die Friedensbewegung? Erfahrungen, Probleme und nächste Aufgaben im Kampf gegen die atomare Bedrohung," round table talk on the peace movement with Gert Bastian, Karl D. Bredthauer, Volkmar Deile, Ulrich Frey, Petra K. Kelly, Klaus Mannhardt, Gunnar Matthiessen, Eva Quistorp, and Claudia Wörmann-Adam, in *Blätter für deutsche und internationale Politik* 27 (1982): 789–90.
16. Ibid.
17. Bundespressestelle des DGB, ed., *Informationsdienst ID* 13 from 7 July 1983, quoted according to Strutz, *Der fremde Freund*, 121.
18. "Frieden durch Abrüstung! Friedensaufruf und Unterschriftenaktion des DGB zum Antikriegstag 1981," *Blätter für deutsche und internationale Politik* 26 (1981): 1278–80.
19. Interview of *Der Spiegel* with the head of German Trade Union Movement, Ernst Breit, "Ein Generalstreik scheidet aus," *Der Spiegel*, 24 October 1983.
20. Regional activities are documented by Industriegewerkschaft Bergbau und Energie, ed., *Dokumentation, Presseberichte, Fotos, Kurzberichte aus den Bezirken und Geschäftsstellen zu den Aktivitäten der IGBE und des DGB am 5.10.1983. 5 Mahn-Minuten für den Frieden* (Bochum, 1983).
21. "Polizei verläßt die weiche Linie," *Metall*, 6 January 1984, 6.
22. "Mörderische Aufrüstung" *Der Gewerkschafter* 9 (1979).
23. "Den Frieden muss man sich hohlen," *Der Gewerkschafter* 9 (1981).
24. Wolfgang Schultze, "Alle sind aufgerufen," *Gewerkschaftspost* 9 (1981): 4.
25. "Auf einem Auge blind," in *Gewerkschaftspost* 8 (1981): 4.
26. Kempter, *Eugen Loderer*, 389.
27. Strutz, *Der fremde Freund*, 392–93.
28. Stefan Müller, "Linkssozialistische Erneuerung in der IG Metall? Eine neue Konzeption von Arbeiterbildung in den 1960ern," in *Linkssozialismus in Deutschland: Jenseits von Sozialdemokratie und Kommunismus?* ed. Christoph Jünke (Hamburg, 2010), 153–70; in particular see Heinz Dürrbeck, *Gewerkschafter, Sozialist und Bildungsarbeiter: Heinz Dürrbeck (1912–2001)* (Essen, 2010).
29. Heinz O. Vetter, "Solidarität mit Solidarność," in *Gewerkschaftliche Monatshefte*, 39 (1982): 5.
30. *Die Zündung*, 22 September 1981; Zeitschrift der DKP-Betriebsgruppe BMW, Archiv des Instituts für Zeitgeschichte, Bestand DKP Südbayern, ED 717–347.

Select Bibliography

No extensive contemporary and historical research has so far been carried out on the relationship between trade unions and the peace movement. Strutz offers copious material and provides a helpful introduction to the subject, which analyzes the difficult process by which the organization acquired experience and knowledge. Kempter's "Eugene Loderer and the IG Metall: Biography of a Trade Union Member" contains valuable information from the perspective of a leading Social Democratic trade unionist. The anthology published by Lauschke offers further instructive reading.

Kempter, Klaus. *Eugen Loderer und die IG Metall: Biografie eines Gewerkschafters.* Filderstadt, 2003.

Lauschke, Karl. *Die Gewerkschaftselite der Nachkriegszeit: Prägung, Funktion, Leitbilder.* Essen, 2006.

Nehring, Holger. *Politics of Security: The British and West German Protests against Nuclear Weapons and the Early Cold War, 1945–1970.* Oxford Historical Monographs. Oxford, 2013.

Strutz, Stefan. *Der fremde Freund: IG-Metall und Friedensbewegung vom NATO-Doppelbeschluss bis zum Bosnienkrieg.* Frankfurt am Main, 1997.

Chapter 15

The Police
Michael Sturm

Its name already linked to the German peace movement's rallying cry for nuclear disarmament, the city of Krefeld, on 25 June 1983, was braced for public unrest during a visit from US Vice President George Bush, but the anger quickly got out of control. Bush had come to visit this city in the Lower Rhine valley to attend a ceremony marking the occasion of the three hundredth anniversary of the emigration of Krefeld families to North America. The atmosphere was tense, for Chancellor Helmut Kohl was not the only one accompanying the high-profile visitor to the prestigious guild house of the silk weavers. Peace activists were also on hand, using the event to protest against the planned deployment of US medium-range missiles in the city where in November 1980 they had adopted one of their key documents, known as the Krefeld Appeal. At least twenty thousand (according to the organizers forty thousand) people followed the call to protest. The demonstration itself passed without incident.

During the ceremony, however, more demonstrators had gathered at the Krefeld railway station. Principally autonomous and anti-imperialist groups had called for this demonstration, and many of the one thousand participants were masked and wore helmets and black leather jackets. These mainly young and martially decorated activists considered themselves part of the peace movement. However, most of these activists were not content with mere symbolic protests against Bush's visit. This demonstration at the railway station did not last long. En route into the city, the police dispersed the demonstrators. Some were injured and a number of arrests made.

At this point the police thought that the situation had been resolved. But then, after the ceremonial activities in the guildhall had finished, an incident occurred with serious aftermath. The motorcade of cars with George Bush deviated from the set route and drove past a crowd of protesters from both demonstrations who lost no time in surrounding the vice president's limousine. George Bush responded calmly, "It's just like in Chicago. We get cheered and have rocks thrown at us, both here and there."[1]

The Krefeld riots stirred up considerable controversy about the police response and its consequences in the Federal Republic of Germany, as a total of 138 persons were arrested and dozens injured. The German Minister of the Interior, Friedrich Zimmermann (CSU), criticized the measures taken by the police in Krefeld as lacking in rigor. He also reiterated his intention to strengthen criminal law with respect to demonstrations. Herbert Schnoor (SPD), Minister of the Interior in North Rhine-Westphalia, rejected this out of hand. He warned against "putting people who demonstrate because of the strength of their convictions automatically into the same basket as stone-throwing individuals." The right of assembly needed to be protected, as this was "the lifeblood of our democracy."[2]

The disputes over the police action in Krefeld in June 1983 epitomize the points of contention in the relationship between state power and the peace movement during the 1980s. As a matter of fact, the police faced a tremendously heterogeneous social and political assortment of citizens who were willing to take to the streets in protest against the plans about the arms upgrade. In Krefeld and elsewhere the label "peace movement" subsumed members of parties, communities, and church groups, as well as trade unions, women's groups, and occupational groups, as activists of a subculture-oriented autonomous scene that had developed since the early 1980s.

In this context, police presence, action, and strategy assumed a "political quality."[3] The police in general were supposed to follow a range of exceedingly different demands and expectations when dealing with protests, not just in the case of Krefeld. These even sparked heated debates within the police force. At issue were not just technocratic aspects of the rules of engagement but the social role of the police as an institution that could "not make policy decisions" but, nonetheless, had to "act politically" in the context of protest events.[4]

Protest and Action Strategies of the Peace Movement

The number of registered demonstrations and rallies increased exponentially between 1979 and 1983. On average there had been about 2,800 protest events between 1975 and 1978 annually. This ratio doubled in the period thereafter to about 5,600. It culminated in 1983 with some 9,237 rallies and demonstrations.[5]

In its early years, participants in the antinuclear movement were the most capable of mobilizing for demonstrations. Then, from 1981 onward, more people joined in as the protests of the peace movement created more and more resonance. The movement's political, cultural, and social complexities expressed themselves in a wide range of action, which resulted in immediate tensions between different segments of the movement. A general typology might distinguish among (1) (mass-) demonstrations and rallies; (2) direct, militant, and violent forms of protest; and (3) actions of "civil disobedience." In reality the lines between such distinct forms of protest became blurred during actual events. Moreover, classifications were subject to individual perspectives on what constituted "violence," "nonviolence," and "civil disobedience"—and these views varied significantly.

Rallies and Mass Demonstrations

The peace movement mobilized the largest-ever demonstrations and rallies in the history of West Germany. Some 300,000 people participated at the Hofgarten rally "Let's Act Together against the Nuclear Threat" in Bonn on 10 October 1981. When the NATO summit was held in the West German capital on 10 June 1982, a total of 400,000 demonstrators gathered. The very same day at least sixty thousand people in West Berlin demonstrated against the visiting US President Ronald Reagan. In October of the following year, approximately half a million people protested again at the Hofgarten in Bonn, while simultaneously at least a quarter of a million formed a 108-kilometer-long human chain stretching from the of the US Army's European command center in Stuttgart-Vahingen to the Wiley barracks on the US military base of Neu-Ulm. The vast majority of these events, which reached their peak in the fall of 1983 and comprised not only mass protests but also countless smaller rallies, vigils, silent circles, and other symbolic-expressive forms of action, were nonviolent.[6]

Militancy and Direct Forms of Action

All the same, large-scale protests did offer a framework for violent action that emanated mostly from sections of the autonomous spectrum of the peace movement and led to violent confrontations with the police, who reacted with force. Apart from the aforementioned riots in Krefeld, the massive clashes that took place on the occasion of the visiting US Secretary of State Alexander Haig and US President Ronald Reagan in West Berlin in September 1981 and in June 1982 deserve mention here.

In addition, the public pledging of recruits to the Bundeswehr (West German Army) occasionally became the scene of violent protests. One instance was a clash between a few thousand protesters and the police when 1,200 recruits pledged their oath of allegiance on 6 May 1980 in Weser stadium in Bremen. Over the course of the fighting, 257 officers and fifty protesters were injured. Moreover, several military vehicles went up in flames. The protests against the recruits pledging allegiance to the Constitution in the Hanseatic city had been supported by a broad coalition and illustrated at an early stage the heterogeneous composition of the emerging peace movement, as the assessment of events among the demonstrators was far from unanimous.

Civil Disobedience

The biggest challenge for the police proved to be acts of "civil disobedience," a form of protest that various factions of the peace movement increasingly defended as legitimate in relation to the seemingly inevitable deployment of weapons of mass destruction. "Civil disobedience" was seen to be the demonstrative and nonviolent "deliberate transgression of rules, laws and precepts" on ethical and normative grounds, which found their expression

Figure 15.1. Federal border officials guard the barracks of the US Carl Schurz Barracks in Bremerhaven on 15 October 1983 (ullstein bild / Pflaum)

in the blockade of barracks and weapons depots, as well as in the attempts to occupy military building installations or entering restricted military zones.[7]

August 1982 was the first time a large group—around seven hundred people—blocked a Bundeswehr munitions depot, in Groß-Engstingen close to the town of Tübingen. In the same year members of peace groups attempted to obstruct the transport of munitions and missile spare parts from the port of Nordenham bound for southern Germany. A sit-in protest with three hundred participants in front of the European headquarters of the US Armed Forces in Stuttgart-Vahingen was staged on 12 December 1982, the third anniversary of the NATO Double-Track Decision. By the time the breakdown of the Geneva disarmament talks became increasingly likely, in the following year, and deployment of the first Pershing II missiles was announced for November 1983, (sit-in) blockades had turned into an essential element in the repertoire of the peace movement.[8]

The US missile depot in Mutlangen became a special symbolic location of civil disobedience. The events of a so-called celebrities blockade from 1 to 3 September 1983 attended by about 150 well-known personalities such as author Heinrich Böll, the politicians Petra Kelly (Green Party) and Erhard Eppler (SPD), and the satirist Dieter Hildebrandt, unfolded in front of its gates. Public attention focused to a large degree on the reactions of the police, who did not intervene at this time. The interior minister of Baden-Württemberg, Roman Herzog (CDU), declared well before the protest action and after consultations with the Ministry of the Interior and the US Army that he did not intend to do the celebrities "the favor" of having them carried away in front of cameras.[9]

Up until 1987 there were, however, numerous other blockades involving an estimated ten thousand people, among whom were judges, clergy, politicians, and other public figures. As a rule, the police cleared the access routes to military bases with the help of officers who carried peace activists off the streets. Over the years about three thousand protesters were taken into custody in Mutlangen alone and subsequently charged with "causing an obstruction" as indicated in the German Penal Code (§240 Strafgesetzbuch, StGB entitled with coersion). The police and the judicial administration took corresponding steps at other protest sites against similar blockades. Disputes about an appropriate response to the varying forms of civil disobedience furthered an intense discourse on the police's own guiding principles and self-image since the early 1980s. Helmut Gerbert, police inspector of the State of Baden-Württemberg, conceded that "it had been extremely difficult to assess the protest movement as well as those addressed in protest" by his government agency and that this posed "particular problems" as it was "faced with a completely new situation."[10]

"Reprehensible" or Legitimate? Discussions about Civil Disobedience

The area of conflict in which the police had to carry out their duties was informed not only by intra-governmental perceptions and experiences but also by diverging social, legal, and political claims from the outside. Different ongoing discussions were closely monitored in professional police journals. At the same time representatives of the police force repeatedly participated in public debates.

Proponents of civil disobedience were found in nearly all areas of society.[11] Opinions on how this should be assessed legally and legislatively, however, varied a great deal despite its importance to the police force and its strategies. Arguing from basic principles, Helmut Simon, a judge on the Federal Constitutional Court, warned against the indiscriminate criminalization of all acts of civil disobedience. He noted that "we live in a transitory situation with respect to the means of mass destruction, and ethics and law no longer coincide completely." Simon also pointed out that an essential structural principle of democracy, that is, the ability to change decisions reached by a majority, no longer applied in case of the arms upgrade because of its potentially "catastrophic" and "irreversible" consequences.

The public prosecutors and magistrates at the court in Schwäbisch Gmünd (where procedures relating to the Mutlangen blockades were heard), as elsewhere, frequently took contrary views on this legal matter. Legal disputes over acts of civil disobedience hardly touched on its constitutional legitimacy or assessed it by standards of international law. The issue was rather limited to a more narrow technical definition of whether causing an obstruction could be prosecuted as a form of "coercion" as this was not permitted in German law. The first paragraph of §240 of the Penal Code ("coercion"), which applies, states, "The person who unlawfully induces by force or threat thereof to carry out appreciable harm, or the toleration or the omission thereof, will be punished with imprisonment of three years or with a fine." The second paragraph of §240 StGB, however, qualifies "unlawful" as a form of "coercion" only if "the use of force or the threat to cause evil for all intents and purposes needs to be considered reprehensible." This raised the question of whether sitting on an access road to a military facility can be classified as "violence." And could it be assumed that persons who engaged in blocking action of this nature harbored "reprehensible" motives?

The courts assessed these questions differently. District courts in Erlangen, Nuremberg, Ulm, Stuttgart, Reutlingen, Frankfurt, Munster, and Wuppertal judged sit-ins as being devoid of "reprehensibility" and acquitted those prosecuted accordingly, while the judges in Schwäbisch Gmünd accorded the motives of the accused demonstrators with minor importance. They regarded the offense as fulfilling the criteria for "coercion" as the court stated that merely the intent of forcing the driver of a vehicle to stop was reprehensible.[12]

Civil Disobedience as a Challenge to Strategies of Police Action

The police more or less followed this interpretation of the law. When a number of higher-ranking courts ruled that sit-in blockades rated as a form of "coercion," Ralf Krüger, executive chief inspector in Karlsruhe, stated that the buzzword "nonviolent action" was a "semantic deception" that "the executive authority and the jurisdiction of our state should not accept."[13] His likeminded colleague Karl-Heinz Braun of the Higher State Police School in Munster saw the criminality of sit-ins as raising no questions in relation to §240 of the Penal Code. The case of the prosecution, however, frequently suffered because the "injured third party" rarely pressed charges. He therefore suggested that when the police cleared sit-ins, they should call in field officers to make notes and recordings during events, so that injured police could press charges as "victims."[14] What this suggestion implies is that sit-in blockades should be legally assessed primarily under technocratic considerations in an effort to consolidate its freedom of action in the choices of action taken and the professionalization of potential criminal prosecution. It called for "no complicated discussions just clear-cut legal regulations."[15]

In practice the police tended to make some effort to avoid grand displays of martial power as far as protests of civil disobedience were concerned. Only in exceptional cases did the police use batons or water cannons when clearing blockages before military facilities. In Stuttgart-Vahingen the police employed a cavalry division against protesters blocking the US European Command Headquarters in December 1982 and in the city of Bitburg, in Rhineland-Palatinate, the riot police resorted to the use of water cannons and dogs to break up a blockade in front of a US military base in early September 1983.[16] The public reacted in both cases with criticism.[17] Thus the police changed strategies and mainly relied on carrying demonstrators away. This, however, was a physically demanding form of intervention and required certain "manual skills." Teaching grip and carrying techniques became an important function of training programs.

In practice, the carrying away of protesters varied from one situation to another. Elisa Kauffeld described her impressions of a police operation during a blockade by senior citizens at Mutlangen in early May 1986 as follows: "The police dragged, pushed and kicked blockaders to the side [of the

Figure 15.2. Blockade of the US Andrews Barracks in West Berlin, Lichterfelde on 15 October 1983. Dirk Schneider, member of parliament for Berlin (Alternative List), is being carried by police officers in order to clear the street (ullstein bild / Harry Hampel)

road.] Before this happened we had been told that they would carry us away after having warned us three times. This time everything was different … I received a powerful, well-aimed kick, and fell to one side into a puddle."[18] Hanne Narr participated at the senior blockade in May of the following year and reported that "demonstrators and policemen [stood] peacefully together … Many talked to each other. When a higher-ranking officer approached, conversations ceased."[19] It seems remarkable that police officers rarely reported their own perceptions of this or similar operations. Certainly numerous publications have appeared since the 1980s in which police officers described the daily service routine and their impressions from demonstration missions, but such contributions revolved mainly around experiences in the context of violent confrontations. There were repeated reports of statements from representatives of the Gewerkschaft der Polizei (GdP, Trade Union of the Police) indicating that the officers involved experienced a high level of psychological distress when clearing sit-in blockades. Consequently there was an appeal in advance of the "Heated Autumn" in 1983 put forward by the police union to peace groups and politicians asking them to seriously respect the feelings and stress that officials experienced when having to move persons blocking the way.[20]

Overall, it needs to be said that the anger of many protestors was primarily directed against the judiciary, which slowly prosecuted thousands of cases of "coercion." However, the various media and even the protagonists of civil disobedience attested that the police "in practice by and large ... dealt with politically motivated violations in more of a tolerant than a rigid manner."[21] It was remarkable that the vehemently conducted conflict on the political level pertaining to the appropriate responses to protest played only a minor role for the immediate police action against sit-in protests in the various regional states, as the use of police strategies in general appeared to hardly vary among regions.

The police assessed the political protests of the peace movement in a number of ways. Its union, the GdP, played a key part within the force, but also in public debates. As a single union under the umbrella of the German Trade Union Federation (DGB), it considered itself part of the trade union wing of the peace movement, and made efforts to be recognized as such. This claim was echoed in some of its peace policy resolutions and in symbolic actions, such as heeding the call by the DGB on 5 October 1983 to protest against the deployment of nuclear weapons by stopping work for five minutes. As may be expected, the position of the GdP often resulted in tension, not only with representatives of other sections of the peace movement but also within the organization itself.

The GdP urged, on the one hand, immediate and consistent punishment of violence committed by protesters, as was the case in the aforementioned riots in Bremen following the pledge of recruits in the stadium, and to provide the officers with standard crowd control equipment, for instance irritants and water cannons. On the other hand, the national board under the leadership of Günter Schröder decisively rejected proposals that were principally put forward by the CDU/CSU coalition parties with particular rigor since the early 1980s; the rejected proposals included plans to tighten up the right of assembly, which in turn led to controversy at delegates' conferences and in the professional journal of the organization.[22]

This attitude found its exemplary expression on the occasion of a congress in St Pauls Church (Frankfurt am Main) that the GdP had convoked to commemorate the thirty-third anniversary of the promulgation of the Grundgesetz (meaning "constitution" or, literally, "basic law") of the FRG on 23 May 1982 under the motto "Peace within." German Chancellor Helmut Schmidt (SPD) and about seven hundred police officers attended the event and the union had placed it in the context of other peace movement events.[23] Noteworthy is that in its publications the GdP largely refrained from polemical statements against sit-in blockades and even invited authors who judged forms of civil disobedience as a legitimate form of protest to write for the journal *Deutsche Polizei* (German police).[24] In sum, it may be said that the GdP predominantly published moderate statements about the protests of the peace movement and demanded greater citizen orientation and a willingness on the side of the police to enter into a dialogue, especially during the course of demonstrations.

Considered in this perspective, the police's understanding of the state seemed to shift slightly away from hitherto dominant guiding principles of representative parliamentarism. Since the slowdown of the social reform euphoria at the beginning of the 1970s, public protest in police discourses was often perceived as a challenge to a parliamentary majority.[25] This seemed to be a turning point when gradually and under the impact of broadly based protest actions by the peace movement there was a growing acknowledgment that it might be legitimate to influence political and social relations outside the state's institutional structure.

This view was, however, by no means shared by all within the police force. For example, the police chief of Brunswick, Detlef Dommaschk, complained about a "lack of respect toward majority decisions reached in statutory ways." These "changes in political reality and legal culture," however, "increasingly impeded the success of police work." He particularly held "politicizing pastors" responsible for the developments referred to earlier as they demonstrated a "lack of leadership among church pastors," which led to a "general political agitation of certain elected officials that related to issues such as the police, the army, the peace issue, and nuclear power."[26] His perspective was rigidly state-focused. Social protest was therefore primarily considered an impairment of the state and its administration, and it was characterized by seemingly unquestionable procedures and ways of reaching a decision. Moreover the display of the police chief's resentment about the political commitment of the Lutheran pastors shows a lingering ideal within the police of a largely depoliticized society.

The police discourses about activists and the peace movement's protests revealed different ideas and conceptions of "the police and policing." Whereas Detlef Dommaschk epitomizes the traditionally authoritarian conception of a "state police," other, more liberal-minded, voices spoke out for the ideal of a "citizens' police force."[27]

"Culture Clash" over Internal Security

The disputes on the status of the police were also part of the discussion in political controversies, which concerned the internal security of West Germany and increased in intensity after the accession of the conservative-liberal

CDU-FDP coalition in October 1982. Prior to this, there had been a largely bipartisan consensus in the context of combating terrorism and on issues of internal security. This grand coalition broke apart and a period of far-reaching consensus in this field ended in the late 1970s.

From the perspective of the coalition in government, a (spiritual and moral) "change" should be reflected in tighter restrictions on real, or publicly perceived, violent demonstrations. The new Interior Minister, Friedrich Zimmermann, who had assumed his office in 1982 with the intention of at least partially revoking the liberalization of the criminal law on demonstrations introduced by the preceding social-liberal coalition. The intention had been to broaden the terms of the criminal offense of "breaching the peace" (§125 StGB) and to ban protesters from covering their faces and using so-called passive arming, that is, wearing helmets, waterproof clothing, protective goggles against tear gas, and padding to reduce blows from riot sticks. Statements by the interior ministry announced that the existing right of assembly served primarily as an opportunity for violent riots. Although, as Secretary of the Interior Carl-Dieter Spranger (CSU) conceded, the percentage of the "non-peacefully conducted" demonstrations was only 4.3 percent in 1982, he regarded it as "short-sighted to take a statistical analysis as the only standard" by which to assess the situation, especially since in view of the planned actions against the implementation of the NATO Double-Track Decision there prevailed a "fear that the discussion controlled by left-wing forces about the extent to which the use of violence could be considered legitimate … indicated that riots could be expected."[28]

In the conflicts on internal security policy as well as in evaluations of the widespread and frequent protest actions in the Federal Republic, the SPD-ruled North Rhine-Westphalia constituted a counterbalance to the legislative advances of the Union at the federal and regional state levels. Herbert Schnoor, minister of the interior in this most populous state since June 1980, stressed the importance he accorded to the right to demonstration in matters of policymaking. Although violent groups needed to be restrained, it was of overriding importance to ensure that "we do not contribute through clumsy or excessive measures to push parts of the young generation into becoming outsiders."[29] He turned his focus, therefore, onto behavioral patterns of the police and pointed out that there is always a need to reflect on the political consequences of police deployments. The police had to base its actions not only on principles of legality but also on the principle of proportionality, which was determined by the political environment.

In arguing this case, the Minister of the Interior of North Rhine-Westphalia tried to profile himself as an advocate of a comparatively liberal policy on police missions. He rejected a tightening of the right of assembly as demanded by the CDU/CSU and the introduction of "enforcement costs regulation" (*Vollstreckungskostenverordnung*) like those in Baden-Württemberg under Roman Herzog, which was intended to make activists using blocking methods pay for the police assignment. Likewise he did not agree with supplying the police force with chemical irritants and rubber bullets, as the states of Bavaria and Baden-Württemberg did, because these posed an "incalculable risk to [their] victims."[30] Such considerations were informed by ideas about policing taken from the citizens' perspective and were labeled the "North Rhine-Westphalian strategy," which was supported by a number of senior police officers. A more sensitive approach could also be noticed in attempts to find suitable communication-oriented de-escalation strategies.[31] The "politicization of the security policy" had divided the FRG along political lines since the beginning of the 1980s into Social Democratic-governed regional states on one side and those ruled by the conservative Union on the other.[32] The different strategies employed in "protest policing," which could be observed in the police intervention against squatters, did not, however, apply in dealing with the protests of the peace movement, as has already been pointed out.

En Route to Community Policing?

The demonstrations and actions of the peace movement induced noticeable changes in "protest policing" since the early 1980s. Moreover, they caused intense discussions about "the position of the state, state power, and state authority"[33] in social struggles within the police and in wider society. Although the respective positions, when viewed in light of the already outlined "politicization of the policy on security," showed different results in the various regional states, there were a number of general factors that influenced the course of discussions in a nationwide perspective.

First of all, the self-image and the behavioral patterns of police received more public attention. In the context of the new social movements since the late 1970s, many civil rights groups had formed that treated the police "apparatus" critically. Under the heading "Citizens Observe the Police," groups in several cities keenly observed the appearance of state power, meticulously documented police activities, and brought them to public attention.[34] This initiative was connected to a study group on civil rights, based at the Freie Universität Berlin under the leadership of Wolf-Dieter Narr. Since 1978 this group had published a magazine, *Civil Rights & the Police / CILIP*, in a social science research context as part of a movement critically minded toward the police—a "counter-public" that increasingly caught the attention of the mainstream media.

Second, the public discourse about the police, which began in the mid-1980s, enabled individual police officers to voice their opinions either publicly or also anonymously and to relate their daily routine from the "inside" of the police force,[35] denouncing official internal grievances and demanding the "formation of a new police." Frequently complaints were made about police action against protesters. In organizational terms, this development resulted in the establishment of the Federal Association of Critical Police Officers in January 1987. Even if the "critical policemen" constituted only a tiny fraction and at most a few dozen officials, the statements of the initiative were received with great public media interest, possibly even because of the initiative's small size.

Third, it was probably the first time in the history of protests in West Germany that in various places discussion groups were set up in which peace activists and police officers shared their respective perceptions, resentments, fears, and expectations. For instance, in October 1982 the first "Stuttgart discussions" were held between representatives of the police in Baden-Württemberg and members of social and peace initiatives, trade unions, and churches to exchange "the concerns and possibly ... 'fears' of the opposite side."[36] The third round of talks in September 1983 resulted in the so-called Stuttgart document, which was to serve as "a guide for future conflicts" in Baden-Württemberg and stressed the readiness for dialogue on either side. Although legally nonbinding and lacking in a general consensus on the legitimacy of civil disobedience, the efforts reflected a certain form of citizen policing that had been worked out in a negotiation process with parties on all sides.

Fourth, the discussion on police models and deployment strategies were largely coined by the Brokdorf decision of May 1985 in which the West German Federal Constitutional Court dealt with a complaint about a ban on demonstrations at the building site of the Brokdorf Nuclear Power Station in February 1981. In its ruling, the Constitutional Court had underlined the fundamental right to freedom of assembly and imposed various "commandments" that needed to be respected by the police at future protest events. It was stipulated that policing on demonstrations must generally be conducted in a friendly demeanor and serve "de-escalation." The senior police officer in control of the operation and the applicant for the demonstration should behave in a cooperative spirit. The actions of "troublemakers" in a meeting did not constitute grounds for police intervention against all demonstrators. Even though the federal government amended the law of assembly in July 1985 to prohibit disguising and passive arming, the Brokdorf decision became the Magna Carta of the right to demonstrate.[37] The decision was informed by the impressions and experiences of protest events in previous years. The police already reviewed the Brokdorf decision internally and intensified a debate about its self-image and deployment strategies.[38] Police interaction with the peace movement thus led quite independently from the embattled conflicts over internal security during the 1980s to a greater openness to approaches of citizen policing.

Whether the lively protest events during those years truly shaped protest policing in the long run and made it conducive to peaceful demonstrations is open to debate. The anecdotal event described at the beginning, when George Bush, while visiting Krefeld, was all of a sudden confronted with disgruntled demonstrators, no longer need worry his son a couple of decades later. When US President George W. Bush stopped in Mainz during his visit to Germany in February 2005, his motorcade passed through largely deserted streets. Large sections of the city had been preventively closed off. The peace movement had to stage its protests, unlike in Krefeld, a few hundred meters away from the stately procedures.

Michael Sturm is a research fellow at the Villa ten Hompel in Münster. He studied history, political science, and German at the University of Göttingen. He is the coeditor of the following publications on the protest and police history: *Dagegen! Und dann…?! Rechtsextreme Straßenpolitik und zivilgesellschaftliche Gegenstrategien in NRW* (with Heiko Klare, 2011); *Polizei, Gewalt und Staat im 20. Jahrhundert* (with Alf Lüdtke and Herbert Reinke, 2011); *Die 1970er Jahre als schwarzes Jahrzehnt: Politisierung und Mobilisierung zwischen christlicher Demokratie und extremer Rechter* (with Massimiliano Livi and Daniel Schmidt, 2010).

Notes

1. Quotation according to *Der Spiegel* 27, 4 July 1983, 32.
2. *Der Spiegel* 37, 12 September 1983, 24.
3. Martin Winter, *Politikum Polizei: Macht und Funktion der Polizei in der Bundesrepublik Deutschland* (Münster, 1998).
4. Günter Freund, "Bürgernähe im Konfliktfeld," *Die Polizei* 72 (1981): 267.
5. Information provided by Thomas Balistier, *Straßenprotest: Formen oppositioneller Politik in der Bundesrepublik* (Münster, 1996), 14–15.
6. A typological compilation of protest and action forms employed by the peace movement is to be found in Balistier, *Straßenprotest*, 33–113. On this point, see also the contribution by Kathrin Fahlenbrach and Laura Stapane in this volume.
7. The definition of "civil disobedience" is discussed by Andreas Buro, "Friedensbewegung," in Roland Roth and Dieter Rucht, eds., *Die sozialen Bewegungen in Deutschland seit 1945: Ein Handbuch* (Frankfurt am Main and New York, 2008), 281; Balistier, *Straßenprotest*, 33–113; "Horst Schüler-Springorum: Strafrechtliche

Aspekte zivilen Ungehorsams," in *Ziviler Ungehorsam im Rechtsstaat*, ed. Peter Glotz (Frankfurt am Main, 1983), 79.
8. Jürgen Bruhn, '... *dann, sage ich, brich das Gesetz': Ziviler Ungehorsam. Von Gandhis Salzmarsch bis zum Generalstreik* (Frankfurt am Main, 1985), 141.
9. Quotation according to *Der Spiegel* 36, 5 September 1983, 117.
10. Helmut Gerbert, "Polizeiliche Maßnahmen zum Schutz militärischer Einrichtungen," *Die Polizei* 74 (1983): 299.
11. On this wide-ranging discussion, Martin Stöhr, ed., *Ziviler Ungehorsam und rechtsstaatliche Demokratie*, Schriften aus der Arbeit der Evangelischen Akademie Arnoldshain, Arnoldshainer Texte, vol. 43 (Frankfurt am Main, 1986).
12. The different court decisions were discussed in *Der Spiegel* 18, 30 April 1984; *Der Spiegel* 12, 18 March 1985; *Der Spiegel* 13, 25 March 1985.
13. Ralf Krüger, "Rechtsfragen zu polizeilichen Maßnahmen beim Schutz militärischer Anlagen," *Die Polizei* 74 (1983): 316.
14. Karl-Heinz Braun, "Blockaden und ähnliche demonstrative Aktionen als polizeilich zu bewältigende Einsatzlagen," *Die Polizei* 76 (1985): 67.
15. Werner Hamacher, "Zur Diskussion: Ist Sitzblockade Nötigung?" *Deutsche Polizei* 10 (1983): 27.
16. *Der Spiegel* 42, 17 October 1983, 37–38.
17. See also the contribution by Kathrin Fahlenbrach and Laura Stapane in this volume.
18. Elisa Kauffeld, "Erfahrungen einer Seniorin," in *Ziviler Ungehorsam: Traditionen, Konzepte, Erfahrungen, Perspektiven*, ed. Komitee für Grundrechte und Demokratie (Sensbachtal, 1992), 118–20.
19. Hanne Narr, "Muttertagsblockade: Mutlangen, May 10, 1987" in Komitee für Grundrechte und Demokratie, *Ziviler Ungehorsam*, 111.
20. *Deutsche Polizei* 10 (1983): 6.
21. Theodor Ebert, *Ziviler Ungehorsam: Von der APO zur Friedensbewegung* (Waldkirch, 1984), 254.
22. *Deutsche Polizei* 9 (1983): 3–4.
23. In particular the speech delivered by Schröders, *Deutsche Polizei* 7 (1982): 7.
24. Erich Küchenhoff, "Ziviler Ungehorsam als aktiver Verfassungsschutz," *Deutsche Polizei* 9 (1983): 26–31.
25. Winter, *Politikum Polizei*, 198–99.
26. Detlef Dommaschk, "Polizei in der öffentlichen Meinung: Aus Sicht der Polizei," *Die Polizei* 75 (1984): 38 and 43.
27. See, for example, Siegfried Bleck, "Staatsgewalt und Friedensbewegung: Problemfelder des Widerstands und des Zivilen Ungehorsams aus polizeilicher Sicht und Wertung," in *Die Polizei* 75 (1984): 80.
28. Carl-Dieter Spranger, "'Friedensbewegung' und extremistische Aktionsplanung zum NATO-Doppelbeschluss," in *Die Polizei* 74 (1983): 306.
29. Herbert Schnoor, "Politische Aspekte bei der Beurteilung polizeilicher Lagen," *Die Polizei* 73 (1982): 66.
30. *Der Spiegel* 52, 27 December 1982, 28–31; *Der Spiegel* 5, 31 January 1983, 61; *Der Spiegel* 37, 12 September 1983, 24.
31. Dierk H. Schnitzler, "Demonstrationseinsätze in Bonn: Die Entstehung der nord-

rhein-westfälischen Linie für den bürgernahen Polizeieinsatz bei polizeilichen Großlagen," *Archiv für Polizeigeschichte* 37 (2002): 55–59.
32. Winter, *Politikum Polizei*, 196.
33. Schnoor, "Politische Aspekte," 66.
34. Rolf Gössner and Uwe Herzog, *Der Apparat: Ermittlungen in Sachen Polizei* (Cologne, 1982).
35. Lothar Ferstl and Harald Hetzel, *"Für mich ist das Alltag": Innenansichten der Polizei* (Bonn, 1989); Manfred Such, *Bürger statt Bullen: Streitschrift für eine andere Polizei* (Essen, 1988), 148.
36. Alfred Stümper, "'Stuttgarter Gespräche' Überlegungen zur Handhabung von Konflikten anlässlich von Umwelt- oder Friedensdemonstrationen," *Die Polizei* 76 (1985): 345.
37. Manfred Ganschow, "Die Novellierung des Straf- und Versammlungsrechts und ihre Auswirkungen auf die polizeiliche Praxis," *Die Polizei* 76 (1985): 351–54.
38. Winter, *Politikum Polizei*, 197.

Select Bibliography

Historical research has so far paid little attention to the role and the employed practices of the police in connection with the protests of the new social movements during the 1980s. The focus of interest rested up to now on the development of individual protest movements. Usually the police are mentioned only in passing.

There are now a number of social- and cultural-history-oriented studies about the police force in the 1960s and early 1970s in West Germany. Among these, Weinhauer should be especially mentioned. Compulsive reading is presented by Bush's political science exploration/investigation published in the 1980s but still considered an authoritative piece of work. The same applies to Winter's comprehensive study. Both works analyze in detail not only changes of police deployment concepts but also structures, and self-images, especially in the wake of types of action to be found in the new social movements. A number of publications written in a critical spirit from the perspective of the peace movement are also helpful. Gössner is an example, although his book may also be read at the same time as source texts.

Busch, Heiner, Albrecht Funk, Udo Kauß, Wolf-Dieter Narr, and Falco Werkentin. *Die Polizei in der Bundesrepublik*. Frankfurt am Main and New York, 1985.
Gössner, Rolf, and Uwe Herzog. *Der Apparat: Ermittlungen in Sachen Polizei*. Cologne, 1982.
Weinhauer, Klaus. *Schutzpolizei in der Bundesrepublik: Zwischen Bürgerkrieg und Innerer Sicherheit: Die turbulenten sechziger Jahre*. Paderborn, 2003.
Weinhauer, Klaus, Jörg Requate, and Heinz-Gerhard Haupt. *Terrorismus in der Bundesrepublik: Medien, Staat und Subkulturen in den 1970er Jahren*. Frankfurt am Main and New York, 2006.
Winter, Martin. *Politikum Polizei: Macht und Funktion der Polizei in der Bundesrepublik Deutschland*. Münster, 1998.

Chapter 16

"Men Build Missiles":
The Women's Peace Movement

Reinhild Kreis

When Herbert Grönemeyer's album *Bochum* was released a few months after the onset of the intermediate-range nuclear missiles upgrade, many listeners might have recognized in the lyrics echoes of the peace movement's concerns. In "Amerika," one of the album's songs, the singer called on the United States to end hostilities with the Soviet Union and reach an agreement. The popular song "Männer" (Men), off the same album, also touched on the current issue of defense. Grönemeyer sang the lines "Men make war" and "Men build missiles" and thus underlined that the responsibility for war, armament, and the dangers of a "nuclear holocaust" rested not only with governments but also with the male gender. In a somewhat ironic tone the singer alluded to what had become an essential question to many women in the peace movement: how do violence and gender correlate?[1]

Grönemeyer was quite unconventional in addressing the gender dimensions of peace and war. Usually it was women who raised the question of how masculinity and femininity structured society and who integrated these categories in their analyses of peace and war. Women MPs such as Antje Huber and Renate Schmidt (both members of the Social Democratic Party, SPD) and Petra Kelly and Antje Vollmer (both members of the Green Party) tried to draw attention to the specific situation and particular concern of women in parliamentary debates about missile deployment, while male parliamentarians ignored this aspect.[2] Actual definitions of masculinity, femininity, peace, war, and violence varied according to the context in which women were active, but most women (though by no means all) working in the peace movement shared a sensitivity toward the relationship between these categories.

Indirectly, and subconsciously to most contemporary actors, gender dimensions underlay all rhetoric on arms, war, and peace during the Second Cold War.[3] The peace movement shared a "feminist rhetoric" that emphasized characteristics such as sensitivity, living in harmony with nature, nonviolence, and love, all of which were typically attributed to women.[4] This corresponded to the zeitgeist of the 1970s and 1980s, when emotional feelings received high social significance and men too could admit to feelings of fear or anxiety.[5] However, a thorough integration of gender perspectives into the study of the actions, concepts, and the rhetorical and visual strategies of the peace movement has yet to be done.[6]

This article focuses on the women's peace movement, whose activists reflected and discussed gender dimensions as a central theme. In this approach, they differed from other factions within the general peace movement. The women's faction consisted of women from diverse affiliations and political beliefs. Not all women who participated in the peace movement joined the women's peace movement, just as not all supporters of the women's peace movement were part of the women's movement. They considered themselves a distinct initiative.

Far from being confined to West Germany, the women's peace movement was an international phenomenon reaching even across the East-West divide. In East Germany too women struggled for the goals of peace, albeit under very different conditions. They campaigned in a state that suppressed any form of criticism of its system and also all public opposition. Moreover, this state claimed to have already implemented the equality of women and thus regarded all criticism of women's situations as tantamount to criticizing the prevailing system.

The Female Activists: Women's Peace Movement and Women in the Peace Movement

Women participated in all segments of the heterogeneously composed peace movement in which, to mention but a few, Social Democrats, the Greens, Christians, Communists, and a plethora of independent groups and initiatives came together.[7] Within and in addition to the peace movement, a dedicated women's peace movement evolved. It overlapped thematically and in terms of organization and personnel with the protest movement against the arms upgrade, but at the same time went beyond it. The women's peace movement itself was just as diverse as the general peace movement. Karola Maltry identifies three subdivisions within the women's peace movement: first, representatives of the autonomous feminists; second, women who had not joined the women's movement; and third, members of the traditional women's movement.[8] Especially the first two categories formed loose, that is, barely institutionalized, alliances.

Women started quite a few of the initiatives and groups within the peace movement. Eva Quistorp and Mechthild Jansen cofounded initiatives such as Anstiftung der Frauen für den Frieden (Instigation of Women for Peace) and Frauen in der Bundeswehr? Wir sagen NEIN! (Women in the Armed Forces? We say NO), respectively, and were both members of the Coordination Committee of the Peace Movement, which prepared and organized nationwide mass protests. Barbara Hövener contributed significantly to the founding of the German section of IPPNW (International Physicians for the Prevention of Nuclear War), which she initiated along with other doctors and physicians. Similarly it was often women as members of other groups and organizations, such as the SPD, who provided the driving force for the commitment to peace.[9] The same applies to the East, where women like Bärbel Bohley, Katja Havemann, Irina Kukutz, Ulrike Poppe, and others initiated the East German group Frauen für den Frieden (Women for Peace) and established other peace groups.[10] Nevertheless, female leadership figures such as Petra Kelly were an exception, and the public face of the peace movement was otherwise male-dominated. For the most part, women remained in the shadow of male protagonists such as Gert Bastian, Rainer Eppelmann, Erhard Eppler, Robert Havemann, and Jo Leinen in the public perception of both German states.

The disputes over the NATO Double-Track Decision and the deployment of nuclear weapons came at a time when women increasingly engaged politically and sought to represent their interests, especially in the women's movement and the lesbian movement since the 1970s. Other examples of particularly female protest actions were a women's boycott of imported goods from South Africa, which was to demonstrate solidarity in the struggle against apartheid,[11] or gender-specific actions in the environmental and antinuclear movement.[12] In East Germany, by contrast, the alternative women's movement only grew out of the peace movement.[13]

On the political level, the formation of the Green Party in Germany put the established parties under pressure, since the nascent party made issues of gender equity and equality a priority.[14] Also, the governments at the federal and state levels began to take up the issue of gender equality, and the UN announced in 1975 a "Women's Decade" and within the next ten years convened the first three world conferences on women.

The women involved in the peace movement covered all ages, professions, and religions, they came from urban as well as rural areas, and displayed a wide range of political orientations. Some had previously been politically active but many were entering the field of politics for the first time. They did not constitute a homogeneous group but differed with respect to theoretical positions, goals, and ways of tackling the issues concerning women, peace, and the women's peace movement.[15] Roughly we may distinguish two categories: those for whom gender issues were at the very center of the debate about the arms upgrade and those who did not connect these two issues.

This difference led to the formation of a distinct women's peace movement. Two motives stood behind this initiative. First, many women felt that the general peace movement lacked feminist perspectives and a genuine interest in exploring the relationship between violence and gender. Second, a substantial share of women experienced difficulties or felt ill at ease competing in mixed-gender assemblies. They preferred women's groups, in which they did not have to struggle against dominant men.[16] The same applied to the women's peace groups in East Germany and was the motive for restricting access only to women. The formation of exclusive women's initiatives, however, also attracted criticism. Some activists feared that women ran the risk of not being taken seriously or seeking refuge in a "repression-free environment" rather than acting effectively.[17]

Strategies and cooperation were determined by the political affiliations of female activists within the wide scope of groups, ranging from the autonomous women's movement to pacifists to established parties. Thus the issue of cooperation among different divisions of the women's peace movement, as well as with the various groups of the general peace movement, led to conflicts. Feminists complained that women would once again subordinate their own agenda, in this case to the topic of peace.[18] Members of the overall peace movement, on the other hand, considered the women-only actions, at least partly, as counterproductive. Since they regarded a non-destroyed world and world peace the precondition for everything else, including gender equality, they disliked women to take away resources, energy, and attention from this overall goal.

"From Barracks to Sex Shop": Issues and Positions in the Women's Peace Movement

A specific feature of the women's peace movement was the thematic linking of military force with patterns of violence in everyday life and, in particular, violence directed against women. Two examples are Helke Sander's speech "Love and Medium-Range Missiles" and a call by women from Bielefeld who, in the autumn of 1983, organized a "chain of women … from military barracks to sex shops" in order to point out "the connection between sexism and militarism."[19] As a group of women from Kassel put it at a demonstration during a visit of US President Ronald Reagan on 10 June 1982, "For us, the struggle for peace necessarily also is a struggle against male domination."[20]

Depending on their ideological perspective, the various strands of the women's peace movement differed in what issues they regarded most important. Women from the Social Democratic Party or the trade unions, for example, also highlighted the role of capitalism in the development of inequalities and disadvantages. Keywords such as *patriarchy, sexism,* or *militarization* remained highly controversial and reflected rather different political preferences and ideas about society.

There was, however, no doubt within the women's peace movement that it was not enough to prevent an arms upgrade and the stationing of nuclear weapons to create conditions for peace, but that violence and oppression also needed to be overcome in everyday life. Representatives from all sections agreed that women were severely affected by war and rearmament. Rape in particular served as a central point of reference, a topic that had received a great deal of attention in the feminist movement since the 1970s.[21] Others stressed that the increase in arms production was accomplished at the expense of social services, jobs, and measures to promote gender equality and the advancement of women.[22] Women considered patriarchal structures to be at the base of both military and everyday violence and therefore focused their actions on this connection. A modified peace symbol, extended downward and crossed at the vertical bar, symbolically fused images of peace and femininity.[23]

It was the issue of female military service that led to the creation of women's peace groups in both East and West Germany. The debate had commenced in West Germany in the late 1970s, whereas in East Germany the Military Service Act of 1982 actually introduced military service for women in case of war. This debate was particularly suited to reveal the close linkage between questions of military, emancipation, and feminism. Under the prevailing conditions in East Germany, no public discussion on this issue was possible and women had to act very carefully, whereas women in West Germany publicly debated the issue. Some criticized the "male monopoly of power," and considered it discriminatory to deny women access to the Bundeswehr (German armed forces). Alice Schwarzer and the magazine *Emma* represented this position. Others argued that female military service was a step toward a militarization of the entire population and a means to discipline women, an opinion expressed by Sibylle Plogstedt and the magazine *Courage* and by initiatives such as Frauen in die Bundeswehr?—Wir sagen NEIN (Women in the Armed Forces?—We say NO!).[24]

The language of West German feminist magazines mirrors the deeply felt need to distance themselves from topics perceived as "male." Here, female writers used terms and phrases like *machismo* and *peace dudes* to express their criticism, and referred to "the dream of men to finally use their weapons in war."[25] American gender scholar Carol Cohn described in the mid 1980s "nukespeak" as a particular language used to discuss nuclear weapons and nuclear war. She identified it as a type of male language that trivialized facts and that was crammed with sexual connotations. She therefore asked feminists to deconstruct this biased language and to oppose it with a new way of speaking.[26]

Whether to cooperate with men or not remained a highly controversial topic among women in the peace movement. Female trade unionists, female Social Democrats, and female members of the Green Party in particular worked closely with the general peace movement in an often male-dominated environment. For these women gender was not the main impetus, even if they acknowledged a special concern for women. A few feminist groups such as the Munich-based Förderkreis zum Aufbau der feministischen Partei (Initiative for the Formation of a Feminist Party) even tolerated men in their ranks.[27] Both female and male members of this group took part in actions such as a fasting event in the Munich cathedral, which convoked under the slogan "Help mothers fight violence."[28] Occasionally men even insisted on signing the "Women for Peace" appeal.[29] Other groups, predominantly from the autonomous women's movement, rejected any form of cooperation with men.

The situation of feminist groups in East Germany was quite different, since under the repressive conditions of the regime, collaboration with others potentially increased their safety. Therefore, while carefully protecting their independence, women's groups cooperated with other peace and opposition groups across gender boundaries and often under the umbrella of the Protestant Church, which provided a certain degree of protection.

Of overriding importance was the question of whether women are innately more peaceful than men, or whether peaceful qualities in women are a product of their social upbringing. Female authors writing for the magazines *Emma* and *Courage* criticized the taboo that prevented the relationship between women and violence, which they said was based on the myth of women being peaceful by nature, from being addressed. They demanded a discussion about the relationship between women, power, and violence.[30] The debate revealed different positions. While some women demanded to deny men any right to decide on war, peace, or arms, but leave this privilege exclusively to women, others rejected the idea of power being vested in a single gender or a single social group on principle.[31]

Closely interlinked with this discussion were references to the concept of motherhood and women's ability to bear and nurse children. References to motherhood usually served to morally legitimize protest actions and to appeal to women's moral consciousness to join in. Their focus on children and

Figure 16.1. Women and children protesters blocking a road between the US military base in Mutlangen and Schwäbisch Gmünd on 3 September 1983 (ullstein bild / R. Janke)

the protection of future generations corresponded very well with the general peace movement's use of "the future" as a major argument and point of reference.[32] Again, this viewpoint was not universally accepted among women peace advocates. In 1981 the magazine *Emma* accused the Arbeitsgemeinschaft sozialdemokratischer Frauen (AsF, Association of Social Democratic Women) and Friedensfrauen (Women for Peace) of deriving their personal identities only from being mothers and wives, and asked, "Should we not fear for ourselves and for other women?"[33]

"Women against War, But How?" Forms of Action and Protest

The peace movement employed various forms of action, including classical demonstrations, appeals, petitions, and blockades (usually at US military bases), as well as human chains, bike demonstrations, fasts, peace camps, die-ins, and boycotts.[34] Usually both men and women joined in such actions. There were no forms of protest restricted to a single gender, but certain events were directed only at women.[35] Only calls to join "birth strikes" constituted a gender-specific exception. They aimed at highlighting the relationship between peace and violence against women and expressed women's resistance to bearing and rearing future soldiers. Such appeals did not find much support, however.

Bringing together activists of both movements, women's peace camps such as the camp at Reckershausen in the region of the Hunsrück helped to integrate the women's movement and the women's peace movement. Situated in an area with a high density of military installations, the international camp took place every summer for eleven years. It was considered a "utopia in the form of a 'women's world' that turned into reality, at least temporarily" and it influenced other women and lesbian projects.[36] Similar to women's peace marches, which sometimes marched through several countries, the camps were meant to anticipate the goal of better coexistence by implementing such utopian forms of social relations across boundaries on a small scale.[37]

State proscriptions prevented public actions of this kind in East Germany. Under the umbrella of the Protestant Church, however, women's groups managed to send out invitations to parish events, information booths, and political night prayers. With the establishment of working groups even interregional meetings became possible. Part of the agenda for these women's groups was writing letters of protest to East and West German politicians, participating in fasts (which reached across political factions), and even forming a human chain in East Berlin. The female activists risked being monitored, interrogated, and arrested. Supported by the West European peace movements and West Germany's Women for Peace, East German women peace activists therefore aimed part of their efforts at promoting the release of their imprisoned members.[38]

Up to a certain degree, protests in East and West Germany were fairly similar in nature. Collecting signatures against a possible or a real draft of women into military service stood at the inception of women's peace movements in both states. In West Germany sixty thousand women signed the appeal "Women in the Armed Forces?—We say NO!" in 1979. Three years later, a remarkable 150 women in East Germany signed a joint petition to the head of state, Erich Honecker, to demand a public discussion on the new Military Service Act.[39] In both countries, Women for Peace initiated boycott campaigns in which women signed forms and staged demonstrations to let authorities know that they were unwilling to undertake military service of any kind.[40]

A number of publications from the early 1980s took up the issue of peace in its gender dimension and reflected women's activities in the West German peace movement. These publications dealt with women in peace movements from a historical perspective, for example in Herrad Schenk's

Frauen kommen ohne Waffen (Women come without weapons) and a compilation of brief biographies edited by Elisabeth Braendle-Zeile, *Seit 90 Jahren: Frauen für Frieden* (For 90 years: Women for peace).[41] Other works compiled key political texts of the women's peace movement: for example, *Frauen machen Frieden: Lesebuch für Großmütter, Mütter und Töchter* (Women make peace: A reader for grandmothers, mothers, and daughters) and Eva Quistorp's *Frauen für den Frieden* (Women for peace).[42] The story *Kassandra* by Christa Wolf, an East German writer, was an important reference text for many supporters of the women's movement, the peace movement, and the women's peace movement. These publications can be seen as instruments of self-understanding and identity formation in which women documented and reflected their actions as well as their perspectives.

The Positioning of Identity

Most of these publications situated female involvement in the peace movement in a historical context. Pacifist Bertha von Suttner served as a central reference point, as did female peace activists of World War I and women's peace initiatives of the early days of the Federal Republic. Numerous texts and speeches mentioned the "mothers" of the new women's movement of the 1970s.[43] Furthermore, some publications started to ask critical questions about the role of women as mothers, wives, military workers, partisans, paramedics, and so forth who participated in wars and supported military efforts. These historical reflections can be seen as contributions to a women's history that aimed at helping women to become aware of their own history through self-historization.[44]

International relations were a second important factor in the self-positioning of the women's peace movement. Women in West as well as East Germany were very aware of being part of an international (women's) peace movement. The call "Instigation of Women for Peace" was based on a text that had been published shortly before by the Danish Women for Peace and triggered a wave of international follow-up.[45] A total of half a million signatures from different countries were presented to the UN World Conference on Women in 1980.

The Women of Greenham Common are another example for such international role models. In 1981 they besieged the American military base near London with a permanent peace camp and continued to protest against the deployment of nuclear missiles up until 2000.[46] Greenham Common became a central symbol of female protest and a frequent point of reference. The Women's Pentagon Action between 1980 and 1981 had a similar appeal: an

Figure 16.2. Poster "Stand up for Peace!" (Netzwerk Friedenskooperative / FFBIZ Archive, Berlin)

estimated two to four thousand women formed a human chain around the US Defense Department in Arlington, Virginia. They wept and sang to draw attention to the belligerent and dangerous policy of the Defense Department, whose large budget they said took resources away from social programs.[47]

Activist groups from different countries were in close contact, as was the case in the broader peace movement, and international events further strengthened these ties. In many cases they were based on personal contacts. Female representatives of various alliances visited protest events in other countries: among these were Helen Caldicott, the prominent Australian who had been crucial in the founding of the International Physicians for the Prevention of Nuclear War (IPPNW), and Petra Kelly. Feminist magazines such as *Emma* and *Courage* regularly reported on international peace activities; the latter even in a special section.

The relationship between Women for Peace in East and West Germany was of particular significance. Cooperation across the blocs was an important feature of the peace movement in general, but the female networks were even closer. These contacts led to joint protest actions that demonstrated the general peace movement's and the women's peace movement's vision of peace beyond the frontiers of the Cold War.

Finally, the self-description as "fighters" is a third element of the self-positioning of women in the peace movement. Female activists stressed their combative side, regardless of whether they considered women inherently more peaceful than men, or not. "I am a woman, and the persons to whom I turn now, are women. I am a fighter, and the women whom I address speak of fighting," journalist Peggy Parnass noted at the beginning of the 1980s.[48] This kind of rhetoric can be seen as a strategy to draw attention to the seriousness of the situation, and to break the stereotype of weak women in need of harmony. This was, however, not supposed to invoke violence. Women rather wished to demonstrate their own efforts and their anger, and to show that they were willing to stand up for their concerns even at the cost of negative results such as being arrested or ridiculed.

A Forgotten Fight?

The self-positioning strategies of the women's peace movement aimed at making women visible in their commitment to peace and as women, not only to the public but also to themselves. The politics of visibility was also evident in contemporary posters of the general peace movement, which often depicted women participating in demonstrations and protesting.[49] At least in illustrations of the general peace movement women took an equal position alongside men. To what degree images of women have actually changed remains an open question. Karola Maltry has expressed concerns that although women displayed "feminine skills in a male political field" when actively participating in the arena of defense and security policy, they reaffirmed at the same time a prejudice of female peacefulness by their commitment to a peaceful world.[50]

Both at the time and in retrospect, many women complained that their contribution to the peace movement was and continues to be invisible and that their activities were concealed and forgotten. Indeed, there have been few historical studies that systematically address the social profile and actions of women in the new peace movement. This is not meant as a call for a history of "Men versus Women." Instead, gender issues and notions of femaleness and maleness need to be explored in the rhetoric and practice of both the different factions of the peace movement and of the supporters and proponents of the arms upgrade, and put in the context of the New Social Movements, the Cold War, and the gender history of the two German states.

Reinhild Kreis is Assistant Professor at the University of Mannheim. She received her PhD from the Ludwig Maximilians University of Munich with a study on US public diplomacy in West Germany from the 1960s to the 1980s. She was awarded the ifa-Forschungspreis für Auswärtige Kulturpolitik and the Edmund Spevack Award of the Lasky Center for Transatlantic Studies. Her research interests include history of consumption, transatlantic relations, diplomatic and protest history, as well as the history of emotions. Kreis is the author of *Orte für Amerika: Deutsch-Amerikanische Institute und Amerikahäuser seit den 1960er Jahren* (2012), editor of *Diplomatie mit Gefühl. Vertrauen, Misstrauen und die Außenpolitik der Bundesrepublik Deutschland* (2015), as well as coeditor of *'Trust, but Verify': The Politics of Uncertainty & the Transformation of the Cold War Order, 1969–1991* (2016). She is currently working on a research project entitled "Making Things Oneself in an Age of Consumption. Values, Social Orders, and Practices from the 1880s to the 1980s."

Notes

1. Album "4630 Bochum" by Herbert Grönemeyer, EMI, 1984. It is one of the best-selling audio CDs in Germany.
2. *Die Nachrüstungsdebatte im Deutschen Bundestag: Protokoll einer historischen Entscheidung* (Reinbek, 1984).
3. Belinda Davis, "Women's Strength against Crazy Male Power: Gendered Language in the West German Peace Movement of the 1980s," in *Frieden, Gewalt, Geschlecht*,

Friedens- und Konfliktforschung als Geschlechterforschung, ed. Jennifer A. Davy, Karen Hagemann, and Ute Kätzel (Essen, 2005), 244–65; Belinda Davis, "Europe is a Peaceful Woman, America is a War-Mongering Man? The 1980s Peace Movement in NATO-Allied Europe," Themenportal Europäische Geschichte (2009), http://www.europa.clio-online.de/2009/Article=409.

4. Davis, "Women's Strength," 245, 259.
5. Frank Biess, "Die Sensibilisierung des Subjekts: Angst und 'Neue Subjektivität' in den 1970er Jahren," *Werkstatt Geschichte* 49 (2008): 51–71.
6. To research what may be called the "gendering" of discourses about war and peace is a central demand made by Karen Hagemann and was directed at the field of Peace and Conflict Research. See Karen Hagemann, "Krieg, Frieden und Gewalt: Friedens- und Konfliktforschung als Geschlechterforschung. Eine Einführung," in Davy, Hagemann, and Kätzel, *Frieden, Gewalt, Geschlecht*, 47.
7. Andreas Wirsching, *Abschied vom Provisorium: Geschichte der Bundesrepublik Deutschland 1982–1990* (Munich, 2006), 87–93; Thomas Leif, *Die strategische (Ohn-)Macht der Friedensbewegung: Kommunikations- und Entscheidungsstrukturen in den achtziger Jahren* (Opladen, 1990). Both authors do not mention women's groups specifically, but categorize them under other group categories of the peace movement.
8. Karola Maltry distinguishes four movements, as she subdivides the representatives of the autonomous women's movement. See Karola Maltry, *Die neue Frauenfriedensbewegung: Entstehung, Entwicklung, Bedeutung* (Frankfurt am Main, 1993), 231–46.
9. See the chapter by Jan Hansen in this volume.
10. Ehrhart Neubert, *Geschichte der Opposition in der DDR 1949–1989* (Bonn, 2009), 335–498.
11. On the women's movement, see Kristina Schulz, *Der lange Atem der Provokation: Die Frauenbewegung in der Bundesrepublik und in Frankreich 1968–1976* (Frankfurt am Main, 2002). For the lesbian movement, see Gabriele Dennert, Christine Leidinger, and Franziska Rauchut, eds., *In Bewegung bleiben: 100 Jahre Politik, Kultur und Geschichte von Lesben* (Berlin, 2007). For more information on the boycotts, see Angelika Schmidt-Biesalski, ed., *Früchte aus Südafrika: Geschichte und Ergebnisse einer Frauen-Kampagne* (Berlin, 1993).
12. Asta Elbholz, "'Ich hab' noch nie so geheult," *Courage* 5, no. 5 (1980): 4–5. See also the chapter by Silke Mende and Birgit Metzger in this volume.
13. Irena Kukutz, "Die Bewegung Frauen für den Frieden als Teil der unabhängigen Friedensbewegung der DDR," in *Enquete-Kommission Aufarbeitung von Geschichte und Folgen der SED-Diktatur in Deutschland*, vol. VII/2, ed. Deutscher Bundestag (Baden-Baden, 1995): 1333. On this point, see also the essay by Rainer Eckert in this volume.
14. The actual implementation of this policy, however, was not unproblematic. The magazine *Courage*, for example, headlined its February 1980 issue "Grüne Frauen im Dilemma" (The dilemma of "Green" women).
15. For example Maltry, *Die neue Frauenfriedensbewegung*.
16. Ibid., 229, 230; Christiane Leidinger, "11 Jahre Widerstand: Frauenwiderstandscamps im Hunsrück von 1983–1993," *Wissenschaft & Frieden* 28 (2010–12): 47–50; Herrad

Schenk, *Frauen kommen ohne Waffen: Feminismus und Pazifismus* (Munich, 1983), 166.
17. Ibid.; Maltry, *Die neue Frauenfriedensbewegung*, 278.
18. Alice Schwarzer, "Der Generalsekretär und die Friedensengel," *Emma* 4, no. 5 (1980): 5–7.
19. Helke Sanders, "Über Beziehungen zwischen Liebesverhältnissen und Mittelstreckenraketen," lecture delivered on 17 February 1980, and printed in *Courage* 5, no. 4 (1980): 16–29, especially 29; "Aktionen gegen den Krieg/Bielefeld," *Courage* 8, no. 10 (1983): 16.
20. "Frieden im Patriarchat ist Krieg für Frauen," in *Frauen für den Frieden: Analysen, Dokumente und Aktionen aus der Frauenfriedensbewegung*, ed. Eva Quistorp (Frankfurt am Main, 1982), 98–99.
21. One example is the cover story of *Courage* from June 1980 which was titled "Vergewaltigung" (Rape).
22. See, for example, Gisela Kessler, "Gewerkschafterinnen in der Friedensbewegung," interview with the journal *Wir Frauen 1982*, reprinted in Quistorp, ed., *Frauen für den Frieden*, 106–9; Renate Schmidt (SPD) in the debate of the Bundestag on 22 November 1983, in *Die Nachrüstungsdebatte im Deutschen Bundestag*, 209.
23. See for example the poster "Frauen Widerstandscamp," Reckershausen 1983, http://plakat.nadir.org/; cover picture of Quistorp's book *Frauen für den Frieden*.
24. See for example the discussion forum in the magazine *Emma* titled "Frauen ins Militär?" with contributions by Alice Schwarzer and Sibylle Plogstedt in *Emma* 3, no. 12 (1979): 18–22. The political class and society at large was also divided on this subject.
25. Eva Quistorp, "Vorwort," in Quistorp, *Frauen für den Frieden*, 9–10; Theresa Wobbe, "Planung des begrenzten Atomkriegs," *Courage* 5, no. 12 (1980): 11; "Friedens-Macker," in *Courage* 8, no. 8 (1983): 63.
26. Carol Cohn, "Slick 'Ems, Glick 'Ems, Christmas Trees, and Cookie Cutters: Nuclear Language and How We Learned to Pat the Bomb," *Bulletin of the Atomic Scientists* 43, no. 5 (1987): 17–24.
27. Elisabeth Zellmer, *Töchter der Revolte: Frauenbewegung und Feminismus in den 1970er Jahren in München* (Munich, 2011), 134.
28. *Der Feminist* 7, no. 1 (1984).
29. Heidemarie Langer and Brigitte Engert, *Frauen Für Frieden: Erster Erfahrungsbericht einer Bewegung. Die Unterschriftenaktion* (n.p., [1981]), 33.
30. For example, see Anna Dorothea Brockmann, "Krieg und Frieden," *Emma* 5, no. 9 (1981): 10–13; see also the letters to the editor in *Courage* 6, no. 4 (1981): 58 and *Courage* 6, no. 5 (1981): 59.
31. Petra Kelly, "Anleitung zum Sturz des Internationalen Patriarchats," speech delivered to the congress "Feminismus und Ökologie," 1986; reprinted in Eva Quistorp and Barbara Bussfeld, eds., *Scheherazade: Stimmen von Frauen gegen die Logik des Krieges* (Hamburg, 1992), 63, 65; letter to the editor by K. W. in *Courage* 7, no. 5 (1981): 59.
32. The initiative Frauen gegen Atomtod—Unsere Kinder sollen leben (Women against Nuclear Death—Our Children Shall Live), founded in 1983, should be mentioned

as an example; see Anja Becker, "Ein Leben lang gegen Atomkraft," interview with Renée Meyer zur Capellen, in *Frauen aktiv gegen Atomenergie: Wenn aus Wut Visionen werden. 20 Jahre Tschernobyl,* ed. Ulrike Röhr (Norderstedt, 2006), 53–60. A number of texts that call for action can be found in "Anstiftung der Frauen zum Frieden," in Quistorp, *Frauen für den Frieden,* 20–21.

33. "Nachdenken statt nachrüsten!" *Emma* 4, no. 6 (1980): 7.
34. See also the chapter by Kathrin Fahlenbrach and Laura Stapane in this volume.
35. See also the publicity and appeals for a number of planned actions in *Courage* 8, no. 10 (1983): 16–17.
36. Leidinger, "11 Jahre Widerstand"; Sabine Zurmühl, "Im Hunsrück-Camp: Todesbasis Hasselbach von Frauen besetzt," *Courage* 8, no. 9 (1983): 8–9.
37. Eva Quistorp, "Frauen gehen meilenweit—für atomwaffenfreie Lande: Frauenfriedensmarsch '81," in Quistorp, *Frauen für den Frieden,* 44–46.
38. Kukutz, "Die Bewegung 'Frauen für den Frieden'"; see also the chapter by Rainer Eckert in this volume.
39. Kukutz, "Die Bewegung 'Frauen für den Frieden,'" 1295–302.
40. "Wir werden nicht bereit sein … Frauen verweigern den Kriegsdienst," in Quistorp, *Frauen für den Frieden,* 90–91; Dorothea Brockmann, "Verweigert die Hilfsdienste," *Emma* 6, no. 2 (1982): 16–17; Kukutz: "Die Bewegung 'Frauen für den Frieden,'" 1306–7.
41. Schenk, *Frauen kommen ohne Waffen*; Elisabeth Brändle-Zeile, *Seit 90 Jahren: Frauen für den Frieden* (Stuttgart, 1983).
42. Elisabeth Burmeister, *Frauen machen Frieden: Lesebuch für Großmütter, Mütter und Töchter* (Gelnhausen, 1981); Quistorp, ed., *Frauen für den Frieden*.
43. Letter to the editor by B. K. in *Emma* 5, no. 4 (1981): 59–60; Quistorp, "Vorwort," in Quistorp, *Frauen für den Frieden* 9.
44. Claudia Opitz, *Um-Ordnung der Geschlechter: Einführung in die Geschlechtergeschichte* (Tübingen, 2005), 25–26, 49–50.
45. Both appeals are reprinted in Quistorp, ed., *Frauen für den Frieden,* 20–21.
46. Alice Cook and Gwyn Kirk, *Greenham Women Everywhere: Dreams, Ideas and Actions from the Women's Peace Movement* (London, 1984).
47. Women Pentagon Action in Quistorp, ed., *Frauen für den Frieden,* 40–42.
48. Peggy Parnass, "Unzucht mit Abhängigen," in Quistorp, *Frauen für den Frieden,* 83.
49. Benjamin Ziemann, "The Code of Protest: Images of Peace in the West German Peace Movement, 1945–1990," *Contemporary European History* 17, no. 2 (2008): 249; Fabio Crivellari, "Blockade: Friedensbewegung zwischen Melancholie und Ironie," in *Das Jahrhundert der Bilder,* vol. 2: 1949 bis heute, ed. Gerhard Paul (Göttingen, 2008), 482–89.
50. Maltry, *Die neue Frauenfriedensbewegung,* 272.

Select Bibliography

An introduction to gender-historical studies and their potential in peace and conflict research is provided in the anthology by Davy, Hagemann, and Kätzel. While a systematic investigation of the peace movement from the angle of gender-historical perspectives is still pending, Davis has taken first steps (2005 and 2009) toward such an analysis. Up to now most studies on the women's peace movement in Germany have been written by the activists themselves. Maltry has written on West Germany, and Kukutz, the cofounder of the East German Women for Peace, on the women's peace movement in the GDR. More recent publications are from Stern and Bieschke. Promising are also approaches that incorporate visual strategies and communication through images, in the way Ziemann has analyzed the period 1945–1990.

Bieschke, Anne. "Frauen streiten um den Frieden: Kontroversen und Debatten um die neue Frauenfriedensbewegung." *Ariadne: Forum für Frauen- und Geschlechtergeschichte* 66 (2014): 50–59.
Davis, Belinda. "Europe is a Peaceful Woman, America is a War-Mongering Man? The 1980s Peace Movement in NATO-Allied Europe." Themenportal Europäische Geschichte (2009). http://www.europa.clio-online.de/2009/Article=409.
———. "Women's Strength against Crazy Male Power: Gendered Language in the West German Peace Movement of the 1980s," in *Frieden, Gewalt, Geschlecht. Friedens- und Konfliktforschung als Geschlechterforschung*, ed. Jennifer A. Davy, Karen Hagemann, and Ute Kätzel, 244–65. Essen, 2005.
Davy, Jennifer A., Karen Hagemann, and Ute Kätzel, eds., *Frieden, Gewalt, Geschlecht. Friedens- und Konfliktforschung als Geschlechterforschung*. Essen, 2005.
Kukutz, Irena. "Die Bewegung 'Frauen für den Frieden' als Teil der unabhängigen Friedensbewegung der DDR," in *Enquete-Kommission Aufarbeitung von Geschichte und Folgen der SED-Diktatur in Deutschland*, vol. VII/2, ed. Deutscher Bundestag, 1285–408. Baden-Baden, 1995.
Maltry, Karola. *Die neue Frauenfriedensbewegung: Entstehung, Entwicklung, Bedeutung*. Frankfurt am Main, 1993.
Stern, Kathrin. "Grenzen, Grenzverschiebungen, Grenzverschärfungen. Die Handlungsräume der Frauen für den Frieden/Ostberlin." *Ariadne: Forum für Frauen- und Geschlechtergeschichte* 57 (2010): 48–53.
Ziemann, Benjamin. "The Code of Protest: Images of Peace in the West German Peace Movements, 1945–1990." *Contemporary European History* 17, no. 2 (2008): 237–61.

Chapter 17

Nuclear Attack and Civil Defense: Preparing for the Worst-Case Scenario in Politics and Science

Claudia Kemper

The use of atomic bombs on Hiroshima and Nagasaki introduced an entirely new sort of military confrontation and had far-reaching consequences for the preventative protection of the population in the event of conflict. During the Cold War, civil defense planning mostly fell back on the experience of the previous two world wars, especially in the field of civil protection preparedness and civil air defense. In addition there were simulated scenarios carried out in nuclear tests above ground up until the early 1970s. The principles of air defense soon influenced the establishment of a complex preparation system that was labeled "civil defense" in the 1960s. All experts agreed that apart from the question of the scale of the war, any event involving a nuclear explosion would immediately affect a large mass of people. Against this backdrop, arrangements, preparedness, and safeguards in the case of a nuclear strike were combined with those measures meant to deal with technical or natural disasters.

Civil defense preparations integrated into the "state of defense" underwent cycles parallel to the periods of heightened tensions during the Cold War.[1] In European countries in particular the discussions about the possibilities and limits of civil defense policy became a strikingly ambiguous characteristic of this era. First, discussions about technical conviction and the controllability of a nuclear strike formed a communicative framework in which issues of progress always held center stage. Second, the historical perspective at the heart of all civil defense measures highlighted the extent to which nuclear policy was based on experience of and assumptions about conventional warfare. Even contemporaries noted the chasm between the optimistic promises concerning civil nuclear use and the outdated precautions against military nuclear aftermaths in the form of shelters, evacuation plans, and self-protection. Although the experience of Hiroshima helped preparations for emergencies in the medical field, the atomic bomb of 1945 belonged to an outdated arsenal of superpower arms, and bomb silos contained considerably more highly charged destructive arms. Ultimately simulations and disaster scenarios that relied on conventional warfare were the only means to predict possible nuclear war situations, and these appeared to be quite uncertain. Civil defense planning always faced this predicament. The anticipated dimensions of a nuclear war were increasingly seen as unimaginable, unthinkable, and therefore also unpredictable.[2]

Civil Defense in the Nuclear Age

Civil defense in nearly all countries, despite considerable differences, had four aspects in common during the Cold War: first, in the case of nuclear defense, all relevant agencies, authorities, and institutions were to be prepared by having plans for evacuation, water supply, and the functioning of infrastructure. Second, in addition to the construction of public shelters, the focus of civil defense was directed to individual self-defense. The general public needed to be informed, motivated, and trained. This included guidelines for procedures in case of an acute bomb alarm as well as preparations for remaining in a sealed cellar in the domestic domain over an extended period or, in the best case, in a personal bomb shelter. Third, civil defense policy endeavored to convey the meaningfulness of its arrangements. To make preparations effective, the underlying nuclear weapons policy had to be understood as plausible and even necessary, in both the East and West. Civil defense measures logically implied a belief that a nuclear conflict could be won by at least one of the two sides and that part of its population would survive. This served as an argument for civil defense officials and government leaders that the development of civil defenses would increase the chances of survival and thus heighten the country's defense capability.

Therefore, and fourth, the explanatory rhetoric and propaganda of civil defense backed up the ideological self-representation of one's own side, as well as that of the enemy.[3] At the same time, the propaganda of an effective civil defense on either side conveyed to the population the paradigm of security in which the population existed within a technically, scientifically, and politically superior system. However, this strategy presented a certain dilemma in that the information and concepts that were used to promote civil protection created the impression that a nuclear war would be, in fact, more feasible than it really was.[4] On the one hand, officials tried to exacerbate mostly vague fears with regard to a nuclear threat and to increase the motivation for self-protection. On the other hand, the state agency needed to avoid an explicit listing of dangers that detailed potential damage scenarios in order not to discredit its own nuclear defense policies.[5] Overall the civil defense rhetoric accentuated the technical feasibility of measures and, in its early phase, was couched in the characteristically technocratic style of its time. The buildup of civil defense decreased somewhat in a parallel move to the détente policy and a general relaxation of a threat constellation during the late 1960s and early 1970s. Starting in the mid-1970s this changed again.

When looking at individual protagonists in the East-West conflict—for instance, the United States, the Soviet Union, Great Britain, Scandinavia, and West and East Germany—one finds that the 1950s and 1960s represent the developmental phase of civil defense and a period of professionalization in its public relations. Especially the Korean War and the Cuban missile crisis in 1962 resulted in increased efforts. Although US authorities had propagated specific safety installations such as private safe rooms with little success, public life and popular culture made references to bombs on an unparalleled level.[6] The British government made use of its traditional civil defense helper culture, which had evolved from the bombings of World War II and, under Prime Minister Thatcher, delegated responsibilities and contingency plans to municipal authorities.[7] Remarkably the civil defense structures in two neutral countries, Sweden and Switzerland, were far more comprehensive in technical and organizational terms than those in NATO and Warsaw Pact countries.[8]

East Germany developed civil defense as an integral part of a national defense plan that obviously referenced the Soviet Union. After passing an initial law on air protection in 1958, the East German leadership developed all areas of civil defense in its customary hierarchical style. On 1 June 1976, all paramilitary and civilian civil defense organizations were discharged from the authority of the Ministry of the Interior and placed under the authority of the Ministry of National Defense. However, the lack of material and financial means meant that the authorities never accomplished their propagated goal of expanding civil defense into a strategic pillar of its national security. The focus was thus all the more directed at training and disciplining the population, so that in East Germany ideas and practice of civil defense extended into all areas of a citizen's life.[9]

In taking on Soviet specifications, East Germany also adopted the dogma of the feasibility of a nuclear conflict. According to this thinking, nuclear weapons were seen as "significantly improved conventional weapons" and formed part of a military strategy that was based on a conventional concept of war.[10] East German leadership followed Soviet nuclear planning "unconditionally"[11] and prepared the country, due to its strategic military position within the Warsaw Pact, "for a potential armed conflict as well as for an extraordinary situation, not only for the state and its military, but for the whole of society, faithful to the concept of total war."[12]

Civil defense in East Germany did not merely focus on "protection against enemy weapons of mass destruction,"[13] but also served as an instrument of social control. There were nearly half a million full-time and volunteer staff and "Socialist military education" was part of daily life for the citizens of East Germany. In the late 1970s, the militarization of society was once again strongly promoted. Military instruction at school was introduced in 1978; pupils learned not only first-aid measures but also how to use weapons. This was increasingly met by resentment within the population, who apparently regarded these practices as untimely. While some parents complained that their children did not learn about the dramatic consequences of a nuclear explosion and pointed out that "plastic and pantyhose" were hardly adequate materials for producing make-shift protective masks against chemical or nuclear weapons, church representatives and peace activists criticized the military classes and charged the regime for showing a lack of "willingness for peace."[14]

In the mid-1980s East Germany relaxed its compliance to the strict guidelines of the Soviet military and defense system. The clearest sign of this change was a decision reached in 1984, which had been induced by economic pressures and a growing resistance in the population: all responsibility for civil defense matters was transferred to a disaster relief organization. The nuclear disaster at Chernobyl in 1986 put an end to unreserved belief in the feasibility of a nuclear war. All the same, East Germany maintained its civil defense training program and kept up accompanying institutions right until the end. First of all, it complied with obligatory alliance commitments, and second, it counteracted the decline in the population's sense of being threatened.[15]

West Germany established civil defense, initially classified as air-raid protection, from 1955 onwards in the course of integration into the West and, in particular, with NATO admission. The government integrated scientific expertise about the effects of atomic bombs right from the start, e.g., with expertise of the "Commission for the protection of the civilian population against nuclear, biological, and chemical attack" founded in 1950.[16] In 1958 the Bundesanstalt für zivilen Luftschutz (Department of Federal Civil Air-Raid Defense) became the Bundesamt für zivilen Bevölkerungsschutz (BzB) (Federal Agency for the Protection of the Civilian Population). Interestingly, the adopted law entitled "First law on measures to protect the civilian population"[17] regulated responsibilities with the notable omission of any reference to nuclear atomic terminology: "The civil air defense has the task to protect the lives and health of the population, homes, places of work and facilities or goods/utilities, which are important for the general well-being and include goods or sites of cultural heritage against the dangers of air attacks and to remove damage caused by air raids or to mitigate the effects of such attacks. The self-help of the population is supplemented by government action."

Distinctions were drawn between the following categories: self-protection, population warning, shelter, habitation regulations, civil protection, and measures to protect the general health and cultural property.[18] The legal basis constituted a problem, since according to Article 73 of the Basic Law (Constitution), the responsibility for civil defense rested with the federal government, while protection from natural disasters in peacetime was in the hands of regional states. An effective implementation of civil defense measures depended therefore on close cooperation and coordination between private and public institutions for emergencies, such as fire brigades, the German Red Cross, and the Technisches Hilfswerk (THW, German Technical Emergency Service) at the federal and regional state levels.

The Intensification of Civil Defense in the 1980s

Given the international political and military developments from the late 1970s, the East and the West were confronted with the consequences of a nuclear strike and its effects on civil defense.[19] The Bundesamt für Zivilschutz (BfZ) (Federal Office for Civil Protection), successor to the BzB since 1974 and under the authority of the Ministry of the Interior, became an important mediator between scientists and the general public. As of 1975 the BfZ released a series of publications with contributions from civil defense research. The topics covered urgent scientific and technological research relating to the threat posed: radiation damage and radiation sensitivity, combined damage that occurs after nuclear explosions; the effects of a neutron bomb; results from bunker occupation experiments; the effects of wildfires, group dynamics, and individual consequences of nuclear explosions; disaster medicine; and the effects of chemical and biological weapons.[20]

With deteriorating international relations, the continuous work and research of the BfZ returned to the political center stage. Following the NATO Double-Track Decision, government officials stepped up civil defense measures, and public sentiment against NATO's actions intensified. The opposition argued its case against any form of expansion of NATO's military strategy in much stronger and more sophisticated ways than it had previously, and therefore the debate about civil defense became more controversial. The issue of this debate at the beginning of the 1980s was no longer simply about whether West Germany could or should contribute to NATO's military strategy. Instead, at stake was to what extent civil defense, in its protective function, could also serve as a preventive measure and act in support of the defense capability of the country. More than anything else the debate revolved around the general effectiveness of civil protection measures in case of a nuclear strike. However, this fundamental debate about civil defense cannot be schematically reduced to a straightforward conflict between optimistic proponents and pessimistic challengers.

In 1980 Carl Friedrich von Weizsäcker, a prominent peace and conflict researcher, forecast for Europe and particularly Germany "acts of war on all levels of escalation … from conventional tactical weapons up to medium-range and intercontinental ballistic missiles."[21] Unlike certain factions of the peace movement, Weizsäcker steadily argued since his participation in the Declaration of Göttingen[22] in 1957 for a pragmatic approach to the atomic bomb, and in this context for the expansion of civil defense "as a sober precaution with a limited chance of success." Weizsäcker vehemently rejected psychological arguments that the activities of civil defense would only numb the population's awareness of the risk. The resistance against civil defense arose in his view from "the fear of facing a real threat of war in earnest." Instead it could be anticipated that "between the hoped preservation of peace and the feared complete destruction … there was a wide range of possible events in which timely prepared measures would protect human lives, both directly and also for the health necessary for survival thereafter."[23] Other scientists picked up on this differentiated argument to make the point that the policy debate on civil defense merely diverted attention from the actual consequences of a nuclear explosion.[24]

This controversy touched the ethical core of nuclear civil defense. While civil defense advocates regarded the development of civil protection as the basic protection of the population and their participation therein as a humanitarian contribution, civil protection opponents saw it as an internal constraint of the balance of deterrence between superpowers, and consequently as part of war preparations.[25]

The situation assumed the form of a conflict of faith. Opinions on the consequences of nuclear war and what kind of scenario was conceivable or manageable were based on different forecasts; and political consequences were ultimately derived from these.[26] Seen from the government's point of view, the challenge of installing a complete civil defense concept was not only to inform the public about the steps taken in advance, but also to prepare responses and rehearse procedures. Thus federal governmental agencies charged with civil defense made every effort to hit a decidedly sober tone in the early 1980s, as the Minister of the Interior had specified. He deemed that the core of the educational work in matters of civil defense was "honest and frank information to the public." The federal government made no secret of the fact that there was no complete protection against nuclear explosions.[27] However, it was thought that the risk for individuals was reduced considerably by preventive measures and prior training.[28] The Bundesverband für den Selbstschutz (BVS) (Federal Association for Self-Protection) took on a pivotal role between policy-makers and the general public to convince the latter of the rationale behind the national defense preparations. All exercises and provisional arrangements were, unlike in East Germany, voluntary, and therefore, their success was dependent on the local risk assessment. At a municipal level, the BVS offered advice and information on options of private protection. However, responses and risk assessment showed pronounced regional differences. By 1986 the BVS had trained 3,214 self-protection advisers in the state of Baden-Württemberg but none in the city-state of Hamburg.[29]

Survival or Life after a Nuclear Attack

When proponents of civil defense discussed survival after an average nuclear explosion (from a one-megaton bomb, the bomb on Hiroshima was a mere 12,500 tons), they assumed there would be at least a rudimentary functioning environment. On the other hand, opponents predicted that a one-megaton nuclear explosion would obliterate all conditions necessary for life within a 10-kilometer radius. Consequently there were widely divergent assessments of whether and how the wounded could be treated; assessments on medium- and long-term consequences differed accordingly.

Medical prioritization, known as *triage* (selection), was of central importance to civil defense planning. This system, which had been used in emergency medicine since World War I, divides injured persons according to the degree of necessary medical attention and chances of survival. In order to develop a triage system for the event of a nuclear explosion, the planners had to make assumptions. These were, first, that sufficient doctors would be available; and second, that injuries caused by nuclear explosions would correspond to the familiar patterns of injuries known from conventional wars, and could be treated likewise. NATO agreed upon standards and regulations that laid down the principles of triage for efficient emergency treatment of military and civilian casualties in a nuclear war. It distinguished T1 as immediate treatment, T2 as delayed treatment, T3 as minimal treatment, and T4 as postponed treatment. Seriously injured persons in category T4 would therefore receive "postponed treatment" while the wounded in categories T1 and T2 were prioritized as they had better chances of survival.[30]

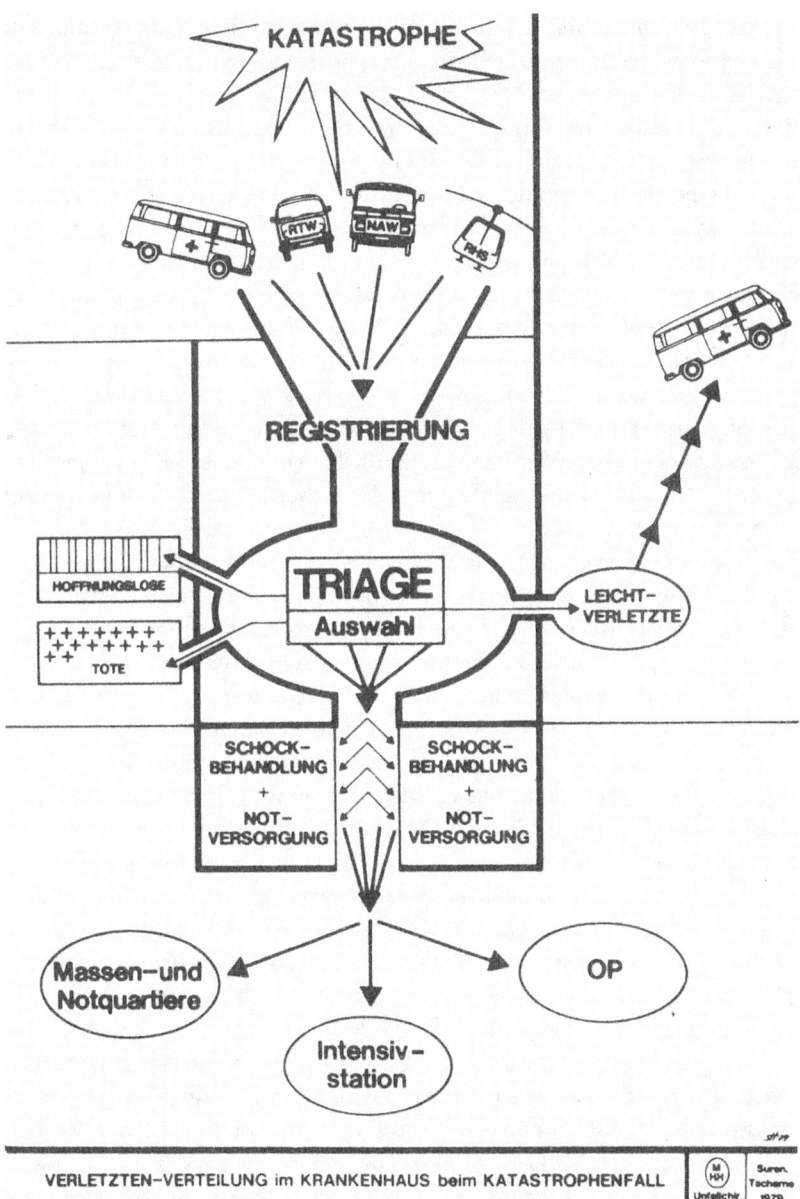

Figure 17.1. Triage System (Doctors' Initiative in the City of Ulm)

In addition to familiar injuries caused by conventional bomb explosions through pressure and heat, reports from Japan had indicated that planners needed to anticipate more substantial injury patterns. First of all, there was likely to be a high proportion of eye injuries caused by mechanical shock, burns or retinal damage induced by long-wave radiation, and bleeding. A second type of injury would be inflicted by radiation exposure, the extent of which depended on the distance from the center of the explosion or the nuclear fallout. As the human body absorbs all radiation to which it is exposed, this adversely affects all biological processes in the body and prevention of radiation sickness is hardly possible.[31] Nausea, vomiting, diarrhea, bleeding, and hair loss are among the common symptoms of acute radiation sickness, which is incurable. The radioactive contamination of cells causes cancer in the long term, especially of the bone marrow. In the early 1980s there were six medical centers in West Germany specializing in bone marrow transplantation. The state did not plan to provide further resources for this kind of complex surgery.

The impact assessment for and against nuclear civil defense went beyond the immediate explosion and the ensuing heat and pressure waves. Two further characteristics differentiated nuclear explosions from conventional bombs or carpet-bombings. The first was radioactive fission products. These are released in an explosion and attach themselves to the dust particles that are raised in ground-level explosions. A contaminated dust cloud extends several miles into the atmosphere and will float afield, depending on wind direction. After the fallout, this cloud continues to disperse radioactive particles from the upper air layers of the Earth's atmosphere, even years after the explosion. As a countermeasure to this delayed consequence, entire areas ought to be evacuated immediately after an explosion to protect the resident population. However, unlike the United States or the Soviet Union, which both had vast land masses, the German civil defense had no way of developing mass evacuation plans because of an overall high population density in central Europe at the beginning of the 1980s.

Civil defense authorities generally advised the construction of private shelters as an effective measure for protection. To boost motivation for the construction of safe rooms or shelters, Minister of the Interior Gerhart Baum conceded in 1980 that "government measures and a willingness of citizens to provide for themselves for potential situations of crisis needed to come together."[32] Brochures, courses, and guidelines usually informed the public that a fourteen-day period in a shelter was considered necessary. But in practice, the suitability of the shelter concepts were tested for only three days, during which, for example, thirty men spent this time in a typical 32 square meter shelter.[33] The last test of this kind was performed in East Germany in 1981 with a satisfying result as far as accommodation and meals were concerned. However, the sanitary situation and "above all psychological problems and the highly unsatisfactory replies to questions of how life would proceed after the nuclear strike" raised major concerns.[34] Although tests of this nature produced technically positive results, opponents of the entire shelter concept criticized that all components of civil defense ignored the fact that the medium-term supply of provisions relied on a still functioning outside world. For survival in a bunker longer than fourteen days, one also required an operational warning system and a minimum of clean air. In a sealed basement room or cellar, persons could only hope to survive the acute phase of the fallout. After this phase the ventilation would deliver unfiltered and contaminated air from outside.

Figure 17.2. Civil protection practice: a safe room shelter for women and children, about 1975/1980 (BArch B 422 Bild-0140 / Kurt Hilberath)

It was intended that the air raid bunkers from the World War II period should protect the city population. These constructions needed to be restored, developed, and strengthened. However, such concrete blocks, seen as relics of a conventional war, inspired little confidence. More telling than these "symbols of a naive illusion of security" was the obvious truth that shelters could accommodate only a fraction of the population. Shelters thus turned into an emotionally charged object of contention in the debate about civil defense. When local authorities, legally responsible for these buildings, wanted to reactivate them, representatives of the peace movement criticized such action as downplaying the scale of the nuclear threat.

One reason for the advocated self-sufficiency in the event of a nuclear explosion was the presumed consequences of an electromagnetic pulse (EMP). A nuclear EMP is created by a nuclear explosion some 100 kilometers above the Earth's atmosphere and cuts off all electrical circuits, so that not only light and water, but also telephone, radio, and other communication technologies no longer function. This point was taken up by the opponents of civil defense when they pointed out that emergency plans and the triage system were based on the assumption that a rudimentary functional technical infrastructure remained at least partly intact after a nuclear explosion. Yet since the EMP necessarily suspends all electrical equipment for an incalculable time, not even basic communication could be taken for granted.

Another point hardly discussed by civil protection authorities, but pointedly addressed by the peace movement, concerned the longer-term consequences of nuclear explosions. The American biologist Paul Ehrlich and the astrophysicist Carl Sagan published a volume titled *The Nuclear Night* summarizing the results of various research projects presented at a scientific conference in 1983. The conference had participants from more than thirty, mostly American, institutions and was organized in cooperation with the Soviet Academy of Sciences. The authors warned against drawing definitive conclusions, but went on to say that "a nuclear war, in which only a fraction of the US and Soviet nuclear weapons were detonated, could change the climate of the northern hemisphere and turn the current climate with alternating seasons into a long, dark, and icy night."[35] Ehrlich and Sagan initiated a widely noted debate within the science community and in the public domain about the "nuclear winter." As they did not predict a final apocalyptic ice age, their prognosis that a few months after the detonation soot and dust would disappear from the atmosphere and then a "new, vicious sunlight" would reach the earth "and blind most animals" seemed absolutely plausible. Nevertheless, a number of physicists and biologists remained skeptical. This opened a broad field of discussion much like today's climate debates, in which civil protection experts and their opponents had to take a stance.[36]

The Militarization of Medicine?

Crosscutting the discussion on civil defense along technological lines, one can also find a civic dimension in this debate. Basic research for self-protection comprised, in addition to technical and medical issues, aspects of "psychobiology," referring to "behavior in stressful situations," and its crucial role in drawing on the experience of previous disaster events.[37] Disaster experts had, up to this point, collected experience with the acute care of a few hundred people. Now they had to anticipate managing with ten to a hundred thousand casualties within a confined space. This required contingency plans and a preventive coordination of civilian institutions. Like others, the federal government of West Germany planned a systematic expansion of the civil defense capacities through the storage of medication or setting up of auxiliary hospitals with mandatory contingency plans. In November 1981 the state in Rhineland-Palatinate issued the first law in its Fire and Disaster Protection Act, which decreed the obligatory participation of physicians in training courses for disaster medicine. The Federal Ministry of Health issued a "health safety law" making it compulsory for physicians to report to authorities and to serve on official duty. It included hospital-use plans for the "state of defense" and mandatory medical disaster instructions for physicians.[38] The choice of terminology was significant, since civil defense preparedness was officially considered part of disaster medicine. Opponents therefore imputed that extended planning provision turned civilian physicians forcibly into the service of military medicine.[39]

Critically minded doctors perceived this process as an attempt to dissolve boundaries between professional emergency, disaster, and war medicine with the purpose of militarizing the healthcare system.[40] The ensuing discussion on the definition of key terms was not an idle academic pastime but related to directives or standards of training and ultimately went beyond the boundaries of disciplines. Peace activists certainly insisted on a strict separation between the effects of natural or technological disasters and deliberately or accidentally induced nuclear explosions. Experts on civil defense tended to sum up both events under the concept of disaster medicine.

While the official side tried to interweave the treatment of civilian and military nuclear aftermath institutionally, it also subsumed different kinds of "emergencies" under the term "disaster." There was an attempt to normalize the unimaginable event of a nuclear explosion by attributing to it the features of a natural disaster, unexpected yet inescapable. The peace movement rejected this approximation rhetoric and resisted all strategies to propagate the bomb as part of normal life.

Conclusion

The civil defense debate was clearly more than purely a trade-off of technology. The intrinsic struggle to control the consequences of a tremendously powerful technology is all the more fascinating from today's perspective. The preparations for the case of emergency cannot be dismissed as little more than the chimera of overburdened politicians, nor can the reactions in the peace movement be seen as sheer hysteria. And the recommendations of civil defense experts for citizens to prepare an airtight basement in the early 1980s was no more the product of feeble thinking than the reduction of twenty or thirty thousand nuclear warheads in the United States and the USSR or Commonwealth of Independent States (CIS) since the early 1990s, when the remaining roughly ten thousand units still wielded enough destructive power to make the Earth uninhabitable. Proponents as well as opponents of civil defense faced a real danger at the beginning of the 1980s, a time of heightened tension during the period of the Second Cold War, and had to grapple with their respective perceptions and views of the world. The nuclear strike was considered the last resort in the Cold War. The dispute over its anticipated consequences mirrors the political culture and mentality of its time.

Claudia Kemper is a researcher in the "Postwar Era" research group at the Hamburg Institute for Social Research. She is currently working on a project on the medial and scientific representation of peaceable and civil societal order in the second half of 20th century. Her publications include "Medizin gegen den Kalten Krieg. Ärzte in der anti-atomaren Friedensbewegung der 1980er Jahre" (Göttingen, 2016); "'The Nuclear Arms Race is Psychological at its Roots': Physicians and their therapies for the Cold War," in: Matthew Grant and Benjamin Ziemann eds., *Understanding the imaginary war: Culture, Thought and Nuclear Conflict, 1945–90*, (Manchester, 2016) (forthcoming); and "Globale Bedrohung und nationale Interessen – die Nichtregierungsorganisation IPPNW," in: Alexander Gallus, Axel Schildt, and Detlef Siegfried eds., *Deutsche Zeitgeschichte – transnational*, (Göttingen, 2015), 45–63.

Notes

1. Bernd Lemke provides a general overview in "Zivile Kriegsvorbereitungen in unterschiedlichen Staats- und Gesellschaftssystemen: Der Luftschutz im 20. Jahrhundert. Ein Überblick," in *Luft- und Zivilschutz in Deutschland im 20. Jahrhundert*, Potsdamer Schriften zur Militärgeschichte, 5, ed. Bernd Lemke (Potsdam, 2007), 67–88.
2. A mastermind of the nuclear deterrent, Herman Kahn, *Thinking about the Unthinkable in the 1980s* (New York, 1984). For a historical assessment, see Sharon Ghamari-Tabrizi, *The Worlds of Herman Kahn: The Intuitive Science of Thermonuclear War* (Cambridge, MA, 2005) and Claus Pias, "'One-Man Think Tank': Herman Kahn, oder wie man das Undenkbare denkt," in *Zeitschrift für Ideengeschichte* 3 (2009): 5–16.
3. Marie Cronqvist, "Survivalism in the Welfare Cocoon: The Culture of Civil Defense in Cold War Sweden," in *Cold War Cultures: Perspectives on Eastern and Western European Societies*, ed. Annette Vowinckel, Marcus Payk, and Thomas M. Lindenberger (New York, 2012), 191–212; about the situation in the United States, see Dee Garrison, *Bracing for Armageddon: Why Civil Defense Never Worked* (New York, 2006).
4. Jochen Molitor, *Mit der Bombe überleben: Die Zivilschutzliteratur der Bundesrepublik 1960–1964* (Cologne, 2011).
5. Joseph Masco, "'Survival Is Your Business': Engineering Ruins and Affect in Nuclear America," in *Cultural Anthropology* 2 (2008): 361–98.
6. Guy Oakes, *The Imaginary War: Civil Defense and American Cold War Culture* (New York, 1994). There is a broad spectrum of approaches, reaching from the famous TV turtle Bert in the 1950s and 1960s, and the civil defense slogan "duck and cover," to the handbook of Ronald Cruit, *Survive the Coming Nuclear War: How to Do It* (New York, 1982).
7. Matthew Grant, *After the Bomb: Civil Defence and Nuclear War in Britain, 1945–68* (Basingstoke, 2010).
8. For a history of the Swiss civil defense system, see Silvia Berger, *Superpower Underground: Switzerland's Rise to Global Bunker Expertise in the Atomic Age*, in *Technology and Culture (2017)* (forthcoming).
9. A detailed description of the organization is given by Holger Beiersdorf and Jörg Welkisch in *Luftschutz, Zivilverteidigung und Zivilschutz in der DDR* (Schkeuditz, 2008).
10. Clemens Heitmann, "Schützen und Helfen? Luftschutz und Zivilverteidigung in der DDR 1955 bis 1989/90," Militärgeschichte der DDR, 12, (Berlin, 2006), 39. Also Wolfgang Jahn, "Der Luftschutz und die Zivilverteidigung (1955–1990)," in *Im Dienste der Partei: Handbuch der bewaffneten Organe der DDR* (Forschungen zur DDR-Gesellschaft), ed. Torsten Diedrich (Berlin, 1998), 551–76.
11. Heitmann, "Schützen und Helfen?" 49.
12. Ibid.
13. Ibid., 89.
14. Christian Th. Müller, "Im Bann der Bombe. Überlegungen zu Luftschutz und Zivilverteidigung in der DDR", in: *Angst im Kalten Krieg*, ed. Bernd Greiner, Christian

Th. Müller and, Dierk Walter (Hamburg, 2009), 94–122, 114. Also Thomas Klein, "Frieden und Gerechtigkeit!" in *Die Politisierung der Unabhängigen Friedensbewegung in Ost-Berlin während der 80er Jahre*, Zeithistorische Studien, 38, (Köln, 2007): 83.
15. Heitmann, "Schützen und Helfen?" 385.
16. The administration was in the hands of the Notgemeinschaft der Deutschen Wissenschaft, which is today's Deutschen Forschungsgemeinschaft. Until 2015 the Schutzkommission (Commission for Protection), founded in 1961, advised the Ministry of the Interior and the federal government as a voluntary organization in matters pertaining to medicine, technical and social sciences, and social aspects of civil protection. See for the history http://www.bbk.bund.de/DE/AufgabenundAusstattung/ForschungundEntwicklung/Schutzkommission/schutzkommission_node.html
17. Axel Schildt, "Die Atombombe und der Wiederaufbau: Luftschutz, Stadtplanungskonzepte und Wohnungsbau 1950–1956," in *1999: Zeitschrift für Sozialgeschichte des 20. und 21. Jahrhunderts* 2 (1987): 52–67.
18. Bundesamt für Bevölkerungsschutz und Katastrophenhilfe, ed., *50 Jahre Zivil- und Bevölkerungsschutz in Deutschland* (Bonn, 2008).
19. The federal office was dissolved only in 2000 and its responsibilities transferred to the Federal Office of Administration with the title Zentralstelle für Zivilschutz (Central Office for Civil Defense). When organizational shortcomings became apparent, a new federal office was founded in 2004, this time with the additional title of "civil protection and disaster management."
20. See e.g.: Bundesamt für Zivilschutz, ed., 25 Jahre Forschung für den Zivil- und Katastrophenschutz, Schutzkommission beim Bundesminister des Innern, (Bad Honnef, 1975); Bundesamt für Zivilschutz, ed., Forschungen für den Zivil- und Katastrophenschutz 1975–1985, (Bonn, 1986).
21. Carl Friedrich von Weizsäcker, "Falls es doch Krieg gibt … Ein Plädoyer für mehr Bevölkerungsschutz," in *Die Zeit*, 16 May 1980.
22. The declaration was conducted and published by several natural scientists and criticized plans to arm the German military with nuclear weapons. See Forschungsstelle für Zeitgeschichte in Hamburg, Institut für Friedensforschung und Sicherheitspolitik, Carl-Friedrich von Weizsäcker-Zentrum für Naturwissenschaft und Friedensforschung, ed., *"Kampf dem Atomtod!" Die Protestbewegung 1957/58 in zeithistorischer und gegenwärtiger Perspektive* (Munich and Hamburg, 2009).
23. Weizsäcker, "Falls es doch Krieg gibt … Ein Plädoyer für mehr Bevölkerungsschutz."
24. Carl Nedelmann, ed., *Zur Psychoanalyse der nuklearen Drohung: Vorträge einer Tagung der Deutschen Gesellschaft für Psychotherapie, Psychosomatik und Tiefenpsychologie* (Göttingen, 1985); Susanne Schregel, "Konjunktur der Angst: 'Politik der Subjektivität' und 'neue Friedensbewegung,' 1979–1983," in Greiner, Müller, and Walter, *Angst*, 495–520.
25. For the debate about the psychological impact on society see Claudia Kemper, "The Nuclear Arms Race is Psychological at its Roots: Physicians and their Therapies for the Cold War," in *Understanding the Imaginary War: Culture, Thought and Nuclear Conflict, 1945–90*, ed. Benjamin Ziemann and Matthew Grant (Manchester, 2016) (forthcoming).

26. Concerning the imaginary dimension of the Cold War, see David Eugster and Sibylle Marti, eds., *Das Imaginäre des Kalten Krieges: Beiträge zu einer Kulturgeschichte des Ost-West-Konfliktes in Europa* (Essen, 2015). See also Heinrich Hartmann and Jakob Vogel, eds., *Zukunftswissen: Prognosen in Wirtschaft, Politik und Gesellschaft seit 1900* (Frankfurt am Main, 2010).
27. Rudolf Baum, "Zivilverteidigung als Schwerpunkt liberaler Sicherheitspolitik," speech delivered by the Minister of the Interior at a convention of the Free Democratic Party on security in Münster on 28 April 1979. Quoted in Johannes Kurt Klein, *Realität Krise: Elemente der psychologischen Lage in Krisenzeiten der Bundesrepublik Deutschland*, Zivilschutz, 13, (Bonn-Bad Godesberg, 1979).
28. See, for example, Bundesverband für den Selbstschutz ed., *Selbstschutz: Ihr Beitrag zum Zivilschutz* (Cologne, 1984), 7.
29. Volker Grünewald and Georg Thiel, "Daten und Fakten," in *Zivilschutz: BZS-Schriftenreihe*, 20, ed. Bundesamt für Zivilschutz (Bonn, 1990), 17.
30. "NATO STANAG 2879: Principles of Medical Policy in the Management of a Mass Casualty Situation," with annotation in *Fleet Medicine Pocket Reference 1999*, ed. Surface Warfare Medicine Institute (San Diego, 1999). See also Hartmut Hanauske-Abel and Gustav Obermayr, "Zivilisten haben keine Chance," in *Die Zeit*, 18 September 1981.
31. Ulmer Ärzteinitiative, ed., *Tausend Grad Celsius: Das Ulm-Szenario für einen Atomkrieg* (Darmstadt, 1983), 42.
32. "Kein Platz im Bunker: Die Bayern haben nicht die geringste Chance," in *Die Zeit*, 16 May 1980.
33. Konradin Kreuzer, "Zivilschutz in einem Atomkrieg," in *Die Überlebenden werden die Toten beneiden: Ärzte warnen vor dem Atomkrieg*, documentation of the Medical Congress for the Prevention of Nuclear War in Hamburg on 19–20 September 1981 (Cologne, 1982), 65.
34. Müller, "Im Bann der Bombe," 110.
35. Ibid. 31.
36. See also Lawrence Badash, *A Nuclear Winter's Tale: Science and Politics in the 1980s* (Cambridge, MA, 2009).
37. Bundesamt für Zivilschutz, ed., *Zivilschutz-Forschung: Forschungen für den Zivil- und Katastrophenschutz 1975–1985* (Bonn, 1986).
38. "Notfalls mit Ohrfeigen behandeln," in *Der Spiegel* 49, 1 December 1980.
39. This conflict also resulted in the foundation of a German chapter of the International Physicians for the Prevention of Nuclear War (IPPNW).
40. In a textbook from 1980, the effects of nuclear, biological, and chemical weapons were listed under the heading "disaster medicine," next to "nuclear power accidents" and "massive car crashes." Ernst Rebentisch, "Katastrophenmedizin: Eine Aufgabe besonderer Art," in *Medizinische Klinik* 75, no. 19 (1980): 672–77. For an opposing view, see Kurt Sroka, "Katastrophenmedizin: Flankenschutz für die Aufrüstung," in *psychosozial* 6, no. 3 (1983): 57–74.

Chapter 18

Nuclear Doomsday Scenarios in Film, Literature, and Music

Philipp Baur

"Aren't they wonderful, these Americans? They give us Pershing and 'The Day After': the bomb and the instruction manual."[1] Ulrich Greiner, journalist for the German national weekly newspaper *Die Zeit,* perceived a certain historical irony as the upgrade of the NATO forces in early December 1983 coincided with the release of an American television film in German cinemas that projected the potential disaster onto the screen. *The Day After* (USA, 1983) depicts a nuclear exchange between the American and Soviet superpowers. Out of the blue, the atomic inferno strikes the inhabitants of a small university town, Lawrence, Kansas, and shows—a fictionalized version of—the worst-case scenario of the Cold War.

When the film was broadcast during primetime on the ABC television network in the United States on 20 November 1983, the American public was shocked. The broadcast became a national event and nearly a hundred million Americans, about half the entire adult population of the United States, are said to have seen the film.[2] US President Ronald Reagan was impressed by an exclusive preview at the White House. On 10 October, he noted in his diary, "It [*The Day After*] is powerfully done—all $7 mil. worth. It's very effective & left me greatly depressed."[3] It is unknown whether Chancellor Helmut Kohl was also shown *The Day After*. The day before the all-decisive parliamentary debate on 21 and 22 November 1983 the film was shown to some members of the Bundestag in Bonn and sparked political banter. Yet neither *The Day After,* nor the emphatic speeches delivered the next day changed the MPs' voting pattern. The parliamentary majority voted on 22 November for the atomic upgrade and, promptly on 26 November, the first Pershing II medium-range missiles were stationed on German territory.

In the course of the following weeks more than three million German citizens watched *The Day After* and the film evoked a wide response from the public and the media, albeit not always positive.[4] It marked the high point of cultural expression featuring the nuclear confrontation between the opposing political blocs, which took place across all kinds of media in the early 1980s. As a matter of fact, this was not a new phenomenon, as previous crises and phases of détente during the Cold War had also been accompanied by a nearly synchronous wave of cultural elaborations of confrontation.[5] An early highlight was the atomic mushroom cloud in the late 1940s, which became a positively associated symbol of American strength and power, while the actual nuclear threat was downplayed, for example, in the infamous *Duck and Cover* civil defense film. Later on, and certainly after the Cuban missile crisis in 1962, popular culture developed a decidedly more critical perspective. Stanley Kubrick's *Dr. Strangelove or: How I Learned to Stop Worrying and Love the Bomb* (USA, 1964) is paradigmatic of this change, and portrayed the logic of a "Mutual Assured Destruction" (MAD) as an insane and suicidal form of automatism.[6]

There was a decline in the number of cultural confrontations in the phase of global political détente during the late 1960s and early 1970s, but when issues surrounding the neutron bomb and the NATO Double-Track Decision renewed discord between the opposing blocs in the late 1970s, musicians, writers, and filmmakers were called yet again onto the scene. Significantly, West German popular culture at this point also took up the theme enthusiastically. Although the 1950s movement Kampf dem Atomtod (Fighting the atomic death) had received eloquent support by writers and intellectuals,[7] it took the rearmament debate of the 1980s to spark a widespread cultural response. This response comprised all parts of media including beat and pop music, new wave and punk rock, cinema and television films, youth and adult literature, comics, and some of the first video games. These cultural expressions can be read like a seismograph registering the threats of the Cold War in detail and reflecting prevailing fears as well as hopes. In many cases, artists deliberately meant to warn their audience and saw their work as a form of protest.[8]

"The Day After": The Nuclear Apocalypse in Film

In 1965, Susan Sontag criticized the imagination of popular culture as exemplified in science fiction disaster films by suggesting two possible effects: they distract from the very real dangers in this world and lull the audience with happy endings, or they help normalize real threats and serve the purpose of making people accustomed to it. In either case they therefore trivialize rather than scare people into action.[9] Nuclear doomsday scenarios of the 1980s, however, clearly distanced themselves from this criticism. Only in rare instances is the catastrophe prevented, as in the movie *War Games* (USA,

1983). In this scenario a youthful hacker inadvertently sets off the automatism of computerized warfare. The countdown to the launch of nuclear missiles can nevertheless be stopped at the last moment. Likewise in *Octopussy* (UK, 1983) James Bond succeeds in thwarting the plan of a renegade Soviet general and saves the world from a nuclear war provoked by a bomb attack on a US military base in West Germany (FRG).

The vast majority of nuclear disaster films of this period do not portray the survival of humankind. They develop the theme of the day after a nuclear attack, counteracting right from the start possible objections of belittling the situation. Director Nicholas Meyer commented in the epilogue to his film *The Day After* that "[t]he catastrophic events you have just witnessed are, in all likelihood, less severe than the destruction that would actually occur in the event of a full nuclear strike against the United States. It is hoped that the images of this film will inspire the nations of this earth, their peoples and leaders, to find the means to avert the fateful day."[10] His remark that *The Day After* understates, rather than exaggerates, is typical of the genre and so serves as a warning that every effort should be made to preclude the possibility of the film turning into reality.

Meyer's film contrasts the day before and the day after a nuclear attack on the United States. Aiming for maximum realism, it reflects popular scenarios of nuclear war and dismantles any hope of survival: all civil defense measures fail. Those who were not killed in the actual explosion soon show the symptoms of radiation sickness: hair loss, skin lesions, nausea. The nuclear explosion and its blinding flash of light are accompanied by an electromagnetic pulse that stalls all electronic equipment and vehicles. Simultaneously, dust raised into the atmosphere darkens the skies, the climate cools down, and a nuclear winter begins.[11] Claims to credibility and authenticity are attempted through the use of documentary material from the US Department of Defense, showing actual missile launches and how the US military might respond to a real catastrophe of this nature.[12]

The recourse to original footage can also be found in other examples at the time. The documentary *Atomic Café* (USA, 1982) received attention similar to that of *The Day After*. It consists of a collage of American propaganda films glorifying the atom, together with musical hits and uncritical media coverage from the 1940s and 1950s, and reveals the nuclear optimism of the postwar period. The early atomic culture thus became a reference point and a projection screen for the exploration of a new nuclear threat in the 1980s. *Atomic Café* could not be more topical noted a critic from the *New York Times* in 1982, who further identified a trend in playing down the dangers of nuclear arms up to the present day.[13] Drawing on the genre of "found-footage-films," *Atomic Café* self-critically reveals the role of the media in perpetuating images of nuclear doomsdays.[14]

A BBC docudrama *Threads* (UK, 1984) shows the effects of a nuclear strike on the city of Sheffield in north England. Much like *The Day After,* the film follows the fate of a few surviving people and depicts in detail the breakdown of social structures and how Britain is thrown back into a pre-industrial age. The content and style of *Threads* make reference to an earlier BBC production, *The War Game* (1965), in which Peter Watkins developed a plot about the effects of a nuclear war on British soil. It was first broadcast full-length in 1985 on British television—in the 1960s the film was considered too shocking for television and was shown only in a small number of cinemas.[15] Both films characterize state civil defense plans like "Protect and Survive" as unbelievable and unrealistic propaganda.

Raymond Briggs's graphic novel *When the Wind Blows* (UK, 1982) draws the same conclusion as its protagonists consult the "Protect and Survive" instruction booklet and call into question its effectiveness. The book echoes the sentiments of those, like the British Campaign for Nuclear Disarmament (CND), who considered existing civil defense plans to be a farce and called for resistance by publishing a counter-booklet "Protest and Survive."[16] The graphic novel *When the Wind Blows* served as model for a number of further works in various media. A radio play version released in 1986 was followed by an eponymous film adaptation that received prominent musical support from David Bowie, Roger Waters (Pink Floyd), and the group Genesis.

All these films were also intensively discussed in Germany and shown at events put on by the peace movement. A *Medienhandbuch Friedensarbeit* (Media guide for peacemaking) published in 1983 by the Youth Film Club of Cologne and the Verein für Friedenspädagogik Tübingen (Association for Teaching Peace) recommended showing them to protest against the arms upgrade.[17] An American CBS television documentary from 1981 also had an enormous impact. It appointed the town Hattenbach near Fulda in Hesse (Fulda Gap) as the setting for a World War III drama of the same name. Although the film *Hattenbach* was not shown on German television, peace activists from the eastern parts of Hesse managed to obtain copies and put it to use for educational purposes.[18] The commercial success of films like *The Day After* and the distribution of *Hattenbach* illustrate how films not only reflected the nuclear threat but also sometimes themselves became media events that could be enlisted as strong arguments against the arms upgrade.

The European Theater of War: Nuclear Apocalypse in Literature

When hostilities increased in the late 1970s, authors also contributed to public debate. This took in part the form of an "Appeal by the Writers in

Europe" for peace and disarmament, which was initiated by members of the West as well as East German writers' associations. Some four thousand Europeans put their name to the document.[19] Moreover, Günther Grass, Heinrich Böll, Bernt Engelmann, Walter Jens, and Rolf Hochhuth, among others, took part in the blockade of the US base at Mutlangen on 1 September 1983 and thus supported the protesters in several ways: the writers served equally as figures of integration within the peace movement and as enemy figure heads to arms upgrade proponents. In addition, the celebrities promised almost certain media attention for the blockade and generated an audience well beyond the local protest area, all over West Germany.[20]

A series of publications came out in the early 1980s in which a nuclear war scenario was played through to the end. On the one hand, these included nonfiction essays, which, despite empirical emphasis, also employed fictitious scenes to make the unimaginable imaginable. On the other hand, we find novels that aimed at a high degree of realism and credibility. The transition between established facts and literary fiction was fluent in both cases. Sir John Hackett, former NATO general and commander of the British Rhine Army, had as early as 1978 written a book of this genre, *The Third World War*. More than three million copies of Hackett's book were printed worldwide. The German translation of 1980 sold sixty thousand copies. Hackett analyzes the consequences of NATO's "flexible response" strategy in all military details and concludes that NATO is insufficiently prepared for a Soviet invasion of Germany. According to Hackett, anyone who wished to prevent a nuclear war would want to press for arms upgrades among the NATO partners.[21]

In contrast, the popular bestseller of the time, *The Fate of the Earth* by American journalist Jonathan Schell, was a clear call for disarmament. The book stayed for weeks at the top of the bestseller list of the German weekly news magazine *Der Spiegel*. Schell's work was the result of five years of research on the consequences of a nuclear war and based on numerous scientific predictions, such as the US Congress-commissioned study "The Effects of Nuclear War," and drawing upon research undertaken by Japanese scientists about the long-term environmental consequences of radioactivity. Schell describes in detail the effects and consequences of an atomic bomb explosion over New York. His gloomy end-of-the-world scenario was balanced with a suggestion for alternative ways to move forward. Humankind was at a crossroads of history and only disarmament promised a chance of survival.[22]

Anton-Andreas Guha took considerably more literary license when he was writing about a nuclear war in Europe in his novel *Ende: Tagebuch aus dem 3. Weltkrieg* (The end: A diary from the Third World War) (1982).[23] Guha, who had been editor of the social liberal *Frankfurter Rundschau* since

1967, specialized in the Americas and security policy issues. In the course of discussing the neutron bomb during the late 1970s, he became one of the most prolifically active advocates for disarmament. He published *Die Neutronenbombe oder die Perversion menschlichen Denkens* (The neutron bomb, or the perversion of human thought) in 1977 and, in 1980, *Der Tod in der Grauzone* (Death in the gray zone).[24] While these two books are works of journalism based on research dealing with armament, with *Ende* Guha turned to the literary form of the novel. He defended this move by arguing that the unthinkable had to be transformed into "sensual experience" to communicate and explain the determinism of nuclear armament. At the same time, he stressed that the book was not mere fantasy but employed realistic scenarios based on NATO's military strategy.[25]

In the early 1980s Matthias Horx, editor at the Frankfurter left-wing magazine *Pflasterstrand,* also chose the format of a diary for his novel *Es geht voran* (Things are moving ahead) (1982). In a transformed dystopian Germany, only a small number of people survived a nuclear catastrophe in bunkers and are thereafter eking out an existence, troubled by hunger, disease, and injuries. Unlike Guha, who works in the genre of documentary realism, Horx contrives the end of the world as a dark satire. The world may offer humans the potential for utter destruction but complete annihilation of the human race proves difficult.[26] Horx similarly exploits irony in his second novel about the case of emergency. In *Glückliche Reise* (Happy journey) (1983), the world recovers from nuclear war but quickly resumes a new arms race. This induces the main character, Jonathan, to detonate a leftover nuclear bomb with the purpose of preempting rearmament.[27] History repeating itself is a defining literary theme and asks if progress and rationalism can ultimately prevail.

Probably the best-known example of German fiction on the worst-case scenario is *Die letzten Kinder von Schewenborn* (The last children of Schewenborn) (1983) by Gudrun Pausewang, a prolific author of young-adult fiction renowned for her books dealing with topics like the Third World, Nazism, or environmental issues.[28] At the center of the action are children who accuse the adult generation of having failed to prevent an escalation of the Cold War: "They should have known what was being conjured up because they experienced a war themselves—even if *theirs* was comparatively harmless compared to our day of the bomb."[29] The setting and the imagery of the novel refer explicitly to the German experience of World War II, and serve to warn of a possible third world war. The drastic realism of the novel is supposed to be a warning call to readers and to provoke action. For this reason Pausewang was repeatedly accused of merely inciting fear and panic. She defended herself in an interview in 2003 by saying "I do not want to spread fear, I only wish to warn you."[30]

Figure 18.1. Cover of "Die letzten Kinder von Schewenborn" (The last children of Schewenborn) by Gudrun Pausewang, 1983 (Ravensburger Verlag)

Schewenborn leaves indeed little room for optimism. The book concludes with the birth of a child, usually a powerful metaphor for a new beginning and for hope. However, in this case the baby is severely impaired as a result of the nuclear fallout and unable to live. The novel cannot, strictly speaking, be classified as apocalyptic. In the original, biblical sense of the word, *apocalypse* denotes "unveiling" or "revelation" and announces not only the end of the world but also the beginning of a new divine age. Pausewang's novel does not grant such salvation to the protagonists—World War III ushers in the actual end of humanity.[31]

At the same time, the book lends itself to a dialectal reading. Although any possibility of survival after a nuclear war is clearly rejected, the utopia of a better world seems always implicitly present. Pausewang herself even urges her readers to work in real life for peace. "*Schewenborn* is not fiction" she writes in the afterword to the 1984 edition. Her own town, Schlitz, near Fulda, had provided the template. In this region the inhabitants had managed to prevent the construction of a US Army military training ground and had thus made a small contribution in the struggle against the arms race.[32] Pausewang's novel illustrates three exemplary characteristics of the movement against nuclear arms: first, a close association between popular culture and political protest; second, the importance of local protest directed against a global threat, as reflected also in popular culture;[33] and third, the positive connotation of fear, which disarmament advocates regarded not as crippling, but rather as a stimulant to initiate action. *Mut zur Angst* (The courage to express fear) became a programmatic slogan of the peace movement.[34]

Nuclear Apocalypse and the Desire for Peace as Expressed in Music

At the end of May 1983, the weekly teen magazine *Bravo* staged a reconciliation of the publicly conducted row between two major stars of the German music scene: Udo Lindenberg and Peter Maffay. At issue was supposedly nothing less than artistic credibility and political views on preserving peace. Both singers rose to prominence during the 1970s selling hundreds of thousands of albums of rock music in German but were not associated with any social or protest movement of the time. However, this would change during the nuclear crisis. In 1981, Udo Lindenberg teamed up with ten-year-old Pascal Kravetz, son of a pianist in his band Panic Orchestra, to record a song "Why Are There Wars?" Lindenberg was a founding member of the initiative Artists for Peace, which brought together an international alliance of artists opposing the arms upgrade. Among them were German artists like

Eva Mattes, Joseph Beuys, Marius Müller-Westernhagen, Ulla Meinecke, as well as political singer-songwriters like Franz Josef Degenhardt, Hannes Wader, and Konstantin Wecker; the Dutch band bots; Danish singer Gitte Hænning; Swedish actress Bibi Andersson; Austrian artists André Heller and Erika Pluhar; Greek musicians Mikis Theodorakis and Maria Farantouri; and American musicians and civil rights activists Harry Belafonte and Joan Baez. They regarded their efforts as a collective plea for peace and against the arms upgrade, cutting across borders. Artists for Peace equally believed that they would reach a wide audience from all levels of society and stir them into action using their art as a peaceful means of protest.[35]

German rock musician Peter Maffay had up to this point refrained from explicit political statements. Because of this, fellow musician Udo Lindenberg called him a "Pocket-Rocker who avoided taking a clear political stance with his 'pseudo-songs.'" Maffay responded by saying that he definitely experienced the same fear and a sense of powerlessness as Lindenberg.[36] In 1982 he tried to express the prevailing apocalyptic mood in his song "Ice Age": "When oceans disappear and the Earth breaks up / Then no warhead will find a target any longer / Is this merely utopian?—Red phone, if you fail."[37] Not until 1983, shortly before an interview with *Bravo*, did Maffay finally agree to participate in an event organized by Artists for Peace at the Berlin outdoor venue Waldbühne and thus took a political stand.

The two musicians may in essence have been addressing personal resentments and rivalries rather than the issues of political protest and peace. The conflict nevertheless makes clear that the debate about the arms upgrade became an inevitable topic for pop musicians to grapple with and shows how teen magazines like *Bravo* turned into a platform for discussing armament policies. Equally noteworthy is that this theme was taken up by the entire spectrum of pop music, from commercially minded musicians who caught the zeitgeist and jumped on the band wagon, right up to artists who perceived themselves as lending a critical voice to protests.[38]

Bearing this in mind, we can begin to understand Nicole's success with "A Little Peace," a perfect model of the German *Schlager* genre—popular and politically unsuspicious music, often consisting of light, sentimental, and entertaining tunes with a catchy melody that would classify as easy listening.[39] "A Little Peace" won the Eurovision Song Contest in Harrogate, UK, on 24 April 1982, was translated into seven languages, and it sold over five million copies. Tellingly, Nicole denied any political reference to the Cold War. About three weeks after her success in England, she commented in an interview with the magazine *Bravo*, "My song is not about politics, but about personal peace." When she was asked whether she could imagine participating

Figure 18.2. Poster "Künstler für den Frieden" (Artists for Peace) major event in support of the Appeal of Krefeld, 1982 (BArch Plak 006-030-003)

in a peace rally she replied, "No, because I'm not interested in big politics. I am impressed by those young people who participate in demonstrations, but I do not think that they can make a difference in this world."[40] Nicole's example illustrates how the music industry instrumentalized the idea of a general desire for peace and molded it for profitable mass consumption. Producers Ralph Siegel and Bernd Meinunger had written the music and lyrics exclusively for her and their strategy of making the song conform to the theme of peace (whether on a general or personal level) did not fall short of their commercial expectations.[41]

Apart from the mainstream Eurovision song contest genre, a number of successful pop songs reflected nuclear doomsday scenarios. The disco band Boney M. produced by Frank Farian released "We Kill the World (Do not Kill the World)" in 1981 and complained about not only the nuclear threat and the lack of peace in the world but also the destruction of the environment. The lyrics feature a dialogue between adult and children's voices as a defining, characteristic style: the matter-of-fact line "we kill the world" sung by lead singer Marcia Barrett is responded to by a plea "do not kill the world" sung by a children's choir, which emotionally accentuates a desire for a better world. A similar perspective from the victim's point of view is evoked in "Forever Young" (1984) by the band Alphaville. The lyrics commence with an emotionally detached chant of dancing youths: "Heaven can wait we're only watching the skies / Hoping for the best but expecting the worst / Are you going to drop the bomb or not?" In view of the fact that the world could end at any moment, dreams of eternal youth appeared obsolete. Alphaville translated this disillusioned knowledge into music. The Italo disco group Righeira took this one step further. In "Vamos a la Playa" (1983), they answered fatalism about the nuclear threat with irony as a way out. Only those who listen carefully to the song's lyrics understand that it is not an invitation to a boisterous beach party but to a dance of death. Once the cities had been contaminated by radiation, the beach offered the only refuge.

Nena's hit "99 Luftballons" (1983) is probably the best-known and most successful international example that derives from a nuclear destruction scenario. The German language original version reached number two on the American Billboard charts and introduced an international mainstream pop audience to a new style of German pop music labeled *Neue Deutsche Welle* (New German Wave)—notwithstanding the fact that Nena actually represented the commercial climax and hence the end of a formerly underground punk rock and new wave music movement.[42] Mistaking ninety-nine balloons as a threat, bellicose politicians respond with fighter jets and thus provoke a nuclear war. Carlo Karges, guitarist and lyricist of the song, remarked in an interview that the band intended less of a political statement but rather sought to pinpoint a paranoid mood in society. He said, "A tremendous fear of each other provokes us into unnecessary cruelty when we need to deal with each other. Whoever strikes first, holds the better cards. That is dangerous."[43] Yet the commercial success of the debut album *Nena* may be better explained by its catchy melodies, its professional production, and a marketing approach that promoted the fresh image of the singer Nena. The serious voice of "99 balloons" as an antiwar song was lost and never played a defining role in Nena's artistic career.

In stark contrast a number of musicians decidedly expressed critical views on the arms upgrade and regarded themselves as supporters of the peace movement. The Dutch band bots, for example, in 1979 wrote the song "The Soft Water" in which it pleaded for peaceful coexistence: "Europe experienced twice a war / a third one will be the last / don't give up, don't give in / soft water hollows stone."[44] The song became a hit in the peace movement and was, for instance, performed on 11 September 1982 at the festival of Artists for Peace in Bochum. At this event, performance artist Joseph Beuys delivered the song "Sonne statt Reagan" (Sun instead of Reagan), making a pun on the president's name and the German word for rain, *Regen*. This became one of the protest movements' most catchy lines.[45] Judging by the attendance, the event was a great success, although the hoped-for positive press response did not materialize—instead the reviews were largely critical or negative. For example, the magazine *Stern* asked skeptically "Can songs beat missiles?"[46]

Conclusion

The impressive range of nuclear disaster scenarios demonstrate that art and culture reflected areas of conflict about the nuclear crisis in detail and did indeed assume a function of amplification. The popularity of such doomsday scenarios in fiction also shows that they were not merely symptoms of a period in crisis but formed part of a social process of digestion. This should, however, not obscure the fact that disasters constituted a most welcome motive for the entertainment industry, especially in pop music, where a strategic market orientation cannot be dismissed out of hand. A clear-cut demarcation between consumption and protest is therefore difficult to detect, and the relationship between pop music and politics in the early 1980s, a time when society and media were experiencing rapid change, remains largely unexplored.

Philipp Baur studied at the University of Augsburg (Germany) and the University of Georgia (USA) and has a MA in modern history, English and German literature, and language studies. He is currently completing his doctoral dissertation on the nuclear threat in the popular culture of the 1980s and works as a coordinator for Erasmus+ capacity building projects in the International Office of Uppsala University (Sweden).

Notes

1. Ulrich Greiner, "Apokalypse Now: Über den amerikanischen Film 'The Day After' und neuere apokalyptische Romane," *Die Zeit*, 2 December 1983.
2. Jerome F. Shapiro, *Atomic Bomb Cinema: The Apocalyptic Imagination on Film* (New York, 2001), 186–91.
3. Ronald Reagan, *The Reagan Diaries*, ed. Douglas Brinkley (New York, 2007), 186.
4. Gemeinschaftswerk der Evangelischen Publizistik e.V., ed., *The Atomic Cinema: Fiktion und Wirklichkeit nuklearer Bedrohung*, Arnoldshainer Filmgespräche (Frankfurt am Main, 1984), 1:113; reviews in public media: Velska von Roques, "Ich will tot sein, wenn das passiert," *Der Spiegel*, 28 November 1983; Thomas Kielinger, "Der Tag danach: Eine Film-Idee wird zum Spektakel des Schreckens," *Die Welt*, 22 November, 1983; Sabina Lietzmann, "Die inszenierte Katastrophe," *Frankfurter Allgemeine Zeitung* (henceforth *FAZ*), 24 November 1983.
5. The periods are described by Ulrich Krökel, "'Bombe und Kultur': Künstlerische Reflexionen über die Atombombe von Hiroshima bis Černobyl," in *Das nukleare Jahrhundert: Eine Zwischenbilanz*, ed. Michael Salewski (Stuttgart, 1998), 188–216; Scott C. Zeman and Michael A. Admundson, eds., *Atomic Culture: How We Learned to Stop Worrying and Love the Bomb* (Boulder, CO, 2004); Philipp Gassert, "Popularität der Apokalypse: Zur Nuklearangst seit 1945," *Aus Politik und Zeitgeschichte* 46 (2011): 48–54; Philipp Baur, "Atomkrieg/Atomkraft," in *Metzler Lexikon Moderne Mythen*, ed. Stephanie Wodianka and Juliane Ebert (Stuttgart, 2014), 28–33.
6. Paul Boyer, *By the Bomb's Early Light: American Thought and Culture at the Dawn of the Atomic Age* (Chapel Hill, NC, 1985); Ilona Stölken-Fitschen, *Atombombe und Geistesgeschichte: Eine Studie der fünfziger Jahre aus deutscher Sicht* (Baden-Baden, 1995); Gerhard Paul, "Mushroom Clouds: Bilder des atomaren Holocausts," in *Das Jahrhundert der Bilder*, vol. 1: 1900 bis 1949, ed. Gerhard Paul (Göttingen, 2009), 722–29.
7. Raimund Kurscheid, *Kampf dem Atomtod: Schriftsteller im Kampf gegen eine deutsche Atombewaffnung* (Cologne, 1981).
8. A discussion of theoretical considerations on media, art, and protest is provided by T. V. Reed, *The Art of Protest: Culture and Activism from the Civil Rights Movement to the Streets of Seattle* (Minneapolis, MN, 2005).
9. Susan Sontag, "The Imagination of Disaster," *Commentary*, October (1965).
10. *The Day After*, directed by Nicholas Meyer, *ABC* 1983, DVD: Euro Video 2007.
11. The phenomenon "nuclear winter" is also discussed in the contribution by Claudia Kemper in this volume.
12. Shapiro, *Atomic Bomb*, 186–92.
13. Vincent Canby, "The Atomic Café: Documentary on Views about Atom Bomb," *New York Times*, 17 March 1982.

14. Sascha Simons, "Das Unvermeidliche vermeiden: Jayne Loaders, Kevin und Pierce Raffertys *The Atomic Café* (1982)," in *Das Undenkbare filmen: Atomkrieg im Kino*, ed. Tobias Nanz and Johannes Pause (Bielefeld, 2013), 25–52.
15. James Chapman, "The BBC and the Censorship of *The War Game* (1965)," *Journal of Contemporary History* 41, no. 1 (2006): 75–94.
16. Lawrence Wittner, *Confronting the Bomb: A Short History of the World Nuclear Disarmament Movement* (Stanford, CA, 2009), 118.
17. Jugendfilmclub Köln e.V. and Verein für Friedenspädagogik Tübingen, ed., *Medienhandbuch Friedensarbeit: Filme, Videos, Dias* (Cologne, 1983).
18. Peter Krahulec, "Der Hattenbach-Film: Dokument der Bedrohung: Instrument der Friedensbewegung," in *Fulda Gap* (brochure), ed. Friedensinitiative Osthessen, 98–101. See also Susanne Schregel, *Der Atomkrieg vor der Wohnungstür: Eine Politikgeschichte der neuen Friedensbewegung in der Bundesrepublik, 1970–1985* (Frankfurt am Main and New York, 2011), 164–77.
19. Anne Marie Stokes, *A Chink in the Wall: German Writers and Literature in the INF-Debate of the Eighties* (Bern, 1995), 39–41; "Appell der Schriftsteller Europas," in *Mut zur Angst: Schriftsteller für den Frieden*, ed. Ingrid Krüger (Darmstadt, 1982), 20.
20. Fabio Crivellari, "Blockade: Friedensbewegung zwischen Melancholie und Ironie," in *Das Jahrhundert der Bilder*, ed. Gerhard Paul (Göttingen, 2008), 2:482–89.
21. John Hackett, *The Third World War: A Future History* (London, 1978); see also Andy Hahnemann, "Keiner kommt davon: Der Dritte Weltkrieg in der deutschen Literatur der 50er Jahre," in *Keiner Kommt davon: Zeitgeschichte in der Literatur nach 1945*, ed. Erhard Schütz and Wolfgang Hardtwig (Göttingen, 2008), 151–65.
22. Jonathan Schell, *The Fate of the Earth* (New York, 1982), 47–54.
23. Anton-Andreas Guha, *Ende: Tagebuch aus dem 3. Weltkrieg* (Königstein, 1983).
24. Anton-Andreas Guha, *Die Neutronenbombe oder die Perversion menschlichen Denkens* (Frankfurt am Main, 1977); Anton-Andreas Guha, *Tod in der Grauzone: Ist Europa noch zu verteidigen?* (Frankfurt am Main, 1980).
25. Regine Herrmann, "Das menschliche Denken überfordert: Anton Andreas Guhas Buch 'Ende' im Mittelpunkt einer Diskussion," *Frankfurter Rundschau*, 21 October 1983. See also Hans Krah, *Weltuntergangsszenarien und Zukunftsentwürfe: Narrationen vom Ende in Literatur und Film 1945–1990* (Kiel, 2004), 314–21.
26. Matthias Horx, *Es geht voran: Ein Ernstfall-Roman* (Berlin, 1982); a review: "Heitere Apokalypse," *Der Spiegel*, 3 May 1982.
27. Matthias Horx, *Glückliche Reise: Roman zwischen den Zeiten* (Berlin, 1983).
28. Susan Tebbutt, *Gudrun Pausewang in Context: Socially Critical "Jugendliteratur": Gudrun Pausewang and the Search for Utopia* (Frankfurt am Main, 1994).
29. Gudrun Pausewang, *Die letzten Kinder von Schewenborn* (Ravensburg, 1983), 186.
30. Susanne Gaschke, "Erziehungsmaßnahme: Die Lehrerin der Angst," *Die Zeit*, 31 December 2003.
31. Arthur Herman, *Propheten des Niedergangs: Der Endzeitmythos im westlichen Denken* (Berlin, 1998).
32. Pausewang deals with the success of protests in another novel: *Etwas lässt sich doch bewirken* (Ravensburg, 1984). In "The Cloud" (1987), she describes the potential fallout of a nuclear reactor accident in Germany following the disaster at Chernobyl.

33. Schregel, *Atomkrieg*, 137–84.
34. Ingrid Krüger, *Mut zur Angst: Schriftsteller für den Frieden* (Darmstadt, 1982); Susanne Schregel, "Konjunktur der Angst: 'Politik der Subjektivität' und neue Friedensbewegung, 1979–1983," in *Angst im Kalten Krieg*, ed. Bernd Greiner, Christian Müller, and Dierk Walter (Hamburg, 2009), 495–520.
35. Martin Klimke and Laura Stapane, "From Artists for Peace to the Green Caterpillar: Cultural Activism and Electoral Politics in 1980s West Germany," in *Accidental Armageddons: The Nuclear Crisis and the Culture of the Cold War in the 1980s*, ed. Eckart Conze, Martin Klimke, and Jeremy Varon (New York, forthcoming).
36. "Maffay wies Udo vor die Tür!" *Bravo*, 2 June 1983.
37. Peter Maffay, *Live '82*, Sony Music 1993.
38. For discussions of pop and politics as a domain for social science research, see Dietrich Helms, "Pop Star Wars," *Aus Politik und Zeitgeschichte* 11 (2005), 28–34; Benjamin Ziemann, "A Quantum of Solace? European Peace Movements during the Cold War and Their Elective Affinities," *Archiv für Sozialgeschichte* 49 (2009): 351–89; Sebastian Peters, *Ein Lied mehr zur Lage der Nation: Politische Inhalte in deutschsprachigen Popsongs* (Berlin, 2010); Dietmar Schiller, ed., *A Change Is Gonna Come: Popmusik und Politik: Empirische Beiträge zu einer politikwissenschaftlichen Popmusikforschung* (Münster, 2012); Detlef Siegfried, "Pop und Politik," in *Popgeschichte: Band 1: Konzepte und Methoden*, ed. Alexa Geisthövel and Bodo Mrozek (Bielefeld, 2014), 33–56.
39. For an explanation of the German *Schlager* genre, see Edward Larkey, "Postwar German Popular Music: Americanization, the Cold War, and the Post-Nazi Heimat," in *Music and German National Identity*, ed. Celia Applegate and Pamela Maxine Potter (Chicago, 2002), 234–50.
40. Nicole, "Politik interessiert mich nicht," *Bravo*, 19 May 1982.
41. Philipp Gassert, "Die Vermarktung des Zeitgeistes: Nicoles Ein bißchen Frieden (1982) als akustisches und visuelles Dokument," *Zeithistorische Forschungen/Studies in Contemporary History* 9 (2012), http://www.zeithistorische-forschungen.de/16126041-Gassert-1-2012.
42. Barbara Hornberger, *Geschichte wird gemacht: Die Neue Deutsche Welle: Eine Epoche deutscher Popmusik* (Würzburg, 2011), 304–16.
43. "99 Luftballons und das Chaos der Gefühle," *Der Spiegel*, 26 March 1984, http://magazin.spiegel.de/EpubDelivery/spiegel/pdf/13510424.
44. Bots, *Entrüstung*, EMI Electrola, 1981.
45. Joseph Beuys, "Sonne Statt Reagan: Pop statt Böller," *Fluter*, 21 September 2007.
46. "Können Schlager Raketen schlagen?" *Stern*, 9 September 1982.

Select Bibliography

Kroekel and Stoelken-Fitschen provide a cursory introduction on the subject in their respective essays. Up to now authors in the United States have primarily taken up the topic of cultural history in the nuclear age. Jerome Shapiro and Zeman and Admundson offer good insights. Vowinckel, Payk, and Lindenberger provide European perspectives. Thorough studies on Germany have focused on the early postwar period. These include

Kurscheid and Stoelken-Fitschen. From a perspective of literary studies, Krah covers a wide field. Stokes published on the inner German collaboration of writers during the 1980s, and Schregel analyzed fictional nuclear war scenarios. Klimke, Conze, and Varon supply a series of case studies and therefore offer an overview about the role of the nuclear crisis in the cultural history of the 1970s and 1980s.

Conze, Eckart, Martin Klimke, and Jeremy Varon, eds. *Accidental Armageddons: The Nuclear Crisis and the Culture of the Cold War in the 1980s.* New York, forthcoming.

Krökel, Ulrich. "'Bombe und Kultur': Künstlerische Reflexionen über die Atombombe von Hiroshima bis Černobyl." In *Das nukleare Jahrhundert: Eine Zwischenbilanz,* ed. Michael Salewski, 188–216. Stuttgart, 1998.

Krah, Hans. *Weltuntergangsszenarien und Zukunftsentwürfe: Narrationen vom Ende in Literatur und Film 1945–1990.* Kiel, 2004.

Kurscheid, Raimund. *Kampf dem Atomtod: Schriftsteller im Kampf gegen eine deutsche Atombewaffnung.* Cologne, 1981.

Shapiro, Jerome. *Atomic Bomb Cinema: The Apocalyptic Imagination on Film.* London, 2002.

Stölken-Fitschen, Ilona. *Atombombe und Geistesgeschichte: Eine Studie der fünfziger Jahre aus deutscher Sicht.* Baden-Baden, 1995.

———. "Bombe und Kultur." In *Das Zeitalter der Bombe: Die Geschichte der atomaren Bedrohung von Hiroshima bis heute,* ed. Michael Salewski, 258–81.Munich, 1995.

Stokes, Anne Marie. *A Chink in the Wall: German Writers and Literature in the INF-Debate of the Eighties.* Bern, 1995.

Vowinckel, Annette, Marcus M. Mayk, and Thomas Lindenberger, eds. *Cold War Cultures: Perspektives on Eastern and Western European Societies.* New York, 2012.

Zeman, Scott C., and Michael A. Admundson, eds., *Atomic Culture: How We Learned to Stop Worrying and Love the Bomb.* Boulder, CO, 2004.

Chapter 19

A Triumph of Disarmament? The 1980s and the International Political System
Florian Pressler

"Disarmament triumphant"—Lawrence Wittner summarizes the period of nuclear disarmament between 1985 and 1992 with these words and attributes the success of disarmament talks to the persistent efforts of the European and US protest movements against nuclear weapons.[1] In his eyes, it was the resistance from below that persuaded the governments in Washington and Moscow into launching the far-reaching policy initiatives that marked those years: the summit meeting between US President Ronald Reagan and Soviet General Secretary Mikhail Gorbachev in 1986 in Reykjavík and the signing of the INF Treaty (Intermediate-range Nuclear Forces) on 8 December 1987 committed both superpowers to the total elimination of their European medium-range missiles; while the START Treaty (Strategic Arms Reduction Treaty) on 31 July 1991 provided for a reduction of the strategic nuclear arsenal.

The significance of the protest movement, which certainly succeeded in pressuring the Reagan administration and the governments of the European members of NATO, cannot be disputed. However, taken on its own, it fails to explain the disarmament successes of the late 1980s. It was only in the context of a changing Soviet position that concrete disarmament steps became possible during the course of the second half of the 1980s: Mikhail Gorbachev's "new thinking"—largely independent of protests—targeted the ending of the East-West confrontation in order to create leverage to carry out internal reforms within the USSR. As proxy wars in Central America, Africa, and Afghanistan were abating, this facilitated conditions for a rapprochement between the superpowers. Economic problems in the Soviet Union and the growing national debt in the United States made the political elite increasingly aware of the costs of the arms race. The collapse of the Eastern bloc and the end of the Cold War ushered in the end of the scenario of mutual threats, which had served to justify the proliferation of nuclear arms in the West. In other words, it had been not only the various protest movements that curtailed the arms race but also a fundamental shift in the international political system. Ultimately both factors jointly contributed to make disarmament possible.

Phases of Confrontation

In the middle of the decade, all signs pointed to confrontation. For Ronald Reagan in 1983, the Soviet Union still represented an "Evil Empire," which precluded any possibility of a peaceful settlement.[2] Driven by deep anticommunist convictions and a missionary zeal, Reagan tried to not only contain but also actively repel the USSR.[3] He avoided any direct confrontation, but at the periphery of the two opposing blocs he financed proxy wars to bring down Soviet-influenced regimes. In Afghanistan, he supported anticommunist mujahedeen against the Moscow-backed government in Kabul. In Central America, he financed the struggle of the Contra rebels against the leftist Sandinista regime in Nicaragua while strengthening right-wing governments in El Salvador and Guatemala against Marxist guerrillas. The United States even intervened directly on the tiny Caribbean island of Grenada in 1983 to prevent a further shift toward the left.

The negotiations on nuclear arms limitation were frozen solid. A fair number of posts in the new US administration had been filled by members of the Committee on the Present Danger, a lobby group opposed to the arms control agreements made during Jimmy Carter's presidency.[4] Reagan described the 1979 SALT II treaty (Strategic Arms Limitation Treaty) that had already been signed by Jimmy Carter and Leonid Brezhnev as "fatally flawed" and refused to ratify it.[5] Instead, he proposed negotiations for a treaty that would stipulate not only limits to nuclear long-range weapons, but also lead to an actual reduction of these weapons (START). Above all it demanded from the Soviet Union a reduction of its numerical superiority in long-range nuclear forces and thus had little chance of success. Reagan also proposed a zero solution for medium-range nuclear weapons in 1981, in other words, no arms upgrade in exchange for the withdrawal of all Soviet medium-range missiles from Europe. This was more a public relations ploy than a serious disarmament initiative. The proposal was presented in the sound knowledge that it would not be acceptable to the Soviet Union and thus aimed for a propaganda coup when it was rejected by Moscow.[6] In fact, the Soviet Union was asked to scrap its existing missiles in return for a promise that the United States would not deploy new missiles. Negotiations on the elimination of intermediate-range missiles in Europe and a limitation or disarmament of ICBMs (Intercontinental Ballistic Missiles) were accordingly unsuccessful. Moscow withdrew from START and INF negotiations when the Parliament of the FRG decided in 1983 to implement the deployment of American medium-range missiles.[7] As disarmament efforts came to naught, nuclear arms production increased. During Ronald Reagan's presidency the United States deployed medium-range missiles in Europe, resumed the development of the neutron bomb and the strategic B1 bomber as well as a new generation of land-based intercontinental ballistic missiles (MX missiles), and put new Trident submarines with nuclear weapons in service. In 1985 the budget of the Pentagon was nearly twice as high as it had been in 1980.[8]

Even during this phase of confrontation, there were small steps toward nuclear détente. For instance, the Soviet government vowed in June 1982 that it would never command a first strike with nuclear weapons, and in August 1983 the Kremlin announced a unilateral test ban on antisatellite weapons. Although the United States never ratified the SALT II Treaty, it heeded by and large the limits on nuclear delivery systems outlined in the proposal. However, it should be pointed out that these gestures exerted no lasting impact in the general climate of confrontation that prevailed during the first half of the 1980s.

Gorbachev and the Inception of a Rapprochement

A real change in thinking on all matters related to nuclear arms occurred only in 1985 when transnational protests against nuclear arms had already peaked. The impetus for rethinking the arms race came from a country that had seen few protests and remained untouched by the efforts of the peace movement: the Soviet Union.

A series of superannuated leaders had determined the fate of the Soviet Union during the first half of the 1980s. After Leonid Brezhnev's death in November 1982, Yuri Andropov (who died in February 1984), and then Konstantin Chernenko (who died in March 1985) were elected to head the CPSU. It may be seen as a fateful turning point in the history of the Cold War when Mikhail Gorbachev (then only fifty-four years old) followed these gerontocrats.[9]

Gorbachev's reform program is usually characterized by the terms *glasnost* (a policy of transparency and openness) and *perestroika* (a generic term for the economic and political restructuring of the USSR). Far less known is his concept of "new thinking," which outlined the components of the Soviet reforms in foreign policy.[10] Gorbachev had understood that only less hostile relations between the superpowers would create the conditions for implementing his economic and domestic political programs. The financial burden of arms production and global power projections had to be reduced if the USSR were to overcome its internal petrification and return to a sound economic base. Arms control agreements were an essential step, since the Soviet military would hardly accept unilateral nuclear disarmament.

This prompted Gorbachev immediately to shift course toward nuclear détente. As early as 7 April 1985, in an interview in *Pravda*, he declared a halt to the deployment of new SS-20 missiles in Europe until November of the same year and a complete end to the deployment of new missiles, provided that the United States did not install additional Pershing II and cruise missiles. A unilateral Soviet moratorium on nuclear tests followed in July. Washington initially regarded these steps as a tactical maneuver that sought to maintain an alleged Soviet nuclear superiority.

Ronald Reagan's Offer for Dialogue

Yet starting in the mid-1980s the saber rattling on the side of the Americans began to decrease. In a speech on US-Soviet relations delivered on 16 January 1984, Reagan hit a relatively conciliatory note and offered to enter into a dialogue. He explained that US policy toward the Soviet Union must not be reduced to deterrence alone and offered an expanded vision:

> We must and will engage the Soviets in a dialog as serious and constructive as possible—a dialog that will serve to promote peace in the troubled regions of the world, reduce the level of arms, and build a constructive working relationship ... As I've said before, my dream is to see the day when nuclear weapons will be banished from the face of the Earth.[11]

Reagan's friendly tone was somewhat surprising. His conciliatory wording might have been induced by the upcoming US presidential election. The president feared the public image promoted by the protest movements of himself as an implacable communist hater and militarist, in contrast to the more open-minded persona of his opponent, Walter Mondale, who supported the nuclear freeze movement.[12] Thus Reagan was given to displaying himself as a moderate and balanced candidate. However, events took their own turn and contributed to Reagan's about-face. One of these was "Able Archer 83," a NATO command staff exercise that simulated a nuclear war and came close to creating an actual threat of war, given that Soviet generals believed that preparations for a first strike by the West were actually under way. Another was the tragedy of Korean Airline flight 007 with 269 people on board, which was shot down by Soviet air defenses that mistook the passenger aircraft for a spy plane when it deviated from its usual route.[13]

Geneva 1985: A Summit between Reagan and Gorbachev

The election of Gorbachev as General Secretary of the Soviet Communist Party in early 1985 turned Reagan's offer for dialogue into a real possibility. Mutual distrust and numerous deaths among the Soviet leadership had up to this point prevented a direct meeting at the top level in the early 1980s. Now preparations for a summit were initiated. At this first meeting between Gorbachev and Reagan in Geneva on 19–21 November 1985, arms control was high on the agenda. Gorbachev hoped to end the economically ruinous arms race strangling his country. The US president for his part had also traveled to the meeting with a genuine desire to negotiate arms controls. Shortly before, in July 1985, the US Congress had yielded to public pressure and slashed Reagan's MX missile program from an intended two hundred down to fifty missiles. This threatened to increase further the already existing supremacy of the Soviet Union in "heavy" ICBMs. To Reagan, arms limitation now also appeared to become an attractive option. An additional complication arose in the implementation of the NATO Double-Track Decision, which had led to considerable tensions within the Atlantic alliance as European governments showed lukewarm reactions to the plan due to its hostile reception among their citizens. The Belgian government refused to deploy the originally agreed upon number of cruise missiles as it had failed to secure a majority in parliament.[14] Reagan was therefore rather anxious to defuse the problems with the European medium-range missiles in his talks with Gorbachev, if only to stabilize the NATO alliance.

The reason for the ultimate failure of the summit had been Reagan's other ambitious missile-defense agenda: the SDI (Strategic Defense Initiative).[15] There are strong indications that Reagan not only rhetorically advocated the complete abolition of all nuclear missiles, which would eventually be rendered useless by SDI, but over time concluded that it would actually be a good idea.[16] However, Reagan demanded that the USSR take the first steps toward disarmament and decided that complete disarmament was possible only once a missile defense shield against surprise attacks secured the United States. Irrespective of the findings of a commission sponsored by the president, which reported in 1983 that such a defense system was hardly feasible technically and financially, Reagan staunchly backed it against all opposition.[17] This in-

Figure 19.1. US President Ronald Reagan and Soviet General Secretary of the CPSU Mikhail Gorbachev during their summit on 19–20 November 1985 in Geneva, Switzerland (Ronald Reagan Presidential Library, Ventura, CA)

transigence increasingly alarmed the Kremlin, because although in itself a defensive weapon system, the shield would have put the United States in a position to wage a nuclear first strike and to block the Soviet Union's retaliation.[18] SDI therefore clearly violated, in Russian opinion, the treaty on the limitation of antimissile systems from 1971 (Anti-Ballistic Missile [ABM] Treaty), which had been intended precisely to secure such a second-strike capability by ensuring that a first strike would prove suicidal and therefore unthinkable. As the construction of its own missile shield was just as far beyond the Soviet financial means as a compensation for SDI by increasing the Soviet missile arsenal, Gorbachev's primary objective in negotiations, and a prerequisite for any understanding, was the cessation of the American missile defense program.[19] Consequently no substantial progress was made, and both heads of state departed empty-handed from Geneva. Notwithstanding, this meeting is nowadays thought to be the beginning of the end of the Cold War since it left on both Reagan's as well as Gorbachev's side a (precarious) confidence that the other party was serious and an agreement was in principle feasible. Both leaders declared jointly that "a nuclear war cannot be won and must never be fought"[20] and agreed to further meetings.

Reykjavík 1986: A Second Attempt

A mere two months after the Geneva talks Gorbachev surprised the world with a proposal to entirely abolish nuclear weapons in three steps by the year 2000. Although Reagan welcomed Gorbachev's proposal, against recommendations from his skeptical advisers, there followed a lull in negotiations until Gorbachev took another initiative in late 1986 and proposed a second summit in the Icelandic capital of Reykjavík. Gorbachev's determination to reach an understanding and the economic plight that prevailed in the Soviet Union forced the Kremlin onto this path. Pressure from Western protest movements was never able to force Reagan to make real concessions.

The different approaches of Reagan and Gorbachev became once again apparent in Reykjavík, where the two leaders met in a guesthouse of the Icelandic government in October 1986.[21] Gorbachev arrived prepared to make far-reaching concessions. He dropped his objections to a zero solution about European medium-range missiles on the first day of negotiations and accepted the American demand to exempt French and British nuclear missiles from such a regime. This step was all the more remarkable, since it meant that the Soviet Union would still be under threat from French and British nuclear weapons when it was obliged to scrap its own missiles stationed in Europe in step with the United States. In addition Gorbachev imagined the halving of US and USSR strategic nuclear weapons. In exchange, he demanded from the Americans a fixed agreement on the ABM Treaty for the duration of ten years and the restriction of SDI to the laboratory level. Reagan, however, rejected any compromise with respect to SDI. Gorbachev responded to his offer to share the technology of the missile defense system with the Soviet Union with the laconic remark that the United States had so far not even been willing to share oil-drilling technology. Although Reagan and Gorbachev came closer than ever to a breakthrough in Reykjavík, their negotiations ultimately failed due to the conditions set for SDI. The two leaders parted once more with inconclusive results.

Détente in Conflicts in the Third World

Away from US-Soviet summit diplomacy, in late 1986, conditions in the conflicts in Afghanistan and Central America underwent changes, which in turn impacted the policy of détente in the late 1980s.[22]

Gorbachev, after assuming office, basically concluded that the Russian intervention in Afghanistan was a "bleeding wound" that needed to be closed. Initially somewhat hesitant, he announced in November 1986 that the Soviet intervention was not permanent and that he wished Afghanistan to be independent and neutral.[23] Although it was another year and a half before the Soviet army actually began its retreat, the key decision had been made. Reagan, for his part, regarded the Soviet willingness to withdraw from Afghanistan as a litmus test for the credibility of the "new thinking."[24] That Gorbachev passed this test lay the foundation for the success of arms control negotiations in the years that followed.

Simultaneously, the US government also faced problems in conducting its proxy wars. In Central America, anticommunist Contra rebels operating from camps in Honduras were fighting against the government of Nicaragua, which was backed by Cuba. The neighboring countries El Salvador and Guatemala were also troubled by civil wars, which, according to Washington, had also been instigated by Cuba. The US Congress had cut military aid to the Contra rebels in Honduras continuously since 1982 and eventually banned all military aid to the guerrillas. The Reagan administration, however, circumvented this and continued supplying weapons to the rebels. Employees of the National Security procured the necessary funds through illegal arms sales to Iran. When this scheme was brought to the attention of the public in November 1986, the government came under considerable pressure.[25] Although it could not be proven that Reagan himself had knowledge of any wrong doing, his reputation as president had been seriously damaged by the scandal. Just like Gorbachev in Afghanistan, Reagan was at a dead end with his policies in Central America. His administration appeared once again to be a club of war-mongering communist haters who did not even stop at breaking laws.

The INF Treaty

Thus Reagan had a lot to gain by leading the arms control negotiations with the Soviet Union to a breakthrough. It was his last chance to present himself to the public as a "president of peace" and to compensate for the Iran-Contra fiasco. The Democratic Party's victory in the midterm elections in 1986, which provided the Democrats with majorities in both houses of Congress, seemed to call for a foreign policy success with some urgency. Yet, as before, it was not Reagan but Gorbachev who took the next step and cleared the conditions necessary to clinch a deal. On 28 February 1987, he agreed to separate negotiations on all issues pertaining to European medium-range missiles from the SDI problem. Matthew Evangelista and Lawrence Wittner argue that the general secretary of the CPSU followed the reasoning of Russian and Western military opponents who suggested that SDI would not be constructed if a zero solution for medium-range weapons was implemented.²⁶ This is unconvincing. The medium-range missiles related primarily to a European security structure, while the SDI was always intended to protect the United States against intercontinental ballistic missiles—and on this point no quick solution was in sight. At no time could Gorbachev assume that yielding on the noninclusion of both topics would persuade the United States to depart from SDI, even though the US Congress certainly cut funds for the SDI program. The reasons for taking this risky step rest firmly on the economic and domestic difficulties in the USSR.

Considering everything, Gorbachev made far-reaching concessions toward Reagan, who grabbed the opportunity to conclude an INF Treaty, which essentially contained all major US demands: it remained unrestrained in its SDI program, all European medium-range missiles were withdrawn, with the exception of the Franco-British nuclear weapons, which had been excluded from the zero option, and finally Soviet medium-range missiles east of the Urals were reduced to one hundred. Despite resistance from his own party, Reagan signed the INF treaty with Gorbachev at a ceremony in Washington in December 1987. The US Senate ratified the agreement on 27 May 1988. In the following years the withdrawn medium-range missiles were destroyed in the presence of inspectors from the other nation.

The INF Treaty represents the most decisive breakthrough in arms control talks during the 1980s. It ushered in the end of the Cold War. The relations between the superpowers changed dramatically and permanently in the months and years after its signing. Soviet troops finally began withdrawing from Afghanistan in May 1988, and in Central America a peace process took root and led to the end of civil wars in the region. Europe witnessed developments that ultimately resulted in the fall of the Berlin Wall and the dissolution of the Eastern Bloc. Yet it should not be thought that the INF Treaty was the direct cause of these dramatic changes. Rather it was the result of a general shift in the international political system along with other developments already mentioned. These had been initiated by Gorbachev's domestic reform efforts and fell, thanks to a Western public demanding détente and disarmament and to a reflective Ronald Reagan, on fertile ground.

The SNF Agreement and START Negotiations

As significant as the breakthrough agreement about the European mid-range missiles was, it pertained to only one type of weapon. Although the arms race in short-range nuclear forces (SNFs) and intercontinental ballistic missiles had abated, both sides still commanded significant arsenals, and these also became the subject of disarmament debates in the late 1980s. In George Bush, Sr, the United States had elected a president who shared little of the enthusiasm that Reagan had developed toward arms reduction during his last term and who initially saw Gorbachev less as a friend and more as a strategic adversary. The new US administration in particular had no interest in further arms control agreements in the area of short-range missiles. It feared that an agreement on the disarmament of European short-range missiles and tactical nuclear weapons would be a first step toward a nuclear-free Europe, in which the superiority of the USSR in conventional forces would give it a decisive advantage. An especially contentious political issue constituted outdated short-range Lance missiles stationed in Germany, which were supposed to be replaced by a modern weapon system. There was increasing resistance when this modernization was about to be implemented toward the end of the 1980s. Above all, the German government opposed this policy, which was untenable in the eyes of its citizens. The government coalition would have faced a serious crisis of conflict and it appeared that the general climate of détente between East and West might have been jeopardized by this move. Moreover modernization became all the more questionable when the Soviet Union offered negotiations for this type of weapon in April 1989 and announced a unilateral withdrawal of five hundred SNF weapon systems from Eastern Europe in the following month. Bush responded at first cautiously to the Soviet offer in May 1989 and made an SNF agreement conditional on an agreement on conventional forces. Only one year later the situation looked significantly more favorable when the US president announced on 3 May 1990 his decision to waive modernization. This was owed to unfolding events in Eastern Europe and a recalcitrant refusal by the German Federal government to permit the stationing of new short-range missiles. In September 1991, Bush also announced the complete withdrawal of these weapons from Europe.

The START negotiations, initiated by Reagan for tactical reasons in the early 1980s, were concluded in the early 1990s and reduced a strategic nuclear arsenal for the first time, to 1,600 carrier systems and six thousand warheads on either side. Again we note that shifts in the international political system ultimately produced these changes. Gorbachev's reform program for restructuring the USSR was already out of control and the disintegration of the gigantic Soviet empire began to emerge as a real possibility. When Bush and Gorbachev signed this historic treaty, the Americans no longer regarded the Kremlin as the main threat but feared an uncontrolled dissemination of warheads resulting from the breakup of the USSR.[27] It was, once again, a dramatic changeover in international relations that provided the opportunity for disarmament.

What Made Disarmament Possible?

The peace movement undoubtedly contributed to the gradual steps of disarmament during the 1980s. In the United States as well as in the European NATO countries it exerted pressure on governments to resume a serious dialogue with the USSR. It thus paved the way for a successful policy of détente in the late 1980s, forcing Western politicians to respond to the offers made by the East. However, the truly decisive steps toward arms control were not undertaken by Western governments but by a new Kremlin leadership under Mikhail Gorbachev. The resumption of summit talks, the dissociation of French and British medium-range missiles in INF negotiations, the decoupling of issues surrounding the SDI system from questions and problems with INF: in all these cases it was Gorbachev who took the initiative and who was prepared to propose far-reaching concessions. Wittner's thesis that Gorbachev was influenced by peace activists seems hardly credible. He certainly took up arguments from Western opponents to the arm's race and from an embryonic Russian peace movement. These generally served as additional legitimation for his decisions. Yet the steps he took were first and foremost determined by domestic policy objectives and the grave economic problems in the Soviet Union. He had to stop the arms race to give his reforms a chance.

Does this mean that the Reagan administration intentionally managed to push the USSR to the limits of its capacity in an arms race, as was suggested by some of its former officials?[28] This thesis calls for doubt. Up to a point the USSR was certainly put under economic pressure by US defense initiatives in the early 1980s. There is, however, no evidence that Washington deliberately pursued a strategy of ruining the Kremlin economically through the arms race. The US defense efforts during Reagan's first term in office instead were directed by a wish to boost American confidence, which had been infested with insecurity and ridden by self-doubt, and to stop the expansion of the Soviet sphere of influence.[29] The fact that Reagan was prepared to enter into arms limitation and disarmament negotiations in his second term also contradicts this theory, because the INF Treaty reduced, rather than increased, economic pressure on the Soviet Union.

When George Bush Sr. boasted in his 1992 election campaign that he had ended the Cold War, his opponent Bill Clinton promptly compared him to the proverbial rooster who claimed he made the sun rise with his cry.[30] The metaphor also holds true for those who put forward the suggestion that Ronald Reagan pursued a sophisticated military-economic strategy, or alternatively, for those who wish to give the lion's share of the credit for the disarmament successes of the 1980s to the peace movement.

Florian Pressler is a research fellow Transatlantic Cultural History (TCH) at the University of Augsburg, Germany. He has studied history, political science, and English literature in Heidelberg and Galway, Ireland, and received his Ph.D. at the University of Heidelberg in 2009. His research focuses on Inter-American relations, American economic history and the history of the Caribbean and Central America. He is the author of *From Reaganomics of Development to Free Trade: The Caribbean Basin Initiative (CBI), 1981–2005* (2012) and *Die erste Weltwirtschaftskrise: Eine kleine Geschichte der Großen Depression* (2013).

Notes

1. Lawrence S. Wittner, *Confronting the Bomb: A Short History of the World Nuclear Disarmament Movement* (Stanford, CA, 2009), 177–204. An abridged and edited version of Wittner's scholarly trilogy *The Struggle against the Bomb*, this book is aimed at the popular market. In our context the third volume of the trilogy is of foremost importance: *Toward Nuclear Abolition: A History of the World Nuclear Disarmament Movement, 1971 to the Present* (Stanford, CA, 2003).
2. Ronald Reagan, "Remarks at the Annual Convention of the National Association of Evangelicals in Orlando," Florida, 8 March 1983, http://www.reagan.utexas.edu/archives/speeches/1983/30883b.htm.
3. Odd Arne Westad, *The Global Cold War: Third World Interventions and the Making of Our Times* (Cambridge, 2005), 337–39. See also Bernd Stöver, *Der Kalte Krieg: Geschichte eines radikalen Zeitalters* (Munich, 2007), 416–17.
4. John Lewis Gaddis, "The Reagan Administration and Soviet-American Relations," in *Reagan and the World*, ed. David Kyvig (New York, 1990), 20.
5. Lou Cannon, *President Reagan: The Role of a Lifetime* (New York, 2000), 670.
6. Gaddis, "Reagan Administration," 21.
7. Stefan Bierling, *Geschichte der amerikanischen Außenpolitik: Von 1917 bis zur Gegenwart* (Munich, 2004), 180; Wittner, *Toward Nuclear Abolition*, 302.
8. John Lewis Gaddis, *Der Kalte Krieg: Eine Neue Geschichte* (Munich, 2007), 279.
9. Archie Brown, "Gorbachev and the End of the Cold War," in *Ending the Cold War: Interpretations, Causation, and the Study of International Relations*, ed. Richard Herrmann and Richard Lebow (New York, 2004), 31–57.
10. Michail Gorbatschow, *Perestroika: Die zweite russische Revolution. Eine neue Politik für Europa und die Welt* (Munich, 1987). Cf. Archie Brown, "The Gorbachev Revolution and the End of the Cold War," in *The Cambridge History of the Cold War, Vol. III: Endings*, ed. Melvyn Leffler and Odd Arne Westad (New York, 2010), 245–48.
11. Ronald Reagan, "Address to the Nation and Other Countries on United States-Soviet Relations," 16 January 1984, http://www.reagan.utexas.edu/archives/speeches/1984/11684a.htm.
12. Klaus Schwabe, *Weltmacht und Weltordnung: Amerikanische Außenpolitik von 1998 bis zur Gegenwart: Eine Jahrhundertgeschichte* (Paderborn, 2006), 407.

13. Beth Fischer, *The Reagan Reversal: Foreign Policy and the End of the Cold War* (Columbia, MO, 1997), 112–13 and 122–23. On Able Archer see Arnav Machanda, "When Truth Is Stranger than Fiction: The Able Archer Incident," in *Cold War History* 9 (2009): 111–33; Vojtech Mastny, "'Able Archer': An der Schwelle zum Atomkrieg?" in *Krisen im Kalten Krieg*, ed. Bernd Greiner, Christian Th. Müller, and Dierk Walter (Hamburg, 2008), 505–22; and the following study, which derived from the research department of the CIA and was published in 2007 on its web site: Benjamin B. Fischer, "A Cold War Conundrum: The 1983 Soviet War Scare," http://www.cia.gov/library/center-for-the-study-of-intelligence/csi-publications/books-and-monographs/a-cold-war-conundrum/source.htm.
14. Vincent Dujardin, "From Helsinki to the Missiles Question: A Minor Role for Small Countries? The Case of Belgium (1973–1985)," in *The Crisis of Détente in Europe: From Helsinki to Gorbachev, 1975–1985,* ed. Leopoldo Nuti (London and New York, 2009), 80.
15. A good survey about the SDI and its problems is provided by John Prados, "The Strategic Defense Initiative: Between Strategy, Diplomacy and US Intelligence Estimates," in Nuti, *The Crisis of Détente in Europe,* 86–98.
16. Paul Lettow, *Ronald Reagan and His Quest to Abolish Nuclear Weapons* (New York, 2005), who even suggests that Reagan's nuclear abolitionism was a pervasive belief and his initiation of the arms race merely a tactical strategy intended to force the Soviet Union into negotiations.
17. Thomas Stamm-Kuhlmann, "Rüstungsparität und Rüstungskontrolle zwischen Kuba-Krise und Perestroika," in *Raketenrüstung und internationale Sicherheit von 1942 bis heute,* ed. Thomas Stamm-Kuhlmann and Reinhard Wolf (Stuttgart, 2004), 123.
18. Archie Brown, *Seven Years that Changed the World: Perestroika in Perspective* (Oxford and New York, 2007), 69.
19. Josef Holik, *Die Rüstungskontrolle: Rückblick auf eine kurze Ära* (Berlin, 2008), 77. Compare also Matthew Evangelista, "Turning Points in Arms Control," in Herrmann and Lebow, *Ending,* 98–99.
20. Joint Soviet-United States Statement on the Summit Meeting in Geneva, 21 November 1985, http://www.reagan.utexas.edu/archives/speeches/1985/112185a.htm.
21. James Mann, *The Rebellion of Ronald Reagan: A History of the End of the Cold War* (New York, 2009), 45–46. See also Wittner, *Toward Nuclear Abolition,* 393–95; and Holik, *Rüstungskontrolle,* 57–58.
22. Richard Herrmann, "Regional Conflicts as Turning Points: The Soviet and American Withdrawals from Afghanistan, Angola, and Nicaragua," in Herrmann and Lebow, *Ending,* 60–82.
23. Conrad Schetter, *Kleine Geschichte Afghanistans* (Munich, 2007), 113.
24. Herrmann, "Regional Conflicts," 60–61.
25. John Coatsworth, "The Cold War in Central America, 1975–1991," in Leffler and Westad, *The Cambridge History of the Cold War,* 212–15.
26. Evangelista, "Turning Points," 100; Wittner, *Toward Nuclear Abolition,* 396–97.
27. Christoph Bluth, *The Collapse of Soviet Military Power* (Sudbury, MA, 1995), 159.
28. Caspar Weinberger, *Fighting for Peace* (New York, 1990); Richard Pipes, "Misinterpreting the Cold War: The Hardliners had it Right," *Foreign Affairs* 74, no. 1 (1995):

154–60. See also Martin Malia, *The Soviet Tragedy: A History of Socialism in Russia, 1917–1991* (New York, 1994), 414–15.
29. Marilena Gala, "From INF to SDI: How Helsinki Reshaped the Transatlantic Dimension of European Security," in Nuti, *The Crisis of Détente in Europe*, 115.
30. Michael Beschloss and Strobe Talbott, *At the Highest Levels: The Inside Story of the End of the Cold War* (Boston, MA, 1993), 468.

Select Bibliography

Wittner offers the most detailed discussion of the peace movement's influence on the disarmament negotiations that induced the end of the Cold War and argues that the protests of this transnational peace movement forced the governments in the East and the West to an arms control agreement. Evangelista blows a similar trumpet, while stressing the increasing distribution of the peace movement's ideas in society rather than direct political pressure from protests. There are a number of authors who oppose the revisionist views of Wittner and Evangelista and who look at the disarmament successes of the late 1980s not in isolation, but in concert with the developments at the end of the Cold War and the actors in government at its center: Gorbachev (Brown) and Reagan (Lettow, Fischer). A longtime diplomat and former federal commissioner for disarmament, Holik provides a brief but informative overview on arms control from a German perspective.

Brown, Archie. "The Gorbachev Revolution and the End of the Cold War." In *The Cambridge History of the Cold War, Vol. III: Endings,* ed. Melvyn Leffler and Odd Arne Westad, 244–66. New York, 2010.
Evangelista, Matthew. *Unarmed Forces: The Transnational Movement to End the Cold War.* Ithaca, NY, 1999.
Fischer, Beth. *The Reagan Reversal: Foreign Policy and the End of the Cold War.* Columbia, MO, 1997.
Holik, Josef. *Die Rüstungskontrolle: Rückblick auf eine kurze Ära.* Berlin, 2008.
Lettow, Paul. *Ronald Reagan and His Quest to Abolish Nuclear Weapons.* New York, 2005.
Wittner, Lawrence S. *Toward Nuclear Abolition: A History of the World Nuclear Disarmament Movement, 1971 to the Present.* Stanford, CA, 2003.

Index

Abrasimov, Pyotr, 93
action, 1, 214, 238n34, 238n36, 300
    action mobilization, 232, 238n36, 239n47
    action strategies of police and civil disobedience, 280–83
    AGDF, 159, 163–64, 191, 243–44, 246
    ASF, 159, 163–64, 189, 191, 243–44
    churches and forms of, 251–52
    "nonviolent action," 280
    police and, 275–77
    political action with spaces and places of peace movement, 174–75
    war and women with action and protest forms, 296–98
Action Committee Service for Peace. *See* Aktionsgemeinschaft Dienst für den Frieden
Action Conferences, 156, 164, 165
Action Group of Halle. *See* Aktionskreis Halle
Action Reconciliation Service for Peace. *See* Aktion Sühnezeichen/ Friedensdienste
activists
    peace movement, protagonists, 189, 192–202
    women and peace movement, 291–93
Adams, Eddie, 228
Adenauer, Konrad, 6, 14, 143
Afghanistan, 24, 62, 344–45
AFK. *See* Arbeitsgemeinschaft für Friedens- und Konfliktforschung
Africa, 53, 292, 338

AGDF. *See* Aktionsgemeinschaft Dienst für den Frieden
aggression research, 139, 144
aircraft
    design development, 75–76
    types, 76, 81
AKH. *See* Aktionskreis Halle
Aktionsgemeinschaft Dienst für den Frieden (AGDF, Action Committee Service for Peace), 159, 163–64, 191, 243–44, 246
Aktionskreis Halle (AKH, Action Group of Halle), 214
Aktion Sühnezeichen/Friedensdienste (ASF, Action Reconciliation Service for Peace), 159, 163–64, 189, 191, 243–44
Albertz, Heinrich, 20, 250
Albrecht, Ulrich, 148
Alphaville, 332
Alt, Franz, 11, 192, 200–201, 202, 250–51
Die Alternative (Bahro), 197
"Amerika" (Grönemeyer), 290
Amsterdam Assembly (1948), 253
Andersson, Bibi, 330
Andrews Barracks, US, 281
Andropov, Yuri, 93, 340
Anstiftung der Frauen für den Frieden (Initiative Women for Peace), 191
anti-Americanism. *See* United States
antinuclear protests
    environmental movement and, 121–24
    posters, 128
antitank helicopters, 76–77
antitank weapons, development, 76–78
Antiwar Day, 232, 266, 269

apartheid, 292
Apel, Hans, 190
"Appeal by the Writers in Europe," 325–26
Appeal of Bielefeld, 19
Appeal of Mainz, 142
Arbeitsgemeinschaft für Friedens- und Konfliktforschung (AFK, Association for Peace and Conflict Research), 141
Arbeitskreis Solidarische Kirche (Working Group Church Solidarity), 216
Arche (Ark), 214
armed force, God and, 243
arms, 109, 191, 243
    "Arms race: help, I've been followed" (cartoon), 79
    arms upgrade resolution, 95–99
    trade unions with arms production, 260–62
    See also disarmament; missiles; SALT; weapons
Arms and hunger. *See Der organisierte Wahnsinn*
"The Arms Race—How and Where?," 66
Artists for Peace, 223, 236n9, 329–30, 331, 333
ASF. *See* Aktion Sühnezeichen/Friedensdienste
Association for Peace and Conflict Research. *See* Arbeitsgemeinschaft für Friedens- und Konfliktforschung
Association of Citizens' Initiatives for Environmental Protection. *See* BBU
Association of Evangelical Lutheran Youth, 249
AT-1/-2 Anti-Tank (mine systems), 77, 78
Atomic Café (documentary film), 324
Auschwitz
    God and, 193
    with pacifism, ethics of, 16, 107
Autumn of Peace. *See Friedensherbst*

Backfire bomber. *See* TU-22M bomber
Baez, Joan, 330

Bahr, Egon, 8, 57, 84n1, 87, 91, 108
    "common security" and, 252
    neutron bomb and, 105
Bahro, Rudolf, 110, 192, 197–98, 201
Balistier, Thomas, 186n33
Bannas, Günter, 165
Barrett, Marcia, 332
Bastian, Gert, 11, 95, 159, 162–63, 198
    disarmament and, 109
    with Krefeld Appeal (1980), 190–91
    peace movement and, 189, 190–91, 201, 233, 262, 292
BBU (Association of Citizens' Initiatives for Environmental Protection), 121, 126, 159–61, 192
BDKJ. *See* Federation of German Catholic Youth
Bechert, Karl, 190
Beckmann, Lukas, 214
"Before the (arms) Race Gets Out of Control" (Bastian), 109
BEK. *See* Bund der Evangelischen Kirchen der DDR
Belafonte, Harry, 330
Belgrade, 40, 44–45
Benz, Georg, 268
Berlin Conference of Bishops, 207
Berlin Declaration, 24, 83, 108
Berlin Wall, 24, 43, 52, 161
Bert (TV turtle), 319n6
Beuys, Joseph, 192, 198–99, 202, 330, 333
BfZ. *See* Bundesamt für Zivilschutz
BGM-109G Gryphon, 72
BGM Boosted Guided Missile, 72
the Bible, 255n12
Biermann, Wolf, 42
"birth strikes," 296–97
bishops, 207, 250, 251, 252
Blohm & Voss, 261
"Blutspur" (blood trail) (Schulz), 136n57
BM-27, 77
BM Truck Mounted Multiple Rocket Launcher (boyevaya mashina - combat vehicle), 77

Bochum (Grönemeyer), 290
bodies
  with "die-in," 179, 229, 230, 236n8
  human chain, 1, 65, 130, 167,
    173, 179, 180, 222, 223, 226,
    229, 230, 231, 263, 276, 293,
    296–97, 300
  media and, 229–32
Bohley, Bärbel, 95, 192, 197, 201, 213,
  216, 292
Böll, Annemarie, 189, 192, 198, 200,
  202, 233
Böll, Heinrich, 21, 167, 189, 192, 198,
  200, 202
  celebrities blockade (1983), 278
  nonviolence and, 239n44
  peace movement and, 222, 326
  personalization of protest and, 232,
    233, 234
  scandal, 239n48
Boney M., 332
Bonhoeffer, Dietrich, 216
Borm, William, 106
bots, 330, 333
Bowie, David, 325
boycotts, Olympic Games, 62, 89
Braendle-Zeile, Elisabeth, 298
Brandt, Peter, 144
Brandt, Willy, 7–8, 11, 22, 87, 91
  deterrence and, 109
  peace movement and, 192, 222
  SPD and, 108
Braun, Karl-Heinz, 280
Bräutigam, Hans Otto, 98
Bravo, 329, 330
Bretschneider, Harald, 210
Brezhnev, Leonid, 40, 58, 340
  role of, 59–60, 64, 81
  Warsaw Pact and, 89
Briggs, Raymond, 13, 325
Brokdorf Nuclear Power Station, 286
Bruns, Tissy, 165
Brüsewitz, Oskar, 209–10
Brzezinski, Zbigniew, 43
BUF. *See* Bundeskonferenz Unabhängiger
  Friedensgruppen

BUKO. *See* Bundeskongress
  entwicklungspolitischer
  Aktionsgruppen
BUND. *See* Union for the Environment
  and Nature Conservation
Bund der Evangelischen Kirchen der
  DDR (BEK, Federation of Protestant
  Churches in East Germany), 208, 217
Bundesamt für zivilen
  Bevölkerungsschutz (BzB), 309, 310
Bundesamt für Zivilschutz (BfZ), 310
Bundeskonferenz Unabhängiger
  Friedensgruppen (BUF, Federal
  Conference of Independent Peace
  Groups), 191
Bundeskongress entwicklungspolitischer
  Aktionsgruppen (BUKO, Federal
  Congress of Developmental Action
  Groups), 191
Bundesverband für den Selbstschutz
  (BVS, Federal Association for Self-
  Protection), 312
Bundeswehr (West German Army), 277
Bund Naturschutz, 120
Buschmann, Martha, 192
Bush, George H. W., 274, 287, 347,
  348
Bush, George W., 287
BVS. *See* Bundesverband für den
  Selbstschutz
BzB. *See* Bundesamt für zivilen
  Bevölkerungsschutz

Caldicott, Helen, 300
Callaghan, James, 59, 60
Capra, Fritjof, 125
Carl Schurz Barracks, US, 277
Carter, Jimmy
  disarmament and, 53, 339
  human rights and, 44
  neutron bombs and, 57–58
  role of, 6, 43, 54, 59, 60, 63, 81
  SALT II and, 108
Catholic Student Communities. *See*
  Katholische Studentengemeinden
CDU. *See* Christian Democratic Union

celebrities blockade, 167, 176, 200, 223, 233, 278
Central Committee of German Catholics. *See* Zentralkomitee der deutschen Katholiken
Central Office for Civil Defense. *See* Zentralstelle für Zivilschutz
Challenger (tank), 76
Charter 77, 42–43, 215
Chernenko, Konstantin, 340
Chernobyl, 309, 335n32
children. *See* youth
Christian Democratic Union (CDU)
    CDU-FDP coalitions, 284, 285
    internal disputes, 114n1
    peace movement and, 107–8
    role of, 7, 64, 104, 105–7
Christian Peace Debate, 251–52
Christian Social Union (CSU), 7, 64, 104, 105
Church Congress (1981), 244–48
churches
    Christian protest in transition, 253–54
    ecclesiastical peace discussions, key aspects, 252–53
    Federation of Evangelical Churches, 244, 256n38
    IKvu, 191, 216, 248
    nuclear crisis and upheavals in, 248–51
    organization and action, forms of, 251–52
    peace and security, debates, 242–44
    role of, 8, 143, 191, 216–17
    World Council of Churches, 243, 253
    See also Protestant Church; Roman Catholic Church
circles of silence, 179, 181, 231, 276
citizens
    BBU, 121, 126, 159–61, 192
    with initiatives and environmental movement, 119–21
"Citizens Observe the Police" groups, 285

civil defense
    in context, 13, 306–7
    ethics of, 311–12
    films, 323
    intensification in 1980s, 310–12
    life after nuclear explosion, 312–17
    medicine, militarization of, 317–18
    in nuclear age, 307–10
    Zentralstelle für Zivilschutz, 320n19
civil disobedience
    action strategies of police and challenge of, 280–83
    criminalization of, 279, 280, 284
    police and, 277–83
civilian populations
    with missile survey, 169n9
    neutron bombs and, 75
civil rights movement. *See* independent peace movement, East Germany and
Civil Rights & the Police / CILIP, 285
Clinton, Bill, 348
clothing, 248, 284
    See also scarves
Club of Rome, 119, 200
coercion, 279–80, 282
Cohn, Carol, 295
Cold War, 23–25
    See also Second Cold War
Commission for Protection. *See* Schutzkommission
Committee for Basic Rights and Democracy. *See* Komitee für Grundrechte und Demokratie
Committee for Peace, Disarmament, and Cooperation. *See* Komitee für Frieden, Abrüstung, und Zusammenarbeit
"common security," 252–53
Communist Party of the Soviet Union (CPSU), 55
community policing, 285–87
Confederation of German Trade Union. *See* Deutscher Gewerkschaftsbund
Conference for Security and Cooperation in Europe (CSCE)
    baskets or themes, 38, 39–41, 44, 45

356 | Index

Belgrade (1977–78), follow-up meeting, 40, 44–45
in context, 6, 37–38, 48–49, 162, 209
Helsinki Final Act, 39–45, 46
human rights and, 37–38
Madrid (1980), follow-up meeting, 45–48
negotiations, 39
opponents, 41–42
conflicts
AFK, 141
forms of, 12–14
nuclear crisis and protagonists of, 7–9
Third World and détente in, 344–45
conscientious objectors, military and, 210, 214
"consensus mobilization," 238n36
conservation societies, 119–21
contamination, 79, 314, 315, 332
Conze, Eckart, 14
Coordinating Committee. *See* peace movement, Coordinating Committee
Counsel for Coordination. *See* Koordinationsrat
countervailing strategy. *See Nachrüstung*
Courage, 294, 295, 300, 302n14
CPSU. *See* Communist Party of the Soviet Union
criminalization, of civil disobedience, 279, 280, 284
crisis. *See* Cuban missile crisis; environmental movement; nuclear crisis
Crivellari, Fabio, 234
cruise missiles
capabilities, 70, 72
GLCM, 61, 65
production, 71
sea-launched, 59
Cruit, Ronald, 319n6
CSCE. *See* Conference for Security and Cooperation in Europe
CSSR. *See* Czechoslovak Socialist Republic

CSU. *See* Christian Social Union
Cuban missile crisis (1962), 308, 323
culture
environmental movement with protests and political, 129–31
Germany and cultural identity, 145
police with "culture clash" over internal security, 283–85
Czechoslovak Socialist Republic (CSSR), 41–43, 46, 96

Dahrendorf, Ralf, 270
Daimler-Benz star, 226
dance, 12, 223, 231, 332
Danish Women for Peace, 298
Day of Resistance. *See* Widerstandstag
The Day After (film), 13, 322, 323–25
Declaration of Göttingen, 311
defense, 43, 54
See also civil defense
Degenhardt, Franz Josef, 330
Deile, Volkmar, 161, 163, 165, 258, 271n3
Demokratischen Sozialisten (DS, Democratic Socialists), 192
demonstrations. *See* peace movement; protests
Denmark, 59, 61
destruction
MAD, 323
spaces and places of potential, 178–79
détente
CSCE and, 44–45
end of, 52–56
support for, 109
Third World, in conflicts, 344–45
TNF development (1970s), 71–74
deterrence
peace studies and logic of, 139–41
political parties and, 108–9
role of, 4
support for, 138
Deutsche Friedensgesellschaft—Vereinigte KriegsdienstgegnerInnen

(DFG-VK, German Peace Society / United War Resisters), 126, 161, 192
Deutsche Friedensunion (DFU, German Peace Union), 162, 192
Deutsche Gesellschaft für Friedens- und Konfliktforschung (DGFK, German Society for Peace), 141–42
Deutsche Kommunistische Partei (DKP, German Communist Party), 159, 160, 161–62, 192
Deutsche Polizei (German police), 283
Deutscher Gewerkschaftsbund (DGB, Confederation of German Trade Union), 258, 264, 282
DFG-VK. *See* Deutsche Friedensgesellschaft—Vereinigte KriegsdienstgegnerInnen
DFU. *See* Deutsche Friedensunion
DGB. *See* Deutscher Gewerkschaftsbund
DGFK. *See* Deutsche Gesellschaft für Friedens- und Konfliktforschung
"die-in," 179, 229, 230, 236n8
Diner, Dan, 145–46
disarmament
    confrontation, phases of, 339–40
    in context, 23, 338–39
    END, 11, 25, 198
    France and, 46–47
    Geneva disarmament talks, 278, 342–43
    Gorbachev and rapprochement, 340–41
    INF Treaty for, 345–46
    issues, 348
    KOFAZ, 159, 162, 192, 194, 202n2, 262
    political parties, 109–11
    Reagan and, dialogue offer, 341–42
    Reykjavík talks (1986), 83, 338, 344
    SNF Agreement and START negotiations, 346–47
    Third World, détente in conflicts in, 344–45
    US and, 53, 338–44
    See also SALT

disaster. *See* Fire and Disaster Protection Act; nuclear doomsday
disobedience. *See* civil disobedience
Dithfurth, Hoimar von, 129
DKP. *See* Deutsche Kommunistische Partei
Documenta 5 (Beuys), 199
Documenta 7 (Beuys), 198
"do-it-yourself aesthetic," 225
Dommaschk, Detlef, 283
doomsday. *See* nuclear doomsday
Double-Track Decision. *See* NATO Double-Track Decision
Double-Zero solution, 66
Dresden Peace Forum, 212
Dr. Strangelove or: How I Learned to Stop Worrying and Love the Bomb (Kubrick), 323
DS. *See* Demokratischen Sozialisten
Duck and Cover (civil defense film), 323
"duck and cover," 319n6
Dülffer, Jost, 147, 151n29
Dürr, Hans-Peter, 142
dust cloud, contaminated, 314
Dutschke, Rudi, 42

Easter March movement, 10, 160, 161, 173, 198, 248, 259
East Germany (GDR)
    BEK, 208, 217
    CSCE and, 41, 43, 46
    Military Service Act of 1982, 294, 297
    New Forum and, 197
    Peace Policy, 81
    See also independent peace movement, East Germany and; NATO Double-Track Decision, East-West German relations
eco-feminism, 125
eco-pacifism, 124, 125, 126, 129
Ecumenical Assembly, 217
education, 156
    See also military
Ehrlich, Paul, 316
Eisenmann, Ernst, 265

EKD. *See* Evangelische Kirche in
    Deutschland
election poster, SPD, 112
electromagnetic pulse (EMP), 316
*Elements of a New Policy: The Relationship
    between Ecology and Socialism* (Bahro),
    197
Emma, 294, 295, 296, 300
EMP. *See* electromagnetic pulse
END. *See* European Nuclear
    Disarmament
Ende: Diary of a Third World War (Guha),
    13, 326–27
Engelmann, Bernt, 326
enhanced radiation weapon. *See* ERW
Environmental Library, Zion Church, 214
environmental movement
    antinuclear protest and, 121–24
    cartoons, 127–28
    in context, 9–10, 131–32
    crisis perceptions and
        interpretations, 124–25
    networks, 126–29
    "new peace movement" and, 124
    of 1970s, 119–21
    protest and political culture, forms
        of, 129–31
    See also Green Party
environmental protection. *See* BBU
Eppelmann, Rainer (Rev.), 95, 212, 218,
    292
Eppler, Erhard, 2, 110, 129, 192, 250
    celebrities blockade (1983), 278
    peace movement and, 195, 202, 292
ERW (enhanced radiation weapon),
    56–58, 79
    See also neutron bomb
ESG. *See* Evangelische
    Studentengemeinde
Es geht voran (Things are moving ahead)
    (Horx), 327
d'Estaing, Valéry Giscard, 59, 60
ethics
    Auschwitz and ethics of pacifism,
        16, 107
    of civil defense, 311–12

Etwas lässt sich doch bewirken
    (Pausewang), 335n32
European Nuclear Disarmament (END),
    11, 25, 198
evacuation plans, 306, 307, 314
Evangelische Kirche in Deutschland
    (EKD, Protestant Church in
    Germany), 208, 246–47
Evangelische Studentengemeinde
    (ESG, Protestant Student Parish
    Organization), 191, 209
Evangelista, Matthew, 345
explosions. *See* nuclear explosions

F-15. *See* McDonnell Douglas F-15 Eagle
F-16. *See* General Dynamics F-16
    Fighting Falcon
"Fall Action Week 1983," 1
Farantouri, Maria, 330
Farian, Frank, 332
fasting, 213, 251, 295
The Fate of the Earth (Schell), 326
FBS. *See* Forward Based Systems
FDP. *See* Free Democratic Party
fear
    civil defense and, 307–8
    literature inciting, 327
    persuasion and, 130
    See also peace movement,
        intellectual foundations
Federal Association for Self-Protection.
    See Bundesverband für den
    Selbstschutz
Federal Association of Critical Police
    Officers, 286
Federal Conference of Independent
    Peace Groups. *See* Bundeskonferenz
    Unabhängiger Friedensgruppen
Federal Congress of Developmental
    Action Groups. *See* Bundeskongress
    entwicklungspolitischer
    Aktionsgruppen
Federation of Evangelical Churches, 244,
    256n38
Federation of German Catholic Youth
    (BDKJ), 248, 249

Federation of Nonviolent Action
  Groups. *See* Föderation gewaltfreier
  Aktionsgruppen
Federation of Protestant Churches
  in East Germany. *See* Bund der
  Evangelischen Kirchen der DDR
femininity, symbolism, 294
feminism
  eco-feminism, 125
  peace movement and, 201
  See also peace movement, women
    and
"fighters," women as, 300
Fighting the atomic death. *See* Kampf
  dem Atomtod
film, nuclear doomsday in, 13, 322,
  323–25
Fire and Disaster Protection Act (West
  Germany), 317
"first wave," 85n9
Fischer, Joschka, 16
Fischer, Oskar, 93
Fitter. *See* Sukhoi 22
"5 Minutes to Midnight," 258, 263, 270
flexible response. *See* NATO
Flogger. *See* MiG 23
Flogger D. *See* MiG 27
Föderation gewaltfreier Aktionsgruppen
  (FÖGA, Federation of Nonviolent
  Action Groups), 191
Ford, Gerald, 40, 41, 43, 53, 81, 90
"Forever Young" (Alphaville), 332
Forward Based Systems (FBS), 63
France, 3
  disarmament and, 46–47
  with NATO Double-Track
    Decision, 4
Frauen für den Frieden (Women for
  Peace), 212, 214
Frauen gegen Atomtod—Unsere Kinder
  sollen leben (Women against Nuclear
  Death), 303n32
Free Democratic Party (FDP), 7
  CDU-FDP coalitions, 284, 285
  eco-pacifism and, 126, 129
  internal disputes, 114n1

  peace movement and, 108
  role of, 64, 104, 113, 123
  SPD and, 59
The Freiburg Institute for Applied
  Ecology, 122
Freundeskreis Wehrdiensttotalverweigerer
  (Friends of Conscientious Objectors
  to Military Service), 214
Frey, Ulrich, 163–64, 165
"Der Friede muss bewaffnet sein" (Peace
  must be armed), 212
Frieden konkret (Peace, here and now)
  seminars, 214
Friedensherbst (Autumn of Peace), 258
Die friedfertige Frau (The peaceful sex)
  (Mitscherlich, M.), 151n38
Friends of Conscientious Objectors to
  Military Service. *See* Freundeskreis
  Wehrdiensttotalverweigerer
Friends of Nature. *See* Naturfreunde
Fulcrum. *See* MiG 29

Galtung, Johan, 139–40, 142, 148
Gandhi, Mahatma, 19, 251
Gaus, Günter, 152n49, 152n51
GdP. *See* Gewerkschaft der Polizei
GDR. *See* East Germany
Geissler, Heiner, 16, 107
gender, 294
  with peace and war, 290–91, 293
  women and peace movement, 295
General Dynamics F-16 Fighting Falcon,
  75
Generals for Peace, 194
Genesis (band), 325
Geneva disarmament talks, 278, 342–43
genocide. *See* Holocaust
Genscher, Hans-Dietrich, 2–3
  NATO Double-Track Decision and,
    92
  role of, 59, 64, 106, 113
Gerbert, Helmut, 278
"German Autumn," 122
German Bishops Conference, 251, 252
German Communist Party. *See* Deutsche
  Kommunistische Partei

German Lutheran Church Congress, 247–48
German Peace Society. *See* Deutsche Friedensgesellschaft—Vereinigte KriegsdienstgegnerInnen
German Peace Union. *See* Deutsche Friedensunion
German Penal Code, 278, 279–80
German police. *See Deutsche Polizei*
German Red Cross, 310
German Society for Peace. *See* Deutsche Gesellschaft für Friedens- und Konfliktforschung
German Technical Emergency Service. *See* Technisches Hilfswerk
German-US relationship, 5, 6–7, 21–22, 33n70
Germany
    cultural identity, 145
    See also East Germany; Socialist Unity Party of Germany; West Germany
Gewerkschaft der Polizei (GdP, Trade Union of the Police), 281–82, 283
Gewerkschafter (The Trade Unionist), 261
Ginsburg, Alexander, 44
GLCM Ground Launched Cruise Missile, 61, 65
"glocalization," 180
Glückliche Reise (Happy journey) (Horx), 327
God
    armed force and, 243
    Auschwitz and, 193
    war and will of, 253
Goldberg, Arthur, 44
Gollwitzer, Brigitte, 193
Gollwitzer, Helmut, 193, 250
Gonzalez, Felipe, 48
Gorbachev, Mikhail
    Geneva disarmament talks, 342–43
    INF Treaty and, 345–46
    nuclear crisis and, 24
    rapprochement and, 340–41
    Reykjavík disarmament talks (1986), 338, 344
    role of, 70, 83–84, 348

Gorski, Philip S., 159
"Granite 86," 84n14
Grass, Günter, 16–17, 167, 326
Greece, 59
Green Party, 10, 11
    disarmament and, 109, 110–11
    eco-pacifism and, 126
    internal disputes, 114n1
    party politics and, 15, 22–23
    peace movement and, 158, 160, 162, 192, 193–94
    posters, 237n18
    role of, 65, 94–95, 113–14, 123
    SPD and, 195
    with women and peace movement, 290
Greiner, Ulrich, 322
Grohmann, Peter, 165
Gromyko, Andrei, 60
Grönemeyer, Herbert, 290
Grundgesetz, 282
Guha, Anton-Andreas, 13, 152n61, 326–27

Hackett, John (Sir), 326
Haeber, Herbert, 96
Hænning, Gitte, 330
Haftendorn, Helga, 6, 58
Hagemann, Karen, 302n6
Haig, Alexander, 276
Hans-Böckler-Stiftung (Hans Böckler Foundation), 262
Happy journey. *See Glückliche Reise*
harassment, police, 216
Harmel Report (1967), 4, 53, 104
Hattenbach (film), 325
Hauswedell, Corinna, 150n16
Havemann, Katja, 197, 292
Havemann, Robert, 197, 212, 292
"Heated Autumn" (1983), 281
Heilbronn, 176, 184n17
Heinemann, Gustav, 143
helicopters, antitank, 76–77
Heller, André, 330
Helsinki Final Act
    CSCE and, 39–45, 46
    societal implications, 41–44

Herf, Jeffrey, 14
Herzog, Roman, 278, 285
High Level Group (HLG), 54, 58
Hildebrandt, Dieter, 278
Hiroshima, 125, 228, 231, 306–7, 314
HLG. *See* High Level Group
Hochhuth, Rolf, 326
Hofgarten rally
    1981, 146, 163, 174, 189, 268, 276
    1982, 174, 276
    1983, 174, 200, 222, 237n25
Holocaust, 16, 18, 125
Honecker, Erich, 40, 88, 100n10
    with NATO Double-Track Decision, 88–92, 96, 98
    peace movement and, 93–95, 99, 214
Horx, Matthias, 327
Hövener, Barbara, 292
Huber, Antje, 290
human chain. *See* bodies
human rights, 216
    CSCE and, 37–38
    groups, 25, 217
    US and, 44
Hungary, 25

ICBMs. *See* Intercontinental Ballistic Missiles
"Ice Age" (Maffay), 330
identity
    Germany and cultural, 145
    women with peace movement and positioning of, 298–300
IG-Metall Jugend (IG Metall Youth), 260, 263
IG Metall trade union, 258, 261, 263, 265, 267, 268
IISS. *See* International Institute for Strategic Studies
IKV. *See* Interchurch Peace Council
IKvu. *See* Initiative Kirche von unten
Inability to mourn. *See* "Die Unfähigkeit zu trauern"
independent peace movement, East Germany and
    civil rights movement and development of, 209–12
    in context, 11–12, 207, 217–18
    peace contacts across border, 214–15
    peace efforts, spectrum of, 208
    peace movement in second half of 1980s, 216–17
    peace policy, official, 215–16
    peace without weapons, 212–14
INF. *See* Intermediate-Range Nuclear Forces; Shorter-Range INF; Zero Solution for Long-range
"Information about the strategic offensive forces' exercises of the USSR noted during the maneuver, SAPAD 81," 84n1
Initiative Church from Below. *See* Initiative Kirche von unten
Initiative Frieden und Menschenrechte (Initiative for Peace and Human Rights), 217
Initiative Kirche von unten (IKvu, Initiative Church from Below), 191, 216, 248
Initiative Women for Peace. *See* Anstiftung der Frauen für den Frieden
injuries, in nuclear explosion, 314, 324
Interchurch Peace Council (IKV), 244, 246
Intercontinental Ballistic Missiles (ICBMs), 53, 70
Intermediate-Range Nuclear Forces (INF), 64
Intermediate-Range Nuclear Forces (INF) Treaty, 24, 62, 70, 84, 345–46
internal security. *See* security
International Institute for Strategic Studies (IISS), 3, 56
IPPNW (International Physicians for the Prevention of Nuclear War), 11, 292, 300
Israel, 76
Italy, 6, 57, 61, 65, 177

Jäger, Thomas, 145
Jahn, Roland, 216

Jansen, Mechthild, 292
Jaruzelski, Wojciech, 47
JEF. *See* Junge Europäische Föderalisten
Jens, Walter, 21, 326
Jews, 16, 18, 125
Joffe, Josef, 9
Jørgensen, Anker, 89
Jungdemokraten (Young Democrats), 192
Junge Europäische Föderalisten (JEF, Young European Federalists), 126
Jungk, Robert, 123, 129
    influence of, 143
    as peace movement protagonist, 189, 192, 200–201, 202
Jungmännerwerk (Young Men's Association), 209

Kade, Gerhard, 192, 194, 201–2
Kampf dem Atomtod (Fighting the atomic death), 323
Karges, Carlo, 332–33
Kassandra (Wolf), 298
Katholische Studentengemeinden (Catholic Student Communities), 209
Kauffeld, Elisa, 280–81
Kelly, Petra, 11, 22, 94, 95, 126
    celebrities blockade (1983), 278
    Krefeld Appeal and, 190
    peace movement and, 162–63, 198, 214, 222, 233, 262, 300
    as peace movement protagonist, 192, 195–96, 201
    with women and peace movement, 290, 292
Kielmansegg, Peter Graf, 14
Kiesinger, Kurt Georg, 6
King, Martin Luther, Jr., 19, 251
Kissinger, Henry, 43
Klemm, Barbara, 234
KOFAZ. *See* Komitee für Frieden, Abrüstung, und Zusammenarbeit
Kohl, Helmut, 2, 3, 18, 65
    on German-US relationship, 21–22, 33n70
    with NATO Double-Track Decision, 16, 52, 92, 94
    peace movement and, 6–7, 107
    role of, 9, 92, 274
Komitee für Frieden, Abrüstung, und Zusammenarbeit (KOFAZ, Committee for Peace, Disarmament, and Cooperation), 159, 162, 192, 194, 202n2, 262
Komitee für Grundrechte und Demokratie (Committee for Basic Rights and Democracy), 191
Koordinationsrat (Counsel for Coordination), 146
Korean Airline, flight 007, 342
Korean War, 308
Kravetz, Pascal, 329
Krefeld Appeal (1980), 19, 20, 146, 155, 162, 190–91
    Artists for Peace and, 223, 236n9
    influence of, 263, 266
Krefeld riots, police and, 274–75
Krolikowski, Werner, 93
Krüger, Ralf, 280
Kubrick, Stanley, 323
Kukutz, Irina, 292
Kvitsinsky, Yuli, 64

"labor for peace," trade unions and, 260–62
Lafontaine, Oskar, 11, 110, 192, 233
LARS 1, 77–78
LARS Light Artillery Rocket System, 77
The Last Children of Schewenborn. *See Die letzten Kinder von Schewenborn*
"The Last Stand" (*Der Spiegel*), 55
laws
    Fire and Disaster Protection Act (West Germany), 317
    Military Service Act of 1982 (GDR), 294, 297
    See also martial law, in Poland
LD. *See* Liberale Demokraten
Leclerc (tank), 76
Lehnert, Detlef, 144
Leif, Thomas, 183n8, 192
Leinen, Jo, 126, 165, 258, 271n2, 292
Leopard 2 (tank), 76

Lettow, Paul, 350n16
Die letzten Kinder von Schewenborn (The Last Children of Schewenborn) (Pausewang), 13, 178, 327–29
Liberale Demokraten (LD, Liberal Democrats), 192
life, after nuclear explosion, 312–17
    See also civil defense
The Limits to Growth (Club of Rome), 119, 200
Lindenberg, Udo, 329–30
literature, nuclear doomsday in, 325–29
"A Little Peace" (Nicole), 330
Living without Arms. *See* Ohne Rüstung Leben
Loderer, Eugen, 260, 266
Long-Term Defense Program (LTDP), 54
"Love and Medium-Range Missiles" (Sander), 293
LRINF. *See* Zero Solution for Long-range
LTDP. *See* Long-Term Defense Program

M1 Abrams (tank), 76
Machtbesessenheit (obsession with power), 14
Machtvergessenheit (obliviousness to power), 14
MAD. *See* "Mutual Assured Destruction"
Madrid. *See* Conference for Security and Cooperation in Europe
Maffay, Peter, 329, 330
Maltry, Karola, 291, 301, 302n8
Maneuverable Reentry Vehicle (MARV), 72
"Männer" (Men) (Grönemeyer), 290
Mannhardt, Klaus, 165, 192
Markovits, Andrei S., 159
martial law, in Poland, 47, 91, 269
martyrs, 209–10
MARV. *See* Maneuverable Reentry Vehicle
Maser, Peter, 217, 219n5
mass demonstrations, of peace movement 1981–82, 163–65, 174
    October 15–22, 1983, 222
    police with rallies and, 276

Mattes, Eva, 330
Matthiesen, Gunnar, 262
"Mayors for Peace," 181, 186n44
MBFR. *See* Mutual and Balanced Force Reductions
McDonnell Douglas F-15 Eagle, 75
Mechtersheimer, Alfred, 20, 159
Meckel, Markus, 218
media, 325
    bodies and, 229–32
    NATO Double-Track Decision in, 52, 96
    See also peace movement, visual and media strategies
Media guide for peacemaking. *See Medienhandbuch Friedensarbeit*
medicine, militarization of, 317–18
Medienhandbuch Friedensarbeit (Media guide for peacemaking) (Youth Film Club), 325
Meinecke, Ulla, 330
Meinhof, Ulrike, 239n48
Meinunger, Bernd, 332
memory, nuclear crisis and politics of, 15–18
Men. *See* "Männer"
metall, 263, 265
Meyer, Nicholas, 324
MGM Mobile Guided Missile, 72
MiG 23 (Flogger), 75
MiG 27 (Flogger D), 75
MiG 29 (Fulcrum), 75
MiG Mikoyan-Gurevich (Soviet aircraft company), 75
militancy, police and, 276–77
militarization, of medicine, 317–18
Militarization Atlas of West Germany, 20
military, 84n10
    Bundeswehr, 277
    conscientious objectors and, 210, 214
    education, 210, 309
    environmental movement and, 125
    peace movement and sites of military importance, 175–77
    planning, changes in, 70, 78–80

protests against, 277–78, 281
RMA, 76
sexism and militarism, 293–95
symbolism, 238n30
techniques, development of, 74–78
Military Service Act of 1982 (GDR), 294, 297
The Millennium Man: From the Future Workshops of our Society (Jungk), 200
MIRVs. *See* Multiple Independently Targetable Re-entry Vehicles
Mischnik, Adam, 42
missiles, 293
    capabilities, 77
    civilian populations, survey, 169n9
    GLCM, 61, 65
    ICBMs, 53, 70
    See also cruise missiles; Cuban missile crisis; Pershing II missiles; SS-20 missiles
Mitscherlich, Alexander, 144
Mitscherlich, Margarete, 151n38
Mitterrand, François, 3
mobilization, 232, 238n36, 239n47
Moderamen, 246–47
Mondale, Walter, 341
Moral in Zeiten der Krise (Morality in times of crisis) (Richter), 138
Moscow Helsinki Group, 41–42, 43
motherhood, 295–96, 298
MRCA (Multi-Role Combat Aircraft) Tornado, 75
Müller-Westernhagen, Marius, 330
Multiple Independently Targetable Re-entry Vehicles (MIRVs), 53, 73
Multi-Role Combat Aircraft Tornado. *See* MRCA Tornado
music
    nuclear doomsday in, 329–33
    "nuclear pop," role of, 13
    protests and musical code, 224
Mutual and Balanced Force Reductions (MBFR), 37, 44, 53
"Mutual Assured Destruction" (MAD), 323
myth, of peace movement, 183n8

Nachrüstung (retrofitting/countervailing strategy), 2
Nagasaki, 228, 231, 306
Narr, Hanne, 281
Narr, Wolf-Dieter, 285
nationalism, in peace movement, 142–46
National Youth Committee, 258
NATO
    flexible response and, 3, 28n14
    Harmel Report (1967), 4, 53, 104
    members, meeting of, 5
NATO Double-Track Decision
    in context, 2–3, 5, 6, 159
    détente era, end of, 52–56
    genesis of, 56–62
    implementation, 62–66
    in media, 52, 96
    opponents, 9, 174, 268
    poster, 97
    protests, 1, 97, 246, 278
    role of, 22, 192
    supporters, 1–2, 4, 16, 19–20, 104, 192, 266
NATO Double-Track Decision, East-West German relations
    arms upgrade resolution influencing, 95–99
    in context, 5–6, 99–100
    interests of West and East Germany, 87–88
    political developments (1979–81) before and after, 88–91
    politics (1982–83), 91–95
natural sciences, 150n22
nature, 120, 125, 126, 233, 240n51, 290–91
Naturfreunde (Friends of Nature), 126
Nazis, 200, 207
Nena, 332, 333
Netherlands, 59, 61, 62
Neue Deutsche Welle (New German wave), 332
neutron bomb, 4, 186n33
    development, 74–75
    ERW, 56–58, 79
    guidelines, 57–58

opponents, 105
New Age movement, 125
New Forum, 197
New German wave. *See Neue Deutsche Welle*
New Social Movements, 9, 109
   in context, 120–21, 132, 224
   influence of, 174–75
   protest and political culture, 129–31
   with protests, forms of, 263
   trade unions and, 259–60
Nicaragua, 345
Nicole (singer), 330, 332
Niemöller, Martin, 190
"99 Luftballons" (Nena), 332, 333
Nitze, Paul, 64
Nixon, Richard, 81, 141
nonviolence, 191, 231, 239n44, 276, 280
Norway, 59, 61
Notgemeinschaft der Deutschen Wissenschaft, 320n16
"No to Nuclear Armament," 1
nuclear crisis
   anti-Americanism and "Western ties," 17, 18–22, 19
   with Cold War, end of, 23–25
   conflict, forms of, 12–14
   in context, 1–2
   history and legacy, 14–15
   issues, 2–7, 14–15
   memory, politics of, 15–18
   party politics and, 15, 22–23
   peace movement with, 9–12
   protagonists, 7–9
   with Roman Catholic Church, upheavals in, 248–51
nuclear doomsday
   Chernobyl, 309, 335n32
   in context, 13, 17–18, 321n40
   film and, 13, 322, 323–25
   literature and, 325–29
   music and, 329–33
nuclear explosions
   capabilities, 73, 74, 312
   injuries, 314, 324
   life after, 312–17
"nuclear pop." *See* music
nuclear power
   balance and SS-20 missiles, 3
   Brokdorf Nuclear Power Station, 286
   "Superpower Deal" (1977), 81
The Nuclear Night (Ehrlich and Sagan), 316
The Nuclear State (Jungk), 123, 129, 200
nuclear weapon-free zones, 180–81
"nuclear winter," 316, 324, 334n11
"nukespeak," 295

obliviousness to power. *See Machtvergessenheit*
obsession with power. *See Machtbesessenheit*
Octopussy (film), 324
Ohne Rüstung Leben (ORL, Living without Arms), 191, 243
oil, 88, 119, 215, 344
Olympic Games, boycotts, 62, 89
Der organisierte Wahnsinn (Arms and hunger) (Brandt, W.), 109
ORL. *See* Ohne Rüstung Leben
Orlov, Yuri, 41, 44
Oslo International Peace Research Institute, 139

pacifism, 16, 107
   See also eco-pacifism
PAH Anti-Tank Helicopter (Panzerabwehrhubschrauber), 76
Pahlavi, Mohammad Reza, 199
Palme, Olaf, 216
Palme Report, 252
Pappi, Franz Urban, 155, 159
Paris Charter (1990), 48
Parnass, Peggy, 300
patriarchy, 259, 294
Pauling, Linus, 142
Paulskirchenbewegung (Paul's Church Movement), 143

Pausewang, Gudrun, 13, 178, 327–29, 335n32
Pax Christi, 191, 248–49, 250
peace, 151n38, 217, 298, 325, 330
    AGDF, 159, 163–64, 191, 243–44, 246
    Anstiftung der Frauen für den Frieden, 191
    ASF, 159, 163–64, 189, 191, 243–44
    DFU, 162, 192
    ecclesiastical peace discussions, 252–53
    GDR and Peace Policy, 81
    gender with war and, 290–91, 293
    groups, 126, 139, 141–42, 161, 162, 181, 186n44, 192, 208, 211, 212, 214, 243, 244, 246, 252, 258
    Initiative Women for Peace, 194
    KOFAZ, 159, 162, 192, 194, 202n2, 262
    "labor for peace," trade unions and, 260–62
    peaceful coexistence, 91, 110, 139, 215, 333
    Protestant Church with security and, 242–44
    symbolism and, 222–23, 294
    "World Peace Week," 258
    See also Artists for Peace
Peace, here and now seminars. *See Frieden konkret* seminars
The peaceful sex. *See Die friedfertige Frau*
Peace is Possible: The Policy of the Sermon on the Mount (Alt), 201, 250
peace movement
    Action Conferences, 156, 164, 165
    in context, 1–2, 6
    environmental movement and "new," 124
    failure of, 9
    feminism and, 201
    forms of interest aggregation and decision-making in, 157
    influences on, 9–10, 131–32
    institutional organization of
        in context, 9, 10, 167–68
        decentralization (1983–86), 165–67
        establishment (1975–81), 159–63
        mass demonstration (1981–82), 163–65, 174
        organizational network of, 154–59
    intellectual foundations
        characteristics, 138–39
        in context, 10
        nationalism in, 142–46
        peace studies and logic of deterrence, 139–41
        as political movement, 146–49
        rearmament debate, 141–42
    members, 10–11, 19, 154, 164–65
    myth of, 183n8
    with nuclear crisis, 9–12
    "people" in, 236n16
    police with protest and action strategies of, 275–76
    populations in protest, 235n1
    posters, 12, 166, 225–26, 231, 300, 331
    as protagonist of conflict, 7–9
    protagonists
        activists, 189, 192–202
        Alt, 192, 200–201, 202
        Bahro, 192, 197–98, 201
        Bastian, 189, 190–91, 201
        Beuys, 192, 198–99, 202
        Bohley, Bärbel, 192, 197, 201
        Böll, Annemarie, 189, 192, 200, 202
        Böll, Heinrich, 189, 192, 200, 202
        in context, 11, 189, 201–2
        Eppler, 195, 202
        groups, 191–92
        Jungk, 189, 192, 200–201, 202
        Kade, 192, 194, 201–2
        Kelly, 192, 195–96, 201

Quistorp, 193–94, 201
Sölle, Dorothee, 189, 191, 193, 201
Vack, Klaus, 192, 198, 202
spaces and places of
   in context, 12–13, 173–74, 181–82
   destruction, spaces and places of potential, 178–79
   military importance, sites of, 175–77
   peace, counter-places of, 179–81
   political action between center and periphery, 174–75
supporters, 8, 93–95, 99, 106, 107–8, 154–58, 214, 233, 262, 326
trade unions with forms of protest and, 262–70
visual and media strategies
   in context, 12, 13–14, 222–23
   demonstration, expressive codes of, 223–25
   media protest as performance, 229–32
   posters and protest, expressive pathos of, 225–26
   protest, personalization of, 232–34
   visual symbols and protest images, 226–29
women and
   activists, 291–93
   in context, 10–11, 290–91
   gender and, 295
   identity, positioning of, 298–300
   issues and positions, 293–96
   militarism and sexism, 293–95
   motherhood and, 295–96, 298
   role of, 10–11, 193–96, 201
   subdivisions of, 291
   visibility, politics of, 300–301
   war, action and protest forms with, 296–98

as youth movement, 10
See also environmental movement; independent peace movement, East Germany and
peace movement, Coordinating Committee
   decentralization (1983–86), 165, 167
   event poster, 231
   with mass demonstrations (1981–82), 163, 164–65
   myth of, 183n8
   organizational network and, 154, 156, 158
   role of, 168, 189, 191, 194
Peace must be armed. *See* "Der Friede muss bewaffnet sein"
Peace Week, 243, 244, 251, 258
Pelikan, Jiri, 42
penal code. *See* German Penal Code
"people," in peace movement, 236n16
"People's Assembly for Peace," 222
performance
   media protest, 229–32
   social action as, 238n34
Pershing II missiles
   capabilities, 70
   construction of, 4, 169n20
   in context, 4, 23–24, 70–71, 83–84
   description, 18
   military importance, sites of, 176–77
   protest posters, 225–26, 227
   TNF development (1970s), 71–74
   war and military planning, changes, 70, 78–80
   Warsaw Pact and TNFs, 70, 80–83
   See also protests
persuasion, fear and, 130
places. *See* peace movement, spaces and places of
Plogstedt, Sibylle, 294
Pluhar, Erika, 330
Poland
   Antiwar Day, 232
   CSCE and, 41, 43
   human rights in, 25

martial law in, 47, 91, 269
PUWP, 43
role of, 78, 79, 80, 82
trade unions, 269–70
police
    "Citizens Observe the Police" groups, 285
    civil disobedience and, 277–83
    community policing, 285–87
    in context, 14
    with "culture clash" over internal security, 283–85
    Federal Association of Critical Police Officers, 286
    GdP, 281–82, 283
    harassment, 216
    Krefeld riots and, 274–75
    militancy and action, direct forms of, 276–77
    with protest and action strategies of peace movement, 275–76
    rallies and mass demonstrations, 276
    with sit-ins and psychological distress, 281–82
    training programs, 280
    violence, 123, 210, 265, 276–77, 280–81
Polish United Workers' Party (PUWP), 43
political parties
    consequences, 111–13
    in context, 7–8
    deterrence and, 108–9
    disarmament, 109–11
    role of, 105–9
    "self recognition" and criticism of state, 113–14
    signs and omens, 104–5
politics
    environmental movement with protests and political culture, 129–31
    of memory and nuclear crisis, 15–18
    NATO Double-Track Decision (1979–81) and East-West German, 88–91
    NATO Double-Track Decision (1982–83) and East-West German, 91–95
    nuclear crisis influencing party politics, 15, 22–23
    peace movement as political movement, 146–49
    political action with spaces and places of peace movement, 174–75
    religion and, 250–51
    women and politics of visibility, 300–301
Poppe, Ulrike, 95, 197, 216, 292
populations
    civilian, 75, 169n9
    evacuation plans for, 314
    in protest with peace movement, 235n1
posters
    antinuclear protests, 128
    Artists for Peace, 331
    DGB, 264
    Green Party, 237n18
    IG Metall trade union, 267
    NATO Double-Track Decision, 97
    peace movement, 12, 166, 225–26, 231, 300, 331
    peace movement, Coordinating Committee event poster, 231
    peace movement and student movements, 12
    protest, images of, 227
    protest and aesthetics of, 225–26
    SPD election poster, 112
    "Stand up for Peace!," 300
    weapons systems, 228
power, 14
    See also nuclear power
Prague Spring, 161
"Protect and Survive" (booklet), 325
"Protest and Survive" (booklet), 325
Protestant Church, 191
    EKD, 208, 246–47
    with independent peace and civil rights movement, 209, 212

peace and security, debates about, 242–44
with peace efforts, 208
peace without weapons and, 212
Protestant Church Congress, 163, 244
role of, 8, 217, 242
Protestant Church in Germany. *See* Evangelische Kirche in Deutschland
Protestant Student Parish Organization. *See* Evangelische Studentengemeinde
protests
    anti-Americanism, 17, 19, 276
    children and, 296
    Christian, in transition, 253–54
    demonstration, expressive codes of, 223–25
    demonstrations, increase of, 275
    environmental movement and antinuclear, 121–24
    environmental movement with political culture and, 129–31
    mass demonstrations, 163–65, 174, 222, 276
    media protest as performance, 229–32
    against military, 277–78, 281
    NATO Double-Track Decision, 1, 97, 246, 278
    neutron bomb, 57
    peace movement and populations in, 235n1
    personalization of, 232–34
    police violence with, 123
    police with action strategies of peace movement and, 275–76
    posters, 128, 225–26, 227
    "Protest and Survive," 325
    rights at, 286
    trade unions with peace movement and forms of, 262–70
    visual symbols and images of, 226–29
    war and women with action and forms of, 296–98
    See also peace movement

psychological distress
    militarization of medicine and, 317
    in police with sit-in, 281–82
PUWP. *See* Polish United Workers' Party

Quinlan, Michael (Sir), 3
Quistorp, Eva, 11, 165, 193–94, 201, 292

radioactive fission products, 314
RAF terrorism. *See* Red Army Fraction terrorism
rallies, police with, 276
    See also peace movement; protests
rape, 294
Rappe, Hermann, 8, 258–59
rapprochement, Gorbachev and, 340–41
Raschke, Joachim, 147
Rätz, Werner, 165
Reagan, Ronald, 6, 90, 228
    criticism of, 21, 198–99, 293, 333
    deterrence and, 108
    disarmament and, 338–42, 344
    Geneva disarmament talks, 342–43
    INF Treaty and, 345–46
    nuclear crisis and, 23, 24
    on nuclear doomsday in film, 322
    protests against, 17, 276
    Reykjavík disarmament talks (1986), 338, 344
    role of, 63–64, 66, 70, 350n16
rearmament debate, 141–42
Red Army Fraction (RAF) terrorism, 158, 200
religion
    politics and, 250–51
    symbols, 226, 234
"Report Baden-Baden" (television show), 201
retrofitting. *See Nachrüstung*
"Revolution in Military Affairs" (RMA), 76
Reykjavík disarmament talks (1986), 83, 338, 344
Richter, Horst-Eberhard, 138, 144
Ridder, Helmut, 190

Righeira, 332
rights, 191, 209–12, 285, 286
    See also human rights
riots. *See* Krefeld riots, police and
RMA. *See* "Revolution in Military
    Affairs"
Roman Catholic Church, 209
    AKH and, 214
    nuclear crisis and upheavals in,
        248–51
    with peace movement, 217
    role of, 8, 207, 242
*Ronald Reagan and His Quest to Abolish
    Nuclear Weapons* (Lettow), 350n16
Russell, Bertrand, 130
Russell Peace Foundation, 162
Russell Tribunals, 130

Sagan, Carl, 316
SALT (Strategic Arms Limitation Talks)
    SALT I, 3, 6, 37, 44, 71
    SALT II, 61, 62, 71, 108
Sander, Helke, 293
SBZ. *See* Soviet Occupation Zone
scarves, 226, 237n24, 247, 248
Schalck-Golodkowski, Alexander, 93
Schell, Jonathan, 326
Schenk, Herrad, 297–98
Schmidt, Helmut, 2, 3, 6, 7, 59
    CSCE and, 40
    on détente, 56
    ERWs and, 57
    Grundgesetz and, 282
    NATO Double-Track Decision and,
        19–20, 52, 56, 57, 65, 87–91,
        104, 192, 266
    opposition to, 126
    peace movement and, 173
    role, 60, 63, 81, 109
    SPD and, 105, 113
Schmidt, Renate, 290
Schneider, Dirk, 281
Schnoor, Herbert, 275, 284
Schorlemmer, Friedrich, 210
Schröder, Günter, 282
Schultze, Wolfgang, 266

Schulz, Rolf, 136n57
Schumacher, Hans Günter, 161
Schutzkommission (Commission for
    Protection), 320n16
Schwarz, Hans-Peter, 14
Schwarzer, Alice, 294
sea-launched cruise missiles, 59
"Second Cold War," 53, 124, 290, 318
"second wave," 85n9
Securing Peace. *See* Sicherung des
    Friedens
security, 252–53
    police and internal security, 283–85
    Protestant Church with peace and,
        242–44
    See also Conference for Security and
        Cooperation in Europe
"security partnership," 252
SED. *See* Socialist Unity Party of
    Germany
selection (*triage*), 312–13
Senghaas, Dieter, 148, 153n66
Seventh Pentecost Festival, 243, 244
sex, 151n38
    militarism and sexism, 293–95
    rape and, 294
Seyfried, Gerhard, 237n18
shelters, 178, 307, 315–16
ship building, 262
Shorter-Range INF (SRINF), 66
short-range nuclear force Agreement. *See*
    SNF Agreement
Sicherung des Friedens (Securing Peace),
    243, 252
Siegel, Ralph, 332
silence, circles of, 179, 181, 231, 276
silent vigils, 173, 174, 231, 251
Simon, Helmut, 279
sit-ins
    criminalization of, 280
    police and psychological distress
        with, 281–82
    role of, 1, 14, 123, 193, 223, 229,
        231, 263, 278, 279
Sixth Assembly of the World Council of
    Churches, 216–17

Skorpion, 77
SNF (short-range nuclear force) Agreement, 346–47
social action, as performance, 238n34
Social Democratic Party (SPD), 2
    Appeal of Bielefeld and, 19
    deterrence and, 108–9
    disarmament and, 109–10
    eco-pacifism and, 126
    election poster, 112
    FDP, 59
    Green Party and, 195
    internal disputes, 114n1
    Kohl on, 21
    peace movement and, 108, 160, 195
    role of, 7, 11, 59, 64, 96, 104, 105, 123
    Schmidt, Helmut, and, 105, 113
Socialist Unity Party of Germany (SED), 43, 197, 208, 216, 217–18
Soelle, Dorothee, 18
"The Soft Water" (bots), 333
Solidarity, 43, 47, 269–70
Sölle, Dietrich, 193
Sölle, Dorothee, 18, 189, 191, 193, 201, 250, 252
"Sonne statt Reagan" (Sun instead of Reagan) (Beuys), 198–99, 333
Sontag, Susan, 323
sound effects, 229, 231
South Africa, 292
Southeast Asia, 53
Soviet Occupation Zone (SBZ), 208
Soviet Union, 84n1
    in Afghanistan, 24, 62, 344–45
    CPSU or Communist Party of the Soviet Union, 55
    CSCE and, 40–42, 46
    with détente, end of, 54–56
    NATO and, 3, 4
    oil and, 88, 215
    role of, 60–61, 64, 65
    US-Soviet relationship, 44, 53, 66, 70–71, 81, 290, 339–44
    weapons innovation and technology, 4–5

SOYUS 8, 82–83
spaces. *See* peace movement, spaces and places of
SPD. *See* Social Democratic Party
Der Spiegel, 16, 52, 55, 197, 245, 250, 326
"spirituality of resistance," 252
Sponti, 225
Spranger, Carl-Dieter, 284
squatter scene, 10
SRINF. *See* Shorter-Range INF
SS-20 missiles
    capabilities, 70, 72–73
    controversy, 4, 5
    increase in, 54–56, 82
    nuclear power balance and, 3
    response to, 58, 72
SS Surface-to-Surface Missiles (NATO category for Soviet missiles). *See* SS-20 missiles
"Stand up for Peace!" poster, 300
START negotiations, 338, 346–47
Straesser, Christoph, 192
Strategic Arms Limitation Talks. *See* SALT
Strauss, Franz Josef, 88, 93, 106
strikes
    "birth strikes," 296–97
    "wildcat strikes," 263
structural violence, 140, 150n15
students, 12, 191, 209
submarines
    with cruise missiles, 71
    trade unions and, 262
Sukhoi 22 (Fitter), 75
Sun instead of Reagan. *See* "Sonne statt Reagan"
"Superpower Deal" (1977), 81
survival, after nuclear explosion, 312–17
    See also civil defense
Survive the Coming Nuclear War: How to Do It (Cruit), 319n6
Suttner, Bertha von, 298
"Swords into Plowshares," 210, 211, 214, 218, 226, 234

symbolism
    civil disobedience, 278
    military, 238n30
    peace and femininity, 294
    peace movement and, 222–23
    religious symbols, 226, 234
    visual symbols and images of protest, 226–29

tanks, 76–78
Technisches Hilfswerk (THW, German Technical Emergency Service), 310
technology
    military techniques, development, 74–78
    MIRVs, 53, 73
    weapons innovation and, 4–5, 54
terrorism, 123, 284
    "German Autumn," 122
    RAF, 158, 200
Thatcher, Margaret, 308
Theater Nuclear Forces (TNFs), 54, 56, 58
    development (1970s), 71–74
    Warsaw Pact and, 70, 80–83
Theodorakis, Mikis, 330
Things are moving ahead. See *Es geht voran*
The Third World War (Hackett), 326
Third World, in conflicts, 344–45
"Third World" movement, 124
Thompson, Edward Palmer, 142
Thoreau, Henry David, 19
Threads (docudrama), 325
THW. See Technisches Hilfswerk
TNFs. See Theater Nuclear Forces
Tomorrow is Already Here (Jungk), 200
The Trade Unionist. See *Gewerkschafter*
Trade Union Monthly, 258
Trade Union of the Police. See Gewerkschaft der Polizei
trade unions
    with Antiwar Day, 266
    with arms production and "labor for peace," 260–62
    in context, 8, 258–59, 270

GdP, 281–82, 283
new social movements and, 259–60
peace movement and forms of protest with, 262–70
Solidarity and, 47
youth organizations, 265
"Training and Doctrine Command" (TRADOC), 85n10
training programs, police, 280
Trapp, Horst, 192
Traube, Klaus, 122–23
triage (selection), 312–13
TU-22M (Backfire) bomber, 76, 81
Tübingen Association for Peace Education, 156
Turkey, 59, 262
The Turning Point (Capra), 125
TU Tupolev (Soviet aircraft company), 76, 81

Uexküll, Gösta von, 190
UK. See United Kingdom
UN. See United Nations
unemployment, 261, 265
"Die Unfähigkeit zu trauern" (Inability to mourn), 144
Union for the Environment and Nature Conservation (BUND), 120
unions. See trade unions
United Kingdom (UK), 60, 61
United Nations (UN), 292, 298
United States (US)
    anti-Americanism and nuclear crisis, 17, 19, 22–23, 276
    CSCE and, 40, 41, 43
    détente and, 53
    disarmament and, 53, 338–44
    German-US relationship, 5, 6–7, 21–22, 33n70
    human rights and, 44
    role of, 60, 63–65, 71
    Soviet-US relationship, 44, 53, 66, 70–71, 81, 290, 339–44
United War Resisters. See Deutsche Friedensgesellschaft—Vereinigte KriegsdienstgegnerInnen

UN World Conference on Women
    (1980), 298
US barracks
    Andrews Barracks, 281
    Carl Schurz Barracks, 277
US Bishops Conference, 250

Vack, Hanne, 198, 202
Vack, Klaus, 167, 192, 198, 202
"Vamos a la Playa" (Righeira), 332
Vance, Cyrus, 44
Verheugen, Günter, 112
Vetter, Heinz Oskar, 269
Vietnam War
    influence of, 141
    protest, images of, 228
Vietnam War Crimes Tribunal (1966–67), 130
vigils, silent. *See* silence
violence, 124, 150n10
    coercion and, 279
    FÖGA, 191
    legitimacy of, 284
    nonviolence and, 191, 231, 239n44, 276, 280
    police, 123, 210, 265, 276–77, 280–81
    rape, 294
    structural, 140, 150n15
    women and, 295, 297
    See also terrorism
visibility, women and politics of, 300–301
visual strategies. *See* peace movement, visual and media strategies
visual symbols, protest, 226–29
Vogel, Hans-Jochen, 113
Vogt, Roland, 126, 160, 170n28
Voigt, Karsten D., 108
Volkshochschule Wyhler Wald, 129
Vollmer, Antje, 290

Wader, Hannes, 330
"Walk in the Woods" proposal, 65
war, 13, 308, 319n6, 325, 326–27, 329
    changes in, 70, 78–80
    DFG-VK, 126, 161, 192
    gender with peace and, 290–91, 293
    IPPNW, 11, 292, 300
    will of God and, 253
    women, with action and protest forms, 296–98
    See also Cold War; Vietnam War
War Games (film), 13, 323–24
Warneke, Tim, 236n6, 236n16
Warsaw Pact, 3, 4, 24, 89, 308
    CSCE and, 45
    "Granite 86," 84n14
    SOYUS 8, 82–83
    TNFs and, 70, 80–83
    with war and military planning, 78–80
The War Game (docudrama), 325
Wasmuht, Ulrike C., 146–47
Waters, Roger, 325
WDC. *See* Workers' Defense Committee
weapons
    antitank, 76–78
    innovation and technology, 4–5, 54
    peace without, 212–14
    posters, weapons systems, 228
Weber, Josef, 190
Wecker, Konstantin, 330
Wehner, Herbert, 21, 105
Weisskopf, Victor F., 142
Weizsäcker, Carl Friedrich von, 150n19, 252, 311
Weizsäcker, Richard von, 18
"We Kill the World (Do not Kill the World)" (Boney M.), 332
welfare system, 265
"Western ties," nuclear crisis and anti-Americanism with, 18–22
West German Army. *See* Bundeswehr
West Germany, 277
    CSCE and, 41
    Fire and Disaster Protection Act, 317
    party politics and, 22–23
    role of, 60, 61, 64
    See also NATO Double-Track Decision, East-West German relations

When the Wind Blows (Briggs), 13, 325
When the Wind Blows (film), 13
"Why Are There Wars?" (Lindenberg), 329
Widerstandstag (Day of Resistance), 251
"wildcat strikes," 263
Winkler, Heinrich August, 14
Wischnewski, Hans-Juergen, 92
Wissmann, Matthias, 107
Der Wittenberger Friedenskreis (The Wittenberg Peace Group), 211
The Wittenberg Peace Group. *See* Der Wittenberger Friedenskreis
Wittner, Lawrence S., 23, 338, 345
Woermann-Adam, Claudia, 262
Wolf, Christa, 298
women
    Anstiftung der Frauen für den Frieden, 191
    feminism, 125, 201
    as "fighters," 300
    Frauen gegen Atomtod—Unsere Kinder sollen leben, 303n32
    nature and, 290–91
    violence and, 295, 297
    See also peace movement, women and; UN World Conference on Women
Women against Nuclear Death. *See* Frauen gegen Atomtod—Unsere Kinder sollen leben
Women for Peace. *See* Frauen für den Frieden
Women for Peace on the Coordination Committee of the Peace Movement, 191
Women of Greenham Common, 298
"Women's Decade," 292
Women's Pentagon Action, 298, 300

Workers' Defense Committee (WDC), 43
Working Group Church Solidarity. *See* Arbeitskreis Solidarische Kirche
World Council of Churches, 243, 253
World Economic Summit, 63
World Peace Council, 208
"World Peace Week," 258
writers, 325–26
Wulf, Christoph, 238n34
Wulff, Christian, 7, 107
Wüstenhagen, Hans-Helmuth, 160

Young Democrats. *See* Jungdemokraten
Young European Federalists. *See* Junge Europäische Föderalisten
Young Men's Association. *See* Jungmännerwerk
youth, 10, 248, 249, 258
    children, 13, 178, 180, 223, 296, 309, 315, 327–29, 332
    groups, 126, 192, 209
    IG-Metall Jugend, 260, 263
    students, 12, 191, 209
    trade unions and, 265
Youth Film Club, 325

Zagladin, Vadim, 96
Zentralkomitee der deutschen Katholiken (ZdK, Central Committee of German Catholics), 248
Zentralstelle für Zivilschutz (Central Office for Civil Defense), 320n19
Zero Solution for Long-range (LRINF), 66
Ziemann, Benjamin, 147, 150n15
Zimmermann, Friedrich, 129, 275, 284
Zink, Jörg, 129

www.ingramcontent.com/pod-product-compliance
Lightning Source LLC
Chambersburg PA
CBHW072141100526
44589CB00015B/2040